THE LIVES OF THE CAESARS

THE LIVES OF THE CAESARS

Suetonius

Introduction by Molly Dauster, Ph.D.

BARNES
& NOBLE
BOOKS
NEW YORK

Originally published circa AD 117

This edition published by Barnes & Noble Publishing, Inc.

Cover Design by Pronto Design, Inc.

2004 Barnes & Noble Publishing, Inc.

ISBN 0-7607-5758-5

Printed and bound in the United States of America

1 3 5 7 9 10 8 6 4 2

CONTENTS

INTRODUCTION

SUETONIUS' *The Lives of the Caesars* quite often resembles a modern sensationalized tabloid, stuffed with insinuations, scandal, and royal shenanigans, but it is really much more. Written by a "palace insider" and published during the reign of Hadrian (c. AD 117) at the height of the Roman Empire, *The Lives of the Caesars* is a unique, intense, and individual portrait of each emperor. Despite its antiquity, *The Lives of the Caesars* is neither remote nor obscure; it remains the most readable and most significant biography of the ruling families of the early Roman Empire ever written. A "bestseller" in its own day, it has been in almost continual reprint since its first publication, and the passage of nearly two thousand years has dimmed neither its appeal to historically minded readers nor its importance to scholars. *The Lives of the Caesars* was both the inspiration and major source for Robert Graves' *I, Claudius,* as well as the award-winning BBC/PBS dramatization of the same name. Suetonius' animated and assured account of the emperors of Rome brings the mundane, tragic, humorous, and scandalous activities of Rome's elite—the emperors, their families, friends, enemies, successes, failures, loves, and ambitions—to vivid life.

Modern scholars and readers generally refer to Gaius Suetonius Tranquillus, the author of *The Lives of the Caesars,* as Suetonius, but his fellow Romans most often called him Tranquillus. We know very little about his life. The most widely accepted birth date for Suetonius is around AD 70, and he probably died sometime before

AD 130 or 140. He may have been born in Betriacum (near modern Modena, Italy) while his father was serving as an officer under Vespasian. Where he spent his boyhood is unknown; claims have been made for Pisarum in Umbrian Italy, although a commemorative tablet found in 1952 in northern Africa (the Roman province of Numidia) speaks of him as if he were a "hometown boy." It is clear that Suetonius spent at least some of his early years in Rome in the emperor's palace, since he displays an easy familiarity with the education and daily life of young people in that setting. Suetonius practiced law very briefly, but found that he was more suited to a life of letters than to the politically charged atmosphere of the law courts of ancient Rome. This phase of Suetonius' life is documented in the collected letters of the Younger Pliny, with whom Suetonius enjoyed a long friendship. Pliny acted as a mentor to Suetonius' literary ambitions and aided his efforts to obtain official positions at court. He supported Suetonius' decision to leave law, and, most important, he persistently urged Suetonius to continue his work on *The Lives of the Caesars.*

Pliny's recommendations to the emperors resulted in several key appointments for Suetonius, including the official court posts of *a studiis, a bibliotheca,* and *ab epistulis* under the emperors Trajan and Hadrian. These positions have no precise counterparts in today's bureaucracy, but an *a studiis* can be thought of as an expert advisor to the emperor, an *ab epistulis* was a more responsible and demanding version of a personal executive secretary, and an *a bibliotheca* was a sort of combination acquisitions librarian, archivist, and government documents librarian. It is clear that in all of his works Suetonius not only relied on his court background and contacts but also drew heavily on his ready access to official sources, archives, and expert texts.

The Lives of the Caesars is "historical" in its chronological arrangement, and covers a period of nearly one hundred twenty years, from the founder of the Julian-Claudian dynasty, Julius Caesar (49-44 BC), to the Flavian Emperor Domitian (AD 81-96). This period saw the final dissolution of the Republic and the institution of the Empire. While many factors led to the end of the Republic, the key factors were control of the army, new wealth from far-flung provinces, and unchecked ambition among Rome's powerful families. By the time of Julius Caesar it was clear that elected officials could no longer hold the Roman state together. Citizens gradually lost the power to vote on issues and senators eventually lost the power to decide the issues on which to vote. While Republican Rome had been at least nominally flexible, all classes of society in the Empire became more established, hierarchical, and separate. The one theme that is a constant throughout the Empire, although it is not always clear in Suetonius, is that most emperors came to the throne on tides of blood—civil wars, mutinies, and rebellions in the provinces were common ways to gain the palace. After an emperor gained power there were often purges, sometimes on a huge scale, of known and suspected enemies. Rome became a great city, home to millions, but life there was not always easy, especially for those in the public eye.

Because Suetonius not only wrote in a new style of personal history but also evidently assumed his audience had a background in the basics of Roman history, the historical context of *The Lives of the Caesars* is somewhat sketchy. Two dynasties ruled during the period about which he wrote; the Julio-Claudian and the Flavian. The Julio-Claudian line began with Julius Caesar (born July 12, 100 BC), who, strictly speaking, was not an emperor. In fact, it was the fear that he might become one that led to his assassination in 44 BC. Caesar began the process of consolidating all state power in the hands of one man, but he did it within the guidelines and traditions of the Republic. Before he died Caesar had already named Octavian (born September 23, 63 BC), his great-nephew and adoptive son, as his heir. In 27 BC, Octavian emerged the victor in the civil war that followed Caesar's murder, and he set about restructuring the entire administration of the Roman state. Renamed Augustus by the Senate, Octavian apparently retained many features of the Republic, but the army and the finances were now both in the control of the emperor. The one problem Augustus did not solve was succession—in too many future cases the army would decide. He himself adopted Tiberius (born 42 BC), his wife's son, as his successor. While Augustus showed a positive genius for administration and self-promotion, Tiberius seemed both bitter and withdrawn. He eventually left Rome for the isle of Capri, abandoning administration of the state to underlings. Tiberius died of natural causes in AD 37 and was followed by Gaius (born August 31, AD 12), nicknamed Caligula—or "little boot"—from the miniature army boots he wore while on campaign with his father in Germany. After four years of perfectly wretched administration, with murders, confiscations, scandals, and exiles the norm, Gaius was assassinated by a tribune of the guard in AD 41. Claudius (born August 10 BC), the hero of Robert Graves' novel, was declared emperor by the same guardsmen who murdered Gaius. Claudius had been kept out of public life by his family because of physical infirmities. Although Graves thought Claudius was not as mentally negligent as was assumed, the verdict of history is still out on that point. Claudius was the last adult male of the Julio-Claudian line; he was succeeded by Nero, his nephew and stepson. It is likely that Nero and his mother, the appalling Agrippina, murdered Claudius. Nero (born December 15, AD 37) left much to be desired as an emperor. Even though he was emperor, what Nero really desired was to be the ancient equivalent of a pop-star. His failure to placate—and pay—the army led to his forced suicide in AD 68.

A period of civil war followed Nero's death during which rival generals fought for the throne in AD 68-69. Galba, Otho, and Vitellius each held power briefly, but in the end the winner was Vespasian (born AD 9), the founder of the Flavian dynasty. Vespasian was a tough old soldier, without many pretenses or much polish. The army adored him and he ruled for ten years, dying of natural causes in AD 79. While his sons and heirs were more sophisticated, they also displayed his practical and efficient approach to administration. Vespasian's son Titus (born December 30, AD 39), followed him as emperor and ruled from AD 79 to 81. It is possible that Titus was killed by his brother

Domitian. Of all the emperors profiled in *The Lives of the Caesars,* Domitian is the most hated by Suetonius, probably because he had direct contact with his eccentricities. Domitian (born October 31, AD 51), ruled autocratically and very badly for fifteen years, until his wife led a palace coup against him.

Trajan (born AD 53, ruled AD 98-117) and Hadrian (born January 24, AD 76, ruled AD 138) were the emperors under whom Suetonius served. Hadrian dismissed Suetonius for alleged improprieties toward the empress around AD 122; these charges are obscure but probably represent only some lapse on Suetonius' part in the increasingly strict and ritualized palace protocol. Suetonius put his newfound leisure and expert knowledge to use and finished his monumental biography on the ruling families of Rome.

From the few surviving references by other ancient authors that have come down to us—quotes, attributions, and fragments—we know that Suetonius wrote a number of well-received little books in both Latin and Greek on a large number of popular topics. The audience for any of his works, especially *The Lives of the Caesars,* is a source of evergreen disputation among Classical scholars, but most likely included people from much of the top strata of Roman society—a society which was literate at a level unmatched for centuries. Evidently his audience, whatever its composition, had a wide range of interests because his most successful works covered such topics as famous courtesans, games and sports, the Roman calendar and year, public spectacles and shows, clothes and fashion, human physical defects—both as curiosities and as a sign of character, names and omens of winds, the derivation of names of rivers and seas, public offices, and a few more serious and technical commentaries on grammar. He wrote at least one other long, scholarly and very important study on the lives of the Roman poets, orators and historians, a few fragments of which have come down to us as the *De viris illustribus* ("On the lives of the famous"). It is clear that he recycled some of his previous writings, especially on games and public offices, in composing his most famous and most complete work, *The Lives of the Caesars.*

Even before he wrote *The Lives of the Caesars* or the other, smaller works, Suetonius was a noted philologist and a recognized antiquarian among Rome's Greco-Roman literary circle—a circle that included the emperors. The extant writings of Roman antiquarians display a fondness for puns, word-play, often dubious or superficial derivations of place-names, and an extraordinary passion for hunting out recognizably old forms of words and grammatical construction (as if someone today insisted on writing and speaking like Chaucer's characters). As a group, they seemed to share a somewhat uncritical acceptance of the absolute truthfulness of folklore and fable, and had a rather sentimental attraction to obscure rituals and quaint customs. Many antiquarian authors of the early Empire, such as Aulus Gellius and the Elder Pliny, wrote in a sort of grab-bag fashion, with information about diverse subjects thrown in wherever and whenever the author happened to remember them. Suetonius, however, brought his remarkable memory and notable talent for arranging information—invaluable in a librarian—to all of his works. His simple, direct style of presentation (based in part on Cato the Censor *c.* 234-149 BC) as well as his precision in arrangement had a great effect on other authors, especially biographers. For example, St. Jerome used Suetonius' biographies as a model and source when he compiled his own *Chronicle.*

In Suetonius' hands, biography focuses on personal and, especially, moral character as demonstrated in various situations, rather than how individual character either shaped events in history or was shaped by them. Suetonius seems more concerned with the operations of chance than with the cause and effects of history. He appears to have deliberately set out to create personal, rather than historical, biography as a Roman literary genre; no earlier examples of his particular style of biography are known. History was a well-established literary genre in Rome, and Tacitus had published his monumental *Histories* and *Annales,* which cover more or less the same period and people as *The Lives of the Caesars* only about thirty years earlier; but Suetonius deliberately avoids history as it was understood by the Romans.

In some respects this is a positive gain for modern readers, since it was common and accepted practice for historians of that time to construct speeches and letters of great men to be more in accord with what was considered they "ought" to have said or written. Suetonius, however, had direct access to the letters of the emperors themselves, as well as eyewitness accounts, court gossip, court connections, and traditional palace lore, and he often uses these sources to correct popular impressions or to fill gaps in contemporary histories. The result is that Suetonius is often the only ancient source for the actual words of the emperors and their families. Suetonius' quotation of actual speech and letters redirected biography into a new, and uniquely Roman, form of literature.

The major criticism of Suetonius in his own day came from those who considered him not an "artist" but merely a reporter because he did not embellish speeches. Most modern complaints come from scholars and readers who are dismayed by his cavalier approach to history and his lack of interest in the politics of his day. Suetonius' avoidance of history may stem from a number of causes beside a conscious decision to create a new genre of literature, including personal preference, the sources to which he had access, and even self-protection—it was seldom prudent to be involved in politics in imperial Rome. Suetonius, however, carries his avoidance of history to extremes, and his focus on the individual and his personal motivation often result in weak or doubtful explanations for major national events. In a few cases, Suetonius merely seems to repeat what today we would call "urban legends." A prime example is the still widely accepted story of how Nero fiddled (or played the lyre) while Rome burned; because of convincing contradictory evidence, most modern scholars have rejected this appealing tableau. Nevertheless, Suetonius' lack of historical precision in *The Lives of the Caesars* should seriously affect no one but a professional scholar, and it has little or no bearing on the overall importance of the text or the undeniable enjoyment of his portraits as a whole.

Because life and success in ancient times were so uncertain, Suetonius' major theme is the role of chance in human affairs. The aspect of The *Lives of the Caesars* that causes the most consternation among modern scholars is Suetonius' belief in astrology and its ability to predict character and events. Since there is still no reliable, external means of judging character, and since Suetonius and his fellow Romans had no way to show the falsity of astrology's astronomical basis, perhaps he should be forgiven this lapse.

Suetonius also seems to have been attracted to the idea of reading peoples' fortunes and character in the shape of their faces. Even at the time, this was most often seen as a sort of parlor game, but one that could have far-reaching consequences. The major point about chance and its role in Roman life is that most Romans believed the gods revealed their desires, favors, and intentions through signs, omens, and portents—and nothing was too large or too small to ignore. Although it is often claimed that emperors among others cynically used any sign for personal gain or advancement, Suetonius makes it clear that they just as often believed the signs themselves. If advancement could be, might be, or was influenced by chance, no one could afford to disdain any premonition, fail to use any good-luck charm, or laugh off any warning.

Notables in both the Republic and the Empire were also very much concerned with their reputations. In an age without credit bureaus, identification cards, or extensive public records, a man was literally who his friends and family said he was. This individual anxiety about reputation, or *dignitas*, is another persistent theme in Suetonius' *The Lives of the Caesars. Dignitas* meant much more in ancient Rome than mere dignity: it encompassed a whole family's reputation, and affected all political, social, and financial transactions. *Dignitas* was revealed in dress, bearing, mannerisms, positions, and associates. It was something deserved because of personal character. The closest modern counterpart might be the concept of "face"; loss or gain in *dignitas* can be viewed as similar to "loss of face" or "gain of face." Personal dignity had to be protected, gained, vindicated, and proven in every interaction between public men. As an example of how *dignitas* affected actions, Suetonius advances the convincing hypothesis that Julius Caesar crossed the Rubicon and plunged Rome into civil war because the alternative would have been to submit to an unrecoverable loss of *dignitas.*

Chance, personal dignity, and the desire for honor all played a role in the rise and fall of personal character as shown by each emperor in *The Lives of the Caesars.* Occasionally Suetonius' lack of historicity forces him into simplistic, and mistaken, positions, but taking each portrait as an exposition of character rather than as a judgement of history, he at least displays a fresh and unique viewpoint. Suetonius was not concerned with wars, politics, law, or the sweep of history. As an antiquarian and an archivist, he consistently shows a preference for the maintenance, or even reinstatement, of old customs, practices, and rituals. It is on the basis of whether a given emperor built on or destroyed established Roman customs that Suetonius awards marks and states which emperor was "*good*" or "*bad.*" Above all else he asks the question, "What sort of man was he?" It is Suetonius' concern with the life of the individual, his petty as well as great actions, that has kept *The Lives of the Caesars* fresh, absorbing, and entertaining for nearly two thousand years.

Molly Dauster holds a Ph.D. in Ancient History from Texas Tech University. Her area of specialization is Republican Rome, and she has taught at Ohio University and Texas Tech University.

PREFACE

THE translation of *The Lives of the Caesars* is based upon the text of Maximilian Ihm, Leipzig, 1907 (editio minor, 1909) with some slight changes in punctuation, capitalisation, and orthography, to conform more nearly with English and American usage. Where Ihm does not offer a readable text, conjectures have been admitted and mentioned in the footnotes, and in a few other cases a different reading from his has been adopted.

The aim has been a translation, rather than the easier task of a paraphrase. The version of Philemon Holland (London, 1606) cannot be surpassed in style and spirit, and it is more accurate than any other English translation. An attempt has been made to compete with it in the only possible way, namely in greater fidelity to a better text than was available in his day, and in a nearer approach to the manner of Suetonius. The text and interpretation of Suetonius offer many difficulties, all of which have received careful consideration; but it is hardly to be hoped that the results have been satisfactory in all cases.

I am indebted for many valuable suggestions to the excellent German translation of Adolf Stahr, Stuttgart, 1857, in the new edition published at Munich in 1912.

To *The Lives of the Caesars* have been added those extracts from the *Lives of Illustrious Men* which afford a continuous text and are generally regarded as authentic. See the Prefatory Note to Part II.

A complete Index to the whole work will be found at the end of Volume II.

JOHN C. ROLFE.

PHILADELPHIA, *April*, 1913.

VOLUME I

PART I

THE LIVES OF THE CAESARS

GENERAL CHARACTERISTICS

THE biographies of Suetonius are interesting both for their contents and as a form of literature. Strictly speaking they are neither history nor biography. Great historical events, such as Caesar's campaigns in Gaul, are dismissed in a brief chapter, or with a casual allusion, like the defeat of Varus. The acts of the senate and people, and the edicts of the emperors, receive fuller attention, but are wholly subordinate to the personal element. On the other hand no ideal life is presented, to inspire imitation and point a moral, and no attempt is made to trace the development of character as influenced by heredity, education, and environment. The *Lives,* as Leo has shown,[1] are of the "grammatical" type,[2] and they furnish material for biographies in the true sense of the word, giving the thoughtful reader abundant opportunity for the reflexions and deductions which the writer has omitted.

Suetonius was rather a student and a searcher of records than an observer or inquirer, and his interests lay in the past rather than in the present. The *Lives* become shorter as he approaches his own time, when the written sources were fewer and the opportunities for obtaining personal information greater. He had at his disposal a great amount of material in the form of histories and memoirs which are now lost; he had access either directly or indirectly through his colleague *Ab studiis,* to the imperial archives while he was Hadrian's secretary; and his intimacy with Pliny must have made him familiar with senatorial records and opinions. Occasionally he made use of hearsay evidence[3] and of personal observation.[4] That he seems to have made little use of inscriptions[5] is doubtless due in large measure to his possession of other material which is not available to-day.

On the rare occasions when he gives us an insight into his method of handling his sources, as in *Calig.* viii, it seems clear that he examined conflicting statements with care and intelligence, whenever he thought it necessary to do so; but the plan of his work does not often call for such an investigation. Although he aims to be strictly impartial, scrupulously recounting the virtues and vices of the emperors in separate lists,[6] he seems as a rule to pay little regard to the source from which his information comes, and rarely makes any personal comment .[7]

This apparent impartiality does not give us a fair and unbiassed estimate of the emperors. To be convinced of this we have only to imagine a biography of some prominent man of our own day, made up of praise and blame drawn indiscriminately from the organs of his own party and of the opposition, and presented without comment. Just as such a method would yield a considerable number of absolute falsehoods, so many of the statements of Suetonius must be rejected for one reason or another.

He is often, perhaps generally, regarded as a scandal-monger and a man of prurient mind, but neither of these charges seems justified. The details which give rise to the latter are relatively few in number and are presented with the same judicial coldness which characterises his work in general; while the so-called scandal-mongery is in reality a feature of the development of realism[8] in the writing of the early Empire and of the prevailing interest in the personality and private life of prominent men.

The style of Suetonius is rather that of the scholar and investigator than of the man of letters. It is plain and concise, with no attempt at fine writing or rhetorical embellishment, and has been well characterised as "businesslike." His brevity is rarely obscure, and when it is, the obscurity is generally the result of our imperfect knowledge. At times his conciseness yields sentences worthy of Tacitus, but these, like his intensely dramatic passages, are due rather to the subject matter than to any departure from his usual style. He has the grammarian's feeling for language, and his words are always well chosen and effective. While at times the catalogues of crimes and of petty personal details are somewhat monotonous, the *Lives* as a whole are of absorbing interest, and give us a wealth of anecdotes, witticisms, and curious information of great variety.

THE MANUSCRIPTS

Two critical editions of *The Lives of the Caesars* have appeared within the past few years, those of M. Ihm, Leipzig, 1907, and of L. Preud'homme, Groningen, 1906, each based on a painstaking and independent study of the manuscripts. These show remarkably few deviations from the work of Roth (1858) and from each other. The text therefore may be regarded as practically settled, at least until the independent value of the fifteenth century codices has been demonstrated. (See p. xxv.)

It is generally agreed that all our existing manuscripts are derived from one at Fulda, written in rustic capitals (Ihm) or uncials (Preud'homme). This seems to have been the only one in existence at the time, and it is known to us from a letter of Servatus Lupus, abbot of Ferriéres, of the year 884. This codex and a copy of it in minuscules, which was sent to Servatus Lupus at his request, are now lost; but the latter was extensively copied, and the number of manuscripts at present existing is very large. The Fulda codex (Ω, Ihm; P, Preud'homme[1]) lacked the beginning of the *Life of Julius Caesar* and had other lesser lacunae and numerous errors, but seems to have been free from interpolation. The copies however were extensively emended, so that by the twelfth century the text was in bad condition.

The manuscripts used by Ihm, with the sigla which he employs, are the following; the sigla of Preud'homme are given in parentheses:

M (A). The *codex Memmianus* of the ninth century. Our oldest and best manuscript, either a copy of the one sent to Servatus Lupus or closely related to it, apparently free from interpolations, though not without errors and lacunae. None of our other manuscripts is derived from it. It contains corrections made by another hand, not later than the twelfth century (M^2).

This codex came originally from the monastery of St. Martin of Tours, was later in the possession of Henri de Mesmes, and is now in the National Library in Paris. It is commonly called Memmianus, from de Mesmes, but was formerly called Turonensis; its present designation is Codex Parisinus, 6115, formerly 5984.

G (C). The *codex Gudianus* of the eleventh century, now at Wölffenbuttel (Gudianus, 268). Closely related to M and derived from a similar original, but inferior to it. It has numerous corrections, made in part by the scribe (M^2) and in part in the fifteenth century (M^3).

V (B). The *codex Vaticanus,* 1904, of the eleventh century, a little younger than G but more trustworthy. It frequently agrees with M, and is of almost equal value; but it comes to an end at *Calig* iii, *delecta sua re.* It was used by Lipsius in 1574. It contains glosses of the same general character as M^2.

Preud'homme regards his D (Parisinus, 5804), of the fourteenth century, as in the same class with the above; Ihm, who assigns it to the fifteenth century, rates it much less highly.

The other important manuscripts fall into two classes, each represented by a large number of examples. The first class is represented by the following:

L (a). The *codex Laurentianus,* 68. 7, of the twelfth century, in the Medicean Library at Florence, the *Mediceus Tertius* of Oudendorp. It also contains Caesar, *De Bella Gallico,* and has corrections by an earlier (L^2) and a later hand (L^3).

P (b). The *codex Parisinus,* 5801, of the twelfth century, with corrections from a manuscript of the second class (P^2), according to Ihm.

O (c). The *codex Laurentianus,* 66. 39, of the twelfth century, in the Medicean Library at Florence. Has corrections similar to those in P (O^2).

S (f). The *codex Montepessulanus,* 117, of the twelfth century, at Montpelier. Corrected in the same manner as P and O.

T. The *codex Berolinensis,* Lat. 337, of the fourteenth century, formerly *Hulsianus* or *Hagianus* Frequently agrees with V and L. Corrected by a hand of about the same date as the original scribe.

From the agreement of L, P, O, S, and T, the readings of their archetype are recovered, a lost manuscript from the same original as V, but inferior to V, designated by X (X′). The agreement of X and V gives the readings of X′, a lost codex of the class of M and V.

The second class contains more errors and interpolations than the first. It is represented by a very large number of manuscripts, of which Ihm uses the following:

II (*β*). The *codex Parisinus,* 6116, of the twelfth century, corrected from a manuscript of the variety represented by R.

Q (*γ*). The *codex Parisinus,* 5802, of the twelfth century, corrected in the fifteenth.

R (*α*). The *codex Regius of* the twelfth century, in the British Museum (15. C. iii), and rated high by Bentley. It comes to an end with *Dom.* xiv, *non alias magis,* but seems to have been complete in the sixteenth century.

The agreement of these codices gives the readings of their archetype (Υ), a lost codex of about the same date as X, but inferior to it; and since P, O, S, and T were corrected from a manuscript of this class, their agreement with Υ gives the readings of another lost manuscript Υ′.

Besides the manuscripts of the whole work we have two collections of selections, which have some critical value. The earliest of these was made by Heiric of Auxerre between 871 and 876 and based on Lupus's copy of the codex Fuldensis. It is of considerable value, but has suffered from emendation; H (Y). A fuller epitome of the thirteenth century, of comparatively little value, is preserved in codex Parisinus, 17903, formerly Notre-Dame, 188; N.

Ihm and Preud'homme are in substantial agreement in their classification of the manuscripts. The latter divides them into two classes, X and Z, the first including M, V, X, G, δ, and H (or in his nomenclature, A, B, X′, C, D, and Y); the second, R, Π, Q, and Suessionensis, 119 (in his nomenclature, α, β, γ, ε).

The only important difference of opinion is as to the independent value of the fifteenth-century manuscripts, which frequently offer good readings not found in the earlier codices. Roth came to the conclusion that these were mere conjectures, without value in determining the readings of the archetype, and the careful and independent investigations of Ihm and Preud'homme led them to the same opinion. The contrary view is held by some scholars,[2] but cannot be regarded as sufficiently established.[3]

BIBLIOGRAPHICAL NOTE

THE earliest editions are two published in Rome in 1470, one in July by Johannes Campanus, and the other in December by Johannes Aleriensis; these were immediately followed by a Venetian edition of 1471, and all three are regarded as *editiones principes*. Among other early editions are those of Beroaldus, Bologna, 1493 and 1506, the latter with a valuable commentary; Erasmus, Basle, 1518; R. Stephanus (Robert Étienne), Paris, 1543; and Casaubon, Geneva, 1595 and Paris, 1610.

Down to 1820 more than forty editions were issued, including some second editions, among them those of Gronovius, Leyden, 1698; Burman, Amsterdam, 1763, with the full commentary of a number of his predecessors and selections from those of others; Ernesti, Leipzig, 1748 and 1775; Oudendorp, Leyden, 1751; Baumgarten-Crusius, Leipzig, 1816, with a commentary and very full indices (*Clavis Suetoniana*). This is still the standard annotated edition. It was issued with some additions by C. B. Hase at Paris in 1828. Bentley planned an edition which was never finished, but his material is preserved in the British Museum.

In later times the editions have been few in number. That of C. L. Roth, Leipzig, 1858, was the standard text until the appearance of those of Ihm and Preud'homme.

The Lives of the Caesars still lacks a commentary in English and a full and satisfactory one in any language. There are annotated editions of separate lives by H. T. Peck, *Julius and Augustus,* New York, 1893[2]; E. S. Shuckburgh, *Augustus,* Cambridge, 1896; and J. B. Pike, *Tiberius, Caligula, Claudius and Nero,* Boston, 1903; to these maybe added H. Smilda, *Claudius,* Groningen, 1896, and C. Hofstee, *Galba, Olho and Vitellius,* Groningen, 1898.

The *Caesars* have been translated into English by Philemon Holland, London, 1606; John Clarke, London, 1732, with the Latin text; and by Alexander Thomson, London, 1796. A revision of Thomson's translation was made by T. Forester, and published in the Bohn Library (London) without a date.

Of books and monographs dealing with Suetonius the following may be mentioned: A. Macé, *Essai sur Suétone,* Paris, 1900; Fr. Leo, *Die griechisch-römischen Biographie,* Leipzig, 1901; L. Preud'homme, *Premiére, deuxiéme, troisiéme étude sur l' histoire du lexte de Suétone de vita Caesarum, Bulletins de l' Académie royale de Belgique,* 1902 and 1904; Ihm, *Hermes,* 36, 37 and 40; H. R. Thimm, *De usu alque elocutione C. Suet. Tranq.*, Regimonti, 1867; P. Bagge, *De elocutione C. Suet. Tranq.*, Upsala, 1875; I. W. Freund, *De Suetonii usu atque genere dicendi,* Breslau, 1901; W. Dennison, "The Epigraphic Sources of Suetonius," *Amer. Jour. of Archœology,* Second Series, II., pp. 26 ff.; L. Damasso, *La Grammatica di C. Suet. Tranq.*, Turin, 1906; C. L. Smith, *Harvard Studies in Class. Phil.*, xii. pp. 54 ff; A. A. Howard, *idem,* vii, 210 ff., x. pp. 23 ff., and xii. pp. 261 ff.; J. C. Rolfe, "Suetonius and his Biographies," *Proc. Amer. Philosophical Soc.* lii, pp. 206 ff.

The reader may be reminded of S. Baring-Gould's *Tragedy of the Caesars,* London, 1902; Sienkiewicz's *Quo Vadis;* Gardthausen's *Augustus und seine Zeit,* Leipzig, 1891; Shuckburgh's *Augustus,* London, 1903; and of other general and special works dealing with the period.

SIGLA

Ω=the archetype of our existing codices, restored by the agreement of X′ and Y′.

M=Codex Memmianus.

G=Codex Gudianus.

X′=the archetype of V and X.

V=Codex Vaticanus.

X=the archetype of

L=Codex Laurentianus, 68 .7.

P=Codex Parisinus, 5801.

O=Codex Laurentianus, 66 .39.

S=Codex Montepessulanus.

T=Codex Berolinensis.

Υ=the archetype of

Π=Codex Parisinus, 6116.

Q=Codex Parisinus, 5802.

R=Codex Regius.

Υ′=the agreement of Υ with S and T, usually accompanied by that of P^2 and O (O^2).

ζ=all the codices not included in the above list.

BOOK I

THE DEIFIED JULIUS

I. In the course of his sixteenth year[1] he lost his father. In the next consulate, having previously been nominated priest of Jupiter,[2] he broke his engagement with Cossutia, a lady of only equestrian rank, but very wealthy, who had been betrothed to him before he assumed the gown of manhood, and married Cornelia, daughter of that Cinna who was four times consul, by whom he afterwards had a daughter Julia; and the dictator Sulla could by no means force him to put away his wife. Therefore besides being punished by the loss of his priesthood, his wife's dowry, and his family inheritances, Caesar was held to be one of the opposite party. He was accordingly forced to go into hiding, and though suffering from a severe attack of quartan ague, to change from one covert to another almost every night, and save himself from Sulla's detectives by bribes. But at last, through the good offices of the Vestal virgins and of his near kinsmen, Aemilius Mamercus and Aurelius Cotta, he obtained forgiveness. Everyone knows that when Sulla had long held out against the most devoted and eminent men of his party who interceded for Caesar, and they obstinately persisted, he at last gave way and cried, either by divine inspiration or a shrewd forecast: "Have your way and take him; only bear in mind that the man you are so eager to save will one day deal the death blow to the cause of the aristocracy, which you have joined with me in upholding; for in this Caesar there is more than one Marius."

81 B.C. II. He served his first campaign in Asia on the personal staff of Marcus Thermus, governor of the province. Being sent by Thermus to Bithynia, to fetch a fleet, he dawdled so long at the court of Nicomedes that he was suspected of improper relations with the king; and he lent colour to this scandal by going back to Bithynia a few days after his return, with the alleged purpose of
80 B.C. collecting a debt for a freedman, one of his dependents. During the rest of the campaign he enjoyed a better reputation, and at the storming of Mytilene Thermus awarded him the civic crown.[3]

III. He served too under Servilius Isauricus in Cilicia, but only for a short time; for learning of the death of Sulla, and at the same
78 B.C. time hoping to profit by a counter revolution which Marcus Lepidus was setting on foot, he hurriedly returned to Rome. But he did not make common cause with Lepidus, although he was offered highly favourable terms, through lack of confidence both in that leader's capacity and in the outlook, which he found less promising than he had expected.

IV. Then, after the civil disturbance had been quieted, he brought a charge of extortion against Cornelius Dolabella, an ex-
77 B.C. consul who had been honoured with a triumph. On the acquittal of Dolabella Caesar determined to withdraw to Rhodes, to escape from the ill-will which he had incurred, and at the same time to
74 B.C. rest and have leisure to study under Apollonius Molo, the most eminent teacher of oratory of that time. While crossing to Rhodes, after the winter season had already begun, he was taken by pirates near the island of Pharmacussa and remained in their custody for nearly forty days in a state of intense vexation, attended only by a single physician and two body-servants; for he had sent off his travelling companions and the rest of his attendants at the outset, to raise money for his ransom. Once he was set on shore on payment of fifty talents, he did not delay then and there to launch a fleet and pursue the departing pirates, and the moment they were in his power to inflict on them the punishment which he had often threatened when joking with them.[4] He then proceeded to Rhodes, but as Mithridates was devastating the

neighbouring regions, he crossed over into Asia, to avoid the appearance of inaction when the allies of the Roman people were in danger. There he levied a band of auxiliaries and drove the king's prefect from the province, thus holding the wavering and irresolute states to their allegiance.

V. While serving as military tribune, the first office which was conferred on him by vote of the people after his return to Rome, he ardently supported the leaders in the attempt to re-establish the authority of the tribunes of the commons, the extent of which Sulla had curtailed. Furthermore, through a bill proposed by one 70 B.C. Plotius, he effected the recall of his wife's brother Lucius Cinna, as well as of the others who had taken part with Lepidus in his revolution and after the consul's death had fled to Sertorius; and he personally spoke in favour of the measure.

VI. When quaestor, he pronounced the customary orations from 67 B.C. the rostra in praise of his aunt Julia and his wife Cornelia, who had both died. And in the eulogy of his aunt he spoke in the following terms of her paternal and maternal ancestry and that of his own father: "The family of my aunt Julia is descended by her mother from the kings, and on her father's side is akin to the immortal Gods; for the Marcii Reges (her mother's family name) go back to Ancus Marcius, and the Julii, the family of which ours is a branch, to Venus. Our stock therefore has at once the sanctity of kings, whose power is supreme among mortal men, and the claim to reverence which attaches to the Gods, who hold sway over kings themselves."

In place of Cornelia he took to wife Pompeia, daughter of Quintus Pompeius and granddaughter of Lucius Sulla. But he afterward divorced her, suspecting her of adultery with Publius 62 B.C. Clodius; and in fact the report that Clodius had gained access to her in woman's garb during a public religious ceremony[5] was so persistent, that the senate decreed that the pollution of the sacred rites be judicially investigated.

VII. As quaestor it fell to his lot to serve in Farther Spain. When he was there, while making the circuit of the assize-towns, to hold court under commission from the praetor, he came to Gades, and noticing a statue of Alexander the Great in the temple of Hercules, he heaved a sigh, and as if out of patience with his own incapacity in having as yet done nothing noteworthy at a time of life when Alexander had already brought the world to his feet, he straightway asked for his discharge, to grasp the first opportunity for greater enterprises at Rome. Furthermore, when he was dismayed by a dream the following night (for he thought that he had offered violence to his mother) the soothsayers inspired him with high hopes by their interpretation, which was: that he was destined to rule the world, since the mother whom he had seen in his power was none other than the earth, which is regarded as the common parent of all mankind.

VIII. Departing therefore before his term was over, he went to the Latin colonies which were in a state of unrest and meditating a demand for citizenship[6]; and he might have spurred them on to some rash act, had not the consuls, in anticipation of that very danger, detained there for a time the legions which had been enrolled for service in Cilicia.

IX. For all that he presently made a more daring attempt at Rome; for a few days before he entered upon his aedileship he was suspected of having made a conspiracy with Marcus Crassus, an ex-consul, and likewise with Publius Sulla and Lucius Autronius, who, after their election to the consulship, had been found guilty of
65 B.C. corrupt practices. The design was to set upon the senate at the opening of the year and put to the sword as many as they thought good; then Crassus was to usurp the dictatorship, naming Caesar as his master of horse, and when they had organized the state according to their pleasure, the consulship was to be restored to Sulla and Autronius. This plot is mentioned by Tanusius Geminus in his History, by Marcus Bibulus in his edicts, and by Gaius Curio the elder in his speeches. Cicero too seems to hint at it in a letter to Axius, where he says that Caesar in his consulship established the despotism which he had had in mind when he was aedile. Tanusius adds that Crassus, either conscience-stricken or moved by fear, did not appear on the day appointed for the massacre, and

that therefore Caesar did not give the signal which it had been agreed that he should give; and Curio says that the arrangement was that Caesar should let his toga fall from his shoulder. Not only Curio, but Marcus Actorius Naso as well declare that Caesar made another plot with Gnaeus Piso, a young man to whom the province of Spain had been assigned unasked and out of the regular order, because he was suspected of political intrigues at Rome; that they agreed to rise in revolt at the same time, Piso abroad and Caesar at Rome, aided by the Ambrani and the peoples beyond the Po; but that Piso's death brought both their designs to naught.

X. When aedile, Caesar decorated[7] not only the Comitium and 65 B.C. the Forum with its adjacent basilicas, but the Capitol as well, building temporary colonnades for the display of a part of his material. He exhibited combats with wild beasts and stage-plays too, both with his colleague and independently. The result was that Caesar alone took all the credit even for what they spent in common, and his colleague Marcus Bibulus openly said that his was the fate of Pollux: "For," said he, "just as the temple erected in the Forum to the twin brethren, bears only the name of Castor, so the joint liberality of Caesar and myself is credited to Caesar alone." Caesar gave a gladiatorial show besides, but with somewhat fewer pairs of combatants than he had purposed; for the huge band which he assembled from all quarters so terrified his opponents, that a bill was passed limiting the number of gladiators which anyone was to be allowed to keep in the city.

XI. Having won the goodwill of the masses, Caesar made an attempt through some of the tribunes to have the charge of Egypt given him by a decree of the commons, seizing the opportunity to ask for so irregular an appointment because the citizens of Alexandria had deposed their king, who had been named by the senate an ally and friend of the Roman people, and their action was generally condemned. He failed however because of the opposition of the aristocratic party; wishing therefore to impair their prestige in every way he could, he restored the trophies commemorating the victories of Gaius Marius over Jugurtha and over the Cimbri and Teutoni, which Sulla had long since demolished. Furthermore in conducting prosecutions for murder,[8] he included in the number of murderers even those who had received moneys from the public treasury during the proscriptions for bringing in the heads of Roman citizens, although they were expressly exempted by the Cornelian laws.

XII. He also bribed a man to bring a charge of high treason against Gaius Rabirius, who some years before had rendered conspicuous service to the senate in repressing the seditious designs of the tribune Lucius Saturninus; and when he had been selected by lot to sentence the accused,[9] he did so with such eagerness, that when Rabirius appealed to the people, nothing was so much in his favour as the bitter hostility of his judge.

XIII. After giving up hope of the special commission,[10] he announced his candidacy for the office of pontifex maximus, resorting to the most lavish bribery. Thinking on the enormous debt which he had thus contracted, he is said to have declared to his mother on the morning of the election, as she kissed him when he was starting for the polls, that he would never return except as pontifex. And in fact he so decisively defeated two very strong competitors (for they were greatly his superiors in age and rank), that he polled more votes in their tribes than were cast for both of them in all the tribes.

XIV. When the conspiracy of Catiline was detected, and all the rest of the senate favoured inflicting the extreme penalty on those implicated in the plot, Caesar, who was now praetor elect, alone proposed that their goods be confiscated and that
63 B.C. they be imprisoned each in a separate town. Nay, more, he inspired such fear in those who favoured severer measures, by picturing the hatred which the Roman commons would feel for them for all future time, that Decimus Silanus, consul elect, was not ashamed to give a milder interpretation to his proposal (since it would have been humiliating to change it) alleging that it had been understood in a harsher sense than he intended. Caesar would have prevailed too, for a number had

already gone over to him, including Cicero, the consul's brother, had not the address of Marcus Cato kept the wavering senate in line. Yet not even then did he cease to delay the proceedings, but only when an armed troop of Roman knights that stood on guard about the place threatened him with death as he persisted in his headstrong opposition. They even drew their swords and made such passes at him that his friends who sat next him forsook him, while a few had much ado to shield him in their embrace or with their robes. Then, in evident fear, he not only yielded the point, but for the rest of the year kept aloof from the House.

XV. On the first day of his praetorship he called upon 62 B.C.
Quintus Catulus to render an account to the people touching the restoration of the Capitol, proposing a bill for turning over the commission to another.[11] But he withdrew the measure, since he could not cope with the united opposition of the aristocrats, seeing that they had at once dropped their attendance on the newly elected consuls[12] and hastily gathered in throngs, resolved on an obstinate resistance.

XVI. Nevertheless, when Caecilius Metellus, tribune of the commons, brought forward some bills of a highly seditious nature in spite of the veto of his colleagues, Caesar abetted him and espoused his cause in the stubbornest fashion, until at last both were suspended from the exercise of their public functions by a decree of the senate. Yet in spite of this Caesar had the audacity to continue in office and to hold court; but when he learned that some were ready to stop him by force of arms, he dismissed his lictors, laid aside his robe of office, and slipped off privily to his house, intending to remain in retirement because of the state of the times. Indeed, when the populace on the following day flocked to him quite of their own accord, and with riotous demonstrations offered him their aid in recovering his position, he held them in check. Since this action of his was wholly unexpected, the senate, which had been hurriedly convoked to take action about that very gathering, publicly thanked him through its leading men; then summoning him to the House and lauding him in the strongest terms, they rescinded their former decree and restored him to his rank.

XVII. He again fell into danger by being named among the accomplices of Catiline, both before the commissioner[13] Novius Niger by an informer called Lucius Vettius and in the senate by Quintus Curius, who had been voted a sum of money from the public funds as the first to disclose the plans of the conspirators. Curius alleged that his information came directly from Catiline, while Vettius actually offered to produce a letter to Catiline in Caesar's handwriting. But Caesar, thinking that such an indignity could in no wise be endured, showed by appealing to Cicero's testimony that he had of his own accord reported to the consul certain details of the plot, and thus prevented Curius from getting the reward. As for Vettius, after his bond was declared forfeit and his goods seized, he was roughly handled by the populace assembled before the rostra, and all but torn to pieces. Caesar then put him in prison, and Novius the commissioner went there too, for allowing an official of superior rank to be arraigned before his tribunal.

61 B.C. XVIII. Being allotted the province of Farther Spain after his praetorship, Caesar got rid of his creditors, who tried to detain him, by means of sureties and contrary both to precedent and law was on his way before the provinces were provided for[14]; possibly through fear of a private impeachment or perhaps to respond more promptly to the entreaties of our allies for help. After restoring order in his province, he made off with equal haste, and without waiting for the arrival of his successor, to sue at the same time for a triumph and the consulship. But inasmuch as the day for the elections had already been announced and no account could be taken of Caesar's candidacy unless he entered the city as a private citizen, and since his intrigues to gain exemption from the laws met with general protest, he was forced to forgo the triumph, to avoid losing the consulship.

59 B.C. XIX. Of the two other candidates for this office, Lucius Lucceius and Marcus Bibulus, Caesar joined forces with the former, making a bargain with him that since Lucceius had less influ-

ence but more funds, he should in their common name promise largess to the electors from his own pocket. When this became known, the aristocracy authorized Bibulus to promise the same amount, being seized with fear that Caesar would stick at nothing when he became chief magistrate, if he had a colleague who was heart and soul with him. Many of them contributed to the fund, and even Cato did not deny that bribery under such circumstances was for the good of the commonwealth.

So Caesar was chosen consul with Bibulus. With the same motives the aristocracy took care that provinces of the smallest importance should be assigned to the newly elected consuls; that is, mere woods and pastures.[15] Thereupon Caesar, especially incensed by this slight, by every possible attention courted the goodwill of Gnaeus Pompeius, who was at odds with the senate because of its tardiness in ratifying his acts after his victory over king Mithridates. He also patched up a peace between Pompeius and Marcus Crassus, who had been enemies since their consulship, which had been one of constant wrangling. Then he made a 60 B.C.
compact with both of them, that no step should be taken in public affairs which did not suit any one of the three.

XX. Caesar's very first enactment after becoming consul was, that the proceedings both of the senate and of the people should day by day be compiled and published. He also revived a by-gone custom, that during the months when he did not have the fasces an orderly should walk before him, while the lictors followed him. He brought forward an agrarian law too, and when his colleague announced adverse omens,[16] he resorted to arms and drove him from the Forum; and when next day Bibulus made complaint in the senate and no one could be found who ventured to make a motion, or even to express an opinion about so high-handed a proceeding (although decrees had often been passed touching less serious breaches of the peace), Caesar's conduct drove him to such a pitch of desperation, that from that time until the end of his term he did not leave his house, but merely issued proclamations announcing adverse omens.

From that time on Caesar managed all the affairs of state alone and after his own pleasure; so that sundry witty fellows, pretending by way of jest to sign and seal testamentary documents,[17] wrote "Done in the consulship of Julius and Caesar," instead of "Bibulus and Caesar," writing down the same man twice, by name and by surname. Presently too the following verses were on everyone's lips:—

"In Caesar's year, not Bibulus', an act took place of late;
For naught do I remember done in Bibulus' consulate."

The plain called Stellas, which had been devoted to public uses by the men of by-gone days, and the Campanian territory, which had been reserved to pay revenues for the aid of the government, he divided without casting lots[18] among twenty thousand citizens who had three or more children each. When the publicans asked for relief, he freed them from a third part of their obligation, and openly warned them in contracting for taxes in the future not to bid too recklessly. He freely granted everything else that anyone took it into his head to ask, either without opposition or by intimidating anyone who tried to object. Marcus Cato, who tried to delay proceedings,[19] was dragged from the House by a lictor at Caesar's command and taken off to prison. When Lucius Lucullus was somewhat too outspoken in his opposition, he filled him with such fear of malicious prosecution,[20] that Lucullus actually fell on his knees before him. Because Cicero, while pleading in court, deplored the state of the times, Caesar transferred the orator's enemy Publius Clodius that very 60 B.C. same day from the patricians to the plebeians, a thing for which Clodius had for a long time been vainly striving; and that too at the ninth hour.[21] Finally taking action against all the opposition in a body, he bribed an informer to declare that he had been egged on by certain men to murder Pompey, and to come out upon the rostra and name the guilty parties according to a prearranged plot. But when the informer had named one or two to no purpose and not without suspicion of double-dealing, Caesar, hopeless of the success of his over-hasty attempt, is supposed to have had him taken off by poison.

XXI. At about the same time he took to wife Calpurnia, daughter of Lucius Piso, who was to succeed him in the consulship, and affianced his own daughter Julia to Gnaeus Pompeius, breaking a previous engagement with Servilius Caepio, although the latter had shortly before rendered him conspicuous service in his contest with Bibulus. And after this new alliance he began to call upon Pompey first to give his opinion in the senate, although it had been his habit to begin with Crassus, and it was the rule for the consul in calling for opinions to continue throughout the year the order which he had established on the Kalends of January.

XXII. Backed therefore by his father-in-law and son-in-law, out of all the numerous provinces he made the Gauls his choice, as the most likely to enrich him and furnish suitable material for triumphs. At first, it is true, by the bill of Vatinius he received only Cisalpine Gaul with the addition of Illyricum; but presently he was assigned Gallia Comata as well by the senate, since the members feared that even if they should refuse it, the people would give him this also. Transported with joy at this success, he could not keep from boasting a few days later before a crowded house, that having gained his heart's desire to the grief and lamentation of his opponents, he would therefore from that time mount on their heads;[22] and when someone insultingly remarked that that would be no easy matter for any woman, he replied in the same vein that Semiramis too had been queen in Syria and the Amazons in days of old had held sway over a great part of Asia.

XXIII. When at the close of his consulship the praetors Gaius Memmius and Lucius Domitius moved an inquiry into his conduct during the previous year, Caesar laid the matter before the senate; and when they failed to take it up, and three days had been wasted in fruitless wrangling, went off to his province. Whereupon his quaestor was at once arraigned on several counts, as a preliminary to his own impeachment. Presently he himself too was prosecuted by Lucius Antistius, tribune of the commons, and it was only by appealing to the whole college that he contrived not to be brought to trial, on the ground that he was absent on public service. Then to secure himself for the future, he took great pains always to put the magistrates for the year under personal obligation, and not to aid any candidates or suffer any to be elected, save such as guaranteed to defend him in his absence. And he did not hesitate in some cases to exact an oath to keep this pledge or even a written contract.

55 B.C. XXIV. When however Lucius Domitius, candidate for the consulship, openly threatened to effect as consul what he had been unable to do as praetor, and to take his armies from him, Caesar compelled Pompeius and Crassus to come to Luca, a city in his province, where he prevailed on them to stand for a second consulship, to defeat Domitius; and he also succeeded through their influence in having his term as governor of Gaul made five years longer. Encouraged by this, he added to the legions which he had received from the state others at his own cost, one actually composed of men of Transalpine Gaul and bearing a Gallic name too (for it was called Alauda[23]), which he trained in the Roman tactics and equipped with Roman arms; and later on he gave every man of it citizenship. After that he did not let slip any pretext for war, however unjust and dangerous it might be, picking quarrels as well with allied, as with hostile and barbarous nations; so that once the senate decreed that a commission be sent to inquire into the condition of the Gallic provinces, and some even recommended that Caesar be handed over to the enemy. But as his enterprises prospered, thanksgivings were appointed in his honour oftener and for longer periods than for anyone before his time.

58/49 B.C. XXV. During the nine years of his command this is in substance what he did. All that part of Gaul which is bounded by the Pyrenees, the Alps and the Cévennes, and by the Rhine and Rhone rivers, a circuit of some 3,200[24] miles, with the exception of some allied states which had rendered him good service, he reduced to the form of a province; and imposed upon it a yearly tribute of

40,000,000 sesterces.[25] He was the first Roman to build a bridge and attack the Germans beyond the Rhine; and he inflicted heavy losses upon them. He invaded the Britons too, a people unknown before, vanquished them, and exacted moneys and hostages. Amid all these successes he met with adverse fortune but three times in all: in Britain, where his fleet narrowly escaped destruction in a violent storm; in Gaul; when one of his legions was routed at Gergovia; and in the land of Germany, when his lieutenants Titurius and Aurunculeius were ambushed and slain.

XXVI. Within this same space of time he lost first his mother, then his daughter, and soon afterwards his grandson. Meanwhile, as the community was aghast at the murder of Publius Clodius, the senate had voted that only one consul should be chosen, and expressly named Gnaeus Pompeius. When the tribunes planned to make him Pompey's colleague, Caesar urged them rather to propose to the people that he be permitted to stand for a second consulship without coming to Rome, when the term of his governorship drew near its end, to prevent his being forced for the sake of the office to leave his province prematurely and without finishing the war. On the granting of this, aiming still higher and flushed with hope, he neglected nothing in the way of lavish expenditure or of favours to anyone, either in his public capacity or privately. He began a forum with the proceeds of his spoils, the ground for which cost more than a hundred million sesterces. He announced a combat of gladiators and a feast for the people in memory of his daughter, a thing quite without precedent. To raise the expectation of these events to the highest possible pitch, he had the material for the banquet prepared in part by his own household, although he had let contracts to the markets as well. He gave orders too that whenever famous gladiators fought without winning the favour of the people,[26] they should be rescued by force and kept for him. He had the novices trained, not in a gladiatorial school by professionals, but in private houses by Roman knights and even by senators who were skilled in arms, earnestly beseeching them, as is shown by his own letters, to give the recruits individual attention and personally direct their exercises. He doubled the pay of the legions for all time. Whenever grain was plentiful, he distributed it to them without stint or measure, and now and then gave each man a slave from among the captives.

XXVII. Moreover, to retain his relationship and friendship with Pompey, Caesar offered him his sister's granddaughter Octavia in marriage, although she was already the wife of Gaius Marcellus, and asked for the hand of Pompey's daughter, who was promised to Faustus Sulla. When he had put all Pompey's friends under obligation, as well as the great part of the senate, through loans made without interest or at a low rate, he lavished gifts on men of all other classes, both those whom he invited to accept his bounty and those who applied to him unasked, including even freedmen and slaves who were special favourites of their masters or patrons. In short, he was the sole and ever ready help of all who were in legal difficulties or in debt and of young spendthrifts, excepting only those whose burden of guilt or of poverty was so heavy, or who were so given up to riotous living, that even he could not save them; and to these he declared in the plainest terms that what they needed was a civil war.

XXVIII. He took no less pains to win the devotion of princes and provinces all over the world, offering prisoners to some by the thousand as a gift, and sending auxiliary troops to the aid of others whenever they wished, and as often as they wished, without the sanction of the senate or people, besides adorning the principal cities of Asia and Greece with magnificent public works, as well as those of Italy and the provinces of Gaul and Spain. At last, when all were thunder-struck at his actions and wondered what their
51 B.C. purpose could be, the consul Marcus Claudius Marcellus, after first making proclamation that he purposed to bring before the senate a matter of the highest public moment, proposed that a successor to Caesar be appointed before the end of his term, on the ground that the war was ended, peace was established, and the victorious army ought to be disbanded; also that no account be taken of Caesar at the elections, unless he were present, since

Pompey's subsequent action[27] had not annulled the decree of the people. And it was true that when Pompey proposed a bill touching the privileges of officials, in the clause where he debarred absentees from candidacy for office he forgot to make a special exception in Caesar's case, and did not correct the oversight until the law had been inscribed on a tablet of bronze and deposited in the treasury. Not content with depriving Caesar of his provinces and his privilege, Marcellus also moved that the colonists whom Caesar had settled in Novum Comum by the bill of Vatinius should lose their citizenship, on the ground that it had been given from political motives and was not authorized by the law.

XXIX. Greatly troubled by these measures, and thinking, as they say he was often heard to remark, that now that he was the leading man of the state, it was harder to push him down from the first place to the second than it would be from the second to the lowest, Caesar stoutly resisted Marcellus, partly through vetoes of the tribunes and partly through the other consul, Servius Sulpicius. When next year Gaius Marcellus, who had succeeded his cousin Marcus as consul, tried the same thing, Caesar by a heavy bribe secured the support of the other consul, Aemilius Paulus, and of Gaius Curio, the most reckless of the tribunes. But seeing that everything was being pushed most persistently, and that even the consuls elect were among the opposition, he sent a written appeal to the senate, not to take from him the privilege which the people had granted, or else to compel the others in command of armies to resign also; feeling sure, it was thought, that he could more readily muster his veterans as soon as he wished, than Pompey his newly levied troops. He further proposed a compromise to his opponents, that after giving up eight legions and Transalpine Gaul, he be allowed to keep two legions and Cisalpine Gaul, or at least one legion and Illyricum, until he was elected consul.

XXX. But when the senate declined to interfere, and his opponents declared that they would accept no compromise in a matter affecting the public welfare, he crossed to Hither Gaul, and after holding all the assizes, halted at Ravenna, intending to resort to war if the senate took any drastic action against the tribunes of the commons who interposed vetoes in his behalf.[28] Now this was his excuse for the civil war, but it is believed that he had other motives. Gnaeus Pompeius used to declare that since Caesar's own means were not sufficient to complete the works which he had planned, nor to do all that he had led the people to expect on his return, he desired a state of general unrest and turmoil. Others say that he dreaded the necessity of rendering an account for what he had done in his first consulship contrary to the auspices and the laws, and regardless of vetoes; for Marcus Cato often declared, and took oath too, that he would impeach Caesar the moment he had disbanded his army. It was openly said too that if he was out of office on his return, he would be obliged, like Milo, to make his defence in a court hedged about by armed men. The latter opinion is the more credible one in view of the assertion of Asinius Pollio, that when Caesar at the battle of Pharsalus saw his enemies slain or in flight, he said, word for word: "They would have it so. Even I, Gaius Caesar, after so many great deeds, should have been found guilty, if I had not turned to my army for help." Some think that habit had given him a love of power, and that weighing the strength of his adversaries against his own, he grasped the opportunity of usurping the despotism which had been his heart's desire from early youth. Cicero too was seemingly of this opinion, when he wrote in the third book of his *De Officiis*[29] that Caesar ever had upon his lips these lines of Euripides,[30] of which Cicero himself adds a version:

> "If wrong may e'er be right, for a throne's sake were wrong most right:—be God in all else feared."[31]

XXXI. Accordingly, when word came that the veto of the tribunes had been set aside and they themselves had left the city, he at once sent on a few cohorts with all secrecy, and then, to disarm
49 B.C. suspicion, concealed his purpose by appearing at a public show,

inspecting the plans of a gladiatorial school which he intended building, and joining as usual in a banquet with a large company. It was not until after sunset that he set out very privily with a small company, taking the mules from a bakeshop hard by and harnessing them to a carriage; and when his lights went out and he lost his way, he was astray for some time, but at last found a guide at dawn and got back to the road on foot by narrow bypaths. Then, overtaking his cohorts at the river Rubicon, which was the boundary of his province, he paused for a while, and realising what a step he was taking, he turned to those about him and said: "Even yet we may draw back; but once cross yon little bridge, and the whole issue is with the sword."

XXXII. As he stood in doubt, this sign was given him. On a sudden there appeared hard by a being of wondrous stature and beauty, who sat and played upon a reed; and when not only the shepherds flocked to hear him, but many of the soldiers left their posts, and among them some of the trumpeters, the apparition snatched a trumpet from one of them, rushed to the river, and sounding the war-note with mighty blast, strode to the opposite bank. Then Caesar cried: "Take we the course which the signs of the gods and the false dealing of our foes point out. The die is cast," said he.

XXXIII. Accordingly, crossing with his army, and welcoming the tribunes of the commons, who had come to him after being driven from Rome, he harangued the soldiers with tears, and rending his robe from his breast besought their faithful service. It is even thought that he promised every man a knight's estate, but that came of a misunderstanding; for since he often pointed to the finger of his left hand as he addressed them and urged them on, declaring that to satisfy all those who helped him to defend his honour he would gladly tear his very ring from his hand, those on the edge of the assembly, who could see him better than they could hear his words, assumed that he said what his gesture seemed to mean; and so the report went about that he had promised them the right of the ring and four hundred thousand sesterces[32] as well.

XXXIV. The sum total of his movements after that is, in their order, as follows: He overran Umbria, Picenum, and Etruria, took prisoner Lucius Domitius, who had been irregularly[33] named his successor, and was holding Corfinium with a garrison, let him go free, and then proceeded along the Adriatic to Brundisium, where Pompey and the consuls had taken refuge, intending to cross the sea as soon as might be. After vainly trying by every kind of hindrance to prevent their sailing, he marched off to Rome, and after calling the senate together to discuss public business, went to attack Pompey's strongest forces, which were in Spain under command of three of his lieutenants—Marcus Petreius, Lucius Afranius, and Marcus Varro—saying to his friends before he left "I go to meet an army without a leader, and I shall return to meet a leader without an army." And in fact, though his advance was delayed by the siege of Massilia, which had shut its gates against him, and by extreme scarcity of supplies, he nevertheless quickly gained a complete victory.

XXXV. Returning thence to Rome, he crossed into Macedonia, and after blockading Pompey for almost four months behind
48 B.C. mighty ramparts, finally routed him in the battle at Pharsalus, followed him in his flight to Alexandria, and when he learned that his rival had been slain, made war on King Ptolemy, whom he perceived to be plotting against his own safety as well; a war in truth of great difficulty, convenient neither in time nor place, but carried on during the winter season, within the walls of a well-provisioned and crafty foeman, while Caesar himself was without supplies of
47 B.C. any kind and ill-prepared. Victor in spite of all, he turned over the rule of Egypt to Cleopatra and her younger brother, fearing that if he made a province of it, it might one day under a headstrong governor be a source of revolution. From Alexandria he crossed to Syria, and from there went to Pontus, spurred on by the news that Pharnaces, son of Mithridates the Great, had taken advantage of the situation to make war, and was already flushed with numerous successes; but Caesar vanquished him in a single battle within five days after his arrival and four hours after getting sight of him,

often remarking on Pompey's good luck in gaining his principal fame as a general by victories over such feeble foemen. Then he 46 B.C. overcame Scipio and Juba, who were patching up the remnants of their party in Africa, and the sons of Pompey in Spain. 45 B.C.

XXXVI. In all the civil wars he suffered not a single disaster except through his lieutenants, of whom Gaius Curio perished in Africa, Gaius Antonius fell into the hands of the enemy in Illyricum, Publius Dolabella lost a fleet also off Illyricum, and Gnaeus Domitius Calvinus an army in Pontus. Personally he always fought with the utmost success, and the issue was never even in doubt save twice; once at Dyrrachium, where he was put to flight, and said of Pompey, who failed to follow up his success, that he did not know how to use a victory; again in Spain, in the final struggle, when, believing the battle lost, he actually thought of suicide.

XXXVII. Having ended the wars, he celebrated five triumphs, four in a single month, but at intervals of a few days, after vanquishing Scipio; and another on defeating Pompey's sons. The first and most splendid was the Gallic triumph, the next the Alexandrian, then the Pontic, after that the African, and finally the Spanish, each differing from the rest in its equipment and display of spoils. As he rode through the Velabrum on the day of his Gallic triumph, the axle of his chariot broke, and he was all but thrown out; and he mounted the Capitol by torchlight, with forty elephants bearing lamps on his right and his left. In his Pontic triumph he displayed among the show-pieces of the procession an inscription of but three words, "I came, I saw, I conquered," not indicating the events of the war, as the others did, but the speed with which it was finished.

XXXVIII. To each and every foot-soldier of his veteran legions he gave twenty-four thousand sesterces by way of booty, over and above the two thousand apiece which he had paid them at the beginning of the civil strife. He also assigned them lands, but not side by side, to avoid dispossessing any of the former owners. To every man of the people, besides ten pecks of grain and the same number of pounds of oil, he distributed the three hundred sesterces which he had promised at first, and one hundred apiece to boot because of the delay. He also remitted a year's rent in Rome to tenants who paid two thousand sesterces or less, and in Italy up to five hundred sesterces. He added a banquet and a dole of meat, and after his Spanish victory two dinners;[34] for deeming that the former of these had not been served with a liberality creditable to his generosity, he gave another five days later on a most lavish scale.

XXXIX. He gave entertainments of divers kinds: a combat of gladiators and also stage-plays in every ward all over the city, performed too by actors of all languages, as well as races in the circus, athletic contests, and a sham sea-fight. In the gladiatorial contest in the Forum Furius Leptinus, a man of praetorian stock, and Quintus Calpenus, a former senator and pleader at the bar, fought to a finish. A Pyrrhic dance was performed by the sons of the princes of Asia and Bithynia. During the plays Decimus Laberius, a Roman knight, acted a farce of his own composition, and having been presented with five hundred thousand sesterces and a gold ring,[35] passed from the stage through the orchestra and took his place in the fourteen rows.[36] For the races the circus was lengthened at either end and a broad canal[37] was dug all about it; then young men of the highest rank drove four-horse and two-horse chariots and rode pairs of horses, vaulting from one to the other. The game called Troy was performed by two troops, of younger and of older boys. Combats with wild beasts were presented on five successive days, and last of all there was a battle between two opposing armies, in which five hundred foot-soldiers, twenty elephants, and thirty horsemen engaged on each side. To make room for this, the goals were taken down and in their place two camps were pitched over against each other. The athletic competitions lasted for three days in a temporary stadium built for the purpose in the region of the Campus Martius. For the naval battle a pool was dug in the lesser Codeta and there was a contest of ships of two, three, and four banks of oars, belonging to the Tyrian and Egyptian fleets, manned by a large force of fighting men. Such a throng flocked to all these shows from every quarter, that many strangers had to lodge in tents pitched in the streets or along the roads, and the press was often such that many were crushed to death, including two senators.

XL. Then turning his attention to the reorganisation of the state, he reformed the calendar, which the negligence of the pontiffs had long since so disordered, through their privilege of adding months or days at pleasure, that the harvest festivals did not come in summer nor those of the vintage in the autumn; and he adjusted the year to the sun's course by making it consist of three hundred and sixty-five days, abolishing the intercalary month,[38] and adding one day every fourth year. Furthermore, that the correct reckoning of time might begin with the next Kalends of January, he inserted two other months between those of November and December; hence the year in which these arrangements were made was one of fifteen months, including the intercalary month, which belonged to that year according to the former custom.

XLI. He filled the vacancies in the senate, enrolled additional patricians, and increased the number of praetors, aediles, and quaestors, as well as of the minor officials; he reinstated those who had been degraded by official action of the censors or found guilty of bribery by verdict of the jurors. He shared the elections with the people on this basis: that except in the case of the consulship, half of the magistrates should be appointed by the people's choice, while the rest should be those whom he had personally nominated. And these he announced in brief notes like the following, circulated in each tribe: "Caesar the Dictator to this or that tribe. I commend to you so and so, to hold their positions by your votes." He admitted to office even the sons of those who had been proscribed. He limited the right of serving as jurors to two classes, the equestrian and senatorial orders, disqualifying the third class, the tribunes of the treasury.[39]

He made the enumeration of the people neither in the usual manner nor place, but from street to street aided by the owners of blocks of houses, and reduced the number of those who received grain at public expense from three hundred and twenty thousand to one hundred and fifty thousand. And to prevent the calling of additional meetings at any future time for purposes of enrolment, he provided that the places of such as died should be filled each year by the praetors from those who were not on the list.

XLII. Moreover, to keep up the population of the city, depleted as it was by the assignment of eighty thousand citizens to colonies across the sea, he made a law that no citizen older than twenty or younger than forty, who was not detained by service in the army, should be absent from Italy for more than three successive years; that no senator's son should go abroad except as the companion of a magistrate or on his staff; and that those who made a business of grazing should have among their herdsmen at least one-third who were men of free birth. He conferred citizenship on all who practised medicine at Rome, and on all teachers of the liberal arts, to make them more desirous of living in the city and to induce others to resort to it.

As to debts, he disappointed those who looked for their cancellation, which was often agitated, but finally decreed that the debtors should satisfy their creditors according to a valuation of their possessions at the price which they had paid for them before the civil war, deducting from the principal whatever interest had been paid in cash or pledged through bankers; an arrangement which wiped out about a fourth part of their indebtedness. He dissolved all guilds, except those of ancient foundation. He increased the penalties for crimes; and inasmuch as the rich involved themselves in guilt with less hesitation because they merely suffered exile, without any loss of property, he punished murderers of freemen[40] by the confiscation of all their goods, as Cicero writes, and others by the loss of one-half.

XLIII. He administered justice with the utmost conscientiousness and strictness. Those convicted of extortion he even dismissed from the senatorial order. He annulled the marriage of an ex-praetor, who had married a woman the very day after her divorce, although there was no suspicion of adultery. He imposed duties on foreign wares. He denied the use of litters and the wearing of scarlet robes or pearls to all except to those of a designated position and age, and on set days. In particular he enforced the law against extravagance, setting watchmen in various parts of the market, to seize and bring to him dainties which were exposed for sale in violation of the law; and sometimes he sent his lictors and soldiers to take from a dining-room any articles which had escaped the vigilance of his watchmen, even after they had been served.

XLIV. In particular, for the adornment and convenience of the city, also for the protection and extension of the Empire, he formed more projects and more extensive ones every day: first of all, to rear a temple to Mars, greater than any in existence, filling up and levelling the pool in which he had exhibited the sea-fight, and to build a theatre of vast size, sloping down from the Tarpeian rock; to reduce the civil code to fixed limits, and of the vast and prolix mass of statutes to include only the best and most essential in a limited number of volumes; to open to the public the greatest possible libraries of Greek and Latin books, assigning to Marcus Varro the charge of procuring and classifying them; to drain the Pomptine marshes; to let out the water from Lake Fucinus; to make a highway from the Adriatic across the summit of the Apennines as far as the Tiber; to cut a canal through the Isthmus; to check the Dacians, who had poured into Pontus and Thrace; then to make war on the Parthians by way of Lesser Armenia, but not to risk a battle with them until he had first tested their mettle.

All these enterprises and plans were cut short by his death. But before I speak of that, it will not be amiss to describe briefly his personal appearance, his dress, his mode of life, and his character, as well as his conduct in civil and military life.

XLV. He is said to have been tall of stature, with a fair complexion, shapely limbs, a somewhat full face, and keen black eyes; sound of health, except that towards the end he was subject to sudden fainting fits and to nightmare as well. He was twice attacked by the falling sickness[41] during his campaigns. He was somewhat overnice in the care of his person, being not only carefully trimmed and shaved, but even having superfluous hair plucked out, as some have charged; while his baldness was a disfigurement which troubled him greatly, since he found that it was often the subject of the gibes of his detractors. Because of it he used to comb forward his scanty locks from the crown of his head, and of all the honours voted him by the senate and people there was none which he received or made use of more gladly than the privilege of wearing a laurel wreath at all times. They say, too, that he was fantastic in his dress; that he wore a senator's tunic[42] with fringed sleeves reaching to the wrist, and always had a girdle[43] over it, though rather a loose one; and this, they say, was the occasion of Sulla's *mot,* when he often warned the nobles to keep an eye on the ill-girt boy.

XLVI. He lived at first in the Subura in a modest house, but after he became pontifex maximus, in the official residence on the Sacred Way. Many have written that he was very fond of elegance and luxury; tliat having laid the foundations of a country-house on his estate at Nemi and finished it at great cost, he tore it all down because it did not suit him in every particular, although at the time he was still poor and heavily in debt; and that he carried tesselated and mosaic floors about with him on his campaigns.

XLVII. They say that he was led to invade Britain by the hope of getting pearls, and that in comparing their size he sometimes weiged them with his own hand; that he was always a most enthusiastic collector of gems, carvings, statues, and pictures by early artists; also of slaves of exceptional figure and training at enormous prices, of which he himself was so ashamed that he forbade their entry in his accounts.

XLVIII. It is further reported that in the provinces he gave banquets constantly in two dining-halls, in one of which his officers or Greek companions, in the other Roman civilians and the more distinguished of the provincials reclined at table. He was so punctilious and strict in the management of his household, in small matters as well as in those of greater importance, that he put his baker in irons for serving him with one kind of bread and his guests with another; and he inflicted capital punishment on a favourite freedman for adultery with the wife of a Roman knight, although no complaint was made against him.

XLIX. There was no stain on his reputation for chastity except his intimacy with King Nicomedes, but that was a deep and lasting reproach, which laid him open to insults from every quarter. I say nothing of the notorious lines of Licinius Calvus:

"Whate'er Bithynia had, and Caesar's paramour."

I pass over, too, the invectives of Dolabella and the elder Curio, in which Dolabella calls him "the queen's rival, the inner partner of the royal couch," and Curio, "the brothel of Nicomedes and the stew of Bithynia." I take no account of the edicts of Bibulus, in which he posted his colleague as "the queen of Bithynia," saying that "of yore he was enamoured of a king, but now of a king's estate." At this same time, so Marcus Brutus declares, one Octavius, a man whose disordered mind made him somewhat free with his tongue, after saluting Pompey as "king" in a,crowded assembly, greeted Caesar as "queen." But Gaius Memmius makes the direct charge that he acted as cupbearer to Nicomedes with the rest of his wantons at a large dinner-party, and that among the guests were some merchants from Rome, whose names Memmius gives. Cicero, indeed, is not content with having written in sundry letters that Caesar was led by the king's attendants to the royal apartments, that he lay on a golden couch arrayed in purple, and that the virginity of this son of Venus was lost in Bithynia; but when Caesar was once addressing the senate in defence of Nysa, daughter of Nicomedes, and was enumerating his obligations to the king, Cicero cried: "No more of that, pray, for it is well known what he gave you, and what you gave him in turn." Finally, in his Gallic triumph his soldiers, among the bantering songs which are usually sung by those who follow the chariot, shouted these lines, which became a by-word:

"All the Gauls did Caesar vanquish, Nicomedes vanquished him;
Lo! now Caesar rides in triumph, victor over all the Gauls,
Nicomedes does not triumph, who subdued the conqueror."

L. That he was unbridled and extravagant in his intrigues is the general opinion, and that he seduced many illustrious women, among them Postumia, wife of Servius Sulpicius, Lollia, wife of Aulus Gabinius, Tertulla, wife of Marcus Crassus, and even Gnaeus Pompey's wife Mucia. At all events there is no doubt that Pompey was taken to task by the elder and the younger Curio, as well as by many others, because through a desire for power he had afterwards married the daughter of a man on whose account he divorced a wife who had borne him three children, and whom he had often referred to with a groan as an Aegisthus. But beyond all others Caesar loved Servilia, the mother of Marcus Brutus, for whom in his first consulship he bought a pearl costing six million sesterces. During the civil war, too, besides other presents, he knocked down some fine estates to her in a public auction at a nominal price, and when some expressed their surprise at the low figure, Cicero wittily remarked: "It's a better bargain than you think, for there is a third off."[44] And in fact it was thought that Servilia was prostituting her own daughter Tertia to Caesar.

LI. That he did not refrain from intrigues in the provinces is shown in particular by this couplet, which was also shouted by the soldiers in his Gallic triumph:

"Men of Rome, keep close your consorts, here's a bald adulterer.
Gold in Gaul you spent in dalliance, which you borrowed here in Rome."

LII. He had love affairs with queens too, including Eunoe the Moor, wife of Bogudes, on whom, as well as on her husband, he bestowed many splendid presents, as Naso writes;[45] but above all with Cleopatra, with whom he often feasted until daybreak, and he would have gone through Egypt with her in her state-barge almost to Aethiopia, had not his soldiers refused to follow him. Finally he called her to Rome and did not let her leave until he had ladened her with high honours and rich gifts, and he allowed her to give his name to the child which she bore. In fact, according to certain Greek writers, this child was very like Caesar in looks and carriage. Mark Antony declared to the senate that Caesar had really acknowledged the boy, and that Gaius Matius, Gaius Oppius, and other friends of Caesar knew this. Of these Gaius Oppius, as if admitting that the situation required apology and defence, published a book, to prove that the child whom Cleopatra fathered on Caesar was not his. Helvius Cinna, tribune of the commons, admitted to several that he had a bill drawn up in due form, which Caesar had ordered him to propose to the people in his absence, making it lawful for Caesar to marry what wives he wished, and as many as he wished, "for the purpose of begetting children."[46] But to remove all doubt that he had an evil reputation both for shameless vice and for adultery, I have only to add that the elder Curio in one of his speeches calls him "every woman's man and every man's woman."

LIII. That he drank very little wine not even his enemies denied. There is a saying of Marcus Cato that Caesar was the only man who undertook to overthrow the state when sober. Even in the matter of food Gaius Oppius tells us that he was so indifferent, that once when his host served stale oil instead of fresh, and the other guests would have none of it, Caesar partook even more plentifully than usual, not to seem to charge his host with carelessness or lack of manners.

LIV. Neither when in command of armies nor as a magistrate at Rome did he show a scrupulous integrity; for as certain men have declared in their memoirs, when he was proconsul in Spain,[47] he not only begged money from the allies, to help pay his debts, but also attacked and sacked some towns of the Lusitanians although they did not refuse his terms and opened their gates to him on his arrival. In Gaul he pillaged shrines and temples of the gods filled with offerings, and oftener sacked towns for the sake of plunder than for any fault. In consequence he had more gold than he knew what to do with, and offered it for sale throughout Italy and the provinces at the rate of three thousand sesterces the pound.[48] In his first consulship he stole three thousand pounds of gold from the Capitol, replacing it with the same weight of gilded bronze. He made alliances and thrones a matter of barter, for he extorted from Ptolemy alone in his own name and that of Pompey nearly six thousand talents, while later on he met the heavy expenses of the civil wars and of his triumphs and entertainments by the most bare-faced pillage and sacrilege.

LV. In eloquence and in the art of war he either equalled or surpassed the fame of their most eminent representatives. After his accusation of Dolabella, he was without question numbered with the leading advocates. At all events when Cicero reviews the orators in his *Brutus*,[49] he says that he does not see to whom Caesar ought to yield the palm, declaring that his style is elegant as well as brilliant, even grand and in a sense noble. Again in a letter to Cornelius Nepos he writes thus of Caesar: "Come now, what orator would you rank above him of those who have devoted themselves to nothing else? Who has cleverer or more frequent epigrams? Who is either more picturesque or more choice in diction?" He appears, at least in his youth, to have imitated the manner of Caesar Strabo, from whose speech entitled "For the Sardinians" he actually transferred some passages word for word to a trial address[50] of his own. He is said to have delivered himself in a high-pitched voice with impassioned action and gestures, which were not without grace. He left several speeches, including some which are attributed to him on insufficient evidence. Augustus had good reason to think that the speech "For Quintus Metellus" was rather taken down by shorthand writers who could not keep pace with his delivery, than published by Caesar himself; for in some copies I find that even the title is not "For Metellus," but, "Which he wrote for Metellus," although the discourse purports to be from Caesar's lips, defending Metellus and himself against the charges of their common detractors. Augustus also questions the authenticity of the address "To his Soldiers in Spain," although there are two versions of it: one purporting to have been spoken at the first battle, the other at the second, when Asinius Pollio writes that because of the sudden onslaught of the enemy he actually did not have time to make an harangue.

LVI. He left memoirs too of his deeds in the Gallic war and in the civil strife with Pompey; for the author of the Alexandrian, African, and Spanish Wars is unknown; some think it was Oppius, others Hirtius, who also supplied the final book of the Gallic War, which Caesar left unwritten. With regard to Caesar's memoirs Cicero, also in the *Brutus*[51] speaks in the following terms: "He wrote memoirs which deserve the highest praise; they are naked in their simplicity, straightforward yet graceful, stripped of all rhetorical adornment, as of a garment; but while his purpose was to supply material to others, on which those who wished to write history might draw, he haply gratified silly folk, who will try to use the curling-irons on his narrative, but he has kept men of any sense from touching the subject." Of these same memoirs Hirtius uses this emphatic language[52]; "They are so highly rated in the judgment of all men, that he seems to have deprived writers of an opportunity, rather than given them one; yet our admiration for this feat is greater than that of others; for they know how well and faultlessly he wrote, while we know besides how easily and rapidly he finished his task." Asinius Pollio thinks that they were put together somewhat carelessly and without strict regard for truth; since in many cases Caesar was too ready to believe the accounts which others gave of their actions, and gave a perverted account of his own, either designedly or perhaps from forgetfulness; and he thinks that he intended to rewrite and revise them. He left besides a work in two volumes "On Analogy," the same number of "Speeches criticising Cato," in addition to a poem, entitled "The Journey." He wrote the first of these works while crossing the Alps and returning to his army from Hither Gaul, where he had held the assizes; the second about the time of the battle of Munda, and the third in the course of a twenty-four days' journey from Rome to

Farther Spain. Some letters of his to the senate are also preserved, and he seems to have been the first to reduce such documents to pages and the form of a memorial volume,[53] whereas previously consuls and generals sent their reports written right across the sheet. There are also letters of his to Cicero, as well as to his intimates on private affairs, and in the latter, if he had anything confidential to say, he wrote it in cipher, that is, by so changing the order of the letters of the alphabet, that not a word could be made out. If anyone wishes to decipher these, and get at their meaning, he must substitute the fourth letter of the alphabet, namely D, for A, and so with the others. We also have mention of certain writings of his boyhood and early youth, such as the "Praises of Hercules," a tragedy "Oedipus," and a "Collection of Apophthegms"; but Augustus forbade the publication of all these minor works in a very brief and frank letter sent to Pompeius Macer, whom he had selected to set his libraries in order.

LVII. He was highly skilled in arms and horsemanship, and of incredible powers of endurance. On the march he headed his army, sometimes on horseback, but oftener on foot, bareheaded both in the heat of the sun and in rain. He covered great distances with incredible speed, making a hundred miles a day in a hired carriage and with little baggage, swimming the rivers which barred his path or crossing them on inflated skins, and very often arriving before the messengers sent to announce his coming.

LVIII. In the conduct of his campaigns it is a question whether he was more cautious or more daring, for he never led his army where ambuscades were possible without carefully reconnoitring the country, and he did not cross to Britain without making personal inquiries[54] about the harbours, the course, and the approach to the island. But on the other hand, when news came that his camp in Germany was beleaguered, he made his way to his men through the enemies' pickets, disguised as a Gaul. He crossed from Brundisium to Dyrrachium in winter time, running the blockade of the enemy's fleets; and when the troops which he had ordered to follow him delayed to do so, and he had sent to fetch them many times in vain, at last in secret and alone he boarded a small boat at night with his head muffled up; and he did not reveal who he was, or suffer the helmsman to give way to the gale blowing in their teeth, until he was all but overwhelmed by the waves.

LIX. No regard for religion ever turned him from any undertaking, or even delayed him. Though the victim escaped as he was offering sacrifice, he did not put off his expedition against Scipio and Juba. Even when he had a fall as he disembarked, he gave the omen a favourable turn by crying: "I hold thee fast, Africa." Furthermore, to make the prophecies ridiculous which declared that the stock of the Scipios was fated to be fortunate and invincible in that province, he kept with him in camp a contemptible fellow belonging to the Cornelian family, to whom the nickname Salvito[55] had been given as a reproach for his manner of life.

LX. He joined battle, not only after planning his movements in advance but on a sudden opportunity, often immediately at the end of a march, and sometimes in the foulest weather, when one would least expect him to make a move. It was not until his later years that he became slower to engage, through a conviction that the oftener he had been victor, the less he ought to tempt fate, and that he could not possibly gain as much by success as he might lose by a defeat. He never put his enemy to flight without also driving him from his camp, thus giving him no respite in his panic. When the issue was doubtful, he used to send away the horses, and his own among the first, to impose upon his troops the greater necessity of standing their ground by taking away that aid to flight.

LXI. He rode a remarkable horse, too, with feet that were almost human; for its hoofs were cloven in such a way as to look like toes. This horse was foaled on his own place, and since the soothsayers had declared that it foretold the rule of the world for its master, he reared it with the greatest care, and was the first to mount it, for it would endure no other rider. Afterwards, too, he dedicated a statue of it before the temple of Venus Genetrix.

LXII. When his army gave way, he often rallied it single-handed, planting himself in the way of the fleeing men, laying hold of them one by one, and even catching them by the throat and forcing them to face the enemy; that, too, when they were in such a panic that an eagle-bearer made a pass at him with the point[56] as he tried to stop him, while another left the standard in Caesar's hand when he would hold him back.

LXIII. His presence of mind was no less renowned, and the instances of it will appear even more striking. After the battle of Pharsalus, when he had sent on his troops and was crossing the strait of the Hellespont in a small passenger boat, he met Lucius Cassius, of the hostile party, with ten armoured ships,[57] and made no attempt to escape, but went to meet Cassius and actually urged him to surrender; and Cassius sued for mercy and was taken on board.

LXIV. At Alexandria, while assaulting a bridge, he was forced by a sudden sally of the enemy to take to a small skiff; when many others threw themselves into the same boat, he plunged into the sea, and after swimming for two hundred paces, got away to the nearest ship, holding up his left hand all the way, so as not to wet some papers which he was carrying, and dragging his cloak after him with his teeth, to keep the enemy from getting it as a trophy.

LXV. He valued his soldiers neither for their personal character nor their fortune, but solely for their prowess, and he treated them with equal strictness and indulgence; for he did not curb them everywhere and at all times, but only in the presence of the enemy. Then he required the strictest discipline, not announcing the time of a march or a battle, but keeping them ready and alert to be led on a sudden at any moment wheresoever he might wish. He often called them out even when there was no occasion for it, especially on rainy days and holidays. And warning them every now and then that they must keep close watch on him, he would steal away suddenly by day or night and make a longer march than usual, to tire out those who were tardy in following.

LXVI. When they were in a panic through reports about the enemy's numbers, he used to rouse their courage not by denying or discounting the rumours, but by falsely exaggerating the true danger. For instance, when the anticipation of Juba's coming filled them with terror, he called the soldiers together and said:

"Let me tell you that within the next few days the king will be here with ten legions, thirty thousand horsemen, a hundred thousand light-armed troops, and three hundred elephants. Therefore some of you may as well cease to ask further questions or make surmises and may rather believe me, since I know all about it. Otherwise, I shall surely have them shipped on some worn out craft and carried off to whatever lands the wind may blow them."

LXVII. He did not take notice of all their offences or punish them by rule, but he kept a sharp look out for deserters and mutineers, and chastised them most severely, shutting his eyes to other faults. Sometimes, too, after a great victory he relieved them of all duties and gave them full licence to revel, being in the habit of boasting that his soldiers could fight well even when reeking of perfumes. In the assembly he addressed them not as "soldiers," but by the more flattering term "comrades," and he kept them in fine trim, furnishing them with arms inlaid with silver and gold, both for show and to make them hold the faster to them in battle, through fear of the greatness of the loss. Such was his love for them that when he heard of the disaster to Titurius, he let his hair and beard grow long, and would not cut them until he had taken vengeance.

LXVIII. In this way he made them most devoted to his interests as well as most valiant. When he began the civil war, every centurion of each legion proposed to supply a horseman from his own allowance, and the soldiers one and all offered their service without pay and without rations, the richer assuming the care of the poorer. Throughout the long struggle not one deserted and many of them, on being taken prisoner, refused to accept their lives, when offered them on the condition of consenting to serve against Caesar. They bore hunger and other hardships, both when in a state of siege and when besieging others, with such fortitude, that when Pompey saw in the works at Dyrrachium a kind of bread made of herbs, on which they were living, he said that he was fighting wild beasts; and he gave orders that it be put out of sight quickly and shown to none of his men, for fear that the endurance and resolution of the foe would break their spirit.

How valiantly they fought is shown by the fact that when they suffered their sole defeat before Dyrrachium, they insisted on being punished, and their commander felt called upon rather to console than to chastise them. In the other battles they overcame with ease countless forces of the enemy, though decidedly fewer in number themselves. Indeed one cohort of the sixth legion, when set to defend a redoubt, kept four legions of Pompey at bay for several hours, though almost all were wounded by the enemy's showers of arrows, of which a hundred and thirty thousand were picked up within the ramparts. And no wonder, when one thinks of the deeds of individual soldiers, either of Cassius Scaeva the centurion, or of Gaius Acilius of the rank and file, not to mention others. Scaeva, with one eye gone, his thigh and shoulder wounded, and his shield bored through in a hundred and twenty places, continued to guard the gate of a fortress put in his charge. Acilius in the sea-fight at Massilia grasped the stern of one of the enemy's ships, and when his right hand was lopped off, rivalling the famous exploit of the Greek hero Cynegirus, boarded the ship and drove the enemy before him with the boss of his shield.

LXIX. They did not mutiny once during the ten years of the Gallic war; in the civil wars they did so now and then, but quickly resumed their duty, not so much owing to any indulgence of their general as to his authority. For he never gave way to them when they were insubordinate, but always boldly faced them, discharging the entire ninth legion in disgrace before Placentia, though Pompey was still in the field, reinstating them unwillingly and only after many abject entreaties, and insisting on punishing the ringleaders.

LXX. Again at Rome, when the men of the Tenth clamoured for their discharge and rewards with terrible threats and no little peril to the city, though the war in Africa was then raging, he did not hesitate to appear before them, against the advice of his friends, and to disband them. But with a single word, calling them "citizens," instead of "soldiers," he easily brought them round and bent them to his will; for they at once replied that they were his "soldiers" and insisted on following him to Africa, although he refused their service. Even then he punished the most insubordinate by the loss of a third part of the booty and of the land intended for them.

LXXI. Even when a young man he showed no lack of devotion and fidelity to his dependents. He defended Masintha, a youth of high birth, against king Hiempsal with such spirit, that in the dispute he caught the king's son Juba by the beard. On Masintha's being declared tributary to the king, he at once rescued him from those who would carry him off and kept him hidden for some time in his own house; and when presently he left for Spain after his praetorship, he carried the young man off in his own litter, unnoticed amid the crowd that came to see him off and the lictors with their fasces.

LXXII. His friends he treated with invariable kindness and consideration. When Gaius Oppius was his companion on a journey through a wild, woody country and was suddenly taken ill, Caesar gave up to him the only shelter[58] there was, while he himself slept on the ground out-of-doors. Moreover, when he came to power, he advanced some of his friends to the highest positions, even though they were of the humblest origin, and when taken to task for it, flatly declared that if he had been helped in defending his honour by brigands and cut-throats, he would have requited even such men in the same way.

LXXIII. On the other hand he never formed such bitter enmities that he was not glad to lay them aside when opportunity offered. Although Gaius Memmius had made highly caustic speeches against him, to which he had replied with equal bitterness, he went so far as to support Memmius afterwards in his suit for the consulship. When Gaius Calvus, after some scurrilous epigrams, took steps through his friends towards a reconciliation, Caesar wrote to him first and of his own free will. Valerius Catullus, as Caesar himself did not hesitate to say, inflicted a lasting stain on his name by the verses about Mamurra[59]; yet when he apologised, Caesar invited the poet to dinner that very same day, and continued his usual friendly relations with Catullus's father.

LXXIV. Even in avenging wrongs he was by nature most merciful, and when he got hold of the pirates who had captured him, he had them crucified, since he had sworn beforehand that he would do so, but ordered that their throats be cut first. He could never make up his mind to harm Cornelius Phagites, although when he was sick and in hiding,[60] the man had waylaid him night after night, and even a bribe had barely saved him from being handed over to Sulla. The slave Philemon, his amanuensis, who had promised Caesar's enemies that he would poison him, he merely punished by death, without torture. When summoned as a witness against Publius Clodius, the paramour of his wife Pompeia, charged on the same count with sacrilege, Caesar declared that he had no evidence, although both his mother Aurelia and his sister Julia had given the same jurors a faithful account of the whole affair; and on being asked why it was then that he had put away his wife, he replied; "Because I maintain that the members of my family should be free from suspicion, as well as from guilt."

LXXV. He certainly showed admirable self-restraint and mercy, both in his conduct of the civil war and in the hour of victory. While Pompey threatened to treat as enemies those who did not take up arms for the government, Caesar gave out that those who were neutral and of neither party should be numbered with his friends. He freely allowed all those whom he had made centurions on Pompey's recommendation to go over to his rival. When conditions of surrender were under discussion at Ilerda, and friendly intercourse between the two parties was constant, Afranius and Petreius, with a sudden change of purpose, put to death all of Caesar's soldiers whom they found in their camp; but Caesar could not bring himself to retaliate in kind. At the battle of Pharsalus he cried out, "Spare your fellow citizens," and afterwards allowed each of his men to save any one man he pleased of the opposite party. And it will be found that no Pompeian lost his life except in battle, save only Afranius and Faustus, and the young Lucius Caesar; and it is believed that not even these men were slain by his wish, even though the two former had taken up arms again after being pardoned, while Caesar had not only cruelly put to death the dictator's slaves and freedmen with fire and sword, but had even butchered the wild beasts which he had procured for the entertainment of the people. At last, in his later years, he went so far as to allow all those whom he had not yet pardoned to return to Italy, and to hold magistracies and the command of armies: and he actually set up the statues of Lucius Sulla and Pompey, which had been broken to pieces by the populace. After this, if any dangerous plots were formed against him, or slanders uttered, he preferred to quash rather than to punish them. Accordingly, he took no further notice of the conspiracies which were detected, and of meetings by night, than to make known by proclamation that he was aware of them; and he thought it enough to give public warning to those who spoke ill of him, not to persist in their conduct, bearing with good nature the attacks on his reputation made by the scurrilous volume of Aulus Caecina and the abusive lampoons of Pitholaus.

LXXVI. Yet after all, his other actions and words so turn the scale, that it is thought that he abused his power and was justly slain. For not only did he accept excessive honours, such as an uninterrupted consulship, the dictatorship for life, and the censorship of public morals, as well as the forename Imperator, the surname of Father of his Country, a statue among those of the kings, and a raised couch in the orchestra[61]; but he also allowed honours to be bestowed on him which were too great for mortal man: a golden throne in the House and on the judgment seat; a chariot and litter[62] in the procession at the circus; temples, altars, and statues beside those of the gods; a special priest, an additional college of the Luperci, and the calling of one of the months by his name. In fact, there were no honours which he did not receive or confer at pleasure.

He held his third and fourth consulships in name only, content with the power of the dictatorship conferred on him at the same time as the consulships. Moreover, in both years he substituted two consuls for himself for the last three months, in the meantime holding no elections except for tribunes and plebeian aediles, and appointing praefects instead of the praetors, to manage the affairs of the city during his absence. When one of the consuls suddenly died the day before the Kalends of January, he gave the vacant office for a few hours to a man who asked for it. With the same disregard of law and precedent he named magistrates for several years to come, bestowed the emblems of consular rank on ten expraetors, and admitted to the House men who had been given citizenship, and in some cases half-civilised Gauls. He assigned the charge of the mint and of the public revenues to his own slaves, and gave the oversight and command of the three legions which he had left at Alexandria to a favourite of his called Rufio, son of one of his freedmen.

LXXVII. No less arrogant were his public utterances, which Titus Ampius records: that the state was nothing, a mere name without body or form; that Sulla did not know his A. B. C. when he laid down his dictatorship; that men ought now to be more circumspect in addressing him, and to regard his word as law. So far did he go in his presumption, that when a soothsayer once reported direful inwards without a heart, he said: "They will be more favourable when I wish it; it should not be regarded as a portent, if a beast has no heart."[63]

LXXVIII. But it was the following action in particular that roused deadly hatred against him. When the Senate approached him in a body with many highly honorary decrees, he received them before the temple of Venus Genetrix without rising. Some think that when he attempted to get up, he was held back by Cornelius Balbus; others, that he made no such move at all, but on the contrary frowned angrily on Gaius Trebatius when he suggested that he should rise. And this action of his seemed the more intolerable, because when he himself in one of his triumphal processions rode past the benches of the tribunes, he was so incensed because a member of the college, Pontius Aquila by name, did not rise, that he cried: "Come then, Aquila, take back the republic from me,[64] you mighty tribune"; and for several days he would not make a promise to any one without adding, "That is, if Pontius Aquila will allow me."

LXXIX. To an insult which so plainly showed his contempt for the Senate he added an act of even greater insolence; for at the Latin Festival, as he was returning to the city, amid the extravagant and unprecedented demonstrations of the populace, someone in the press placed on his statue a laurel wreath with a white fillet tied to it[65]; and when Epidius Marullus and Caesetius Flavus, tribunes of the commons, gave orders that the ribbon be removed from the crown and the man taken off to prison, Caesar sharply rebuked and deposed them, either offended that the hint at regal power had been received with so little favour, or, as he asserted, that he had been robbed of the glory of refusing it. But from that time on he could not rid himself of the odium of having aspired to the title of monarch, although he replied to the commons, when they hailed him as king, "I am Caesar and no king,"[66] and at the Lupercalia, when the consul Antony several times attempted to place a crown upon his head as he spoke from the rostra, he put it aside and at last sent it to the Capitol, to be offered to Jupiter Optimus Maximus. Nay, more, the report had spread in various quarters that he intended to move to Ilium or Alexandria, taking with him the resources of the state, draining Italy by levies, and leaving it and the charge of the city to his friends; also that at the next meeting of the Senate Lucius Cotta would announce as the decision of the Fifteen,[67] that inasmuch as it was written in the books of fate that the Parthians could be conquered only by a king, Caesar should be given that title. LXXX. It was this that led the conspirators to hasten in carrying out their designs, in order to avoid giving their assent to this proposal.

Therefore the plots which had previously been formed separately, often by groups of two or three, were united in a general conspiracy, since even the populace no longer were pleased with present conditions, but both secretly and openly rebelled at his tyranny and cried out for defenders of their liberty. On the admission of foreigners to the Senate, a placard was posted: "God bless the Commonwealth![68] let no one consent to point out the House to a newly made senator." The following verses too were sung everwhere:—

"Caesar led the Gauls in triumph, led them to the senate house;
Then the Gauls put off their breeches, and put on the laticlave."[69]

When Quintus Maximus, whom he had appointed consul in his place for three months, was entering the theatre, and his lictor called attention to his arrival in the usual manner, a general shout was raised: "He's no consul!" At the first election after the deposing of Caesetius and Marullus, the tribunes, several votes were found for their appointment as consuls. Some wrote on the base of Lucius Brutus' statue, "Oh, that you were still alive"; and on that of Caesar himself:

"First of all was Brutus consul, since he drove the kings from Rome;
Since this man drove out the consuls, he at last is made our king."

More than sixty joined the conspiracy against him, led by Gaius Cassius and Marcus and Decimus Brutus. At first they hesitated whether to form two divisions at the elections in the Campus Martius, so that while some hurled him from the bridge[70] as he summoned the tribes to vote, the rest might wait below and slay him; or to set upon him in the Sacred Way or at the entrance to the theatre. When, however, a meeting of the Senate was called for the Ides of March in the Hall of Pompey, they readily gave that time and place the preference.

LXXXI. Now Caesar's approaching murder was foretold to him by unmistakable signs. A few months before, when the settlers assigned to the colony at Capua by the Julian Law were demolishing some tombs of great antiquity, to build country houses, and plied their work with the greater vigour because as they rummaged about they found a quantity of vases of ancient workmanship, there was discovered in a tomb, which was said to be that of Capys, the founder of Capua, a bronze tablet, inscribed with Greek words and characters to this purport: "Whenever the bones of Capys shall be moved, it will come to pass that a son of Ilium shall be slain at the hands of his kindred, and presently avenged at heavy cost to Italy." And let no one think this tale a myth or a lie, for it is vouched for by Cornelius Balbus, an intimate friend of Caesar. Shortly before his death, as he was told, the herds of horses which he had dedicated to the river Rubicon when he crossed it, and had let loose without a keeper, stubbornly refused to graze and wept copiously. Again, when he was offering sacrifice, the soothsayer Spurinna warned him to beware of danger, which would come not later than the Ides of March; and on the day before the Ides of that month a little bird called the king-bird flew into the Hall of Pompey with a sprig of laurel, pursued by others of various kinds from the grove hard by, which tore it to pieces in the hall. In fact the very night before his murder he dreamt now that he was flying above the clouds, and now that he was clasping the hand of Jupiter; and his wife Calpurnia thought that the pediment[71] of their house fell, and that her husband was stabbed in her arms; and on a sudden the door of the room flew open of its own accord. March 15

Both for these reasons and because of poor health he hesitated for a long time whether to stay at home and put off what he had planned to do in the senate; but at last, urged by Decimus Brutus not to disappoint the full meeting which had for some time been waiting for him, he went forth almost at the end of the fifth hour; and when a note revealing the plot was handed him by someone on the way, he put it with others which he held in his left hand, intending to read them presently. Then, after several victims had been slain, and he could not get favourable omens, he entered the House in defiance of portents, laughing at Spurinna and calling him a false prophet, because the Ides of March were come without bringing him harm; though Spurinna replied that they had of a truth come, but they had not gone.

LXXXII. As he took his seat, the conspirators gathered about him as if to pay their respects, and straightway Tillius Cimber, who had assumed the lead, came nearer as though to ask something; and when Caesar with a gesture put him off to another time, Cimber caught his toga by both shoulders; then as Caesar cried, 44 B.C.

"Why, this is violence!" one of the Cascas stabbed him from one side just below the throat.[72] Caesar caught Casca's arm and ran it through with his stylus,[73] but as he tried to leap to his feet, he was stopped by another wound. When he saw that he was beset on every side by drawn daggers, he muffled his head in his robe, and at the same time drew down its lap to his feet with his left hand, in order to fall more decently, with the lower part of his body also covered. And in this wise he was stabbed with three and twenty wounds, uttering not a word, but merely a groan at the first stroke, though some have written that when Marcus Brutus rushed at him, he said in Greek, "You too, my child?" All the conspirators made off, and he lay there lifeless for some time, until finally three common slaves put him on a litter and carried him home, with one arm hanging down. And of so many wounds none turned out to be mortal, in the opinion of the physician Antistius, except the second one in the breast.

The conspirators had intended after slaying him to drag his body to the Tiber, confiscate his property, and revoke his decrees; but they forebore through fear of Marcus Antonius the consul, and Lepidus, the master of horse.

LXXXIII. Then at the request of his father-in-law, Lucius Piso, the will was unsealed and read in Antony's house, which Caesar had made on the preceding Ides of September at his place near Lavicum, and put in the care of the chief of the Vestals. Quintus Tubero states that from his first consulship until the beginning of the civil war it was his wont to write down Gnaeus Pompeius as his heir, and to read this to the assembled soldiers. In his last will, however, he named three heirs, his sisters' grandsons, Gaius Octavius, to three-fourths of his estate, and Lucius Pinarius and Quintus Pedius to share the remainder. At the end of the will, too, he adopted Gaius Octavius into his family and gave him his name. He named several of his assassins among the guardians of his son, in case one should be born to him, and Decimus Brutus even among his heirs in the second degree.[74] To the people he left his gardens near the Tiber for their common use and three hundred sesterces to each man.

Sept. 13, 45 B.C.

LXXXIV. When the funeral was announced, a pyre was erected in the Campus Martius near the tomb of Julia, and on the rostra a gilded shrine was placed, made after the model of the temple of Venus Genetrix; within was a couch of ivory with coverlets of purple and gold, and at its head a pillar hung with the robe in which he was slain. Since it was clear that the day would not be long enough for those who offered gifts, they were directed to bring them to the Campus by whatsoever streets of the city they wished, regardless of any order of precedence. At the funeral games, to rouse pity and indignation at his death, these words from the "Contest for the Arms" of Pacuvius were sung:—

"Saved I these men that they might murder me?"

and words of a like purport from the "Electra" of Atilius. Instead of a eulogythe consul Antonius caused a herald to recite the decree of the Senate in which it had voted Caesar all divine and human honours at once, and likewise the oath with which they had all pledged themselves to watch over his personal safety; to which he added a very few words of his own. The bier on the rostra was carried down into the Forum by magistrates and ex-magistrates; and while some were urging that it be burned in the temple of Jupiter of the Capitol, and others in the Hall of Pompey, on a sudden two beings[75] with swords by their sides and brandishing a pair of darts set fire to it with blazing torches, and at once the throng of bystanders heaped upon it dry branches, the judgment seats with the benches, and whatever else could serve as an offering. Then the musicians and actors tore off their robes, which they had taken from the equipment of his triumphs and put on for the occasion, rent them to bits and threw them into the flames, and the veterans of the legions the arms with which they had adorned themselves for the funeral; many of the women too, offered up the jewels which they wore and the amulets and robes of their children.

At the height of the public grief a throng of foreigners went about lamenting each after the fashion of his country, above all the Jews,[76] who even flocked to the place for several successive nights.

LXXXV. Immediately after the funeral the commons ran to the houses of Brutus and Cassius with firebrands, and after being repelled with difficulty, they slew Helvius Cinna when they met him, through a mistake in the name, supposing that he was Cornelius Cinna, who had the day before made a bitter indictment of Caesar and for whom they were looking; and they set his head upon a spear and paraded it about the streets. Afterwards they set up in the Forum a solid column of Numidian marble almost twenty feet high, and inscribed upon it, "To the Father of his Country." At the foot of this they continued for a long time to sacrifice, make vows, and settle some of their disputes by an oath in the name of Caesar.

LXXXVI. Caesar left in the minds of some of his friends the suspicion that he did not wish to live longer and had taken no precautions, because of his failing health; and that therefore he neglected the warnings which came to him from portents and from the reports of his friends. Some think that it was because he had full trust in that last decree of the senators and their oath that he dismissed even the armed bodyguard of Spanish soldiers that formerly attended him. Others, on the contrary, believe that he elected to expose himself once for all to the plots that threatened him on every hand, rather than to be always anxious and on his guard. Some, too, say that he was wont to declare that it was not so much to his own interest as to that of his country that he remain alive; he had long since had his fill of power and glory; but if aught befell him, the commonwealth would have no peace, but would be plunged in civil strife under much worse conditions.

LXXXVII. About one thing almost all are fully agreed, that he all but desired such a death as he met; for once when he read in Xenophon[77] how Cyrus in his last illness gave directions for his funeral, he expressed his horror of such a lingering kind of end and his wish for one which was swift and sudden. And the day before his murder, in a conversation which arose at a dinner at the house of Marcus Lepidus, as to what manner of death was most to be desired, he had given his preference to one which was sudden and unexpected.

LXXXVIII. He died in the fifty-sixth year of his age, and was numbered among the gods, not only by a formal decree, but also in the conviction of the vulgar. For at the first of the games which 44 B.C. his heir Augustus gave in honour of his apotheosis, a comet shone for seven successive days, rising about the eleventh hour,[78] and was believed to be the soul of Caesar, who had been taken to heaven; and this is why a star is set upon the crown of his head in his statue.

It was voted that the hall in which he was slain be walled up, that the Ides of March be called the Day of Parricide, and that a meeting of the senate should never be called on that day.

LXXXIX. Hardly any of his assassins survived him for more than three years, or died a natural death. They were all condemned, and they perished in various ways—some by shipwreck, some in battle; some took their own lives with the self-same dagger with which they had impiously slain Caesar.

BOOK II

THE DEIFIED AUGUSTUS

I. There are many indications that the Octavian family was in days of old a distinguished one at Velitrae; for not only was a street in the most frequented part of the town long ago called Octavian, but an altar was shown there besides, consecrated by an Octavius. This man was leader in a war with a neighbouring town, and when news of a sudden onset of the enemy was brought to him just as he chanced to be sacrificing to Mars, he snatched the inwards of the victim from the fire and offered them up half raw; and thus he went forth to battle, and returned victorious. There was, besides, a decree of the people on record, providing that for the future too the inwards should be offered to Mars in the same way, and the rest of the victims be handed over to the Octavii.

II. The family was admitted to the senate by king Tarquinius Priscus among the lesser clans;[1] was later enrolled by Servius Tullius among the patricians; in course of time returned to the ranks of the plebeians; and after a long interval was restored to patrician rank by the Deified Julius. The first of the house to be elected by the people to a magistracy was Gaius Rufus, who became quaestor. He begot Gnaeus and Gaius, from whom two branches of the Octavian family were derived, of very different standing; for Gnaeus and all his scions in turn held the highest offices, but Gaius and his progeny, whether from chance or choice, remained in the equestrian order down to the father of

Augustus. Augustus's great grandfather served in Sicily in the second Punic war as tribune of the soldiers under the command of Aemilius Papus. His grandfather, content with the offices of a 205 B.C.
municipal town and possessing an abundant income, lived to a peaceful old age. This is the account given by others; Augustus himself merely writes[2] that he came of an old and wealthy equestrian family, in which his own father was the first to become a senator. Marcus Antonius taunts him with his great-grandfather, saying that he was a freedman and a rope-maker from the country about Thurii, while his grandfather was a money-changer. This is all that I have been able to learn about the paternal ancestors of Augustus.

III. His father Gaius Octavius was from the beginning of his life a man of wealth and repute, and I cannot but wonder that some have said that he too was a money-changer, and was even employed to distribute bribes at the elections and perform other services in the Campus; for as a matter of fact, being brought up in affluence, he readily attained to high positions and filled them with distinction. Macedonia fell to his lot at the end of his praetorsip; on his way to the province, executing a special commission from the senate, he wiped out a band of runaway slaves, refugees from the armies of Spartacus and Catiline, who held possession of the country about Thurii. In governing his province he showed equal justice and courage; for besides routing the Bessi and the other Thracians in a great battle, his treatment of our allies was such, that Marcus Cicero, in letters which are still in existence,[3] urges and admonishes his brother Quintus, who at the time was serving as proconsular governor[4] of Asia with no great credit to 61/58 B.C.
himself, to imitate his neighbour Octavius in winning the favour of our allies.

IV. While returning from Macedonia, before he could declare himself a candidate for the consulship, he died suddenly, survived by three children, an elder Octavia by Ancharia, and by Atia a younger Octavia and Augustus. Atia was the daughter of Marcus Atius Balbus and Julia, sister of Gaius Caesar. Balbus, a native of

Aricia on his father's side, and of a family displaying many senatorial portraits,[5] was closely connected on his mother's side with Pompey the Great. After holding the office of praetor, he was one of the commission of twenty[6] appointed by the Julian law to distribute lands in Campania to the commons. But Antonius again, trying to disparage the maternal ancestors of Augustus as well, twits him with having a great-grandfather of African birth, who kept first a perfumery shop and then a bakery at Aricia. Cassius of Parma also taunts Augustus with being the grandson both of a baker and of a money-changer, saying in one of his letters: "Your mother's meal came from a vulgar bakeshop of Aricia; this a money-changer from Nerulum kneaded into shape with hands stained with filthy lucre."[7]

Sept. 23, 63 B.C. V. Augustus was born just before sunrise on the ninth day before the Kalends of October in the consulship of Marcus Tullius Cicero and Gaius Antonius, at the Ox-Heads in the Palatine quarter, where he now has a shrine, built shortly after his death. For it is recorded in the proceedings of the senate, that when Gaius Laetorius, a young man of patrician family, was pleading for a milder punishment for adultery because of his youth and position, he further urged upon the senators that he was the possessor and as it were the warden of the spot which the deified Augustus first touched at his birth, and begged that he be pardoned for the sake of what might be called his own special god. Whereupon it was decreed that that part of his house should be consecrated.

VI. A small room like a pantry is shown to this day as the emperor's nursery in his grandfather's country-house near Velitrae, and the opinion prevails in the neighbourhood that he was also born there. No one ventures to enter this room except of necessity and after purification, since there is a conviction of long-standing that those who approach it without ceremony are seized with shuddering and terror; and what is more, this has recently been shown to be true. For when a new owner, either by chance or to test the matter, went to bed in that room, it came to pass that, after a very few hours of the night, he was thrown out by a sudden mysterious force, and was found bedclothes and all half-dead before the door.

VII. In his infancy he was given the surname Thurinus in memory of the home of his ancestors, or else because it was near Thurii that his father Octavius, shortly before the birth of his son, had gained his victory over the runaway slaves. That he was surnamed Thurinus I may assert on very trustworthy evidence, since I once owned a little bronze bust, representing him as a boy and inscribed with that name in letters of iron almost illegible from age. This I presented to the emperor,[8] who cherishes it among the Lares of his bed-chamber. Furthermore, he is often called Thurinus in Mark Antony's letters by way of insult; to which 27 B.C.
Augustus merely replied that he was surprised that his former name was thrown in his face as a reproach. Later he took the name of Gaius Caesar and then the surname Augustus, the former by the will of his great-uncle, the latter on the motion of Munatius Plancus. For when some expressed the opinion that he ought to be called Romulus as a second founder of the city, Plancus carried the proposal that he should rather be named Augustus, on the ground that this was not merely a new title but a more honourable one, inasmuch as sacred places too, and those in which anything is consecrated by augural rites are called "august" (*augusta*), from the increase (*auctus*) in dignity, or from the movements or feeding of the birds (*avium gestus gustusve*), as Ennius[9] also shows when he writes:

"After by augury august illustrious Rome had been founded."

VIII. At the age of four he lost his father. In his twelfth year he 59 B.C.
delivered a funeral oration to the assembled people in honour of his grandmother Julia. Four years later, after assuming the gown of manhood, he received military prizes at Caesar's African triumph, although he had taken no part in the war on account of his youth. When his uncle presently went to Spain to engage the sons of Pompey, although Augustus had hardly yet recovered his strength 46 B.C.
after a severe illness, he followed over roads beset by the enemy with only a very few companions, and that too after suffering shipwreck,

and thereby greatly endeared himself to Caesar, who soon formed a high opinion of his character over and above the energy with which he had made the journey.

When Caesar, after recovering the Spanish provinces, planned an expedition against the Dacians and then against the Parthians, Augustus, who had been sent on in advance to Apollonia, devoted his leisure to study. As soon as he learned
44 B.C. that his uncle had been slain and that he was his heir, he was in doubt for some time whether to appeal to the nearest legions, but gave up the idea as hasty and premature. He did, however, return to the city and enter upon his inheritance, in spite of the doubts of his mother and the strong opposition of his stepfather, the ex-consul Marcius Philippus. Then he levied armies and henceforth ruled the State, at first with Marcus Antonius and Marcus Lepidus, then with Antony alone for nearly twelve years, and finally by himself for forty-four.

IX. Having given as it were a summary of his life, I shall now take up its various phases one by one, not in chronological order, but by classes; to make the account clearer and more intelligible.

The civil wars which he waged were five, called by the names of Mutina, Philippi, Perusia, Sicily, and Actium; the first and last of these were against Marcus Antonius, the second against Brutus and Cassius, the third against Lucius Antonius, brother of the triumvir, and the fourth against Sextus Pompeius, son of Gnaeus.

X. The initial reason for all these wars was this: since he considered nothing more incumbent on him than to avenge his uncle's death and maintain the validity of his enactments, immediately on returning from Apollonia he resolved to surprise Brutus and Cassius by taking up arms against them; and when they foresaw the danger and fled, to resort to law and prosecute them for murder in their absence. Furthermore, since those who had been appointed to celebrate Caesar's victory by games did not dare to do so, he gave them himself. To be able to carry out his other plans with more authority, he announced his candidature for the position of one of the tribunes of the people, who happened to die; though he was a patrician, and not yet a senator.[10] But when his designs were opposed by Marcus Antonius, who was then consul, and on whose help he had especially counted, and Antony would not allow him even common and ordinary justice without the promise of a heavy bribe, he went over to the aristocrats, who he knew detested Antony, especially because he was besieging Decimus Brutus at Mutina, and trying to drive him by force of arms from the province given him by Caesar and ratified by the senate. Accordingly at the advice of certain men he hired assassins to kill Antony, and when the plot was discovered, fearing retaliation he mustered veterans, by the use of all the money he could command, both for his own protection and that of the State. Put in command of the army which he had raised, with the rank of propraetor, and bidden to join with Hirtius and Pansa, who had become consuls, in lending aid to Decimus Brutus, he finished the war which had been entrusted to him within three months in two battles. In the former of these, so Antony writes, he took to flight and was not seen again until the next day, when he returned without his cloak and his horse; but in that which followed all agree that he played the part not only of a leader, but of a soldier as well, and that, in the thick of the fight, when the eagle-bearer of his legion was sorely wounded, he shouldered the eagle and carried it for some time.

XI. As Hirtius lost his life in battle during this war, and Pansa shortly afterwards from a wound, the rumour spread that he had caused the death of both, in order that after Antony had been put to flight and the state bereft of its consuls, he might gain sole control of the victorious armies. The circumstances of Pansa's death in particular were so suspicious, that the physician Glyco was imprisoned on the charge of having applied poison to his wound. Aquilius Niger adds to this that Augustus himself slew the other consul Hirtius amid the confusion of the battle.

XII. But when he learned that Antony after his flight had found a protector in Marcus Lepidus, and that the rest of the leaders and armies were coming to terms with them, he abandoned the cause of the nobles without hesitation, alleging as a pretext for his change of allegiance the words and acts of certain of their number, asserting that some had called him a boy, while others had openly said that he ought to be honoured and got rid of,[11] to escape the necessity of making suitable recompense to him or to his veterans. To show more plainly that he regretted his connection with the former party, he imposed a heavy fine on the people of Nursia and banished them from their city when they were unable to pay it, because they had at public expense erected a monument to their citizens who were slain in the battles at Mutina and inscribed upon it: "they fell for liberty."

XIII. Then, forming a league with Antony and Lepidus, he finished the war of Philippi also in two battles, although weakened by illness, being driven from his camp in the first battle and barely making his escape by fleeing to Antony's division. He did not use his victory with moderation, but after sending Brutus's head to Rome, to be cast at the feet of Caesar's statue, he vented his spleen upon the most distinguished of his captives, not even sparing them insulting language. For instance, to one man who begged humbly for burial, he is said to have replied: "The birds will soon settle that question." When two others, father and son, begged for their lives, he is said to have bidden them cast lots or play mora,[12] to decide which should be spared, and then to have looked on while both died, since the father was executed because he offered to die for his son, and the latter thereupon took his own life. Because of this the rest, including Marcus Favonius, the well-known imitator of Cato, saluted Antony respectfully as Imperator,[13] when they were led out in chains, but lashed Augustus to his face with the foulest abuse.

42 B.C.

When the duties of administration were divided after the victory, Antony undertaking to restore order in the East, and Augustus to lead the veterans back to Italy and assign them lands in the municipalities, he could neither satisfy the veterans nor the landowners, since the latter complained that they were driven from their homes, and the former that they were not being treated as their services had led them to hope.

XIV. When Lucius Antonius at this juncture attempted a revolution, relying on his position as consul and his brother's power, he forced him to take refuge in Perusia, and starved him into surrender, not, however, without great personal danger both before and during the war. For at an exhibition of games, when he had given orders that a common soldier who was sitting in the fourteen rows[14] be put out by an attendant, the report was spread by his detractors that he had had the man killed later and tortured as well; whereupon he all but lost his life in a furious mob of soldiers, owing his escape to the sudden appearance of the missing man safe and sound. Again, when he was sacrificing near the walls of Perusia, he was well nigh cut off by a band of gladiators, who had made a sally from the town. 41 B.C. 40 B.C.

XV. After the capture of Perusia he took vengeance on many, meeting all attempts to beg for pardon or to make excuses with the one reply, "You must die." Some write that three hundred men of both orders were selected from the prisoners of war and sacrificed on the Ides of March like so many victims at the altar raised to the Deified Julius. Some have written that he took up arms of a set purpose, to unmask his secret opponents and those whom fear rather than good-will kept faithful to him, by giving them the chance to follow the lead of Lucius Antonius; and then by vanquishing them and confiscating their estates to pay the rewards promised to his veterans. 43/35 B.C.

XVI. The Sicilian war was among the first that he began, but it was long drawn out by many interruptions, now for the purpose of rebuilding his fleets, which he twice lost by shipwreck and storms, and that, too, in the summer; and again by making peace at the demand of the people, when supplies were cut off and there was a severe famine. Finally, after new ships had been built and twenty thousand slaves set free and trained as oarsmen, he made the Julian harbour at Baiae by letting the sea into the Lucrine lake and lake Avernus. After drilling his forces there all winter, he defeated Pompey between Mylae and Naulochus, though just before the battle he was suddenly overcome by so deep a sleep that his friends had to awaken him to give the signal. And it was this, I think, that gave Antony opportunity for the taunt: "He could not even look with steady eyes at the fleet when it was ready for battle, but lay in a stupor on his back, looking up at the sky, and did not rise or appear before the soldiers until the enemy's ships had been put to flight by Marcus Agrippa." Some censured another act and saying of his, declaring that when his fleets were lost in the storm, he cried out, "I will have the victory spite of Neptune," and that on the next day on which there were games in the Circus, he removed the statue of that god from the sacred procession. And it is safe to say that in none of his wars did he encounter more dangers or greater ones. For when he had transported an army to Sicily and was on his way back to the rest of his forces on the mainland, he was surprised by Pompey's admirals Demochares and Apollophanes and barely escaped with but a single ship. Again, as he was going on foot to Regium by way of Locri, he saw some of Pompey's biremes coasting along the shore, and taking them for his own ships and going down to the beach, narrowly escaped capture. At that same time, too, as he was making his escape by narrow bypaths, a slave of his companion Aemilius Paulus, nursing a grudge because Augustus had proscribed his master's father some time before, and thinking that he had an opportunity for revenge, attempted to slay him.

After Pompey's flight, Augustus' other colleague, Marcus Lepidus, whom he had summoned from Africa to help him, was puffed up by confidence in his twenty legions and claimed the first place with terrible threats; but Augustus stripped him of his army; and though he granted him his life when he sued for it, he banished him for all time to Circei.

XVII. At last he broke off his alliance with Marcus Antonius, which was always doubtful and uncertain, and with difficulty kept alive by various reconciliations; and the better to show that his rival had fallen away from conduct becoming a citizen, he had the will which Antony had left in Rome, naming his children by Cleopatra among his heirs, opened and read before the people.

But when Antony was declared a public enemy, he sent back to him all his kinsfolk and friends, among others Gaius Sosius and Titus Domitius, who were still consuls at the time. He also excused the community of Bononia from joining in the rally of all Italy to his standards, since they had been from ancient days dependents of the Antonii. Not long afterwards he won the sea-fight at Actium, 31 B.C.
where the contest continued to so late an hour that the victor passed the night on board. Having gone into winter quarters at Samos after Actium, he was disturbed by the news of a mutiny of the troops that he had selected from every division of his army and sent on to Brundisium after the victory, who demanded their rewards and discharge; and on his way back to Italy he twice encountered storms at sea, first between the headlands of the Peloponnesus and Aetolia, and again off the Ceraunian mountains. In both places a part of his galleys were sunk, while the rigging of the ship in which he was sailing was carried away and its rudder broken. He delayed at Brundisium only twenty-seven days—just long enough to satisfy all the demands of the soldiers—and then went to Egypt by a roundabout way through Asia and Syria, laid siege to Alexandria, where Antony had taken refuge with Cleopatra, and soon took the city. Although Antony tried to make terms at the eleventh hour, Augustus forced him to commit suicide, and viewed his corpse. He greatly desired to save Cleopatra alive for his triumph, and even had Psylli brought to her, to suck the poison from her wound, since it was thought that she died from the bite of an asp. He allowed them both the honour of burial, and in the same tomb, giving orders that the mausoleum which they had begun should be finished. The young Antony, the elder of Fulvia's two sons, he dragged from the image of the Deified Julius, to which he had fled after many vain entreaties, and slew him. Caesarion, too, whom Cleopatra fathered on Caesar, he overtook in his flight, brought back, and put to death. But he spared the rest of the offspring of Antony and Cleopatra, and afterwards maintained and reared them according to their several positions, as carefully as if they were his own kin.

XVIII. About this time he had the sarcophagus and body of Alexander the Great brought forth from its shrine,[15] and after gazing on it, showed his respect by placing upon it a golden crown and strewing it with flowers; and being then asked whether he wished to see the tomb of the Ptolemies as well, he replied, "My wish was to see a king, not corpses." He reduced Egypt to the form of a province, and then to make it more fruitful and better adapted to supply the city with grain, he set his soldiers at work cleaning out all the canals into which the Nile overflows, which in the course of many years had become choked with mud. To extend the fame of his victory at Actium and perpetuate its memory, he founded a city called Nicopolis near Actium, and provided for the celebration of games there every five years; enlarged the ancient temple of Apollo; and after adorning the site of the camp which he had occupied with naval trophies, consecrated it to Neptune and Mars.

XIX. After this he nipped in the bud at various times several outbreaks, attempts at revolution, and conspiracies, which were betrayed before they became formidable. The ringleaders were, first the young Lepidus, then Varro Murena and Fannius Caepio, later Marcus Egnatius, next Plautius Rufus and Lucius Paulus, husband of the emperor's granddaughter, and besides these Lucius Audasius, who had been charged with forgery, and was moreover old and feeble; also Asinius Epicadus, a half-breed of Parthian descent, and finally Telephus, slave and page[16] of a woman; for even men of the lowest condition conspired against him and imperilled his safety. Audasius and Epicadus had planned to take his daughter Julia and his grandson Agrippa by force to the armies from the islands where they were confined, Telephus to set upon both Augustus and the senate, under the delusion that he himself was destined for empire. Even a soldier's servant from the army in Illyricum, who had escaped the vigilance of the door-keepers, was caught at night near the emperor's bed-room, armed with a hunting knife; but whether the fellow was crazy or feigned madness is a question, since nothing could be wrung from him by torture.

XX. He carried on but two foreign wars in person: in Dalmatia, when he was but a youth, and with the Cantabrians after the overthrow of Antony. He was wounded, too, in the former campaign, being struck on the right knee with a stone in one battle, and in another having a leg and both arms severely injured by the collapse of a bridge. His other wars he carried on through his generals, although he was either present at some of those in Pannonia and Germany, or was not far from the front, since he went from the city as far as Ravenna, Mediolanum, or Aquileia.

XXI. In part as leader, and in part with armies serving under his auspices,[17] he subdued Cantabria, Aquitania, Pannonia, Dalmatia, and all Illyricum, as well as Raetia and the Vindelici and Salassi, which are Alpine tribes. He also put a stop to the inroads of the Dacians, slaying great numbers of them, together with three of their leaders, and forced the Germans back to the farther side of the river Albis, with the exception of the Suebi and Sigambri, who submitted to him and were taken into Gaul and settled in lands near the Rhine. He reduced to submission other peoples, too, that were in a state of unrest.

But he never made war on any nation without just and due cause, and he was so far from desiring to increase his dominion or his military glory at any cost, that he forced the chiefs of certain barbarians to take oath in the temple of Mars the Avenger that they would faithfully keep the peace for which they asked; in some cases, indeed, he tried exacting a new kind of hostages, namely women, realizing that the barbarians disregarded pledges secured by males; but all were given the privilege of reclaiming their hostages whenever they wished. On those who rebelled often or under circumstances of especial treachery he never inflicted any severer punishment than that of selling the prisoners, with the condition that they should not pass their term of slavery in a country near their own, nor be set free within thirty years. The reputation for prowess and moderation which he thus gained led even the Indians and the Scythians, nations known to us only by hearsay, to send envoys of their own free will and sue for his

friendship and that of the Roman people. The Parthians, too, readily yielded to him, when he laid claim to Armenia, and at his
20 B.C. demand surrendered the standards which they had taken from Marcus Crassus and Marcus Antonius[18]; they offered him hostages besides, and once when there were several claimants of their throne, they would accept only the one whom he selected.

XXII. The temple of Janus Quirinus, which had been closed but twice before his time since the founding of the city,[19] he closed three times in a far shorter period, having won peace on land and sea. He twice entered the city in an ovation, after the war of Philippi, and again after that in Sicily, and he celebrated three regular triumphs[20] for his victories in Dalmatia, at Actium, and at Alexandria, all on three successive days.

XXIII. He suffered but two severe and ignominious defeats, those of Lollius and Varus, both of which were in Germany. Of
15 B.C. these the former was more humiliating than serious, but the latter
9 A.D. was almost fatal, since three legions were cut to pieces with their general, his lieutenants, and all the auxiliaries. When the news of this came, he ordered that watch be kept by night throughout the city, to prevent any outbreak, and he prolonged the terms of the governors of the provinces, that the allies might be held to their allegiance by experienced men with whom they were acquainted. He also vowed great games to Jupiter Optimus Maximus, in case the condition of the commonwealth should improve, a thing which had been done in the Cimbric and Marsic wars. In fact, they say that he was so greatly affected that for several months in succession he cut neither his beard nor his hair, and sometimes he would dash his head against a door, crying: "Quintilius Varus, give me back my legions!" And he observed the day of the disaster each year as one of sorrow and mourning.

XXIV. He made many changes and innovations in the army, besides reviving some usages of former times. He exacted the strictest discipline. It was with great reluctance that he allowed even his generals to visit their wives, and then only in the winter season. He sold a Roman knight and his property at public auction, because he had cut off the thumbs of two young sons, to make them unfit for military service; but when he saw that some tax-gatherers were intent upon buying him, he knocked him down to a freeman of his own, with the understanding that he should be banished to the country districts, but allowed to live in freedom. He dismissed the entire tenth legion in disgrace, because they were insubordinate, and others, too, that demanded their discharge in an insolent fashion, he disbanded without the rewards which would have been due for faithful service. If any cohorts gave way in battle, he decimated them,[21] and fed the rest on barley.[22] When centurions left their posts, he punished them with death, just as he did the rank and file; for faults of other kinds he imposed various ignominious penalties, such as ordering them to stand all day long before the general's tent, sometimes in their tunics without their sword-belts, or again holding ten-foot poles or even a clod of earth.[23]

XXV. After the civil wars he never called any of the troops "comrades," either in the assembly or in an edict, but always "soldiers"[24]; and he would not allow them to be addressed otherwise, even by those of his sons or stepsons who held military commands, thinking the former term too flattering for the requirements of discipline, the peaceful state of the times, and his own dignity and that of his household. Except as a fire-brigade at Rome, and when there was fear of riots in times of scarcity, he employed freedmen as soldiers only twice: once as a guard for the colonies in the vicinity of Illyricum, and again to defend the bank of the river Rhine; even these he levied on men and women of means while they were still slaves, and at once gave them freedom; and he kept them under their original standard,[25] not mingling them with the soldiers of free birth or arming them in the same fashion.

As military prizes he was somewhat more ready to give trappings[26] or collars, valuable for their gold and silver, than crowns for scaling ramparts or walls, which conferred high honour; the latter he gave as sparingly as possible and without favouritism, often even to the common soldiers. He presented Marcus Agrippa with a blue banner in Sicily after his naval victory. Those who had celebrated triumphs were the only ones whom he thought ineligible for prizes, even though they had been the companions of his campaigns and shared in his victories, on the ground that they themselves had the privilege of bestowing such honours wherever they wished. He thought nothing less becoming in a well-trained leader than haste and rashness, and, accordingly, favourite sayings of his were: "More haste, less speed "; "Better a safe commander than a bold"; and "That is done quickly enough which is done well enough." He used to say that a war or a battle should not be begun under any circumstances, unless the hope of gain was clearly greater than the fear of loss; for he likened such as grasped at slight gains with no slight risk to those who fished with a golden hook, the loss of which, if it were carried off, could not be made good by any catch.

XXVI. He received offices and honours before the usual age, and some of a new kind and for life. He usurped the consulship in the twentieth year of his age, leading his legions against the city as
43 B.C. if it were that of an enemy, and sending messengers to demand the office for him in the name of his army; and when the Senate hesitated, his centurion, Cornelius, leader of the deputation, throwing back his cloak and showing the hilt of his sword, did not hesitate to say in the House, "This will make him consul, if you do
33 B.C. not." He held his second consulship nine years later, and a third
31 B.C. after a year's interval; the rest up to the eleventh were in successive
30/23 B.C. years, then after declining a number of terms that were offered him, he asked of his own accord for a twelfth after a long interval,
5 B.C. no less than seventeen years, and two years later for a thirteenth,
2 B.C. wishing to hold the highest magistracy at the time when he introduced each of his sons Gaius and Lucius to public life upon their coming of age. The five consulships from the sixth to the tenth he held for the full year, the rest for nine, six, four, or three months, except the second, which lasted only a few hours; for after sitting for a short time on the curule chair in front of the temple of Jupiter Capitolinus in the early morning, he resigned the honour

on the Kalends of January and appointed another in his place. He did not begin all his consulships in Rome, but the fourth in Asia, the fifth on the Isle of Samos, the eighth and ninth at Tarraco.

XXVII. He was for ten years a member of the triumvirate for restoring the State to order, and though he opposed his colleagues for some time and tried to prevent a proscription, yet when it was begun, he carried it through with greater severity than either of them. For while they could oftentimes be moved by personal influence and entreaties, he alone was most insistent that no one should be spared, even adding to the list his guardian Gaius Toranius, who had also been the colleague of his father Octavius in the aedileship. Julius Saturninus adds that after the proscription was over Marcus Lepidus addressed the senate in justification of the past and held out hope of leniency thereafter, since enough punishment had been inflicted; but that Augustus on the contrary declared that he had consented to end the proscription only on condition that he was allowed a free hand for the future. However, to show his regret for this inflexibility, he later honoured Titus Vinius Philopoemen with equestrian rank, because it was said that he had hidden his patron, who was on the list.

While he was triumvir, Augustus incurred general detestation by many of his acts. For example, when he was addressing the soldiers and a throng of civilians had been admitted to the assembly, noticing that Pinarius, a Roman knight, was taking notes, he ordered that he be stabbed on the spot, thinking him an eavesdropper and a spy. Because Tedius Afer, consul elect, railed at some act of his in spiteful terms, he uttered such terrible threats that Afer committed suicide.[27] Again, when Quintus Gallius, a praetor, held some folded tablets under his robe as he was paying his respects, Augustus, suspecting that he had a sword concealed there, did not dare to make a search on the spot for fear it should turn out to be something else; but a little later he had Gallius hustled from the tribunal by some centurions and soldiers, tortured him as if he were a slave, and though he made no confession, ordered his execution, first tearing out the man's eyes with his own hand. He himself writes, however, that Gallius made a treacherous attack on him after asking for an audience, and was haled to prison; and that after he was dismissed under sentence of banishment, he either lost his life by shipwreck or was waylaid by brigands.

He received the tribunician power for life, and once or twice chose a colleague in the office for periods of five years each. He was also given the supervision of morals and of the laws for all time, and by the virtue of this position, although without the title of censor, he nevertheless took the census thrice, the first and last time with a colleague, the second time alone.

XXVIII. He twice thought of restoring the republic; first immediately after the overthrow of Antony, remembering that his rival had often made the charge that it was his fault that it was not restored; and again in the weariness of a lingering illness, when he went so far as to summon the magistrates and the senate to his house, and submit an account of the general condition of the empire.[28] Reflecting, however, that as he himself would not be free from danger if he should retire, so too it would be hazardous to trust the State to the control of the populace, he continued to keep it in his hands; and it is not easy to say whether his intentions or their results were the better.[29] His good intentions he not only expressed from time to time, but put them on record as well in an edict in the following words "May it be my privilege to establish the State in a firm and secure position, and reap from that act the fruit that I desire; but only if I may be called the author of the best possible government, and bear with me the hope when I die that the foundations which I have laid for the State will remain unshaken." And he realized his hope by making every effort to prevent any dissatisfaction with the new régime.

Since the city was not adorned as the dignity of the empire demanded, and was exposed to flood and fire, he so beautified it that he could justly boast that he had found it built of brick[30] and left it in marble. He made it safe too for the future, so far as human foresight could provide for this.

XXIX. He built many public works, in particular the following:
his forum with the temple of Mars the Avenger, the temple of Apollo
on the Palatine, and the fane of Jupiter the Thunderer on the
Capitol. His reason for building the forum was the increase in the
number of the people and of cases at law, which seemed to call for a
third forum, since two were no longer adequate. Therefore it was
opened to the public with some haste, before the temple of Mars was 24 B.C.
finished, and it was provided that the public prosecutions be held 28 B.C.
there apart from the rest, as well as the selection of jurors by lot. He 22 B.C.
had made a vow to build the temple of Mars in the war of Philippi,
which he undertook to avenge his father; accordingly he decreed
that in it the senate should consider wars and claims for triumphs,
from it those who were on their way to the provinces with military
commands should be escorted,[31] and to it victors on their return
should bear the tokens of their triumphs. He reared the temple of
Apollo in that part of his house on the Palatine for which the soothsayers declared that the god had shown his desire by striking it with
lightning. He joined to it colonnades with Latin and Greek libraries,
and when he was getting to be an old man he often held meetings of
the senate there as well, and revised the lists of jurors. He dedicated
the shrine to Jupiter the Thunderer because of a narrow escape; for
on his Cantabrian expedition during a march by night, a flash of
lightning grazed his litter and struck the slave dead who was carrying
a torch before him. He constructed some works too in the name of
others, his grandsons to wit, his wife and his sister, such as the colonnade and basilica of Gaius and Lucius; also the colonnades of Livia 12 B.C.
and Octavia, and the theatre of Marcellus. More than that, he often 15 & 33 B.C.
urged other prominent men to adorn the city with new monuments
or to restore and embellish old ones, each according to his means. 13 B.C.
And many such works were built at that time by many men; for example, the temple of Hercules of the Muses by Marcius Philippus, the
temple of Diana by Lucius Cornificius, the Hall of Liberty by Asinius
Pollio, the temple of Saturn by Munatius Plancus, a theatre by
Cornelius Balbus, an amphitheatre by Statilius Taurus, and by
Marcus Agrippa in particular many magnificent structures.

XXX. He divided the area of the city into regions and wards, arranging that the former should be under the charge of magistrates selected each year by lot, and the latter under "masters" elected by the inhabitants of the respective neighbourhoods. To guard against fires he devised a system of stations of night watchmen, and to control the floods he widened and cleared out the channel of the Tiber, which had for some time been filled with rubbish and narrowed by jutting buildings. Further, to make the approach to the city easier from every direction, he personally undertook to rebuild the Flaminian Road all the way to Ariminum, and assigned the rest of the high-ways to others who had been honoured with triumphs, asking them to use their prize-money in paving them.

He restored sacred edifices which had gone to ruin through lapse of time or had been destroyed by fire, and adorned both these and the other temples with most lavish gifts, depositing in the shrine of Jupiter Capitolinus as a single offering sixteen thousand pounds of gold, besides pearls and other precious stones to the value of fifty million sesterces.

13 B.C. XXXI. After he finally had assumed the office of pontifex maximus on the death of Lepidus (for he could not make up his mind to deprive him of the honour while he lived) he collected whatever prophetic writings of Greek or Latin origin were in circulation anonymously or under the names of authors of little repute, and burned more than two thousand of them, retaining only the Sibylline books and making a choice even among those; and he deposited them in two gilded cases under the pedestal of the Palatine Apollo. Inasmuch as the calendar, which had been set in order by the Deified Julius, had later been confused and disordered through negligence, he restored it to its former system; and
8 B.C. in making this arrangement he called the month Sextilis by his own surname, rather than his birth-month September, because in the former he had won his first consulship and his most brilliant victories. He increased the number and importance of the priests, and also their allowances and privileges, in particular those of the

Vestal virgins. Moreover, when there was occasion to choose another vestal in place of one who had died, and many used all their influence to avoid submitting their daughters to the hazard of the lot, he solemnly swore that if anyone of his granddaughters were of eligible age, he would have proposed her name. He also revived some of the ancient rites which had gradually fallen into disuse, such as the augury of Safety,[32] the office of Flamen Dialis, the ceremonies of the Lupercalia, the Secular Games, and the festival of the Compitalia. At the Lupercalia he forbade beardless youths to join in the running, and at the Secular Games he would not allow young people of either sex to attend any entertainment by night except in company with some adult relative. He provided that the Lares of the Crossroads should be crowned twice a year, with spring and summer flowers.

Next to the immortal Gods he honoured the memory of the leaders who had raised the estate of the Roman people from obscurity to greatness. Accordingly he restored the works of such men with their original inscriptions, and in the two colonnades of his forum dedicated statues of all of them in triumphal garb, declaring besides in a proclamation: "I have contrived this to lead the citizens to require[33] me, while I live, and the rulers of later times as well, to attain the standard set by those worthies of old." He also moved the statue of Pompey from the hall in which Gaius Caesar had been slain and placed it on a marble arch opposite the grand door[34] of Pompey's theatre.

XXXII. Many pernicious practices militating against public security had survived as a result of the lawless habits of the civil wars, or had even arisen in time of peace. Gangs of footpads openly went about with swords by their sides, ostensibly to protect themselves, and travellers in the country, freemen and slaves alike, were seized and kept in confinement in the workhouses[35] of the land owners; numerous leagues, too, were formed for the commission of crimes of every kind, assuming the title of some new guild.[36] Therefore to put a stop to brigandage, he stationed guards of soldiers wherever it seemed advisable, inspected the workhouses, and disbanded all guilds, except such as were of long standing and formed for legitimate purposes. He burned the records of old debts to the treasury, which were by far the most frequent source of blackmail. He made over to their holders places in the city to which the claim of the state was uncertain. He struck off the lists the names of those who had long been under accusation, from whose humiliation[37] nothing was to be gained except the gratification of their enemies, with the stipulation that if anyone was minded to renew the charge, he should be liable to the same penalty.[38] To prevent any action for damages or on a disputed claim from falling through or being put off, he added to the term of the courts thirty more days, which had before been taken up with honorary games. To the three divisions of jurors he added a fourth of a lower estate, to be called *ducenarii*[39] and to sit on cases involving trifling amounts. He enrolled as jurors men of thirty years or more, that is five years younger than usual. But when many strove to escape court duty, he reluctantly consented that each division in turn should have a year's exemption, and that the custom of holding court during the months of November and December should be given up.

XXXIII. He himself administered justice regularly and sometimes up to nightfall, having a litter placed upon the tribunal, if he was indisposed, or even lying down at home. In his administration of justice he was both highly conscientious and very lenient; for to save a man clearly guilty of parricide from being sewn up in the sack,[40] a punishment which was inflicted only on those who pleaded guilty, he is said to have put the question to him in this form: "You surely did not kill your father, did you?" Again, in a case touching a forged will, in which all the signers were liable to punishment by the Cornelian Law, he distributed to the jury not merely the two tablets for condemnation or acquittal, but a third as well, for the pardon of those who were shown to have been induced to sign by misrepresentation or misunderstanding. Each year he referred appeals of cases involving citizens to the city praetor, but those between foreigners to ex-consuls, of whom he had put one in charge of the business affairs of each province.

XXXIV. He revised existing laws and enacted some new ones, for example, on extravagance, on adultery and chastity, on bribery, and on the encouragement of marriage among the various classes of citizens. Having made somewhat more stringent changes in the last of these than in the others, he was unable to carry it out because of an open revolt against its provisions, until he had abolished or mitigated a part of the penalties, besides increasing the rewards[41] and allowing a three years' exemption from the obligation to marry after the death of a husband or wife. When the knights even then persistently called for its repeal at a public show, he sent for the children of Germanicus and exhibited them, some in his own lap and some in their father's, intimating by his gestures and expression that they should not refuse to follow that young man's example. And on finding that the spirit of the law was being evaded by betrothal with immature girls and by frequent changes of wives, he shortened the duration of betrothals and set a limit on divorce.

XXXV. Since the number of the senators was swelled by a low-born and ill-assorted rabble (in fact, the senate numbered more than a thousand, some of whom, called by the vulgar Orcivi,[42] were wholly unworthy, and had been admitted after Caesar's death through favour or bribery) he restored it to its former limits and distinction by two enrolments, one according to the choice of the members themselves, each man naming one other, and a second made by Agrippa and himself. On the latter occasion it is thought that he wore a coat of mail under his tunic as he presided, and a sword by his side, while ten of the most robust of his friends among the senators stood by his chair. Cremutius Cordus writes that even then the senators were not allowed to approach except one by one, and after the folds of their robes had been carefully searched. Some he shamed into resigning, but he allowed even these to retain their distinctive dress, as well as the privilege of viewing the games from the orchestra and taking part in the public banquets of the order. Furthermore, that those who were chosen and approved might perform their duties more conscientiously, and also with less inconvenience, he provided that before taking his seat each member should offer incense and wine at the altar of the god in whose temple the meeting was held; that regular meetings of the senate should be held not oftener than twice a month, on the Kalends and the Ides; and that in the months of September and October only those should be obliged to attend who were drawn by lot, to a number sufficient for the passing of decrees. He also adopted the plan of privy councils chosen by lot for terms of six months, with which to discuss in advance matters which were to come before the entire body. On questions of special importance he called upon the senators to give their opinions, not according to the order established by precedent, but just as he fancied, to induce each man to keep his mind on the alert, as if he were to initiate action rather than give assent to others.

XXXVI. He introduced other innovations too, among them these: that the proceedings of the senate should not be published[43]; that magistrates should not be sent to the provinces immediately after laying down their office; that a fixed sum should be allowed the proconsuls for mules and tents, which it was the custom to contract for and charge to the State; that the management of the public treasury should be transferred from the city quaestors to ex-praetors or praetors; and that the centumviral court,[44] which it was usual for ex-quaestors to convoke, should be summoned by the Board of Ten.[45]

XXXVII. To enable more men to take part in the administration of the State, he devised new offices: the charge of public buildings, of the roads, of the aqueducts, of the channel of the Tiber, of the distribution of grain to the people, as well as the prefecture of the city, a board of three for choosing senators, and another for reviewing the companies of the knights whenever it should be necessary. He appointed censors, an office which had long been discontinued. He increased the number of praetors. He also demanded that whenever the consulship was conferred on him, he should have two colleagues instead of one; but this was not granted, since all cried out that it was a sufficient offence to his supreme dignity that he held the office with another and not alone.

XXXVIII. He was not less generous in honouring martial prowess, for he had regular triumphs[46] voted to above thirty generals, and the triumphal regalia to somewhat more than that number.

To enable senators' sons to gain an earlier acquaintance with public business, he allowed them to assume the broad purple stripe immediately after the gown of manhood and to attend meetings of the senate; and when they began their military career, he gave them not merely a tribunate in a legion, but the command of a division of cavalry as well; and to furnish all of them with experience in camp life, he usually appointed two senators' sons to command each division.

He reviewed the companies of knights at frequent intervals, reviving the custom of the procession after long disuse. But he would not allow an accuser to force anyone to dismount as he rode by, as was often done in the past; and he permitted those who were conspicuous because of old age or any bodily infirmity[47] to send on their horses in the review, and come on foot to answer to their names whenever they were summoned. Later he excused those who were over thirty-five years of age and did not wish to retain their horses from formally surrendering them.

XXXIX. Having obtained ten assistants from the senate, he compelled each knight to render an account of his life, punishing some of those whose conduct was scandalous and degrading others; but the greater part he reprimanded with varying degrees of severity. The mildest form of reprimand was to hand them a pair of tablets publicly, which they were to read in silence on the spot. He censured some because they had borrowed money at low interest and invested it at a higher rate.

XL. At the elections for tribunes if there were not candidates enough of senatorial rank,[48] he made appointments from among the knights, with the understanding that after their term they might remain in whichever order they wished. Morever, since many knights whose property was diminished during the civil wars did not venture to view the games from the fourteen rows[49] through fear of the penalty of the law regarding theatres, he declared that none were liable to its provisions, if they themselves or their parents had ever possessed a knight's estate.

He revised the lists of the people street by street, and to prevent the commons from being called away from their occupations too often because of the distributions of grain, he determined to give out tickets for four months' supply three times a year; but at their urgent request he allowed a return to the old custom of receiving a share every month. He also revived the old time election privileges,[50] trying to put a stop to bribery by numerous penalties, and distributing to his fellow members of the Fabian and Scaptian tribes[51] a thousand sesterces a man from his own purse on the day of the elections, to keep them from looking for anything from any of the candidates.

Considering it also of great importance to keep the people pure and unsullied by any taint of foreign or servile blood, he was most chary of conferring Roman citizenship and set a limit to manumission. When Tiberius requested citizenship for a Grecian dependent of his, Augustus wrote in reply that he would not grant it unless the man appeared in person and convinced him that he had reasonable grounds for the request; and when Livia asked it for a Gaul from a tributary province, he refused, offering instead freedom from tribute, and declaring that he would more willingly suffer a loss to his privy purse than the prostitution of the honour of Roman citizenship. Not content with making it difficult for slaves to acquire freedom, and still more so for them to attain full rights, by making careful provision as to the number, condition, and status of those who were manumitted, he added the proviso that no one who had ever been put in irons or tortured should acquire citizenship by any grade of freedom.[52]

He desired also to revive the ancient fashion of dress, and once when he saw in an assembly a throng of men in dark cloaks, he cried out indignantly, "Behold them

Romans, lords of the world, the nation clad in the toga,"[53]

and he directed the aediles never again to allow anyone to appear in the Forum or its neighbourhood except in the toga and without a cloak.

XLI. He often showed generosity to all classes when occasion offered. For example, by bringing the royal treasures to Rome in his Alexandrian triumph he made ready money so abundant, that the rate of interest fell, and the value of real estate rose greatly; and after that, whenever there was an excess of funds from the property of those who had been condemned, he loaned it without interest for fixed periods to any who could give security for double the amount. He increased the property qualification for senators, requiring one million two hundred thousand sesterces, instead of eight hundred thousand, and making up the amount for those who did not possess it. He often gave largess[54] to the people, but usually of different sums: now four hundred, now three hundred, now two hundred and fifty sesterces a man; and he did not even exclude young boys, though it had been usual for them to receive a share only after the age of eleven. In times of scarcity too he often distributed grain to each man at a very low figure, sometimes for nothing, and he doubled the money tickets.[55]

XLII. But to show that he was a prince who desired the public welfare rather than popularity, when the people complained of the scarcity and high price of wine, he sharply rebuked them by saying: "My son-in-law Agrippa has taken good care, by building several aqueducts, that men shall not go thirsty." Again, when the people demanded largess which he had in fact promised, he replied: "I am a man of my word"; but when they called for one which had not been promised, he rebuked them in a proclamation for their shameless impudence, and declared that he would not give it, even though he was intending to do so. With equal dignity and firmness, when he had announced a distribution of money and found that many had been manumitted and added to the list of citizens, he declared that those to whom no promise had been made should receive nothing, and gave the rest less than he had promised, to make the appointed sum suffice. Once indeed in a time of great scarcity when it was difficult to find a remedy, he expelled from the city the slaves that were for sale, as well as the schools of gladiators, all foreigners with the exception of physicians and teachers, and a part of the household slaves; and when grain at last became more plentiful, he writes: "I was strongly inclined to do away forever with distributions of grain, because through dependence on them agriculture was neglected; but I did not carry out my purpose, feeling sure that they would one day be renewed through desire for popular favour." But from that time on he regulated the practice with no less regard for the interests of the farmers and grain-dealers than for those of the populace.

XLIII. He surpassed all his predecessors in the frequency, variety, and magnificence of his public shows. He says that he gave games four times in his own name and twenty-three times for other magistrates, who were either away from Rome or lacked means. He gave them sometimes in all the wards and on many stages with actors in all languages,[56] and combats of gladiators not only in the Forum or the amphi-theatre, but in the Circus and in the Saepta; sometimes, however, he gave nothing except a fight with wild beasts. He gave athletic contests too in the Campus Martius, erecting wooden seats; also a sea-fight, constructing an artificial lake near the Tiber, where the grove of the Caesars now stands. On such occasions he stationed guards in various parts of the city, to prevent it from falling a prey to footpads because of the few people who remained at home. In the Circus he exhibited charioteers, runners, and slayers of wild animals, who were sometimes young men of the highest rank. Besides he gave frequent performances of the game of Troy[57] by older and younger boys, thinking it a time-honoured and worthy custom for the flower of the nobility to become known in this way. When Nonius Asprenas was lamed by a fall while taking part in this game, he presented him with a golden necklace and allowed him and his descendants to bear the surname Torquatus. But soon afterwards he gave up that form of entertainment, because Asinius Pollio the orator complained bitterly and angrily in the senate of an accident to his grandson Aeserninus, who also had broken his leg.

He sometimes employed even Roman knights in scenic and gladiatorial performances, but only before it was forbidden by decree of the senate. After that he exhibited no one of respectable parentage, with the exception of a young man named Lycius, whom he showed merely as a curiosity; for he was less than two feet tall, weighed but seventeen pounds, yet had a stentorian voice. He did however on the day of one of the shows make a display of the first Parthian hostages that had ever been sent to Rome, by leading them through the middle of the arena and placing them in the second row above his own seat. Furthermore, if anything rare and worth seeing was ever brought to the city, it was his habit to make a special exhibit of it in any convenient place on days when no shows were appointed. For example a rhinoceros in the Saepta, a tiger on the stage and a snake of fifty cubits in the Comitium.

It chanced that at the time of the games which he had vowed to give in the circus, he was taken ill and headed the sacred procession lying in a litter; again, at the opening of the games with which he dedicated the theatre of Marcellus, it happened that the joints of his curule chair gave way and he fell on his back. At the games for his grandsons, when the people were in a panic for fear the theatre should fall, and he could not calm them or encourage them in any way, he left his own place and took his seat in the part which appeared most dangerous.

XLIV. He put a stop by special regulations to the disorderly and indiscriminate fashion of viewing the games, through exasperation at the insult to a senator, to whom no one offered a seat in a crowded house at some largely attended games in Puteoli. In consequence of this the senate decreed that, whenever any public show was given anywhere, the first row of seats should be reserved for senators; and at Rome he would not allow the envoys of the free and allied nations to sit in the orchestra, since he was informed that even freedmen were sometimes appointed. He separated the soldiery from the people. He assigned special seats to the married men of the commons, to boys under age their own section and the adjoining one to their preceptors; and he decreed that no one wearing a dark cloak should sit in the middle of the house.[58] He would not allow women to view even the gladiators except from the upper seats, though it had been the custom for men and women to sit together at such shows. Only the Vestal virgins were assigned a place to themselves, opposite the praetor's tribunal. As for the contests of the athletes, he excluded women from them so strictly, that when a contest between a pair of boxers had been called for at the games in honour of his appointment as pontifex maximus, he postponed it until early the following day, making proclamation that it was his desire that women should not come to the theatre before the fifth hour.

XLV. He himself usually watched the games in the Circus from the upper rooms of his friends and freedmen,[59] but sometimes from the imperial box,[60] and even in company with his wife and children. He was sometimes absent for several hours, and now and then for whole days, making his excuses and appointing presiding officers to take his place. But whenever he was present, he gave his entire attention to the performance, either to avoid the censure to which he realized that his father Caesar had been generally exposed, because he spent his time in reading or answering letters and petitions; or from his interest and pleasure in the spectacle, which he never denied but often frankly confessed. Because of this he used to offer special prizes and numerous valuable gifts from his own purse at games given by others, and he appeared at no contest in the Grecian fashion[61] without making a present to each of the participants according to his deserts. He was especially given to watching boxers, particularly those of Latin birth, not merely such as were recognized and classed as professionals, whom he was wont to match even with Greeks, but the common untrained townspeople that fought rough and tumble and without skill in the narrow streets. In fine, he honoured with his interest all classes of performers who took part in the public shows; maintained the privileges of the athletes and even increased them; forbade the matching of gladiators without the right of appeal for quarter; and deprived the magistrates of the power allowed them by an ancient law of punishing actors anywhere and everywhere, restricting it to the time of games and to the theatre. Nevertheless he exacted the severest discipline in the contests in the wrestling halls and the combats of the gladiators. In particular he was so strict in curbing the lawlessness of the actors, that when he learned that Stephanio, an actor of Roman plays, was waited on by a matron with hair cut short to look like a boy, he had him whipped with rods through the three theatres[62] and then banished him. Hylas, a pantomimic actor, was publicly scourged in the atrium of his own house, on complaint of a praetor, and Pylades was expelled from the city and from Italy as well, because by pointing at him with his finger[63] he turned all eyes upon a spectator who was hissing him.

XLVI. After having thus set the city and its affairs in order, he added to the population of Italy by personally establishing twenty-eight colonies; furnished many parts of it with public buildings and revenues; and even gave it, at least to some degree, equal rights and dignity with the city of Rome, by devising a kind of votes which the members of the local senate were to cast in each colony for candidates for the city offices and send under seal to Rome against the day of the elections. To keep up the supply of men of rank and induce the commons to increase and multiply, he admitted to the equestrian military career[64] those who were recommended by any town, while to those of the commons who could lay claim to legitimate sons or daughters when he made his rounds of the city he distributed a thousand sesterces for each child.

XLVII. The stronger provinces, which could neither easily nor safely be governed by annual magistrates, he took to himself; the others he assigned to proconsular governors selected by lot. But he changed some of them at times from one class to the other, and often visited many of both sorts. Certain of the cities which had treaties with Rome, but were on the road to ruin through their lawlessness, he deprived of their independence; he relieved others that were overwhelmed with debt, rebuilt some which had been destroyed by earthquakes, and gave Latin rights[65] or full citizenship 27 B.C.

to such as could point to services rendered the Roman people. I believe there is no province, excepting only Africa and Sardinia, which he did not visit; and he was planning to cross to these from Sicily after his defeat of Sextus Pompeius, but was prevented by a series of violent storms, and later had neither opportunity nor occasion to make the voyage.

XLVIII. Except in a few instances he restored the kingdoms of which he gained possession by the right of conquest to those from whom he had taken them or joined them with other foreign nations. He also united the kings with whom he was in alliance by mutual ties, and was very ready to propose or favour intermarriages or friendships among them. He never failed to treat them all with consideration as integral parts of the empire, regularly appointing a guardian for such as were too young to rule or whose minds were affected, until they grew up or recovered; and he brought up the children of many of them and educated them with his own.

XLIX. Of his military forces he assigned the legions and auxiliaries to the various provinces, stationed a fleet at Misenum and another at Ravenna, to defend the Upper and Lower seas, and employed the remainder partly in the defence of the city and partly in that of his own person, disbanding a troop of Calagurritani which had formed a part of his body-guard until the overthrow of Antony, and also one of Germans, which he had retained until the defeat of Varus. However, he never allowed more than three cohorts to remain in the city and even those were without a permanent camp; the rest he regularly sent to winter or summer quarters in the towns near Rome. Furthermore, he restricted all the soldiery everywhere to a fixed scale of pay and allowances, designating the duration of their service and the rewards on its completion according to each man's rank, in order to keep them from being tempted to revolution after their discharge either by age or poverty. To have funds ready at all times without difficulty for maintaining the soldiers and paying the rewards due to them, he established a military treasury, supported by new taxes.

To enable what was going on in each of the provinces to be reported and known more speedily and promptly, he at first stationed young men at short intervals along the military roads, and afterwards post-chaises. The latter has seemed the more convenient arrangement, since the same men who bring the dispatches from any place can, if occasion demands, be questioned as well.

L. In passports,[66] dispatches, and private letters he used as his seal at first a sphinx, later an image of Alexander the Great, and finally his own, carved by the hand of Dioscurides; and this his successors continued to use as their seal. He always attached to all letters the exact hour, not only of the day, but even of the night, to indicate precisely when they were written.

LI. The evidences of his clemency and moderation are numerous and strong. Not to give the full list of the men of the opposite faction whom he not only pardoned and spared, but allowed to hold high positions in the state, I may say that he thought it enough to punish two plebeians, Junius Novatus and Cassius Patavinus, with a fine and with a mild form of banishment respectively, although the former had circulated a most scathing letter about him under the name of the young Agrippa, while the latter had openly declared at a large dinner party that he lacked neither the earnest desire nor the courage to kill him. Again, when he was hearing a case against Aemilius Aelianus of Corduba and it was made the chief offence, amongst other charges, that he was in the habit of expressing a bad opinion of Caesar, Augustus turned to the accuser with assumed anger and said: "I wish you could prove the truth of that. I'll let Aelianus know that I have a tongue as well as he, for I'll say even more about him;" and he made no further inquiry either at the time or afterwards. When Tiberius complained to him of the same thing in a letter, but in more forcible language, he replied as follows: "My dear Tiberius, do not be carried away by the ardour of youth in this matter, or take it too much to heart that anyone speak evil of me; we must be content if we can stop anyone from doing evil to us."

LII. Although well aware that it was usual to vote temples even to proconsuls, he would not accept one even in a province save jointly in his own name and that of Rome. In the city itself he refused this honour most emphatically, even melting down the silver statues which had been set up in his honour in former times and with the money coined from them dedicating golden tripods to Apollo of the Palatine.

When the people did their best to force the dictatorship upon him, he knelt down, threw off his toga from his shoulders and with bare breast begged them not to insist.

LIII. He always shrank from the title of Lord[67] as reproachful and insulting. When the words

"O just and gracious Lord!"

were uttered in a farce at which he was a spectator and all the people sprang to their feet and applauded as if they were said of him, he at once checked their unseemly flattery by look and gesture, and on the following day sharply reproved them in an edict. After that he would not suffer himself to be called Sire even by his children or his grandchildren either in jest or earnest, and he forbade them to use such flattering terms even among themselves. He did not if he could help it leave or enter any city or town except in the evening or at night, to avoid disturbing anyone by the obligations of ceremony. In his consulship he commonly went through the streets on foot, and when he was not consul, generally in a closed litter. His morning receptions were open to all, including even the commons, and he met the requests of those who approached him with great affability, jocosely reproving one man because he presented a petition to him with as much hesitation "as he would a penny to an elephant." On the day of a meeting of the senate he always greeted the members in the House[68] and in their seats, calling each man by name without a prompter; and when he left the House, he used to take leave of them in the same manner, while they remained seated. He exchanged social calls with many, and did not cease to attend all their anniversaries, until he was well on in years and was once incommoded by the crowd on the day of a betrothal. When Gallus Cerrinius, a senator with whom he was not at all intimate, had suddenly become blind and had therefore resolved to end his life by starvation, Augustus called on him and by his consoling words induced him to live.

LIV. As he was speaking in the senate someone said to him: "I did not understand," and another: "I would contradict you if I had an opportunity." Several times when he was rushing from the House in anger at the excessive bickering of the disputants, some shouted after him: "Senators ought to have the right of speaking their mind on public affairs." At the selection of senators when each member chose another,[69] Antistius Labeo named Marcus Lepidus, an old enemy of the emperor's who was at the time in banishment; and when Augustus asked him whether there were not others more deserving of the honour, Labeo replied that every man had his own opinion. Yet for all that no one suffered for his freedom of speech or insolence.

LV. He did not even dread the lampoons against him which were scattered in the senate house, but took great pains to refute them; and without trying to discover the authors, he merely proposed that thereafter such as published notes or verses defamatory of anyone under a false name should be called to account.

LVI. When he was assailed with scurrilous or spiteful jests by certain men, he made reply in a public proclamation; yet he vetoed a law to check freedom of speech in wills.[70] Whenever he took part in the election of magistrates, he went the round of the tribes with his candidates and appealed for them in the traditional manner. He also cast his own vote in his tribe, as one of the people. When he gave testimony in court, he was most patient in submitting to questions and even to contradiction. He made his forum narrower than he had planned, because he did not venture to eject the owners of the neighbouring houses. He never recommended his sons for office without adding "If they be worthy of it." When they were still under age and the audience at the theatre rose as one man in their honour, and stood up and applauded them, he expressed strong disapproval. He wished his friends to be prominent and influential in the state, but to be bound by the same laws as the rest and equally liable to prosecution. When Nonius Asprenas, a close friend of his, was meeting a charge of poisoning made by Cassius Severus, Augustus asked the senate what they thought he ought to do; for he hesitated, he said for fear that if he should support him, it might be thought that he was shielding a guilty man, but if he failed to do so, that he was proving false to a friend and prejudicing his case. Then, since all approved of his appearing in the case, he sat on the benches[71] for several hours, but in silence and without even speaking in praise of the defendant.[72] He did however defend some of his clients, for instance a certain Scutarius, one of his former officers, who was accused of slander. But he secured the acquittal of no more than one single man, and then only by entreaty, making a successful appeal to the accuser in the presence of the jurors; this was Castricius, through whom he had learned of Murena's conspiracy.

LVII. It may readily be imagined how much he was beloved because of this admirable conduct. I say nothing of decrees of the senate, which might seem to have been dictated by necessity or by awe. The Roman knights celebrated his birthday of their own accord by common consent, and always for two successive days.[73] All sorts and conditions of men, in fulfilment of a vow for his welfare, each year threw a small coin into the Lacus Curtius, and also brought a New Year's gift to the Capitol on the Kalends of January, even when he was away from Rome. With this sum he bought and dedicated in each of the city wards costly statues of the gods, such as Apollo Sandaliarius, Jupiter Tragoedus, and others. To rebuild his house on the Palatine, which had been destroyed by fire, the veterans, the guilds,[74] the tribes, and even individuals of other conditions gladly contributed money, each according to his means; but he merely took a little from each pile as a matter of form, not more than a denarius from any of them. On his return from a province they received him not only with prayers and good wishes, but with songs. It was the rule, too, that whenever he entered the city, no one should suffer punishment.

LVIII. The whole body of citizens with a sudden unanimous impulse proffered him the title of Father of his Country: first the commons, by a deputation sent to Antium, and then, because he declined it, again at Rome as he entered the theatre, which they attended in throngs, all wearing laurel wreaths; the senate afterwards in the House, not by a decree or by acclamation, but tlirough Valerius Messala. He, speaking for the whole body, said: "Good fortune and divine favour attend thee and thy house, Caesar Augustus; for thus we feel that we are praying for lasting prosperity for our country and happiness for our city. The senate in accord with the people of Rome hails thee Father of thy Country." Then Augustus with tears in his eyes replied as follows (and I have given his exact words, as I did those of Messala): "Having attained my highest hopes, Fathers of the Senate, what more have I to ask of the immortal gods than that I may retain this same unanimous approval of yours to the very end of my life."

LIX. In honour of his physician, Antonius Musa, through whose care he had recovered from a dangerous illness, a sum of money was raised and Musa's statue set up beside that of Aesculapius. Some householders provided in their wills that their heirs should drive victims to the Capitol and pay a thank-offering in their behalf, because Augustus had survived them, and that a placard to this effect should be carried before them. Some of the Italian cities made the day on which he first visited them the beginning of their year. Many of the provinces, in addition to temples and altars, established quinquennial games in his honour in almost every one of their towns.

LX. His friends and allies among the kings each in his own realm founded a city called Caesarea, and all joined in a plan to contribute the funds for finishing the temple of Jupiter Olympius, which was begun at Athens in ancient days, and to dedicate it to his Genius[75]; and they would often leave their kingdoms and show him the attentions usual in dependents, clad in the toga and without the emblems of royalty, not only at Rome, but even when he was travelling through the provinces.

LXI. Now that I have shown how he conducted himself in civil and military positions, and in ruling the State in all parts of the world in peace and in war, I shall next give an account of his private and domestic life, describing his character and his fortune at home and in his household from his youth until the last day of his life.

43 B.C. He lost his mother during his first consulship and his sister
9 B.C. Octavia in his fifty-fourth year. To both he showed marked devotion during their lifetime, and also paid them the highest honours after their death.

LXII. In his youth he was betrothed to the daughter of Publius Servilius Isauricus, but when he became reconciled with Antony after their first quarrel, and their troops begged that the rivals be further united by some tie of kinship, he took to wife Antony's
43 B.C. stepdaughter Claudia, daughter of Fulvia by Publius Clodius, although she was barely of marriageable age; but because of a falling out with his mother-in-law Fulvia, he divorced her before they had begun to live together. Shortly after that he married
40 B.C. Scribonia, who had been wedded before to two ex-consuls, and was a mother by one of them. He divorced her also, "unable to put up with her shrewish disposition," as he himself writes, and at once
38 B.C. took Livia Drusilla from her husband Tiberius Nero, although she was with child at the time; and he loved and esteemed her to the end without a rival.

LXIII. By Scribonia he had a daughter Julia, by Livia no children at all, although he earnestly desired issue. One baby was conceived, but was prematurely born. He gave Julia in marriage first to Marcellus, son of his sister Octavia and hardly more than a boy, and then after his death to Marcus Agrippa, prevailing upon his sister to yield her son-in-law to him; for at that time Agrippa had to wife one of the Marcellas and had children from her. When Agrippa also died, Augustus, after considering various alliances for a long time, even in the equestrian order, finally chose his stepson Tiberius, obliging him to divorce his wife, who was with child and by whom he was already a father. Mark Antony writes that

Augustus first betrothed his daughter to his son Antonius and then to Cotiso, king of the Getae, at the same time asking for the hand of the king's daughter for himself in turn.

LXIV. From Agrippa and Julia he had three grandsons, Gaius, Lucius, and Agrippa, and two granddaughters, Julia and Agrippina. He married Julia to Lucius Paulus, the censor's son, and Agrippina to Germanicus his sister's grandson. Gaius and Lucius he adopted at home, privately buying them from their father by a symbolic sale,[76] and initiated them into administrative life when they were still young, sending them to the provinces and the armies as consuls elect. In bringing up his daughter and his granddaughters he even had them taught spinning and weaving, and he forbade them to say or do anything except openly and such as might be recorded in the household diary.[77] He was most strict in keeping them from meeting strangers, once writing to Lucius Vinicius, a young man of good position and character: "You have acted presumptuously in coming to Baiae to call on my daughter." He taught his grandsons reading, swimming, and the other elements of education, for the most part himself, taking special pains to train them to imitate his own handwriting; and he never dined in their company unless they sat beside him on the lowest couch,[78] or made a journey unless they preceded his carriage or rode close by it on either side.

LXV. But at the height of his happiness and his confidence in his family and its training. Fortune proved fickle. He found the 2 B.C.
two Julias, his daughter and granddaughter, guilty of every form of 9 B.C.
vice, and banished them. He lost Gaius and Lucius within the span
of eighteen months, for the former died in Lycia and the latter at 2 A.D.
Massilia. He then publicly adopted his third grandson Agrippa 4 A.D.
and at the same time his stepson Tiberius by a bill passed in the assembly of the *curiae*[79]; but he soon disowned Agrippa because of his low tastes and violent temper, and sent him off to Surrentum.

He bore the death of his kin with far more resignation than their misconduct. For he was not greatly broken by the fate of Gaius and Lucius, but he informed the senate of his daughter's fall through a letter read in his absence by a quaestor, and for very shame would meet no one for a long time, and even thought of putting her to death. At all events, when one of her confidantes, a freedwoman called Phoebe, hanged herself at about that same time, he said: "I would rather have been Phoebe's father." After Julia was banished, he denied her the use of wine and every form of luxury, and would not allow any man, bond or free, to come near her without his permission, and then not without being informed of his stature, complexion, and even of any marks or scars upon his body. It was not until five years later that he moved her from the island[80] to the mainland and treated her with somewhat less rigour. But he could not by any means be prevailed on to recall her altogether, and when the Roman people several times interceded for her and urgently pressed their suit, he in open assembly called upon the gods to curse them with like daughters and like wives. He would not allow the child born to his granddaughter Julia after her sentence to be recognized or reared. As Agrippa grew no more manageable, but on the contrary became madder from day to day, he transferred him to an island[81] and set a guard of soldiers over him besides. He also provided by a decree of the senate that he should be confined there for all time, and at every mention of him and of the Julias he would sigh deeply and even cry out:

"Would that I ne'er had wedded and would I had died without offspring";[82]

and he never alluded to them except as his three boils and his three ulcers.

LXVI. He did not readily make friends, but he clung to them with the utmost constancy, not only suitably rewarding their virtues and deserts but even condoning their faults, provided they were not too great. In fact one cannot readily name any of his numerous friends who fell into disgrace, except Salvidienus Rufus, whom he had advanced to a consul's rank, and Cornelius Gallus, whom he had raised to the prefecture of Egypt, both from the lowest estate. The former he handed over to the senate that it might condemn him to death, because he was plotting revolution; the latter he forbade his house and the privilege of residence in the imperial provinces,[83] because of his ungrateful and envious spirit. But when Gallus too[84] died by his own hand, driven to it by the menaces of his accusers and the decrees of the senate, though commending their loyalty and their indignation on his account, Augustus yet shed tears and bewailed his lot, because he alone could not set what limits he chose to his anger with his friends[85] All the rest continued to enjoy power and wealth to the end of their lives, each holding a leading place in his own class,[86] although sometimes differences arose. Not to mention the others, he occasionally found Agrippa lacking in patience and Maecenas in the gift of silence; for the former because of a slight suspicion of coolness and of a preference shewn for Marcellus, threw up everything and went off to Mytilene, while the latter betrayed to his wife Terentia the secret of the discovery of the conspiracy of Murena.

In return he demanded of his friends affection on their part, both in life and after death.[87] For though he was in no sense a legacy-hunter, and in fact could never bring himself to accept anything from the will of a stranger, yet he was highly sensitive in weighing the death-bed utterances of his friends, concealing neither his chagrin if he was left a niggardly bequest or one unaccompanied with compliments, nor his satisfaction, if he was praised in terms of gratitude and affection. Whenever legacies or shares in inheritances were left him by men of any station who had offspring, he either turned them over to the children at once, or if the latter were in their minority, paid the money back with interest on the day when they assumed the gown of manhood or married.

LXVII. As patron and master he was no less strict than gracious and merciful, while he held many of his freedmen in high honour and close intimacy, such as Licinus, Celadus, and others. His slave Cosmus, who spoke of him most insultingly, he merely put in irons. When he was walking with his steward Diomedes, and the latter in a panic got behind him when they were suddenly charged by a wild boar, he preferred to tax the man with timorousness rather than with anything more serious, and turned a matter of grave danger into a jest, because after all there was no evil intent. But he forced Polus, a favourite freedman of his, to take his own life, because he was convicted of adultery with Roman matrons, and broke the legs of his secretary Thallus for taking five hundred denarii to betray the contents of a letter. Because the tutor and attendants of his son Gaius took advantage of their master's illness and death to commit acts of arrogance and greed in his province, he had them thrown into a river with heavy weights about their necks.

LXVIII. In early youth he incurred the reproach of sundry shameless acts. Sextus Pompey taunted him with effeminacy; Mark Antony with having earned adoption by his uncle through unnatural relations; and Lucius, brother of Mark Antony, that after sacrificing his honour to Caesar he had given himself to Aulus Hirtius in Spain for three hundred thousand sesterces, and that he used to singe his legs with red-hot nutshells, to make the hair grow softer. What is more, one day when there were plays in the theatre, all the people took as directed against him and loudly applauded the following line, spoken on the stage and referring to a priest of the Mother of the Gods, as he beat his timbrel:

"See'st how a wanton's finger sways the world?"[88]

LXIX. That he was given to adultery not even his friends deny, although it is true that they excuse it as committed not from passion but from policy, the more readily to get track of his adversaries' designs through the women of their households. Mark Antony charged him, besides his hasty marriage with Livia, with taking the wife of an ex-consul from her husband's dining room before his very eyes into a bed-chamber, and bringing her back to the table with her hair in disorder and her ears glowing; that Scribonia was divorced because she expressed her resentment too freely at the excessive influence of a rival;[89] that his friends acted as his panders, and stripped and inspected matrons and well-grown girls, as if Toranius the slave-dealer were putting them up for sale. Antony also writes to Augustus himself in the following familiar terms, when he had not yet wholly broken with him privately or publicly: "What has made such a change in you? Because I lie with the queen? She is my wife. Am I just beginning this, or was it nine years ago? What then of you—do you lie only with Drusilla? Good luck to you if when you read this letter you have not been with Tertulla or Terentilla or Rufilla or Salvia Titisenia, or all of them. Does it matter where or with whom you take your pleasure? "

LXX. There was besides a private dinner of his, commonly called that of the "twelve gods," which was the subject of gossip. At this the guests appeared in the guise of gods and goddesses, while he himself was made up to represent Apollo, as was charged not merely in letters of Antony, who spitefully gives the names of all the guests, but also in these anonymous lines, which everyone knows:

"As soon as that table of rascals had secured a choragus[90] and Mallia[91] saw six gods and six goddesses, while Caesar impiously plays the false rôle of Apollo and feasts amid novel debaucheries of the gods; then all the deities turned their faces from the earth and Jupiter himself fled from his golden throne." The scandal of this banquet was the greater because of dearth and famine in the land at the time, and on the following day there was an outcry that the gods had eaten all the grain and that Caesar was in truth Apollo, but Apollo the Tormentor, a surname under which the god was worshipped in one part of the city. He was criticized too as over fond of costly furniture and Corinthian bronzes and as given to gaming. Indeed, as early as the time of the proscriptions there was written on his statue—

"In silver once my father dealt, now in Corinthians[92] I,"

since it was believed that he caused some men to be entered in the list of the proscribed because of their Corinthian vases. Later, during the Sicilian war, this epigram was current:

"After he has twice been beaten at sea and lost his ships, he plays at dice all the time, in the hope of winning one victory."

LXXI. Of these charges or slanders (whichever we may call them) he easily refuted that for unnatural vice by the purity of his life at the time and afterwards; so too the odium of extravagance by the fact that when he took Alexandria, he kept none of the furniture of the palace for himself[93] except a single agate cup, and presently melted down all the golden vessels intended for everyday use. He could not dispose of the charge of lustfulness and they say that even in his later years he was fond of deflowering maidens, who were brought together for him from all quarters, even by his own wife. He did not in the least shrink from a reputation for gaming, and played frankly and openly for recreation, even when he was well on in years, not only in the month of December,[94] but on other holidays as well, and on working days too. There is no question about this, for in a letter in his own handwriting he says: "I dined, dear Tiberius, with the same company; we had besides as guests Vinicius and the elder Silius. We gambled like old men during the meal both yesterday and to-day; for when the dice were thrown, whoever turned up the 'dog'[95] or the six, put a denarius in the pool for each one of the dice, and the whole was taken by anyone who threw the 'Venus.'" Again in another letter: "We spent the Quinquatria[96] very merrily, my dear Tiberius, for we played all day long and kept the gaming-board warm. Your brother made a great outcry about his luck, but after all did not come out far behind in the long run; for after losing heavily, he unexpectedly and little by little got back a good deal. For my part, I lost twenty thousand sesterces, but because I was extravagantly generous in my play, as usual. If I had demanded of everyone the stakes which I let go, or had kept all that I gave away, I should have won fully fifty thousand. But I like that better, for my generosity will exalt me to immortal glory." To his daughter he writes: "I send you two hundred and fifty denarii, the sum which I gave each of my guests, in case they wished to play at dice or at odd and even during the dinner."

LXXII. In the other details of his life it is generally agreed that he was most temperate and without even the suspicion of any fault. He lived at first near the Forum Romanum, above the

Stairs of the Ringmakers, in a house which had belonged to the orator Calvus; afterwards, on the Palatine, but in the no less modest dwelling of Hortensius, which was remarkable neither for size nor elegance, having but a short colonnade with columns of Alban stone,[97] and rooms without any marble decorations or handsome pavements. For more than forty years too he used the same bedroom in winter and summer;[98] although he found the city unfavourable to his health in the winter, yet continued to winter there. If ever he planned to do anything in private or without interruption, he had a retired place at the top of the house, which he called "Syracuse"[99] and "technyphion"[100] In this he used to take refuge, or else in the villa of one of his freedmen in the suburbs; but whenever he was not well, he slept at Maecenas's house. For retirement he went most frequently to places by the sea and the islands of Campania, or to the towns near Rome, such as Lanuvium, Praeneste or Tibur, where he very often held court in the colonnades of the Temple of Hercules. He disliked large and sumptuous country palaces, actually razing to the ground one which his granddaughter Julia built on a lavish scale. His own villas, which were modest enough, he decorated not so much with handsome statues and pictures as with terraces, groves, and objects noteworthy for their antiquity and rarity; for example, at Capreae the monstrous bones of huge sea monsters and wild beasts, called the "bones of the giants," and the weapons of the heroes.

LXXIII. The simplicity of his furniture and household goods may be seen from couches and tables still in existence, many of which are scarcely fine enough for a private citizen. They say that he always slept on a low and plainly furnished bed. Except on special occasions he wore common clothes for the house,[101] made by his sister, wife, daughter or granddaughters; his togas were neither close nor full, his purple stripe neither narrow nor broad, and his shoes somewhat high-soled, to make him look taller than he really was. But he always kept shoes and clothing to wear in public ready in his room for sudden and unexpected occasions.

LXXIV. He gave dinner parties constantly and always formally,[102] with great regard to the rank and personality of his guests. Valerius Messala writes that he never invited a freedman to dinner with the exception of Menas, and then only when he had been enrolled among the freeborn after betraying the fleet of Sextus Pompey. Augustus himself writes that he once entertained a man at whose villa he used to stop,[103] who had been one of his body-guard. He would sometimes come to table late on these occasions and leave early, allowing his guests to begin to dine before he took his place and keep their places after he went out. He served a dinner of three courses or of six when he was most lavish, without needless extravagance but with the greatest goodfellowship. For he drew into the general conversation those who were silent or chatted under their breath, and introduced music and actors, or even strolling players from the circus, and especially story-tellers.[104]

LXXV. Festivals and holidays he celebrated lavishly as a rule, but sometimes only in a spirit of fun. On the Saturnalia, and at any other time when he took it into his head, he would now give gifts of clothing or gold and silver; again coins of every device, including old pieces of the kings and foreign money; another time nothing but hair cloth, sponges, pokers and tongs, and other such things under misleading names of double meaning. He used also at a dinner party to put up for auction lottery-tickets for articles of most unequal value, and paintings of which only the back was shown, thus by the caprice of fortune disappointing or filling to the full the expectations of the purchasers, requiring however that all the guests should take part in the bidding and share the loss or gain.

LXXVI. He was a light eater (for I would not omit even this detail) and as a rule ate of plain food. He particularly liked coarse bread, small fishes, handmade moist cheese, and green figs of the second crop; and he would eat even before dinner, wherever and whenever he felt hungry. I quote word for word from some of his letters: "I ate a little bread and some dates in my carriage." And again: "As I was on my homeward way from the Regia[105] in my litter, I devoured an ounce of bread and a few berries from a cluster of hard-fleshed grapes."[106] Once more: "Not even a Jew, my dear Tiberius, fasts so scrupulously on his sabbaths as I have to-day; for it was not until after the first hour of the night that I ate two mouthfuls of bread in the bath before I began to be anointed." Because of this irregularity he sometimes ate alone either before a dinner party began or after it was over, touching nothing while it was in progress.

LXXVII. He was by nature most sparing also in his use of wine. Cornelius Nepos writes that in camp before Mutina it was his habit to drink not more than three times at dinner. Afterwards, when he indulged most freely he never exceeded a pint; or if he did, he used to throw it up. He liked Raetian wine best, but rarely drank before dinner. Instead he would take a bit of bread soaked in cold water, a slice of cucumber, a sprig of young lettuce, or an apple with a tart flavour,[107] either fresh or dried.

LXXVIII. After his midday meal he used to rest for a while just as he was, without taking off his clothes or his shoes, with his feet uncovered[108] and his hand to his eyes. After dinner he went to a couch in his study,[109] where he remained to late at night, until he had attended to what was left of the day's business, either wholly or in great part. Then he went to bed and slept not more than seven hours at most, and not even that length of time without a break, but waking three or four times. If he could not resume his sleep when it was interrupted, as would happen, he sent for readers or story-tellers, and when sleep came to him he often prolonged it until after daylight. He would never lie awake in the dark without having someone sit by his side. He detested early rising and when he had to get up earlier than usual because of some official or religious duty, to avoid inconveniencing himself he spent the night in the room of one of his friends near the appointed place. Even so, he often suffered from want of sleep, and he would drop off while he was being carried through the streets and when his litter was set down because of some delay.

LXXIX. He was unusually handsome and exceedingly graceful at all periods of his life, though he cared nothing for personal adornment. He was so far from being particular about the dressing of his hair, that he would have several barbers working in a hurry at the same time, and as for his beard he now had it clipped and now shaved, while at the very same time he would either be reading or writing something. His expression, whether in conversation or when he was silent, was so calm and mild, that one of the leading men of the Gallic provinces admitted to his countrymen that it had softened his heart, and kept him from carrying out his design of pushing the emperor over a cliff, when he had been allowed to approach him under the pretence of a conference, as he was crossing the Alps. He had clear, bright eyes, in which he liked to have it thought that there was a kind of divine power, and it greatly pleased him, whenever he looked keenly at anyone, if he let his face fall as if before the radiance of the sun; but in his old age he could not see very well with his left eye. His teeth were wide apart, small, and ill-kept; his hair was slightly curly and inclining to golden; his eyebrows met. His ears were of moderate size, and his nose projected a little at the top and then bent slightly inward.[110] His complexion was between dark and fair. He was short of stature (although Julius Marathus, his freedman and keeper of his records, says that he was five feet and nine inches in height[111]), but this was concealed by the fine proportion and symmetry of his figure, and was noticeable only by comparison with some taller person standing beside him.

LXXX. It is said that his body was covered with spots and that he had birthmarks scattered over his breast and belly, corresponding in form, order and number with the stars of the Bear in the heavens;[112] also numerous callous places resembling ringworm, caused by a constant itching of his body and a vigorous use of the strigil. He was not very strong in his left hip, thigh, and leg, and even limped slightly at times; but he strengthened them by treatment with sand and reeds.[113] He sometimes found the forefinger of his right hand so weak, when it was numb and shrunken with the cold, that he could hardly use it for writing even with the aid of a finger-stall of horn. He complained of his bladder too, and was relieved of the pain only after passing stones in his urine.

LXXXI. In the course of his life he suffered from several severe and dangerous illnesses, especially after the subjugation of Cantabria, when he was in such a desperate plight from abscesses 23 B.C.
of the liver, that he was forced to submit to an unprecedented and hazardous course of treatment. Since hot fomentations gave him no relief, he was led by the advice of his physician Antonius Musa to try cold ones.[114]

He experienced also some disorders which recurred every year at definite times; for he was commonly ailing just before his birthday; and at the beginning of spring he was troubled with an enlargement of the diaphragm, and when the wind was in the south, with catarrh. Hence his constitution was so weakened that he could not readily endure either cold or heat.

LXXXII. In winter he protected himself with four tunics and a heavy toga, besides an undershirt, a woollen chest-protector and wraps for his thighs and shins, while in summer he slept with the doors of his bed-room open, oftentimes in the open court near a fountain, besides having someone to fan him.[115] Yet he could not endure the sun even in winter, and never walked in the open air without wearing a broad-brimmed hat, even at home. He travelled in a litter, usually at night, and by such slow and easy stages that he took two days to go to Praeneste or Tibur; and if he could reach his destination by sea, he preferred to sail. Yet in spite of all he made good his weakness by great care, especially by moderation in bathing; for as a rule he was anointed or took a sweat by a fire, after which he was doused with water either lukewarm or tepid from long exposure to the sun. When however he had to use hot salt water and sulphur baths[116] for rheumatism, he contented himself with sitting on a wooden bath-seat, which he called by the Spanish name *dureta*, and plunging his hands and feet in the water one after the other.

LXXXIII. Immediately after the civil war he gave up exercise with horses and arms in the Campus Martius, at first turning to pass-ball[117] and balloon-ball,[118] but soon confining himself to riding or taking a walk, ending the latter by running and leaping, wrapped in a mantle or a blanket. To divert his mind he sometimes angled and sometimes played at dice, marbles and nuts[119] with little boys, searching everywhere for such as were attractive for their pretty faces or their prattle, especially Syrians and Moors; for he abhorred dwarfs, cripples, and everything of that sort, as freaks of nature and of ill omen.

LXXXIV. From early youth he devoted himself eagerly and with the utmost diligence to oratory and liberal studies. During the war at Mutina, amid such a press of affairs, he is said to have read, written and declaimed every day. In fact he never afterwards spoke in the senate, or to the people or the soldiers, except in a studied and written address, although he did not lack the gift of speaking offhand without preparation. Moreover, to avoid the danger of forgetting what he was to say, or wasting time in committing it to memory, he adopted the practice of reading everything from a manuscript. Even his conversations with individuals and the more important of those with his own wife Livia, he always wrote out and read from a note-book, for fear of saying too much or too little if he spoke offhand. He had an agreeable and rather characteristic enunciation, and he practised constantly with a teacher of elocution; but sometimes because of weakness of the throat[120] he addressed the people through a herald.

LXXXV. He wrote numerous works of various kinds in prose, some of which he read to a group of his intimate friends, as others did in a lecture-room; for example, his "Reply to Brutus on Cato."[121] At the reading of these volumes he had all but come to the end, when he grew tired and handed them to Tiberius to finish, for he was well on in years. He also wrote "Exhortations to Philosophy" and some volumes of an Autobiography, giving an account of his life in thirteen books up to the time of the Cantabrian war, but no farther. His essays in poetry were but slight.

One book has come down to us written in hexameter verse, of which the subject and the title is "Sicily." There is another, equally brief, of "Epigrams," which he composed for the most part at the time of the bath. Though he began a tragedy with much enthusiasm, he destroyed it because his style did not satisfy him, and when some of his friends asked him what in the world had become of Ajax, he answered that "his Ajax had fallen on his sponge."

LXXXVI. He cultivated a style of speaking that was chaste and elegant, avoiding the vanity of attempts at epigram and an artificial order, and as he himself expresses it, "the noisomeness of far-fetched words," making it his chief aim to express his thought as clearly as possible. With this end in view, to avoid confusing and checking his reader or hearer at any point, he did not hesitate to use prepositions with names of cities, nor to repeat conjunctions several times, the omission of which causes some obscurity, though it adds grace. He looked on innovators and archaizers with equal contempt, as faulty in opposite directions, and he sometimes had a fling at them, in particular his friend Maecenas, whose "unguent-dripping curls," as he calls them, he loses no opportunity of belabouring and pokes fun at them by parody. He did not spare even Tiberius, who sometimes hunted up obsolete and pedantic expressions; and as for Mark Antony, he calls him a madman, for writing rather to be admired than to be understood. Then going on to ridicule his perverse and inconsistent taste in choosing an oratorical style, he adds the following: "Can you doubt whether you ought to imitate Annius Cimber or Veranius Flaccus,[122] that you use the words which Sallustius Crispus gleaned from Cato's *Origines*?[123] Or would you rather introduce into our tongue the verbose and unmeaning fluency of the Asiatic orators?"[124] And in a letter praising the talent of his granddaughter Agrippina he writes: "But you must take great care not to write and talk affectedly."

LXXXVII. That in his everyday conversation he used certain favourite and peculiar expressions appears from letters in his own hand, in which he says every now and then, when he wishes to indicate that certain men will never pay, that "they will pay on the

Greek Kalends." Urging his correspondent to put up with present circumstances, such as they are, he says: "Let's be satisfied with the Cato we have;"[125] and to express the speed of a hasty action, "Quicker than you can cook asparagus." He continually used *baceolus* (dolt) for *stultus* (fool), for *pullus* (dark) *pulleiaceus* (darkish), and for *cerritus* (mad) *vacerrosus* (blockhead); also *vapide se habere* (feel flat) for *male se habere* (feel badly), and *betizare*[126] (be like a beet) for *languere* (be weak), for which the vulgar term is *lachanizare.* Besides he used *simus* for *sumus*[127] and *domos* in the genitive singular instead of *domuos.*[128] The last two forms he wrote invariably, for fear they should be thought errors rather than a habit.

I have also observed this special peculiarity in his manner of writing: he does not divide words or carry superfluous letters from the end of one line to the beginning of the next, but writes them just below the rest of the word and draws a loop around them.

LXXXVIII. He does not strictly comply with orthography, that is to say the theoretical rules of spelling laid down by the grammarians, seeming to be rather of the mind of those who believe that we should spell exactly as we pronounce. Of course his frequent transposition or omission of syllables as well as of letters are slips common to all mankind. I should not have noted this, did it not seem to me surprising that some have written that he cashiered a consular governor, as an uncultivated and ignorant fellow, because he observed that he had written *ixi* for *ipsi.* Whenever he wrote in cipher,[129] he wrote B for A, C for B, and the rest of the letters on the same principle, using AA for X.

LXXXIX. He was equally interested in Greek studies, and in these too he excelled greatly. His teacher of declamation was Apollodorus of Pergamon, whom he even took with him in his youthful days from Rome to Apollonia, though Apollodorus was an old man at the time. Later he became versed in various forms of learning through association with the philosopher Areus and his sons Dionysius and Nicanor. Yet he never acquired the ability to speak Greek fluently or to compose anything in it; for if he had occasion to use the language, he wrote what he had to say in Latin and gave it to someone else to translate. Still he was far from being ignorant of Greek poetry, even taking great pleasure in the Old Comedy and frequently staging it at his public entertainments. In reading the writers of both tongues there was nothing for which he looked so carefully as precepts and examples instructive to the public or to individuals; these he would often copy word for word, and send to the members of his household, or to his generals and provincial governors, whenever any of them required admonition. He even read entire volumes to the senate and called the attention of the people to them by proclamations; for example, the speeches of Quintus Metellus "On Increasing the Family," and of Rutilius "On the Height of Buildings"; to convince them that he was not the first to give attention to such matters, but that they had aroused the interest even of their forefathers.

He gave every encouragement to the men of talent of his own age, listening with courtesy and patience to their readings, not only of poetry and history, but of speeches and dialogues as well. But he took offence at being made the subject of any composition except in serious earnest and by the most eminent writers, often charging the praetors not to let his name be cheapened in prize declamations.

XC. This is what we are told of his attitude towards matters of religion.[130] He was somewhat weak in his fear of thunder and lightning, for he always carried a seal-skin about with him everywhere as a protection, and at any sign of a violent storm took refuge in an underground vaulted room;[131] for as I have said,[132] he was once badly frightened by a narrow escape from lightning during a journey by night.

XCI. He was not indifferent to his own dreams or to those which others dreamed about him. At the battle of Philippi, though he had made up his mind not to leave his tent because of illness, he did so after all when warned by a friend's dream; fortunately, as it turned out, for his camp was taken and when the enemy rushed in, his litter was stabbed through and through and torn to pieces, in the belief that he was still lying there ill. All through the spring his own dreams were very numerous and fearful, but idle and unfulfilled; during the rest of the year they were less frequent and more reliable. Being in the habit of making constant visits to the temple of Jupiter the Thunderer, which he had founded on the Capitol, he dreamed that Jupiter Capitolinus complained that his worshippers were being taken from him, and that he answered that he had placed the Thunderer hard by to be his doorkeeper; and accordingly he presently festooned the gable of the temple with bells, because these commonly hung at house-doors. It was likewise because of a dream that every year on an appointed day he begged alms of the people, holding out his open hand to have pennies dropped in it.[133]

XCII. Certain auspices and omens he regarded as infallible. If his shoes were put on in the wrong way in the morning, the left instead of the right, he considered it a bad sign. If there chanced to be a drizzle of rain when he was starting on a long journey by land or sea, he thought it a good omen, betokening a speedy and prosperous return. But he was especially affected by prodigies. When a palm tree sprang up between the crevices of the pavement before his house, he transplanted it to the inner court beside his household gods and took great pains to make it grow. He was so pleased that the branches of an old oak, which had already drooped to the ground and were withering, became vigorous again on his arrival in the island of Capreae, that he arranged with the city of Naples to give him the island in exchange for Aenaria. He also had regard to certain days, refusing ever to begin a journey on the day after a market day,[134] or to take up any important business on the Nones; though in the latter case, as he writes Tiberius, he merely dreaded the unlucky sound[135] of the name.

XCIII. He treated with great respect such foreign rites as were ancient and well established, but held the rest in contempt. For example, having been initiated at Athens[136] and afterwards sitting in judgment of a case at Rome involving the privileges of the priests of Attic Ceres, in which certain matters of secrecy were brought up, he dismissed his councillors and the throng of bystanders and heard the disputants in private. But on the other hand he not only omitted to make a slight detour to visit Apis, when he was travelling through Egypt, but highly commended his grandson Gaius for not offering prayers at Jerusalem as he passed by Judaea.

XCIV. Having reached this point, it will not be out of place to add an account of the omens which occurred before he was born, on the very day of his birth, and afterwards, from which it was possible to anticipate and perceive his future greatness and uninterrupted good fortune.

In ancient days, when a part of the wall of Velitrae had been struck by lightning, the prediction was made that a citizen of that town would one day rule the world. Through their confidence in this the people of Velitrae had at once made war on the Roman people and fought with them many times after that almost to their utter destruction; but at last long afterward the event proved that the omen had foretold the rule of Augustus.

According to Julius Marathus, a few months before Augustus was born a portent was generally observed at Rome, which gave warning that nature was pregnant with a king for the Roman people; thereupon the senate in consternation decreed that no male child born that year should be reared; but those whose wives were with child saw to it that the decree was not filed in the treasury,[137] since each one appropriated the prediction to his own family.

I have read the following story in the books of Asclepias of Mendes entitled *Theologumena*.[138] When Atia had come in the middle of the night to the solemn service of Apollo, she had her litter set down in the temple and fell asleep, while the rest of the matrons also slept. On a sudden a serpent[139] glided up to her and shortly went away. When she awoke, she purified herself,[140] as if after the embraces of her husband, and at once there appeared on her body a mark in colours like a serpent, and she could never get rid of it; so that presently she ceased ever to go to the public baths.

In the tenth month after that Augustus was born and was therefore regarded as the son of Apollo. Atia too, before she gave him birth, dreamed that her vitals were borne up to the stars and spread over the whole extent of land and sea, while Octavius dreamed that the sun rose from Atia's womb.

The day he was born the conspiracy of Catiline was before the House, and Octavius came late because of his wife's confinement; then Publius Nigidius, as everyone knows, learning the reason for his tardiness and being informed also of the hour of the birth, declared that the ruler of the world had been born. Later, when Octavius was leading an army through remote parts of Thrace, and in the grove of Father Liber consulted the priests about his son with barbarian rites, they made the same prediction; since such a pillar of flame sprang forth from the wine that was poured over the altar, that it rose above the temple roof and mounted to the very sky, and such an omen had befallen no one save Alexander the Great, when he offered sacrifice at the same altar. Moreover, the very next night he dreamt that his son appeared to him in a guise more majestic than that of mortal man, with the thunderbolt, sceptre, and insignia of Jupiter Optimus Maximus, wearing a crown begirt with rays and mounted upon a laurel-wreathed chariot drawn by twelve horses of surpassing whiteness. When Augustus was still an infant, as is recorded by the hand of Gaius Drusus,[141] he was placed by his nurse at evening in his cradle on the ground floor and the next morning had disappeared; but after long search he was at last found lying on a lofty tower with his face towards the rising sun.

As soon as he began to talk, it chanced that the frogs were making a great noise at his grandfather's country place; he bade them be silent, and they say that since then no frog has ever croaked there. As he was breakfasting in a grove at the fourth milestone on the Campanian road,[142] an eagle surprised him by snatching his bread from his hand, and after flying to a great height, equally to his surprise dropped gently down again and gave it back to him.

After Quintus Catulus had dedicated the Capitol, he had dreams on two nights in succession: first, that Jupiter Optimus Maximus called aside one of a number of boys of good family, who were playing around his altar, and put in the lap of his toga an image of Roma, which he was carrying in his hand; the next night he dreamt that he saw this same boy in the lap of Jupiter of the Capitol, and that when he had ordered that he be removed, the god warned him to desist, declaring that the boy was being reared to be the saviour of his country. When Catulus next day met Augustus, whom he had never seen before, he looked at him in great surprise and said that he was very like the boy of whom he had dreamed.

Some give a different account of Catulus's first dream: when a large group of well-born children asked Jupiter for a guardian, he pointed out one of their number, to whom they were to refer all their wishes, and then, after lightly touching the boy's mouth with his fingers, laid them on his own lips.[143]

As Marcus Cicero was attending Gaius Caesar to the Capitol,[144] he happened to tell his friends a dream of the night before; that a boy of noble countenance was let down from heaven on a golden chain and, standing at the door of the temple, was given a whip by Jupiter. Just then suddenly catching sight of Augustus, who was still unknown to the greater number of those present and had been brought to the ceremony by his uncle Caesar, he declared that he was the very one whose form had appeared to him in his dream.

When Augustus was assuming the gown of manhood, his senatorial tunic[145] was ripped apart on both sides and fell at his feet, which some interpreted as a sure sign that the order of which the tunic was the badge would one day be brought to his feet.

As the Deified Julius was cutting down a wood at Munda and preparing a place for his camp, coming across a palm tree, he caused it to be spared as an omen of victory. From this a shoot at once sprang forth and in a few days grew so great that it not only equalled the parent tree, but even overshadowed it; moreover many doves built their nests there, although that kind of bird especially avoids hard and rough foliage. Indeed, it was that omen in particular, they say, that led Caesar to wish that none other than his sister's grandson should be his successor

While in retirement at Apollonia, Augustus mounted with Agrippa to the studio of the astrologer Theogenes. Agrippa was the first to try his fortune, and when a great and almost incredible career was predicted for him, Augustus persisted in concealing the time of his birth and in refusing to disclose it, through diffidence and fear that he might be found to be less eminent. When he at last gave it unwillingly and hesitatingly, and only after many urgent requests, Theogenes sprang up and threw himself at his feet. From that time on Augustus had such faith in his destiny, that he made his horoscope public and issued a silver coin stamped with the sign of the constellation Capricornus, under which he was born.

XCV. As he was entering the city on his return from Apollonia after Caesar's death, though the heaven was clear and cloudless, a circle like a rainbow suddenly formed around the sun's disc, and straightway the tomb of Caesar's daughter Julia was struck by lightning. Again, as he was taking the auspices in his first consulship, twelve vultures appeared to him, as to Romulus, and when he slew the victims, the livers within all of them were found to be doubled inward at the lower end, which all those who were skilled in such matters unanimously declared to be an omen of a great and happy future.

XCVI. He even divined beforehand the outcome of all his wars. When the forces of the triumvirs were assembled at Bononia, an eagle that had perched upon his tent made a dash at two ravens, which attacked it on either side, and struck them to the ground. From this the whole army inferred that there would one day be discord among the colleagues, as actually came to pass, and divined its result. As he was on his way to Philippi, a Thessalian gave him notice of his coming victory on the authority of the deified Caesar, whose shade had met him on a lonely road. When he was sacrificing at Perusia without getting a favourable omen, and so had ordered more victims to be brought, the enemy made a sudden sally and carried off all the equipment of the sacrifice; whereupon the soothsayers agreed that all the dangers and disasters with which the sacrificer had been threatened would recoil on the heads of those who were in possession of the entrails; and so it turned out. As he was walking on the shore the day before the sea-fight off Sicily, a fish sprang from the sea and fell at his feet. At Actium, as he was going down to begin the battle, he met an ass with his driver, the man having the name Eutychus[146] and the beast that of Nicon[147]; and after the victory he set up bronze images of the two in the sacred enclosure into which he converted the site of his camp.

XCVII. His death, too, of which I shall speak next, and his deification after death, were known in advance by unmistakable signs. As he was bringing the lustrum[148] to an end in the Campus Martius before a great throng of people, an eagle flew several times about him and then going across to the temple hard by, perched above the first letter of Agrippa's name. On noticing this, Augustus bade his colleague Tiberius recite the vows which it is usual to offer for the next five years; for although he had them prepared and written out on a tablet, he declared that he would not be responsible for vows which he should never pay. At about the same time the first letter of his name was melted from the inscription on one of his statues by a flash of lightning; this was interpreted to mean that he would live only a hundred days from that time, the number indicated by the letter C, and that he would be numbered with the gods, since *aesar* (that is, the part of the name Caesar which was left) is the word for god in the Etruscan tongue.

Then, too, when he was on the point of sending Tiberius to Illyricum and was proposing to escort him as far as Beneventum, and litigants detained him on the judgment seat by bringing forward case after case, he cried out that he would stay no longer in Rome, even if everything conspired to delay him—and this too was afterwards looked upon as one of the omens of his death. When he had begun the journey, he went on as far as Astura and from there, contrary to his custom, took ship by night since it chanced that there was a favourable breeze, and thus contracted an illness beginning with a diarrhoea.

XCVIII. Then after skirting the coast of Campania and the neighbouring islands, he spent four more days at his villa in Capreae, where he gave himself up wholly to rest and social diversions. As he sailed by the gulf of Puteoli, it happened that from an Alexandrian ship which had just arrived there, the passengers and crew, clad in white, crowned with garlands, and burning incense, lavished upon him good wishes and the highest praise, saying that it was through him they lived, through him that they sailed the seas, and through him that they enjoyed their liberty and their fortunes. Exceedingly pleased at this, he gave forty gold pieces to each of his companions, exacting from every one of them a pledge under oath not to spend the sum that had been given them in any other way than in buying wares from Alexandria. More than that, for the several remaining days of his stay, among little presents of various kinds, he distributed togas and cloaks[149] as well, stipulating that the Romans should use the Greek dress and language and the Greeks the Roman. He continually watched the exercises of the ephebi,[150] of whom there was still a goodly number at Capreae according to the ancient usage. He also gave these youths a banquet at which he himself was present, and not only allowed, but even required perfect freedom in jesting and in scrambling for tickets for fruit, dainties and all kinds of things, which he threw to them. In short, there was no form of gaiety in which he did not indulge.

He called the neighbouring part of the island of Capreae Apragopolis[151] from the laziness of some of his company who sojourned there. Besides he used to call one of his favourites, Masgaba by name, Ktistes,[152] as if he were the founder of the island. Noticing from his dining-room that the tomb of this Masgaba, who had died the year before, was visited by a large crowd with many torches, he uttered aloud this verse, composed offhand:

"I see the founder's tomb alight with fire";

and turning to Thrasyllus, one of the suite of Tiberius who was reclining opposite him and knew nothing about the matter, he asked of what poet he thought it was the work. When Thrasyllus hesitated, he added another verse:

"See you with lights Masgaba honoured now?" and asked his opinion of this one also. When Thrasyllus could say nothing except that they were very good, whoever made them, he burst into a laugh and fell a joking about it.

Presently he crossed over to Naples, although his bowels were still weak from intermittent attacks. In spite of this he witnessed a quinquennial gymnastic contest which had been established in his honour, and then started with Tiberius for his destination.[153] But as he was returning his illness increased and he at last took to his bed at Nola, calling back Tiberius, who was on his way to Illyricum, and keeping him for a long time in private conversation, after which he gave attention to no business of importance.

XCIX. On the last day of his life he asked every now and then whether there was any disturbance without on his account; then calling for a mirror, he had his hair combed and his falling[154] jaws set straight.[155] After that, calling in his friends and asking whether it seemed to them that he had played the comedy of life fitly, he added the tag:

"Since well I've played my part, all clap your hands And from the stage dismiss me with applause."

Then he sent them all off, and while he was asking some newcomers from the city about the daughter of Drusus, who was ill, he suddenly passed away as he was kissing Livia, uttering these last words: "Live mindful of our wedlock, Livia, and farewell," thus blessed with an easy death and such a one as he had always longed for. For almost always on hearing that anyone had died swiftly and painlessly, he prayed that he and his might have a like *euthanasia*, for that was the term he was wont to use. He gave but one single sign of wandering before he breathed his last, calling out in sudden terror that forty young men were carrying him off. And even this was rather a premonition than a delusion, since it was that very number of soldiers of the pretorian guard that carried him forth to lie in state.

C. He died in the same room as his father Octavius, in the consulship of two Sextuses, Pompeius and Appuleius, on the fourteenth day before the Kalends of September at the ninth hour, just thirty-five days before his seventy-sixth birthday.

Aug. 19, 14 A.D.

His body was carried by the senators of the municipalities and colonies from Nola all the way to Bovillae, in the night time because of the season of the year, being placed by day in the basilica of the town at which they arrived or in its principal temple. At Bovillae the members of the equestrian order[156] met it and bore it to the city, where they placed it in the vestibule of his house.

In their desire to give him a splendid funeral and honour his memory the senators so vied with one another that among many other suggestions some proposed that his cortege pass through the triumphal gate, preceded by the statue of Victory which stands in the House, while a dirge was sung by children of both sexes belonging to the leading families; others, that on the day of the obsequies golden rings be laid aside and iron ones worn; and some, that his ashes be collected by the priests of the highest colleges. One man proposed that the name of the month of August be transferred to September, because Augustus was born in the latter, but died in the former; another, that all the period from the day of his birth until his demise be called the Augustan Age, and so entered in the Calendar. But though a limit was set to the honours paid him, his eulogy was twice delivered: before the temple of the Deified Julius by Tiberius, and from the old rostra by Drusus, son of Tiberius; and he was carried on the shoulders of senators to the Campus Martius and there cremated. There was even an ex-praetor who took oath that he had seen the form of the Emperor, after he had been reduced to ashes, on its way to heaven. His remains were gathered up by the leading men of the equestrian order, bare-footed and in ungirt tunics, and placed in the Mausoleum. This structure he had built in his sixth consulship between the Via Flaminia and the bank of the Tiber, and at the same time opened to the public the groves and walks by which it was surrounded.

28 B.C.

CI. He had made a will in the consulship of Lucius Plancus and Gaius Silius on the third day before the Nones of April, a year and four months before he died, in two note-books, written in part in his own hand and in part in that of his freedmen Polybius and Hilarion. These the Vestal virgins, with whom they had been deposited, now produced, together with three rolls, which were sealed in the same way. All these were opened and read in the senate. He appointed as his chief heirs Tiberius, to receive two-thirds of the estate, and Livia, one-third; these he also bade assume his name.[157] His heirs in the second degree[158] were Drusus, son of Tiberius, for one-third, and for the rest Germanicus and his three male children.[159] In the third grade he mentioned many of his relatives and friends. He left to the Roman people forty million sesterces; to the tribes[160] three million five hundred thousand; to the soldiers of the pretorian guard a thousand each; to the city cohorts five hundred; and to the legionaries three hundred. This sum he ordered to be paid at once, for he had always kept the amount at hand and ready for the purpose. He gave other legacies to various individuals, some amounting to as much as twenty thousand sesterces, and provided for the payment of these a year later, giving as his excuse for the delay the small amount of his property, and declaring that not more than a hundred and fifty millions would come to his heirs; for though he had received fourteen hundred millions during the last twenty years from the wills of his friends, he said that he had spent nearly all of it, as well as his two paternal estates and his other inheritances, for the benefit of the State. He gave orders that his daughter and his granddaughter Julia should not be put in his Mausoleum, if anything befell them.[161] In one of the three rolls he included directions for his funeral; in the second, an account of what he had accomplished, which he desired to have cut upon bronze tablets and set up at the entrance to the Mausoleum[162]; in the third, a summary of the condition of the whole empire; how

April 3, 13 A.D.

many soldiers there were in active service in all parts of it, how much money there was in the public treasury and in the privy-purse, and what revenues were in arrears. He added, besides, the names of the freedmen and slaves from whom the details could be demanded.

BOOK III

TIBERIUS

I. The patrician branch of the Claudian family (for there was, besides, a plebeian branch of no less influence and prestige) originated at Regilli, a town of the Sabines. From there it moved to Rome shortly after the founding of the city with a large band of dependents, through the influence of Titus Tatius, who shared the kingly power with Romulus (or, according to the generally accepted view, of Atta Claudius, the head of the family) about six years after the expulsion of the kings.[1] It was admitted among the patrician families, receiving, besides, from the State a piece of land on the farther side of the Anio for its dependents, and a burial-site for the family at the foot of the Capitoline hill. Then as time went on it was honoured with twenty-eight consulships, five dictatorships, seven censorships, six triumphs, and two ovations.[2] While the members of the family were known by various forenames and surnames, they discarded the forename Lucius by common consent after two of the family who bore it had been found guilty, the one of highway robbery, and the other of murder. To their surnames, on the other hand, they added that of Nero, which in the Sabine tongue means "strong and valiant."

II. There are on record many distinguished services of the Claudii to their country, as well as many deeds of the opposite character. But to mention only the principal instances, Appius the Blind advised against forming an alliance with king Pyrrhus as not 280 B.C.

at all expedient. Claudius Caudex was the first to cross the straits
264 B.C. with a fleet, and drove the Carthaginians from Sicily. Tiberius
Nero crushed Hasdrubal, on his arrival from Spain with a vast
207 B.C. army, before he could unite with his brother Hannibal. On the
other hand, Claudius Regillianus, decemvir for codifying the laws, through his lawless attempt to enslave a freeborn maid, to gratify his passion for her, was the cause of the second secession of the plebeians from the patricians.[3] Claudius Russus, having set up his statue at Forum Appi with a crown upon its head, tried to take possession of Italy through his dependents. Claudius Pulcher began a
249 B.C. sea-fight off Sicily, though the sacred chickens would not eat when he took the auspices, throwing them into the sea in defiance of the omen, and saying that they might drink, since they would not eat. He was defeated, and on being bidden by the senate to appoint a dictator, he appointed his messenger Glycias, as if again making a jest of his country's peril.

The women also have records equally diverse, since both the famous Claudias belonged to that family: the one who drew the
204 B.C. ship with the sacred properties of the Idaean Mother of the Gods[4] from the shoal in the Tiber on which it was stranded, after first publicly praying that it might yield to her efforts only if her
246 B.C. chastity were beyond question; and the one who was convicted by the people of treason, an unprecedented thing in the case of a woman, because when her carriage made but slow progress through the throng, she openly gave vent to the wish that her brother Pulcher might come to life and lose another fleet, to make less of a crowd in Rome. It is notorious besides that all the Claudii were aristocrats and staunch upholders of the prestige and influence of the patricians, with the sole exception of Publius Clodius, who for the sake of driving Cicero from the city had him-
60 B.C. self adopted by a plebeian and one too who was younger than himself.[5] Their attitude towards the commons was so headstrong and stubborn that not even when on trial for his life before the people did any one of them deign to put on mourning or beg for mercy; and some of them during bickerings and disputes struck the trib-

unes of the commons. Even a Vestal virgin mounted her brother's chariot with him, when he was celebrating a triumph without the sanction of the people, and attended him all the way to the Capitol, in order to make it an act of sacrilege for any one of the tribunes to forbid him or interpose his veto. 143 B.C.

III. Such was the stock from which Tiberius Caesar derived his origin, and that too on both sides: on his father's from Tiberius Nero; on his mother's from Appius Pulcher, both of whom were sons of Appius Caecus. He was a member also of the family of the Livii, through the adoption into it of his maternal grandfather. This family too, though of plebeian origin, was yet of great prominence and had been honoured with eight consulships, two censorships, and three triumphs, as well as with the offices of dictator and master of the horse. It was made illustrious too by distinguished members, in particular Salinator and the Drusi. The former in his censorship put the brand on all the tribes[6] on the charge of fickleness, because having convicted and fined him after a previous consulship, they made him consul a second time and censor as well. 204 B.C. Drusus gained a surname for himself and his descendants by slaying Drausus, leader of the enemy, in single combat. It is also said that when propraetor he brought back from his province of Gaul the gold which was paid long before to the Senones, when they beleaguered the Capitol, and that this had not been wrested from them by Camillus, as tradition has it. 390 B.C. His grandson's grandson, called "Patron of the Senate" because of his distinguished services against the Gracchi, left a son who was treacherously slain by the party of his opponents, while he was busily agitating many plans during a similar dissension. 122 B.C. 91 B.C.

IV. Nero, the father of Tiberius, as a quaestor of Julius Caesar during the Alexandrian war and commander of a fleet, contributed materially to the victory. 48–47 B.C. For this he was made pontiff in place of Publius Scipio and sent to conduct colonies to Gaul, among them Narbo and Arelate. Yet after the murder of Caesar, when all the others voted for an amnesty through fear of mob violence, he even favoured a proposal for rewarding the tyrannicides.

Later on, having held the praetorship, since a dispute arose among the triumvirs at the close of his term, he retained the badges of his rank beyond the legitimate time and followed Lucius Antonius, 41 B.C. consul and brother of the triumvir, to Perusia. When the others capitulated, he alone held to his allegiance and got away first to Praeneste and then to Naples; and after vainly trying to enlist the slaves by a promise of freedom,[7] he took refuge in Sicily. Piqued however because he was not at once given an audience with Sextus Pompeius, and was denied the use of the fasces, he crossed to Achaia and joined Mark Antony. With him he shortly returned to Rome, on the conclusion of a general peace, and gave up to Augustus at his request his wife Livia Drusilla, who was pregnant at the time and had already borne him a son.[8] Not long afterward he died, survived by both his sons, Tiberius Nero and Drusus Nero.

V. Some have supposed that Tiberius was born at Fundi, on no better evidence than that his maternal grandmother was a native of that place, and that later a statue of Good Fortune was set up there by decree of the senate. But according to the most numerous and trustworthy authorities, he was born at Rome, on the Palatine, the sixteenth day before the Kalends of December, in the consulship of Nov. 16, 42 B.C. Marcus Aemilius Lepidus and Lucius Munatius Plancus (the former for the second time) while the war of Philippi was going on. In fact it is so recorded both in the calendar and in the public gazette. Yet in spite of this some write that he was born in the preceding year, that of Hirtius and Pansa, and others in the following year, in the consulate of Servilius Isauricus and Lucius Antonius.

VI. He passed his infancy and his youth amid hardship and tribulation, since he was everywhere the companion of his parents in their flight; at Naples indeed he all but betrayed them twice by his crying, as they were secretly on their way to a ship just as the enemy burst into the town, being suddenly torn from his nurse's breast and again from his mother's arms by those who tried to relieve the poor women of their burden because of the imminent danger. After being taken all over Sicily also and Achaia, and consigned to the public care of the Lacedaemonians, because they were dependents of the Claudii, he almost lost his life as he was leaving there by night, when the woods suddenly took fire all about them, and the flames so encircled the whole company that part of Livia's robe and her hair were scorched. The gifts which were given him in Sicily by Pompeia, sister of Sextus Pompeius, a cloak and clasp, as well as studs of gold, are still kept and exhibited at Baiae. Being adopted, after his return to the city, in the will of Marcus Gallius, a senator, he accepted the inheritance, but soon gave up the name, because Gallius had been a member of the party opposed to Augustus.

At the age of nine he delivered a eulogy of his dead father from the rostra. Then, just as he was arriving at puberty, he accompanied the chariot of Augustus in his triumph after Actium,[9] riding the left trace-horse, while Marcellus, son of Octavia, rode the one on the right. He presided, too, at the city festival, and took part in the game of Troy during the performances in the circus, leading the band of older boys.[10]

VII. The principal events of his youth and later life, from the assumption of the gown of manhood to the beginning of his reign, were these. He gave a gladiatorial show in memory of his father, and a second in honour of his grandfather Drusus, at different times and in different places, the former in the Forum and the latter in the amphitheatre,[11] inducing some retired gladiators[12] to appear with the rest by the payment of a hundred thousand sesterces to each. He also gave stage-plays, but without being present in person. All these were on a grand scale, at the expense of his mother and his stepfather.

He married Agrippina, daughter of Marcus Agrippa, and granddaughter of Caecilius Atticus, a Roman knight, to whom Cicero's letters are addressed; but after he had acknowledged[13] a son from her, Drusus, although she was thoroughly congenial and was a second time with child, he was forced to divorce her and to contract a 11 B.C. hurried marriage with Julia,[14] daughter of Augustus. This caused him no little distress of mind, for he was living happily with Agrippina, and disapproved of Julia's character, having perceived

that she had a passion for him even during the lifetime of her former husband, as was in fact the general opinion. But even after the divorce he regretted his separation from Agrippina, and the only time that he chanced to see her, he followed her with such an intent and tearful gaze that care was taken that she should never again come before his eyes. With Julia he lived in harmony at first, and returned her love; but he soon grew cold, and went so far as to cease to live with her at all, after the severing of the tie formed by a child which was born to them, but died at Aquileia in infancy. He
9 B.C. lost his brother Drusus in Germany and conveyed his body to Rome, going before it on foot all the way.

VIII. He began his civil career by a defence of king Archelaus, the people of Tralles, and those of Thessaly, before the judgment seat of Augustus, the charge in each case being different. He made a plea to the senate in behalf of the citizens of Laodicea, Thyatira and Chios, who had suffered loss from an earthquake and begged
23 B.C. for help. Fannius Caepio, who had conspired with Varro Murena against Augustus, he arraigned for high treason and secured his condemnation. In the meantime he undertook two public charges: that of the grain supply, which, as it happened, was deficient; and the investigation of the slave-prisons[15] throughout Italy, the owners of which had gained a bad reputation; for they were charged with holding in durance not only travellers, but also those whom dread of military service had driven to such places of concealment.

25 B.C. IX. His first military service was as tribune of the soldiers in the campaign against the Cantabrians; then he led an army to the Orient and restored the throne of Armenia to Tigranes, crowning him on the tribunal. He besides recovered the standards which the Parthians had taken from Marcus Crassus.[16] Then for about a year he was governor of Gallia Comata,[17] which was in a state of unrest through the inroads of the barbarians and the dissensions of its chiefs. Next he carried on war with the Raeti and Vindelici, then in Pannonia, and finally in Germany. In the first of these wars he subdued the Alpine tribes, in the second the Breuci and Dalmatians, and in the third he brought forty thousand prisoners

of war over into Gaul and assigned them homes near the bank of the Rhine. Because of these exploits he entered the city both in an ovation and riding in a chariot,[18] having previously, as some think, been honoured with the triumphal regalia, a new kind of distinction never before conferred upon anyone. 7 and 8 B.C.

He entered upon the offices of quaestor, praetor, and consul before the usual age, and held them almost without an interval[19]; then after a time he was made consul again, at the same time receiving the tribunicial power for five years. 6 B.C.

X. At the flood-tide of success, though in the prime of life and health, he suddenly decided to go into retirement and to withdraw as far as possible from the centre of the stage; perhaps from disgust at his wife, whom he dared neither accuse nor put away, though he could no longer endure her; or perhaps, avoiding the contempt born of familiarity, to keep up his prestige by absence, or even add to it, in case his country should ever need him. Some think that, since the children of Augustus were now of age, he voluntarily gave up the position and the virtual assumption of the second rank which he had long held, thus following the example of Marcus Agrippa,[20] who withdrew to Mytilene when Marcellus began his public career, so that he might not seem either to oppose or belittle him by his presence. This was, in fact, the reason which Tiberius himself gave, but afterwards. At the time he asked for leave of absence on the ground of weariness of office and a desire to rest; and he would not give way either to his mother's urgent entreaties or to the complaint which his stepfather openly made in the senate, that he was being forsaken. On the contrary, when they made more strenuous efforts to detain him, he refused to take food for four days. Being at last allowed to depart, he left his wife and son in Rome and went down to Ostia in haste, without saying a single word to any of those who saw him off, and kissing only a very few when he left.

XI. From Ostia he coasted along the shore of Campania, and learning of an indisposition of Augustus, he stopped for a while. But since gossip was rife that he was lingering on the chance of realising his highest hopes, although the wind was all but dead ahead, he sailed directly to Rhodes, for he had been attracted by the charm and healthfulness of that island ever since the time when he put in there on his return from Armenia. Content there with a modest house and a villa in the suburbs not much more spacious, he adopted a most unassuming manner of life, at times walking in the gymnasium without a lictor or a messenger, and exchanging courtesies with the good people of Greece with almost the air of an equal.

It chanced one morning in arranging his programme for the day, that he had announced his wish to visit whatever sick folk there were in the city. This was misunderstood by his attendants, and orders were given that all the sick should be taken to a public colonnade and arranged according to the nature of their complaints. Whereupon Tiberius, shocked at this unexpected sight, and in doubt for some time what to do, at last went about to each one, apologizing for what had happened even to the humblest and most obscure of them.

Only one single instance was noticed of a visible exercise of the rights of the tribunicial authority. He was a constant attendant at the schools and lecture-rooms of the professors of philosophy, and once when a hot dispute had arisen among rival sophists, a fellow had the audacity to ply him with abuse when he took part and appeared to favour one side. Thereupon he gradually backed away to his house, and then suddenly coming out with his lictors and attendants, and bidding his crier to summon the foul-mouthed fellow before his tribunal, he had him taken off to prison.

Shortly after this he learned that his wife Julia had been banished because of her immorality and adulteries, and that a bill of divorce had been sent her in his name by authority of Augustus; but welcome as this news was, he yet considered it his duty to make every possible effort in numerous letters to reconcile the father to his daughter; and regardless of her deserts, to allow her to keep any gifts which he had himself made her at any time. Moreover, when the term of his tribunicial power was at an end, at last admitting that the sole object of his retirement had been to avoid the suspicion of rivalry with Gaius and Lucius, he asked that inasmuch as he was free from care in that regard, since they were now grown up and had an undisputed claim on the succession, he be allowed to visit his relatives, whom he sorely missed. But his request was denied and he was besides admonished to give up all thought of his kindred, whom he had so eagerly abandoned.

XII. Accordingly he remained in Rhodes against his will, having with difficulty through his mother's aid secured permission that, while away from Rome, he should have the title of envoy[21] of Augustus, so as to conceal his disgrace.

Then in very truth he lived not only in private, but even in danger and fear, secluded in the country away from the sea, and shunning the attentions of those that sailed that way; these, however, were constantly thrust on him, since no general or magistrate who was on his way to any province failed to put in at Rhodes. He had besides reasons for still greater anxiety; for when he had crossed to Samos to visit his stepson Gaius, who had been made governor of the Orient, he found him somewhat estranged through the slanders of Marcus Lollius, a member of Gaius' staff and his guardian. He also incurred the suspicion of having through some centurions of his appointment, who were returning to camp after a furlough, sent messages to several persons which were of an ambiguous character and apparently designed to incite them to revolution. On being informed by Augustus of this suspicion, he unceasingly demanded the appointment of someone, of any rank whatsoever, to keep watch over his actions and words.

XIII. He also gave up his usual exercises with horses and arms, and laying aside the garb of his country, took to the cloak and slippers[22]; and in this state he continued for upwards of two years, becoming daily an object of greater contempt and aversion. This went so far that the citizens of Nemausus[23] threw down his statues and busts, and when mention was once made of him at a private dinner party, a man got up and assured Gaius that if he would say the word, he would at once take ship for Rhodes and bring back the head of "the exile," as he was commonly called. It was this act especially, which made his position no longer one of mere fear but of actual peril, that drove Tiberius to sue for his recall with most urgent prayers, in which his mother joined; and he obtained it, although partly owing to a fortunate chance. Augustus had resolved to come to no decision of the question which was not agreeable to his elder son,[24] who, as it happened, was at the time somewhat at odds with Marcus Lollius, and accordingly ready to lend an ear to his stepfather's prayers. With his consent therefore Tiberius was recalled, but on the understanding that he should take no part or active interest in public affairs.

2 A.D. XIV. So he returned in the eighth year after his retirement, with that strong and unwavering confidence in his destiny, which he had conceived from his early years because of omens and predictions.

When Livia was with child with him, and was trying to divine by various omens whether she would bring forth a male, she took an egg from under a setting-hen, and when she had warmed it in her own hand and those of her attendants in turn, a cock with a fine crest was hatched. In his infancy the astrologer Scribonius promised him an illustrious career and even that he would one day be king, but without the crown of royalty; for at that time of
42 B.C. course the rule of the Caesars was as yet unheard of. Again, on his first campaign, when he was leading an army through Macedonia into Syria, it chanced that at Philippi the altars consecrated in bygone days by the victorious legions gleamed of their own accord with sudden fires. When later, on his way to Illyricum, he visited the oracle of Geryon near Patavium, and drew a lot which advised him to seek an answer to his inquiries by throwing golden dice into the fount of Aponus, it came to pass that the dice which he threw showed the highest posssible number; and those dice may be seen to-day under the water. A few days before his recall an eagle, a bird never before seen in Rhodes, perched upon the roof of his house; and the day before he was notified that he might return, his tunic seemed to blaze as he was changing his clothes. It was just at this time that he was

convinced of the powers of the astrologer Thrasyllus, whom he had attached to his household as an adept in the art; for as soon as he caught sight of the ship, Thrasyllus declared that it brought good news—this too at the very moment when Tiberius had made up his mind to push the man off into the sea as they were strolling together, believing him a false prophet and too hastily made the confidant of his secrets, because things were turning out adversely and contrary to his predictions.

XV. On his return to Rome, after introducing his son Drusus to public life,[25] he at once moved from the Carinae[26] and the house of the Pompeys to the gardens of Maecenas on the Esquiline, where he led a very retired life, merely attending to his personal affairs and exercising no public functions.

When Gaius and Lucius died within three years, he was adopted by Augustus along with their brother Marcus Agrippa, being himself first compelled to adopt his nephew Germanicus. And from that time on he ceased to act as the head of a family, or to retain in any particular the privileges which he had given up. For he neither made gifts nor freed slaves, and he did not even accept an inheritance or any legacies, except to enter them as an addition to his personal property.[27] From this time on nothing was left undone which could add to his prestige, especially after the disowning and banishment of Agrippa made it clear that the hope of the succession lay in him alone.

XVI. He was given the tribunician power for a second term of three years, the duty of subjugating Germany was assigned him, and the envoys of the Parthians, after presenting their instructions to Augustus in Rome, were bidden to appear also before him in his province. But when the revolt of Illyricum was reported, he was transferred to the charge of a new war, the most serious of all foreign wars since those with Carthage, which he carried on for three years with fifteen legions and a corresponding force of auxiliaries, amid great difficulties of every kind and the utmost scarcity of supplies. But though he was often recalled, he none the less kept on, for fear that the enemy, who were close at hand and very strong, might assume the offensive if the Romans gave ground. He reaped an ample reward for his perseverance, for he completely subdued and reduced to submission the whole of Illyricum, which is bounded by Italy and the kingdom of Noricum, by Thrace and Macedonia, by the Danube, and by the Adriatic sea.

XVII. Circumstances gave this exploit a larger and crowning glory; for it was at just about that time that Quintilius Varus perished with three legions in Germany, and no one doubted that the victorious Germans would have united with the Pannonians, had not Illyricum been subdued first. Consequently a triumph was voted him and many high honours. Some also recommended that he be given the surname of Pannonicus, others of Invictus, others of Pius. Augustus however vetoed the surname, reiterating the promise that Tiberius would be satisfied with the one which he would receive at his father's death. Tiberius himself put off the triumph, because the country was in mourning for the disaster to Varus; but he entered the city clad in the purple-bordered toga and crowned with laurel, and mounting a tribunal which had been set up in the Saepta, while the senate stood alongside, he took his seat beside Augustus between the two consuls. Having greeted the people from this position, he was escorted to the various temples.

XVIII. The next year he returned to Germany, and realising that the disaster to Varus was due to that general's rashness and lack of care, he took no step without the approval of a council; while he had always before been a man of independent judgment and self reliance, then contrary to his habit he consulted with many advisers about the conduct of the campaign. He also observed more scrupulous care than usual. When on the point of crossing the Rhine, he reduced all the baggage to a prescribed limit, and would not start without standing on the bank and inspecting the loads of the wagons, to make sure that nothing was taken except what was allowed or necessary. Once on the other side, he adopted the following manner of life: he took his meals sitting on the bare turf, often passed the night without a tent, and gave all his orders for the following day, as well as notice of any sudden emergency, in writing; adding the injunction that if anyone was in doubt about any matter, he was to consult him personally at any hour whatsoever, even of the night.

XIX. He required the strictest discipline, reviving bygone methods of punishment and ignominy, and even degrading the commander of a legion for sending a few soldiers across the river to accompany one of his freedmen on a hunting expedition. Although he left very little to fortune and chance, he entered battles with considerably greater confidence whenever it happened that, as he was working at night, his lamp suddenly and without human agency died down and went out; trusting, as he used to say, to an omen in which he had great confidence, since both he and his ancestors had found it trustworthy in all of their campaigns. Yet in the very hour of victory he narrowly escaped assassination by one of the Bructeri, who got access to him among his attendants, but was detected through his nervousness; whereupon a confession of his intended crime was wrung from him by torture.

XX. After two years he returned to the city from Germany and 12 A.D.
celebrated the triumph which he had postponed, accompanied also by his generals, for whom he had obtained the triumphal regalia. And before turning to enter the Capitol, he dismounted from his chariot and fell at the knees of his father, who was presiding over the ceremonies.[28] He sent Bato, the leader of the Pannonians, to Ravenna,[29] after presenting him with rich gifts; thus showing his gratitude to him for allowing him to escape when he was trapped with his army in a dangerous place. Then he gave a banquet to the people at a thousand tables, and a largess of three hundred sesterces to every man. With the proceeds of his spoils he restored and dedicated the temple of Concord, as well as that of Pollux and Castor, in his own name and that of his brother.

XXI. Since the consuls caused a law to be passed soon after this that he should govern the provinces jointly with Augustus and hold the census with him, he set out for Illyricum on the conclusion of the lustral ceremonies[30]; but he was at once recalled, and finding Augustus in his last illness but still alive, he spent an entire day with him in private.

I know that it is commonly believed, that when Tiberius left the room after this confidential talk, Augustus was overheard by his chamberlains to say: "Alas for the Roman people, to be ground by jaws that crunch so slowly!" I also am aware that some have written that Augustus so openly and unreservedly disapproved of his austere manners, that he sometimes broke off his freer and lighter conversation when Tiberius appeared; but that overcome by his wife's entreaties he did not reject his adoption, or perhaps was even led by selfish considerations, that with such a successor he himself might one day be more regretted. But after all I cannot be led to believe that an emperor of the utmost prudence and foresight acted without consideration, especially in a matter of so great moment. It is my opinion that after weighing the faults and the merits of Tiberius, he decided that the latter preponderated, especially since he took oath before the people that he was adopting Tiberius for the good of the country, and alludes to him in several letters as a most able general and the sole defence of the Roman people. In illustration of both these points, I append a few extracts from these letters.

"Fare thee well, Tiberius, most charming of men, and success go with you, as you war for me and for the Muses.[31] Fare thee well, most charming and valiant of men and most conscientious of generals, or may I never know happiness."

"I have only praise for the conduct of your summer campaigns, dear Tiberius, and I am sure that no one could have acted with better judgment than you did amid so many difficulties and such apathy of your army. All who were with you agree that the well-known line could be applied to you:

"'One man alone by his foresight has saved our dear country from ruin.[32]'"

"If anything comes up that calls for careful thought, or if I am vexed at anything, I long mightily, so help me Heaven,[33] for my dear Tiberius, and the lines of Homer come to my mind:

"'Let him but follow and we too, though flames round about us be raging,

Both may return to our homes, since great are his wisdom and knowledge.[34]'"

"When I hear and read that you are worn out by constant hardships, may the Gods confound me if my own body does not wince in sympathy; and I beseech you to spare yourself, that the news of your illness may not kill your mother and me, and endanger the Roman people in the person of their future ruler."

"It matters not whether I am well or not, if you are not well."

"I pray the Gods to preserve you to us and to grant you good health now and forever, if they do not utterly hate the people of Rome."

XXII. Tiberius did not make the death of Augustus public until the young Agrippa had been disposed of. The latter was slain by a tribune of the soldiers appointed to guard him, who received a letter in which he was bidden to do the deed; but it is not known whether Augustus left this letter when he died, to remove a future source of discord, or whether Lavia wrote it herself in the name of her husband; and in the latter case, whether it was with or without the connivance of Tiberius. At all events, when the tribune reported that he had done his bidding, Tiberius replied that he had given no such order, and that the man must render an account to the senate; apparently trying to avoid odium at the time, for later his silence consigned the matter to oblivion.

XXIII. When, however, by virtue of his tribunicial power, he had convened the senate and had begun to address it, he suddenly groaned aloud, as if overcome by grief, and with the wish that not only his voice, but his life as well might leave him, handed the written speech to his son Drusus to finish. Then bringing in the will of Augustus, he had it read by a freedman, admitting of the signers only such as were of the senatorial order, while the others acknowledged their seals outside the House. The will began thus: "Since a cruel fate has bereft me of my sons Gaius and Lucius, be Tiberius Caesar heir to two-thirds of my estate." These words in themselves added to the suspicion of those who believed that he had named Tiberius his successor from necessity rather than from choice, since he allowed himself to write such a preamble.

XXIV. Though Tiberius did not hesitate at once to assume and to exercise the imperial authority, surrounding himself with a guard of soldiers, that is, with the actual power and the outward sign of sovereignty, yet he refused the title for a long time, with barefaced hypocrisy now upbraiding his friends who urged him to accept it, saying that they did not realise what a monster the empire was, and now by evasive answers and calculating hesitancy keeping the senators in suspense when they implored him to yield, and fell at his feet. Finally, some lost patience, and one man cried out in the confusion: "Let him take it or leave it." Another openly voiced the taunt that others were slow in doing what they promised, but that he was slow to promise what he was already doing. At last, as though on compulsion, and complaining that a wretched and burdensome slavery was being forced upon him, he accepted the empire, but in such fashion as to suggest the hope that he would one day lay it down. His own words are: "Until I come to the time when it may seem right to you to grant an old man some repose."

XXV. The cause of his hesitation was fear of the dangers which threatened him on every hand, and often led him to say that he was "holding a wolf by the ears.[35]" For a slave of Agrippa, Clemens by name, had collected a band of no mean size to avenge his master; Lucius Scribonius Libo, one of the nobles, was secretly plotting a revolution; and a mutiny of the soldiers broke out in two places, Illyricum and Germany. Both armies demanded numerous special privileges—above all, that they should receive the same pay as the praetorians. The army in Germany was, besides, reluctant to accept an emperor who was not its own choice, and with the greatest urgency besought Germanicus, their commander at the time, to assume the purple, in spite of his positive refusal. Fear of this possibility in particular led Tiberius to ask the senate for any part in the administration that it might please them to assign him, saying that no one man could bear the whole burden without a colleague, or even several colleagues. He also feigned ill-health, to induce Germanicus to wait with more patience for a speedy succession, or at least for a share in the sovereignty. The mutinies were put down, and he also got Clemens into his power, outwitting him by stratagem. Not until his second year did he finally arraign Libo in the senate, fearing to take any severe measures before his power was secure, and satisfied in the meantime merely to be on his guard. Thus when Libo was offering sacrifice with him among the pontiffs, he had a leaden knife substituted for the usual one,[36] and when he asked for a private interview, Tiberius would not grant it except with his son Drusus present, and as long as the conference lasted he held fast to Libo's right arm, under pretence of leaning on it as they walked together.

XXVI. Once relieved of fear, he at first played a most unassuming[37] part, almost humbler than that of a private citizen. Of many high honours he accepted only a few of the more modest. He barely consented to allow his birthday, which came at the time of the Plebeian games in the Circus, to be recognized by the addition of a single two-horse chariot. He forbade the voting of temples, flamens, and priests in his honour, and even the setting up of statues and busts without his permission; and this he gave only with the understanding that they were not to be placed among the likenesses of the gods, but among the adornments of the temples. He would not allow an oath to be taken ratifying his acts,[38] nor the name Tiberius to be given to the month of September, or that of Livia to October. He also declined the forename Imperator,[39] the surname of Father of his Country, and the placing of the civic crown[40] at his door; and he did not even use the title of Augustus in any letters except those to kings and potentates, although it was his by inheritance.[41] He held but three consulships after becoming emperor—one for a few days, a second for three months, and a third, during his absence from the city, until the Ides of May. 18, 21, and 31 A.D.

XXVII. He so loathed flattery that he would not allow any senator to approach his litter, either to pay his respects or on business, and when an ex-consul in apologizing to him attempted to embrace his knees, he drew back in such haste that he fell over backward. In fact, if anyone in conversation or in a set speech spoke of him in too flattering terms, he did not hesitate to interrupt him, to take him to task, and to correct his language on the spot. Being once called "Lord,"[42] he warned the speaker not to address him again in an insulting fashion. When another spoke of his "sacred duties," and still another said that he appeared before the senate "by the emperor's authority," he forced them to change their language, substituting "advice" for "authority" and "laborious" for "sacred."

XXVIII. More than that, he was self-contained and patient in the face of abuse and slander, and of lampoons on himself and his family, often asserting that in a free country there should be free speech and free thought. When the senate on one occasion demanded that cognizance be taken of such offences and those guilty of them, he said: "We have not enough spare time to warrant involving ourselves in more affairs; if you open this loophole you will find no time for any other business; it will be an excuse for laying everybody's quarrels before you." A most unassuming[43] remark of his in the senate is also a matter of record: "If so and so criticizes me I shall take care to render an account of my acts and words; if he persists, our enmity will be mutual."

XXIX. All this was the more noteworthy, because in addressing and in paying his respects to the senators individually and as a body he himself almost exceeded the requirements of courtesy. In a disagreement with Quintus Haterius in the House, he said: "I crave your pardon, if in my capacity as senator I use too free language in opposing you." Then addressing the whole body: "I say now and have often said before, Fathers of the Senate, that a well-disposed and helpful prince, to whom you have given such great and unrestrained power, ought to be the servant of the senate, often of the citizens as a whole, and sometimes even of individuals. I do not regret my words, but I have looked upon you as kind, just, and indulgent masters,[44] and still so regard you."

XXX. He even introduced a semblance of free government by maintaining the ancient dignity and powers of the senate and the magistrates; for there was no matter of public or private business so small or so great that he did not lay it before the senators, consulting them about revenues and monopolies,[45] constructing and restoring public buildings, and even about levying and disbanding the soldiers, and the disposal of the legionaries and auxiliaries; finally about the extension of military commands and appointments to the conduct of wars, and the form and content of his replies to the letters of kings. He forced the commander of a troop of horse, when charged with violence and robbery, to plead his cause before the senate. He always entered the House alone; and when he was brought in once in a litter because of illness, he dismissed his attendants.

XXXI. When certain decrees were passed contrary to his expressed opinion, he did not even remonstrate. Although he declared that those who were elected to office ought to remain in the city and give personal attention to their duties, a praetor elect obtained permission to travel abroad with the privileges of an ambassador.[46] On another occasion when he recommended that the people of Trebia be allowed to use, in making a road, a sum of money which had been left them for the construction of a new theatre, he could not prevent the wish of the testator from being carried out. When it happened that the senate passed a decree by division and he went over to the side of the minority, not a man followed him.

Other business as well was done solely through the magistrates and the ordinary process of law, while the importance of the consuls was such that certain envoys from Africa presented themselves before them with the complaint that their time was being wasted by Caesar, to whom they had been sent. And this was not surprising, for it was plain to all that he himself actually arose in the presence of the consuls, and made way for them on the street.

XXXII. He rebuked some ex-consuls in command of armies, because they did not write their reports to the senate, and for referring to him the award of some military prizes,[47] as if they had not themselves the right to bestow everything of the kind. He highly complimented a praetor, because on entering upon his office he had revived the custom of eulogizing his ancestors before the people. He attended the obsequies of certain distinguished men, even going to the funeral-pyre.

He showed equal modesty towards persons of lower rank and in matters of less moment. When he had summoned the magistrates of Rhodes, because they had written him letters on public business without the concluding formula,[48] he uttered not a word of censure, but merely dismissed them with orders to supply the omission. The grammarian Diogenes, who used to lecture every Sabbath[49] at Rhodes, would not admit Tiberius when he came to hear him on a different day, but sent a message by a common slave of his, putting him off to the seventh day. When this man waited before the Emperor's door at Rome to pay his respects, Tiberius took no further revenge than to bid him return seven years later. To the governors who recommended burdensome taxes for his provinces, he wrote in answer that it was the part of a good shepherd to shear his flock, not skin it.

XXXIII. Little by little he unmasked the ruler, and although for some time his conduct was variable, yet he more often showed himself kindly and devoted to the public weal. His intervention too was at first limited to the prevention of abuses. Thus he revoked some regulations of the senate and sometimes offered the magistrates his services as adviser, when they sat in judgment on the tribunal, taking his place beside them or opposite them at one end of the platform[50]; and if it was rumoured that any of the accused were being acquitted through influence, he would suddenly appear, and either from the floor or from the judge's[51] tribunal remind the jurors of the laws and of their oath, as well as of the nature of the crime on which they were sitting in judgment. Moreover, if the public morals were in any way affected by laziness or bad habits he undertook to reform them.

XXXIV. He reduced the cost of the games and shows by cutting down the pay of the actors and limiting the pairs of gladiators to a fixed number. Complaining bitterly that the prices of

Corinthian bronzes[52] had risen to an immense figure and that three mullets had been sold for thirty thousand sesterces, he proposed that a limit be set to household furniture and that the prices in the market should be regulated each year at the discretion of the senate; while the aediles were instructed to put such restrictions on cook-shops and eating-houses as not to allow even pastry to be exposed for sale. Furthermore, to encourage general frugality by his personal example, he often served at formal dinners meats left over from the day before and partly consumed, or the half of a boar, declaring that it had all the qualities of a whole one.

He issued an edict forbidding general kissing,[53] as well as the exchange of New Year's gifts[54] after the Kalends of January. It was his custom to return a gift of four-fold value,[55] and in person; but annoyed at being interrupted all through the month by those who did not have access to him on the holiday, he did not continue it.

XXXV. He revived the custom of our forefathers, that in the absence of a public prosecutor matrons of ill-repute be punished according to the decision of a council of their relatives. He absolved a Roman knight from his oath and allowed him to put away his wife, who was taken in adultery with her son-in-law, even though he had previously sworn that he would never divorce her. Notorious women had begun to make an open profession of prostitution, to avoid the punishment of the laws by giving up the privileges and rank of matrons,[56] while the most profligate young men of both orders voluntarily incurred degradation from their rank, so as not to be prevented by the decree of the senate from appearing on the stage and in the arena. All such men and women he punished with exile, to prevent anyone from shielding himself by such a device. He deprived a senator of his broad stripe on learning that he had moved to his gardens just before the Kalends of July,[57] with the design of renting a house in the city at a lower figure after that date. He deposed another from his quaestorship, because he had taken a wife the day before casting lots[58] and divorced her the day after.

XXXVI. He abolished foreign cults, especially the Egyptian and the Jewish rites, compelling all who were addicted to such superstitions to burn their religious vestments and all their paraphernalia. Those of the Jews who were of military age he assigned to provinces of less healthy climate, ostensibly to serve in the army; the others of that same race or of similar beliefs he banished from the city, on pain of slavery for life if they did not obey. He banished the astrologers as well, but pardoned such as begged for indulgence and promised to give up their art.

XXXVII. He gave special attention to securing safety from prowling brigands and lawless outbreaks, He stationed garrisons of soldiers nearer together than before throughout Italy, while at Rome he established a camp for the barracks of the praetorian cohorts, which before that time had been quartered in isolated groups in divers lodging houses.

He took great pains to prevent outbreaks of the populace and punished such as occurred with the utmost severity. When a quarrel in the theatre ended in bloodshed, he banished the leaders of the factions,[59] as well as the actors who were the cause of the dissension; and no entreaties of the people could ever induce him to recall them. When the populace of Pollentia would not allow the body of a chief-centurion to be taken from the forum until their violence had extorted money from his heirs for a gladiatorial show, he dispatched one cohort from the city and another from the kingdom of Cottius, concealing the reason for the move, sent them into the city by different gates, suddenly revealing their arms and sounding their trumpets, and consigned the greater part of the populace and of the decurions[60] to life imprisonment. He abolislied the customary right of asylum[61] in all parts of the empire. Because the people of Cyzicus ventured to commit acts of special lawlessness against Roman citizens, he took from them the freedom which they had earned in the war with Mithridates.

He undertook no campaign after his accession, but quelled outbreaks of the enemy through his generals; and even this he did only reluctantly and of necessity. Such kings as were disaffected and objects of his suspicion he held in check rather by threats and remonstrances than by force; some he lured to Rome by flattering promises and detained there, such as Marobodus the German, Rhascuporis the Thracian, and Archelaus of Cappadocia, whose realm he also reduced to the form of a province.

XXXVIII. For two whole years after becoming emperor he did not set foot outside the gates; after that he went nowhere except to the neighbouring towns, at farthest to Antium, and even that very seldom and for a few days at a time. Yet he often gave out that he would revisit the provinces too and the armies, and nearly every year he made preparations for a journey by chartering carriages and arranging for supplies in the free towns and colonies. Finally he allowed vows to be put up for his voyage and return, so that at last everybody jokingly gave him the name of Callippides, who was proverbial among the Greeks for running without getting ahead a cubit's length.[62]

XXXIX. But after being bereft of both his sons,—Germanicus had died in Syria and Drusus at Rome,—he retired to Campania, and almost everyone firmly believed and openly declared that he would never come back, but would soon die there. And both predictions were all but fulfilled; for he did not return again to Rome, and it chanced a few days later that as he was dining near Tarracina in a villa called the Grotto, many huge rocks fell from the ceiling and crushed a number of the guests and servants, while the emperor himself had a narrow escape.

XL. After traversing Campania and dedicating the Capitolium at Capua and a temple to Augustus at Nola, which was the pretext he had given for his journey, he went to Capreae, particularly attracted to that island because it was accessible by only one small beach, being everywhere else girt with sheer cliffs of great height and by deep water. But he was at once recalled by the constant entreaties of the people, because of a disaster at Fidenae, where more than twenty thousand spectators had perished through the collapse of the amphitheatre during a gladiatorial show. So he crossed to the mainland and made himself accessible to all, the more willingly because he had given orders on leaving the city that no one was to disturb him, and during the whole trip had repulsed those who tried to approach him.[63]

XLI. Then returning to the island, he utterly neglected the conduct of state affairs, from that time on never filling the vacancies in the decuries[64] of the knights, nor changing the tribunes of the soldiers and prefects or the governors of any of his provinces He left Spain and Syria without consular governors for several years, suffered Armenia to be overrun by the Parthians, Moesia to be laid waste by the Dacians and Sarmatians, and the Gallic provinces by the Germans, to the great dishonour of the empire and no less to its danger.

XLII. Moreover, having gained the licence of privacy, and being as it were out of sight of the citizens, he at last gave free rein at once to all the vices which he had for a long time ill concealed; and of these I shall give a detailed account from the beginning. Even at the outset of his military career his excessive love of wine gave him the name of Biberius, instead of Tiberius, Caldius for Claudius, and Mero for Nero.[65] Later, when emperor and at the very time that he was busy correcting the public morals, he spent a night and two whole days feasting and drinking with Pomponius Flaccus and Lucius Piso, immediately afterward making the one governor of the province of Syria and the other prefect of the city, and even declaring in their commissions that they were the most agreeable of friends, who could always be counted on. He had a dinner given him by Cestius Gallus, a lustful and prodigal old man, who had once been degraded by Augustus and whom he had himself rebuked a few days before in the senate, making the condition that Cestius should change or omit none of his usual customs, and that nude girls should wait upon them at table. He gave a very obscure candidate for the quaestorship preference over men of the noblest families, because at the emperor's challenge he had drained an amphora[66] of wine at a banquet. He paid Asellius Sabinus two hundred thousand sesterces for a dialogue, in which he had introduced a contest of a mushroom, a fig-pecker, an oyster and a thrush. Finally he established a new office, master of the imperial pleasures, assigning it to Titus Caesonius Priscus, a Roman knight.

XLV. How grossly he was in the habit of abusing women even of high birth is very clearly shown by the death of a certain Mallonia. When she was brought to his bed and refused most vigorously to submit to his lust, he turned her over to the informers, and even when she was on trial he did not cease to call out and ask her "whether she was sorry"; so that finally she left the court and went home, where she stabbed herself, openly upbraiding the ugly old man for his obscenity. Hence a stigma put upon him at the next plays in an Atellan farce was received with great applause and became current, that "the old goat was licking the does."

XLVI. In money matters he was frugal and close, never allowing the companions of his foreign tours and campaigns a salary, but merely their keep. Only once did he treat them liberally, and then through the generosity of his stepfather, when he formed three classes according to each man's rank and gave to the first six hundred thousand sesterces, to the second four hundred thousand, and to the third, which he called one, not of his friends, but of his Greeks,[67] two hundred thousand.

XLVII. While emperor he constructed no magnificent public works, for the only ones which he undertook, the temple of Augustus and the restoration of Pompey's theatre, he left unfinished after so many years. He gave no public shows at all, and very seldom attended those given by others, for fear that some request would be made of him, especially after he was forced to buy the freedom of a comic actor named Actius. Having relieved the neediness of a few senators, he avoided the necessity of further aid by declaring that he would help no others unless they proved to the senate that there were legitimate causes for their condition. Therefore diffidence and a sense of shame kept many from applying, among them Hortalus, grandson of Quintus Hortensius the orator, who though of very limited means had begotten four children with the encouragement of Augustus.[68]

XLVIII. He showed generosity to the public in but two instances, once when he offered to lend a hundred million sesterces without interest for a period of three years, and again when he made good the losses of some owners of blocks of houses on the Caelian Mount, which had burned down.[69] The former was forced upon him by the clamour of the people for help in a time of great financial stress, after he had failed to relieve the situation by a decree of the senate,[70] providing that the moneylenders should invest two-thirds of their property in land, and that the debtors should at once pay the same proportion of their indebtedness; and the latter also was to relieve a condition of great hardship. Yet he made so much of his liberality in the latter case, that he had the name of the Caelian changed to the Augustan Mount.[71] After he had doubled the legacies provided for in the will of Augustus, he never gave largess to the soldiers, with the exception of a thousand denarii to each of the praetorians, for not taking sides with Sejanus, and some presents to the legions in Syria, because they alone had consecrated no image of Sejanus among their standards.[72] He also very rarely allowed veteran soldiers their discharge, having an eye to their death from years, and a saving of money through their death.[73] He did not relieve the provinces either by any act of liberality, except Asia, when some cities were destroyed by an earthquake.

XLIX. Presently, as time went on, he even resorted to plunder. All the world knows that he drove Gnaeus Lentulus Augur, a man of great wealth, to take his own life through fear and mental anxiety, and to make the emperor his sole heir; that Lepida, too, a woman of very high birth, was condemned to banishment to gratify Quirinius, an opulent and childless ex-consul, who had divorced her, and twenty years later accused her of having attempted to poison him many years before; that besides this the leading men of the Spanish and Gallic provinces, as well as of Syria and Greece, had their property confiscated on trivial and shameless charges, some being accused of nothing more serious than having a part of their property in ready money;[74] that many states and individuals were deprived of immunities of long standing, and of the right of working mines and collecting revenues; that Vonones, king of the Parthians, who on being dethroned by his subjects had taken refuge at Antioch with a vast treasure, in the belief that he was putting himself under the protection of the Roman people, was treacherously despoiled and put to death.

L. He first showed his hatred of his kindred in the case of his brother Drusus, producing a letter of his, in which Drusus discussed with him the question of compelling Augustus to restore the Republic; and then he turned against the rest. So far from showing any courtesy or kindness to his wife Julia, after her banishment, which is the least that one might expect,[75] although her father's order had merely confined her to one town, he would not allow her even to leave her house or enjoy the society of mankind. Nay more, he even deprived her of the allowance[76] granted her by her father and of her yearly income, under colour of observance of the common law, since Augustus had made no provision for these in his will. Vexed at his mother Livia, alleging that she claimed an equal share in the rule, he shunned frequent meetings with her and long and confidential conversations, to avoid the appearance of being guided by her advice; though in point of fact he was wont every now and then to need and to follow it. He was greatly offended too by a decree of the senate, providing that "son of Livia," as well as "son of Augustus" should be written in his honorary inscriptions. For this reason he would not suffer her to be named "Parent of her Country," nor to receive any conspicuous public honour. More than that, he often warned her not to meddle with affairs of importance and unbecoming a woman, especially after he learned that at a fire near the temple of Vesta she had been present in person, and urged the people and soldiers to greater efforts, as had been her way while her husband was alive.

LI. Afterwards he reached the point of open enmity, and the reason, they say, was this. On her urging him again and again to appoint among the jurors a man who had been made a citizen, he declared that he would do it only on condition that she would allow an entry to be made in the official list that it was forced upon him by his mother. Then Livia, in a rage, drew from a secret place[77] and read some old letters written to her by Augustus with regard to the austerity and stubbornness of Tiberius' disposition. He in turn was so put out that these had been preserved so long and were thrown up at him in such a spiteful spirit, that some think that this was the very strongest of the reasons for his retirement. At all events, during all the three years that she lived after he left Rome he saw her but once, and then only one day, for a very few hours; and when shortly after that she fell ill, he took no trouble to visit her. When she died, and after a delay of several days, during which he held out hope of his coining, had at last been buried because the condition of the corpse made it necessary, he forbade her deification, alleging that he was acting according to her own instructions. He further disregarded the provisions of her will, and within a short time caused the downfall of all her friends and intimates, even of those to whom she had on her deathbed entrusted the care other obsequies, actually condemning one of them, and that a man of equestrian rank, to the treadmill.

LII. He had a father's affection neither for his own son Drusus nor his adopted son Germanicus, being exasperated at the former's vices; and, in fact, Drusus led a somewhat loose and dissolute life. Therefore, even when he died, Tiberius was not greatly affected, but almost immediately after the funeral returned to his usual routine, forbidding a longer period of mourning. Nay, more, when a deputation from Ilium offered him somewhat belated condolences, he replied with a smile, as if the memory of his bereavement had faded from his mind, that they, too, had his sympathy for the loss of their eminent fellow-citizen Hector. As to Germanicus, he was so far from appreciating him, that he made light of his illustrious deeds as unimportant, and railed at his brilliant victories as ruinous to his country. He even made complaint in the senate when Germanicus, on the occasion of a sudden and terrible famine, went to Alexandria without consulting him. It is even believed that he caused his death at the hands of Gnaeus Piso, governor of Syria, and some think that when Piso was tried on that charge, he would have produced his instructions, had not Tiberius caused them to be taken from him when Piso privately showed them, and the man himself to be put to death. Because of this the words, "Give us back Germanicus," were posted in many places, and shouted at night all over the city. And Tiberius afterwards strengthened this suspicion by cruelly abusing the wife and children of Germanicus as well.

LIII. When his daughter-in-law Agrippina was somewhat outspoken in her complaints after her husband's death, he took her by the hand and quoted a Greek verse, meaning "Do you think a wrong is done you, dear daughter, if you are not empress?" After that he never deigned to hold any conversation with her. Indeed, after she showed fear of tasting an apple which he handed her at dinner, he even ceased to invite her to his table, alleging that he had been charged with an attempt to poison her; but as a matter of fact, the whole affair had been prearranged, that he should offer her the fruit to test her, and that she should refuse it as containing certain death. At last, falsely charging her with a desire to take refuge, now at the statue of Augustus and now with the armies, he exiled her to Pandataria, and when she loaded him with reproaches, he had her beaten by a centurion until one of her eyes was destroyed. Again, when she resolved to die of starvation, he had her mouth pried open and food crammed into it. Worst of all, when she persisted in her resolution and so perished, he assailed her memory with the basest slanders, persuading the senate to add her birthday to the days of ill omen, and actually taking credit to himself for not having had her strangled and her body cast out on the Stairs of Mourning. He even allowed a decree to be passed in recognition of this remarkable clemency, in which thanks were offered him and a golden gift was consecrated to Jupiter of the Capitol.

LIV. By Germanicus he had three grandsons, Nero, Drusus, and Gaius, and by Drusus one, called Tiberius. Bereft of his own children, he recommended Nero and Drusus, the elder sons of

Germanicus, to the senate, and celebrated the day when each of them came to his majority by giving largess to the commons. But as soon as he learned that at the beginning of the year vows were being put up for their safety also, he referred the matter to the senate, saying that such honours ought to be conferred only on those of tried character and mature years. By revealing his true feelings towards them from that time on, he exposed them to accusations from all quarters, and after resorting to various tricks to rouse them to rail at him, and seeing to it that they were betrayed when they did so, he brought most bitter charges against them both in writing; and when they had in consequence been pronounced public enemies, he starved them to death, Nero on the island of Pontia and Drusus in a lower room of the Palace. It is thought that Nero was forced to take his own life, since an executioner, who pretended that he came by authority of the senate, showed him the noose and hooks,[78] but that Drusus was so tortured by hunger that he tried to eat the stuffing of his mattress; while the remains of both were so scattered that it was with difficulty that they could ever be collected.

LV. In addition to his old friends and intimates, he had asked for twenty of the leading men of the State as advisers on public affairs. Of all these he spared hardly two or three; the others he destroyed on one pretext or another, including Aelius Sejanus, whose downfall involved the death of many others. This man he had advanced to the highest power, not so much from regard for him, as that he might through his services and wiles destroy the children of Germanicus and secure the succession for his own grandson, the child of his son Drusus.

LVI. He was not a whit milder towards his Greek companions, in whose society he took special pleasure. When one Xeno was holding forth in somewhat far-fetched phrases, he asked him what dialect that was which was so affected, and on Xeno's replying that it was Doric, he banished him to Cinaria, believing that he was being taunted with his old-time exile, inasmuch as the Rhodians spoke Doric. He had the habit, too, of putting questions at dinner suggested by his daily reading, and learning that the grammarian Seleucus inquired of the imperial attendants what authors Tiberius was reading and so came primed, he at first banished the offender from his society, and later even forced him to commit suicide.

LVII. His cruel and cold-blooded character was not completely hidden even in his boyhood. His teacher of rhetoric, Theodorus of Gadara, seems first to have had the insight to detect it, and to have characterized it very aptly, since in taking him to task he would now and then call him *πηλὸν αἵματι πεφυραμένον* that is to say, "mud kneaded with blood." But it grew still more noticeable after he became emperor, even at the beginning, when he was still courting popularity by a show of moderation. When a funeral was passing by and a jester called aloud to the corpse to let Augustus know that the legacies which he had left to the people were not yet being paid, Tiberius had the man haled before him, ordered that he be given his due[79] and put to death, and bade him go tell the truth to his father. Shortly afterwards, when a Roman knight called Pompeius stoutly opposed some action in the senate, Tiberius threatened him with imprisonment, declaring that from a Pompeius he would make of him a Pompeian, punning cruelly on the man's name and the fate of the old party.

LVIII. It was at about this time that a praetor asked him whether he should have the courts convened to consider cases of lese-majesty; to which he replied that the laws must be enforced, and he did enforce them most rigorously. One man had removed the head from a statue of Augustus, to substitute that of another; the case was tried in the senate, and since the evidence was conflicting, the witnesses were examined by torture. After the defendant had been condemned, this kind of accusation gradually went so far that even such acts as these were regarded as capital crimes: to beat a slave near a statue of Augustus, or to change one's clothes there; to carry a ring or coin stamped with his image into a privy or a brothel, or to criticize any word or act of his. Finally, a man was put to death merely for allowing an honour to be voted him in his native town on the same day that honours had previously been voted to Augustus.

LIX. He did so many other cruel and savage deeds under the guise of strictness and improvement of the public morals, but in reality rather to gratify his natural instincts, that some resorted to verses to express their detestation of the present ills and a warning against those to come:

"Cruel and merciless man, shall I briefly say all I would utter?
Hang me if even your dam for you affection can feel.
You are no knight. Why so? The hundred thousands are lacking;[80]
If you ask the whole tale, you were an exile at Rhodes.[81]
You, O Caesar, have altered the golden ages of Saturn;
For while you are alive, iron they ever will be.
Nothing for wine cares this fellow, since now 'tis for blood he is thirsting;
This he as greedily quaffs as before wine without water.
Look, son of Rome, upon Sulla, for himself not for you blest and happy,[82]
Marius too, if you will, but after capturing Rome;
Hands of an Antony see, rousing the strife of the people,
Hands stained with blood not once, dripping again and again;
Then say: Rome is no more! He ever has reigned with great bloodshed
Whoso made himself king, coming from banishment home."

These at first he wished to be taken as the work of those who were impatient of his reforms, voicing not so much their real feelings as their anger and vexation; and he used to say from time to time: "Let them hate me, provided they respect my conduct."[83] Later he himself proved them only too true and unerring.

LX. A few days after he reached Capreae and was by himself, a fisherman appeared unexpectedly and offered him a huge mullet; whereupon in his alarm that the man had clambered up to him from the back of the island over rough and pathless rocks, he had the poor fellow's face scrubbed with the fish. And because in the midst of his torture the man thanked his stars that he had not given the emperor an enormous crab that he had caught, Tiberius had his face torn with the crab also. He punished a soldier of the praetorian guard with death for having stolen a peacock from his preserves. When the litter in which he was making a trip was stopped by brambles, he had the man who went ahead to clear the way, a centurion of the first cohorts,[84] stretched out on the ground and flogged half to death.

LXI. Presently he broke out into every form of cruelty, for which he never lacked occasion, venting it on the friends and even the acquaintances, first of his mother, then of his grandsons and granddaughter, and finally of Sejanus. After the death of Sejanus he was more cruel than ever, which showed that his favourite was not wont to egg him on, but on the contrary gave him the opportunities which he himself desired. Yet in a brief and sketchy autobiography which he composed he had the assurance to write that he had punished Sejanus because he found him venting his hatred on the children of his son Germanicus. Whereas in fact he had himself put one of them to death after he had begun to suspect Sejanus and the other after the latter's downfall.

It is a long story to run through his acts of cruelty in detail; it will be enough to mention the forms which they took, as samples of his barbarity. Not a day passed without an execution, not even those that were sacred and holy; for he put some to death even on New Year's day. Many were accused and condemned with their children and even by their children. The relatives of the victims were forbidden to mourn for them. Special rewards were voted the accusers and sometimes even the witnesses. The word of no informer was doubted. Every crime was treated as capital, even the utterance of a few simple words. A poet was charged with having slandered Agamemnon in a tragedy, and a writer of history of having called Brutus and Cassius the last of the Romans. The writers were at once put to death and their works destroyed, although they had been read with approval in public some years before in the presence of Augustus himself. Some of those who were consigned to prison were denied not only the consolation of reading, but even the privilege of conversing and talking together. Of those who were cited to plead their causes some opened their veins at home, feeling sure of being condemned and wishing to avoid annoyance and humiliation, while others drank poison in full view of the senate; yet the wounds of the former were bandaged and they were hurried half-dead, but still quivering, to the prison. Every one of those who were executed was thrown out upon the Stairs of Mourning and dragged to the Tiber with hooks, as many as twenty being so treated in a single day, including women and children. Since ancient usage made it impious to strangle maidens, young girls were first violated by the executioner and then strangled. Those who wished to die were forced to live; for he thought death so light a punishment that when he heard that one of the accused, Carnulus by name, had anticipated his execution, he cried: "Carnulus has given the the slip"; and when he was inspecting the prisons and a man begged for a speedy death, he replied: "I have not yet become your friend." An ex-consul has recorded in his Annals that once at a large dinner-party, at which the writer himself was present, Tiberius was suddenly asked in a loud voice by one of the dwarfs that stood beside the table among the jesters why Paconius, who was charged with treason, remained so long alive; that the emperor at the time chided him for his saucy tongue, but a few days later wrote to the senate to decide as soon as possible about the execution of Paconius.

LXII. He increased his cruelty and carried it to greater lengths, exasperated by what he learned about the death of his son Drusus. At first supposing that he had died of disease, due to his bad habits, on finally learning that he had been poisoned by the treachery of his wife Livilla and Sejanus, there was no one whom Tiberius spared from torment and death. Indeed, he gave himself up so utterly for whole days to this investigation and was so wrapped up in it, that when he was told of the arrival of a host of his from Rhodes, whom he had invited to Rome in a friendly letter, he had him put to the torture at once, supposing that someone had come whose testimony was important for the case. On discovering his mistake, he even had the man put to death, to keep him from giving publicity to the wrong done him.

At Capreae they still point out the scene of his executions, from which he used to order that those who had been condemned after long and exquisite tortures be cast headlong into the sea before his eyes, while a band of marines waited below for the bodies and broke their bones with boathooks and oars, to prevent any breath of life from remaining in them. Among various forms of torture he had devised this one: he would trick men into loading themselves with copious draughts of wine, and then on a sudden tying up their private parts, would torment them at the same time by the torture of the cords and of the stoppage of their water. And had not death prevented him, and Thrasyllus, purposely it is said, induced him to put off some things through hope of a longer life, it is believed that still more would have perished, and that he would not even have spared the rest of his grandsons; for he had his suspicions of Gaius and detested Tiberius as the fruit of adultery. And this is highly probable, for he used at times to call Priam happy, because he had outlived all his kindred.

LXIII. Many things go to show, not only how hated and execrable he was all this time, but also that he lived a life of extreme fear and was even exposed to insult. He forbade anyone to consult soothsayers secretly and without witnesses. Indeed, he even attempted to do away with the oracles near the city, but forbore through terror at the divine power of the Praenestine lots; for though he had them sealed up in a chest and brought to Rome, he could not find them until the box was taken back to the temple.[85] He had assigned provinces to one or two ex-consuls, of whom he did not dare to lose sight, but he detained them at Rome and finally appointed their successors several years later without their having left the city. In the meantime they retained their titles, and he even continued to assign them numerous commissions, to execute through their deputies and assistants.

LXIV. After the exile of his daughter-in-law and grandchildren he never moved them anywhere except in fetters and in a tightly closed litter, while a guard of soldiers kept any who met them on the road from looking at them or even from stopping as they went by.

LXV. When Sejanus was plotting revolution, although he saw the man's birthday publicly celebrated and his golden statues honoured everywhere, yet it was with difficulty that he at last overthrew him, rather by craft and deceit than by his imperial authority. First of all, to remove him from his person under colour of showing him honour, he chose him as his colleague in a fifth
31 A.D. consulship,[86] which, with this very end in view, he assumed after a long interval while absent from the city. Then beguiling him with hope of marriage into the imperial family and of the tribunicial power, he accused him when he least expected it in a shameful and pitiable speech, begging the senators among other things to send one of the consuls[87] to bring him, a lonely old man, into their presence under military protection. Even then distrustful and fearful of an outbreak, he had given orders that his grandson Drusus, whom he still kept imprisoned in Rome, should be set free, if occasion demanded, and made commander-in-chief. He even got ships ready and thought of flight to some of the legions, constantly watching from a high cliff for the signals which he had ordered to be raised afar off[88] as each step was taken, for fear the messengers should be delayed. But even when the conspiracy of Sejanus was crushed, he was no whit more confident or courageous, but for the next nine months he did not leave the villa which is called Io's.

LXVI. His anxiety of mind became torture because of reproaches of all kinds from every quarter, since every single one of those who were condemned to death heaped, all kinds of abuse upon him, either to his face or by billets placed in the orchestra.[89] By these, however, he was most diversely affected, now through a sense of shame desiring that they all be concealed and kept secret, sometimes scorning them and producing them of his own accord and giving them publicity. Why, he was even attacked by Artabanus, king of the Parthians, who charged him in a letter with the murder of his kindred,[90] with other bloody deeds, and with shameless and dissolute living, counselling him to gratify the intense and just hatred of the citizens as soon as possible by a voluntary death.

LXVII. At last in utter self-disgust he all but admitted the extremity of his wretchedness in a letter beginning as follows[91]: "If I know what to write to you, Fathers of the Senate, or how to write it, or what to leave unwritten at present, may all gods and goddesses visit me with more utter destruction than I feel that I am daily suffering." Some think that through his knowledge of the future he foresaw this situation,[92] and knew long beforehand what detestation and ill-repute one day awaited him; and that therefore when he became emperor, he positively refused the title of "Father of his Country" and to allow the senate to take oath to support his acts, for fear that he might presently be found undeserving of such honours and thus be the more shamed. In fact, this may be gathered from the speech which he made regarding these two matters; for example, when he says: "I shall always be consistent and never change my ways so long as I am in my senses; but for the sake of precedent the senate should beware of binding itself to support the acts of any man, since he might through some mischance suffer a change." Again: "If you ever come to feel any doubt," he says, "of my character or of my heartfelt devotion to you (and before that happens, I pray that my last day may save me from this altered opinion of me), the title of Father of my Country will give me no additional honour, but will be a reproach to you, either for your hasty action in conferring the appellation upon me, or for your inconsistency in changing your estimate of my character." 32 A.D.

LXVIII. He was large and strong of frame, and of a stature above the average; broad of shoulders and chest; well proportioned and symmetrical from head to foot. His left hand was the more nimble and stronger, and its joints were so powerful that he could bore through a fresh, sound apple with his finger, and break the head of a boy, or even a young man, with a fillip. He was of fair complexion and wore his hair rather long at the back, so much so as even to cover the nape of his neck; which was apparently a family trait. His face was handsome, but would break out on a sudden with many pimples. His eyes were unusually large and, strange to say, had the power of seeing even at night and in the dark, but only for a short time when first opened after sleep; presently they grew dim-sighted again. He strode along with his neck stiff and bent forward, usually with a stern countenance and for the most part in silence, never or very rarely conversing with his companions, and then speaking with great deliberation and with a kind of supple movement of his fingers. All of these mannerisms of his, which were disagreeable and signs of arrogance, were remarked by Augustus, who often tried to excuse them to the senate and people by declaring that they were natural failings, and not intentional. He enjoyed excellent health, which was all but perfect during nearly the whole of his reign,[93] although from the thirtieth year of his age he took care of it according to his own ideas, without the aid or advice of physicians.

LXIX. Although somewhat neglectful of the gods and of religious matters, being addicted to astrology and firmly convinced that everything was in the hands of fate, he was nevertheless immoderately afraid of thunder. Whenever the sky was lowering, he always wore a laurel wreath, because it is said that that kind of leaf is not blasted by lightning.[94]

LXX. He was greatly devoted to liberal studies in both languages. In his Latin oratory he followed Messala Corvinus, to whom he had given attention in his youth, when Messala was an old man. But he so obscured his style by excessive mannerisms and pedantry, that he was thought, to speak much better offhand than in a prepared address. He also composed a lyric poem, entitled "A Lament for the Death of Lucius Caesar," and made Greek verses in imitation of Euphorion, Rhianus, and Parthenius, poets of whom he was very fond, placing their busts in the public libraries among those of the eminent writers of old; and on that account many learned men vied with one another in issuing commentaries on their works and dedicating them to the emperor. Yet his special aim was a knowledge of mythology, which he carried to a silly and laughable extreme; for he used to test even the grammarians,[95] a class of men in whom, as I have said, he was especially interested, by questions something like this: "Who was Hecuba's mother?" "What was the name of Achilles among the maidens?" "What were the Sirens in the habit of singing?" Moreover, on the first day that he entered the senate after the death of Augustus, to satisfy at once the demands of filial piety and of religion, he offered sacrifice after the example of Minos with incense and wine, but without a fluteplayer, as Minos had done in ancient times on the death of his son.

LXXI. Though he spoke Greek readily and fluently, yet he would not use it on all occasions, and especially eschewed it in the senate; so much so that before using the word "monopolium,"[96] he begged pardon for the necessity of employing a foreign term. Again, when the word ἔμβλημα[97] was read in a decree of the senate, he recommended that it be changed and a native word substituted for the foreign one; and if one could not be found, that the idea be expressed by several words, if necessary, and by periphrasis. On another occasion, when a soldier was asked in Greek to give testimony, he forbade him to answer except in Latin.

LXXII. Twice only during the whole period of his retirement did he try to return to Rome, once sailing in a trireme as far as the gardens near the artificial lake,[98] after first posting a guard along the banks of the Tiber to keep off those who came out to meet him; and again coming up the Appian Way as far as the seventh milestone. But he returned after merely having a distant view of the city walls, without approaching them; the first time for some unknown reason, the second through alarm at a portent. He had among his pets a serpent, and when he was going to feed it from his own hand, as his custom was, and discovered that it had been devoured by ants, he was warned to beware of the power of the multitude. So he went back in haste to Campania, fell ill at Astura, but recovering somewhat kept on to Circeii. To avoid giving any suspicion of his weak condition, he not only attended the games of the soldiers, but even threw down darts from his high seat at a boar which was let into the arena. Immediately he was taken with a pain in the side, and then being exposed to a draught when he was overheated, his illness increased. For all that, he kept up for some time, although he continued his journey as far as Misenum and made no change in his usual habits, not even giving up his banquets and other pleasures, partly from lack of self-denial and partly to conceal his condition. Indeed, when the physician Charicles had taken his hand to kiss it as he left the dining-room, since he was going away on leave of absence, Tiberius, thinking that he was trying to feel his pulse, urged him to remain and take his place again, and prolonged the dinner to a late hour. Even then he did not give up his custom of standing in the middle of the dining-room with a lictor by his side and addressing all the guests by name as they said farewell.

LXXIII. Meanwhile, having read in the proceedings of the senate that some of those under accusation, about whom he had written briefly, merely stating that they had been named by an informer, had been discharged without a hearing, he cried out in anger that he was held in contempt, and resolved to return to Capreae at any cost, since he would not risk any step except from his place of refuge. Detained, however, by bad weather and the increasing violence of his illness, he died a little later in the villa of Lucullus, in
Mar. 16, 37 A.D. the seventy-eighth year of his age and the twenty-third of his reign, on the seventeenth day before the Kalends of April, in the consulship of Gnaeus Acerronius Proculus and Gaius Pontius Nigrinus.

Some think that Gaius gave him a slow and wasting poison; others that during convalescence from an attack of fever food was refused him when he asked for it. Some say that a pillow was thrown upon his face, when he came to and asked for a ring which had been taken from him during a fainting fit. Seneca writes that conscious of his approaching end, he took off the ring, as if to give it to someone, but held fast to it for a time; then he put it back on his finger, and clenching his left hand, lay for a long time motionless; suddenly he called for his attendants, and on receiving no response, got up; but his strength failed him and he fell dead near the couch.

LXXIV. On his last birthday he dreamt that the Apollo of Temenos,[99] a statue of remarkable size and beauty, which he had brought from Syracuse to be set up in the library of the new temple,[100] appeared to him in a dream, declaring that it could not be dedicated by Tiberius. A few days before his death the lighthouse[101] at Capreae was wrecked by an earthquake. At Misenum the ashes from the glowing coals and embers which had been brought in to warm his dining-room, after they had died out and been for a long time cold, suddenly blazed up in the early evening and glowed without cessation until late at night.

LXXV. The people were so glad of his death, that at the first news of it some ran about shouting, "Tiberius to the Tiber," while others prayed to Mother Earth and the Manes to allow the dead man no abode except among the damned. Still others threatened his body with the hook and the Stairs of Mourning, especially embittered by a recent outrage, added to the memory of his former cruelty. It had been provided by decree of the senate that the exe- 21 A.D. cution of the condemned should in all cases be put off for ten days, and it chanced that the punishment of some fell due on the day when the news came about Tiberius. The poor wretches begged the public for protection; but since in the continued absence of Gaius there was no one who could be approached and appealed to, the jailers, fearing to act contrary to the law, strangled them and cast out their bodies on the Stairs of Mourning. Therefore hatred of the tyrant waxed greater, since his cruelty endured even after his death. When the funeral procession left Misenum, many cried out that the body ought rather to be carried to Atella,[102] and half-burned in the amphitheatre; but it was taken to Rome by the soldiers and reduced to ashes with public ceremonies.

LXXVI. Two years before his death he had made two copies of a will, one in his own hand and the other in that of a freedman, but of the same content, and had caused them to be signed and sealed by persons of the very lowest condition. In this will he named his grandsons, Gaius, son of Germanicus, and Tiberius, son of Drusus, heirs to equal shares of his estate, each to be sole heir in case of the other's death. Besides, he gave legacies to several, including the Vestal virgins, as well as to each and every man of the soldiers and the commons of Rome, with separate ones to the masters of the city wards.

BOOK IV

GAIUS CALIGULA

4 A.D. I. Germanicus, father of Gaius Caesar, son of Drusus and the
7 A.D. younger Antonia, after being adopted by his paternal uncle
12 A.D. Tiberius, held the quaestorship five years before the legal age and
14 A.D. passed directly to the consulship.[1] When the death of Augustus was announced, he was sent to the army in Germany, where it is hard to say whether his filial piety or his courage was more conspicuous; for although all the legions obstinately refused to accept
17 A.D. Tiberius as emperor, and offered him the rule of the state,[2] he
18 A.D. held them to their allegiance. And later he won a victory over the enemy and celebrated a triumph. Then chosen consul for a second time, before he entered on his term he was hurried off to restore order in the Orient, and after vanquishing the king of Armenia and reducing Cappadocia to the form of a province, died of a lingering illness at Antioch, in the thirty-fourth year of his age. There was some suspicion that he was poisoned; for besides the dark spots which appeared all over his body and the froth which flowed from his mouth, after he had been reduced to ashes his heart was found entire among his bones; and it is supposed to be a characteristic of that organ that when steeped in poison it cannot be destroyed by fire.

II. Now the belief was that he met his death through the wiles of Tiberius, aided and abetted by Gnaeus Piso.[3] This man had been made governor of Syria at about that time, and realising that he must give offence either to the father or the son, as if there were no alternative, he never ceased to show the bitterest enmity towards Germanicus in word and deed, even after the latter fell ill. In consequence Piso narrowly escaped being torn to pieces by the people on his return to Rome, and was condemned to death by the senate.

III. It is the general opinion that Germanicus possessed all the highest qualities of body and mind, to a degree never equalled by anyone; a handsome person, unequalled valour, surpassing ability in the oratory and learning of Greece and Rome, unexampled kindliness, and a remarkable desire and capacity for winning men's regard and inspiring their affection. His legs were too slender for the rest of his figure, but he gradually brought them to proper proportions by constant horseback riding after meals. He often slew a foeman in hand-to-hand combat. He pleaded causes even after receiving the triumphal regalia; and among other fruits of his studies he left some Greek comedies. Unassuming[4] at home and abroad, he always entered the free and federate towns without lictors. Wherever he came upon the tombs of distinguished men, he always offered sacrifice to their shades. Planning to bury in one mound the old and scattered relics of those who fell in the overthrow of Varus, he was the first to attempt to collect and assemble them with his own hand. Even towards his detractors, whosoever they were and whatever their motives, he was so mild and lenient, that when Piso was annulling his decrees and maltreating his dependents, he could not make up his mind to break with him, until he found himself assailed also by potions and spells.[5] Even then he went no farther than formally to renounce Piso's friendship in the old-time fashion, and to bid his household avenge him, in case anything should befall him.[6]

IV. He reaped plentiful fruit from these virtues, for he was so respected and beloved by his kindred that Augustus (to say nothing of the rest of his relatives) after hesitating for a long time whether to appoint him his successor, had him adopted by Tiberius. He was so popular with the masses, that, according to many writers, whenever he came to any place or left one, he was sometimes in danger of his life from the crowds that met him or saw him off; in fact, when he returned from Germany after quelling the outbreak, all the cohorts of the praetorian guard went forth to meet him, although orders had been given that only two should go, and the whole populace, regardless of age, sex, or rank, poured out of Rome as far as the twentieth milestone.

V. Yet far greater and stronger tokens of regard were shown at the time of his death and immediately afterwards. On the day when he passed away the temples were stoned and the altars of the gods thrown down, while some flung their household gods into the street and cast out their newly born children.[7] Even barbarian peoples, so they say, who were engaged in war with us or with one another, unanimously consented to a truce, as if all in common had suffered a domestic tragedy. It is said that some princes put off their beards and had their wives' heads shaved, as a token of the deepest mourning; that even the king of kings[8] suspended his exercise at hunting and the banquets with his grandees, which among the Parthians is a sign of public mourning.

VI. At Rome when the community, in grief and consternation at the first report of his illness, was awaiting further news, and suddenly after nightfall a report at last spread abroad, on doubtful authority, that he had recovered, a general rush was made from every side to the Capitol with torches and victims, and the temple gates were all but torn off, that nothing might hinder them in their eagerness to pay their vows. Tiberius was roused from sleep by the cries of the rejoicing throng, who all united in singing:—

"Safe is Rome, safe too our country, for Germanicus is safe."

But when it was at last made known that he was no more, the public grief could be checked neither by any consolation nor edict, and it continued even during the festal days of the month of December.[9]

The fame of the deceased and regret for his loss were increased by the horror of the times which followed, since all believed, and with good reason, that the cruelty of Tiberius, which soon burst forth, had been held in check through his respect and awe for Germanicus.

VII. He had to wife Agrippina, daughter of Marcus Agrippa and Julia, who bore him nine children. Two of these were taken off when they were still in infancy, and one just as he was reaching the age of boyhood, a charming child, whose statue, in the guise of Cupid, Livia dedicated in the temple of the Capitoline Venus, while Augustus had another placed in his bed chamber and used to kiss it fondly whenever he entered the room. The other children survived their father, three girls, Agrippina, Drusilla, and Livilla, born in successive years, and three boys, Nero, Drusus, and Gaius Caesar. Nero and Drusus were adjudged public enemies by the senate on the accusation of Tiberius.[10]

VIII. Gaius Caesar was born the day before the Kalends of September in the consulship of his father and Gaius Fonteius Capito. Conflicting testimony makes his birthplace uncertain. Gnaeus Lentulus Gaetulicus writes that he was born at Tibur, Plinius Secundus among the Treveri, in a village called Ambitarvium above the Confluence. Pliny adds as proof that altars are shown there, inscribed "For the Delivery of Agrippina." Verses which were in circulation soon after he became emperor indicate that he was begotten in the winter-quarters of the legions: Aug. 31, 12 A.D.

"He who was born in the camp and reared 'mid the arms of his country,
Gave at the outset a sign that he was fated to rule."

I myself find in the gazette[11] that he first saw the light at Antium. Gaetulicus is shown to be wrong by Pliny, who says that he told a flattering lie, to add some lustre to the fame of a young and vainglorious prince from the city sacred to Hercules; and that he lied with the more assurance because Germanicus really did have a son born to him at Tibur, also called Gaius Caesar, of whose lovable disposition and untimely death I have already spoken.[12] Pliny has erred in his chronology; for the historians of Augustus agree that Germanicus was not sent to Germany until the close of his consulship, when Gaius was already born. Moreover, the inscription on the altar adds no strength to Pliny's view, for Agrippina twice gave birth to daughters in that region, and any childbirth, regardless of sex, is called *puerperium*, since the men of old called girls *puerae*, just as they called boys *puelli*. Furthermore, we have a letter written by Augustus to his granddaughter Agrippina, a few months before he died, about the Gaius in question (for no other child of the name was still alive at that time), reading as follows: "Yesterday I arranged with Talarius and Asillius to bring your boy Gaius on the fifteenth day before the Kalends of June, if it be the will of the gods. I send with him besides one of my slaves who is a physician, and I have written Germanicus to keep him if he wishes. Farewell, my own Agrippina, and take care to come in good health to your Germanicus."

May 18, 14 A.D.

I think it is clear enough that Gaius could not have been born in a place to which he was first taken from Rome when he was nearly two years old. This letter also weakens our confidence in the verses, the more so because they are anonymous. We must then accept the only remaining testimony, that of the public record, particularly since Gaius loved Antium as if it were his native soil, always preferring it to all other places of retreat, and even thinking, it is said, of transferring thither the seat and abode of the empire through weariness of Rome.

IX. His surname Caligula[13] he derived from a joke of the troops, because he was brought up in their midst in the dress of a common soldier. To what extent besides he won their love and devotion by being reared in fellowship with them is especially evident from the fact that when they threatened mutiny after the death of Augustus and were ready for any act of madness, the mere sight of Gaius unquestionably calmed them. For they did not become quiet until they saw that he was being spirited away because of the danger from their outbreak and taken for protection to the nearest town. Then at last they became contrite, and laying hold of the carriage and stopping it, begged to be spared the disgrace which was being put upon them.

X. He attended his father also on his expedition to Syria. On his return from there he first lived with his mother and after her banishment, with his great-grandmother Livia; and when Livia 29 A.D. died, though he was not yet of age, he spoke her eulogy from the rostra. Then he fell to the care of his grandmother Antonia and in the nineteenth year of his age he was called to Capreae by Tiberius, on the same day assuming the gown of manhood and shaving his first beard, but without any such ceremony as had attended the coming of age of his brothers. Although at Capreae every kind of wile was resorted to by those who tried to lure him or force him to utter complaints, he never gave them any satisfaction, ignoring the ruin of his kindred as if nothing at all had happened, passing over his own ill-treatment with an incredible pretence of indifference, and so obsequious towards his grandfather and his household, that it was well said of him that no one had ever been a better slave or a worse master.

XI. Yet even at that time he could not control his natural cruelty and viciousness, but he was a most eager witness of the tortures and executions of those who suffered punishment, revelling at night in gluttony and adultery, disguised in a wig and a long robe, passionately devoted besides to the theatrical arts of dancing and singing, in which Tiberius very willingly indulged him, in the hope that through these his savage nature might be softened. This last was so clearly evident to the shrewd old man, that he used to say now and then that to allow Gaius to live would prove the ruin of himself and of all men, and that he was rearing a viper for the Roman people and a Phaethon for the world.

XII. Not so very long afterward Gaius took to wife Junia Claudilla, daughter of Marcus Silanus, a man of noble rank. Then appointed augur in place of his brother Drusus, before he was invested with the office he was advanced to that of pontiff, with strong commendation of his dutiful conduct and general character; for since the court was deserted and deprived of its other supports, after Sejanus had been suspected of hostile designs and presently put out of the way, he was little by little encouraged to look forward to the succession. To have a better chance of realising this, after losing Junia in childbirth, he seduced Ennia Naevia, wife of Macro, who at that time commanded the praetorian guard, even promising to marry her if he became emperor, and guaranteeing this promise by an oath and a written contract. Having through her wormed himself into Macro's favour, he poisoned Tiberius, as some think, and ordered that his ring be taken from him while he still breathed, and then suspecting that he was trying to hold fast to it, that a pillow be put over his face; or even strangled the old man with his own hand, immediately ordering the crucifixion of a freedman who cried out at the awful deed. And this is likely enough; for some writers say that Caligula himself later admitted, not it is true that he had committed parricide, but that he had at least meditated it at one time; for they say that he constantly boasted, in speaking of his filial piety, that he had entered the bedchamber of the sleeping Tiberius dagger in hand, to avenge the death of his mother and brothers; but that, seized with pity, he threw down the dagger and went out again; and that though Tiberius knew of this, he had never dared to make any inquiry or take any action.

37 A.D. XIII. By thus gaining the throne he fulfilled the highest hopes of the Roman people, or I may say of all mankind, since he was the prince most earnestly desired by the great part of the provincials and soldiers, many of whom had known him in his infancy, as well as by the whole body of the city populace, because of the memory of his father Germanicus and pity for a family that was all but extinct. Accordingly, when he set out from Misenum, though he was in mourning garb and escorting the body of Tiberius, yet his progress was marked by altars, victims, and blazing torches, and he was met by a dense and joyful throng, who called him besides other propitious names their "star," their "chick," their "babe," and their "nursling."

XIV. When he entered the city, full and absolute power was at once put into his hands by the unanimous consent of the senate and of the mob, which forced its way into the House, and no attention was paid to the wish of Tiberius, who in his will had named his other grandson, still a boy, joint heir with Caligula.[14] So great was the public rejoicing, that within the next three months, or less than that, more than a hundred and sixty thousand victims are said to have been slain in sacrifice.

A few days after this, when he crossed to the islands near Campania, vows were put up for his safe return, while no one let slip even the slightest chance of giving testimony to his anxiety and regard for his safety. But when he fell ill, they all spent the whole night about the Palace; some even vowed to fight as gladiators, and others posted placards offering their lives, if the ailing prince were spared.[15] To this unbounded love of his citizens was added marked devotion from foreigners. Artabanus, for example, king of the Parthians, who was always outspoken in his hatred and contempt for Tiberius, voluntarily sought Caligula's friendship and came to a conference with the consular governor; then crossing the Euphrates, he paid homage to the Roman eagles and standards and to the statues of the Caesars.[16]

XV. Gaius himself tried to rouse men's devotion by courting popularity in every way. After eulogising Tiberius with many tears before the assembled people and giving him a magnificent funeral, he at once posted off to Pandateria and the Pontian islands, to remove the ashes of his mother and brother to Rome; and in stormy weather, too, to make his filial piety the more conspicuous. He approached them with reverence and placed them in the urns with his own hands. With no less theatrical effect he brought them to Ostia in a bireme with a banner set in the stern, and from there up the Tiber to Rome, where he had them carried to the Mausoleum[17] on two biers by the most distinguished men of the order of knights, in the middle of the day, when the streets were crowded. He appointed funeral sacrifices, too, to be offered each year with due ceremony, as well as games in the Circus in honour of his mother, providing a carriage to carry her image in the procession. But in memory of his father he gave to the month of September the name of Germanicus. After this, by a single

decree of the senate, he heaped upon his grandmother Antonia whatever honours Livia Augusta had ever enjoyed; took his uncle Claudius, who up to that time had been a Roman knight, as his
37 A.D. colleague in the consulship; adopted his brother Tiberius on the day that he assumed the gown of manhood, and gave him the title of Chief of the Youth.[18] He caused the names of his sisters to be included in all oaths: "And I will not hold myself and my children dearer than I do Gaius and his sisters"; as well as in the propositions[19] of the consuls: "Favour and good fortune attend Gaius Caesar and his sisters."

With the same desire for popularity he recalled those who had been condemned to banishment; took no cognizance of any charges that remained untried from an earlier time; had all documents relating to the cases of his mother and brothers carried to the Forum and burned, to give no informer or witness occasion for further fear, having first loudly called the gods to witness that he had neither read nor touched any of them. He refused a note which was offered him regarding his own safety, maintaining that he had done nothing to make anyone hate him, and that he had no ears for informers.

XVI. He banished from the city the sexual perverts called *spintriae*,[20] barely persuaded not to sink them in the sea. The writings of Titus Labienus, Cremutius Cordus,[21] and Cassius Severus, which had been suppressed by decrees of the senate, he allowed to be hunted up, circulated, and read, saying that it was wholly to his interest that everything which happened be handed down to posterity. He published the accounts of the empire, which had regularly been made public by Augustus,[22] a practice discontinued by Tiberius. He allowed the magistrates unrestricted jurisdiction, without appeal to himself. He revised the lists of the Roman knights strictly and scrupulously, yet with due moderation, publicly taking their horses from those guilty of any wicked or scandalous act, but merely omitting to read the names of men convicted of lesser offences. To lighten the labour of the jurors, he added a fifth division to the previous four. He tried also to restore the suffrage to the people by reviving the custom of elections. He at once paid faithfully and without dispute the legacies named in the will of Tiberius, though this had been set aside, as well as in that of Julia Augusta, which Tiberius had suppressed. He remitted the tax of a two-hundredth[23] on auction sales in Italy; made good to many their losses from fires; and whenever he restored kings to their thrones, he allowed them all the arrears of their taxes and their revenue for the meantime; for example, to Antiochus of Commagene, a hundred million sesterces that had accrued to the Treasury. To make it known that he encouraged every kind of noble action, he gave eight hundred thousand sesterces to a freedwoman, because she had kept silence about the guilt of her patron, though subjected to the utmost torture. Because of these acts, besides other honours, a golden shield was voted him, which was to be borne every year to the Capitol on an appointed day by the colleges of priests, escorted by the senate, while boys and girls of noble birth sang the praises of his virtues in a choral ode. It was further decreed that the day on which he began to reign should be called the Parilia, as a token that the city had been founded a second time.

XVII. He held four consulships, one from the Kalends of July
for two months, a second from the Kalends of January for thirty July 1,
days, a third up to the Ides of January, and the fourth until the sev- 37 A.D.
enth day before the Ides of the same month. Of all these only the Jan. 1,
last two were continuous.[24] The third he assumed at Lugdunum 39 A.D.
without a colleague, not, as some think, through arrogance or dis- Jan. 13,
regard of precedent, but because at that distance from Rome he 40 A.D.
had been unable to get news of the death of the other consul just Jan. 7,
before the day of the Kalends. He twice gave the people a largess 41 A.D.
of three hundred sesterces each, and twice a lavish banquet to the senate and the equestrian order, together with their wives and children. At the former of these he also distributed togas to the men, and to the women and children scarves of red and scarlet. Furthermore, to make a permanent addition to the public gaiety, he added a day to the Saturnalia, and called it *Juvenalis.*

XVIII. He gave several gladiatorial shows, some in the amphitheatre of Taurus[25] and some in the Saepta, in which he introduced pairs of African and Campanian boxers, the pick of both regions. He did not always preside at the games in person, but sometimes assigned the honour to the magistrates or to friends. He exhibited stage-plays continually, of various kinds and in many different places, sometimes even by night, lighting up the whole city. He also threw about gift-tokens[26] of various kinds, and gave each man a basket of victuals. During the feasting he sent his share to a Roman knight opposite him, who was eating with evident relish and appetite, while to a senator for the same reason he gave a commission naming him praetor out of the regular order. He also gave many games in the Circus, lasting from early morning until evening, introducing between the races now a baiting of panthers[27] and now the manœuvres of the game called Troy; some, too, of special splendour, in which the Circus was strewn with red and green, while the charioteers were all men of senatorial rank. He also started some games off-hand, when a few people called for them from the neighbouring balconies,[28] as he was inspecting the outfit of the Circus from the Gelotian house.

XIX. Besides this, he devised a novel and unheard of kind of pageant; for he bridged the gap between Baiae and the mole at Puteoli, a distance of about thirty-six hundred paces,[29] by bringing together merchant ships from all sides and anchoring them in a double line, after which a mound of earth was heaped upon them and fashioned in the manner of the Appian Way. Over this bridge he rode back and forth for two successive days, the first day on a caparisoned horse, himself resplendent in a crown of oak leaves, a buckler, a sword, and a cloak of cloth of gold; on the second, in the dress of a charioteer in a car drawn by a pair of famous horses, carrying before him a boy named Dareus, one of the hostages from Parthia, and attended by the entire praetorian guard and a company of his friends in Gallic chariots. I know that many have supposed that Gaius devised this kind of bridge in rivalry of Xerxes, who excited no little admiration by bridging the much narrower Hellespont; others, that it was to inspire fear in Germany and Britain, on which he had designs, by the fame of some stupendous work. But when I was a boy, I used to hear my grandfather say that the reason for the work, as revealed by the emperor's confidential courtiers, was that Thrasyllus the astrologer had declared to Tiberius, when he was worried about his successor and inclined towards his natural grandson,[30] that Gaius had no more chance of becoming emperor than of riding about over the gulf of Baiae with horses.

XX. He also gave shows in foreign lands, Athenian games[31] at Syracuse in Sicily, and miscellaneous games at Lugdunum in Gaul; at the latter place also a contest in Greek and Latin oratory, in which, they say, the losers gave prizes to the victors and were forced to compose eulogies upon them, while those who were least successful were ordered to erase their writings with a sponge or with their tongue,[32] unless they elected rather to be beaten with rods or thrown into the neighbouring river.

XXI. He completed the public works which had been half finished under Tiberius, namely the temple of Augustus and the theatre of Pompey. He likewise began an aqueduct in the region near Tibur and an amphitheatre beside the Saepta, the former finished by his successor Claudius,[33] while the latter was abandoned. At Syracuse he repaired the city walls, which had fallen into ruin through lapse of time, and the temples of the gods. He had planned, besides, to rebuild the palace of Polycrates at Samos, to finish the temple of Didymaean Apollo at Ephesus, to found a city high up in the Alps, but, above all, to dig a canal through the Isthmus in Greece,[34] and he had already sent a chief centurion to survey the work.

XXII. So much for Caligula as emperor; we must now tell of his career as a monster.

After he had assumed various surnames (for he was called "Pious," "Child of the Camp," "Father of the Armies," and "Greatest and Best of Caesars"), chancing to overhear some kings, who had come to Rome to pay their respects to him, disputing at dinner about the nobility of their descent, he cried:

"Let there be one Lord, one King."[35]

And he came near assuming a crown at once and changing the semblance of a principate into the form of a monarchy.[36] But on being reminded that he had risen above the elevation both of princes and kings, he began from that time on to lay claim to divine majesty; for after giving orders that such statues of the gods as were especially famous for their sanctity or their artistic merit, including that of Jupiter of Olympia,[37] should be brought from Greece, in order to remove their heads and put his own in their place, he built out a part of the Palace as far as the Forum, and making the temple of Castor and Pollux its vestibule, he often took his place between the divine brethren, and exhibited himself there to be worshipped by those who presented themselves; and some hailed him as Jupiter Latiaris. He also set up a special temple to his own godhead, with priests and with victims of the choicest kind. In this temple was a life-sized statue of the emperor in gold, which was dressed each day in clothing such as he wore himself. The richest citizens used all their influence to secure the priesthoods of his cult and bid high for the honour. The victims were flamingoes, peacocks, woodcock, guinea-hens and pheasants, offered day by day each after its own kind. At night he used constantly to invite the full and radiant moon to his embraces and his bed, while in the daytime he would talk confidentially with Jupiter Capitolinus, now whispering and then in turn putting his ear to the mouth of the god, now in louder and even angry language; for he was heard to make the threat: "Lift me up, or I'll lift thee."[38] But finally won by entreaties, as he reported, and even invited to live with the god, he built a bridge over the temple of the Deified Augustus, and thus joined his Palace to the Capitol. Presently, to be nearer yet, he laid the foundations of a new house in the court of the Capitol.

XXIII. He did not wish to be thought the grandson of Agrippa, or called so, because of the latter's humble origin; and he grew very angry if anyone in a speech or a song included Agrippa among the ancestors of the Caesars. He even boasted that his own mother was born in incest, which Augustus had committed with his daughter Julia; and not content with this slur on the memory of Augustus, he forbade the celebration of his victories at Actium and off Sicily by annual festivals,[39] on the ground that they were disastrous and ruinous to the Roman people. He often called his greatgrandmother Livia Augusta "a Ulysses in petticoats,"[40] and he had the audacity to accuse her of low birth in a letter to the senate, alleging that her maternal grandfather had been nothing but a decurion[41] of Fundi; whereas it is proved by public records that Aufidius Lurco held high offices at Rome. When his grandmother Antonia asked for a private interview, he refused it except in the presence of the praefect Macro, and by such indignities and annoyances he caused her death; although some think that he also gave her poison. After she was dead, he paid her no honour, but viewed her burning pyre from his dining-room. He had his brother[42] Tiberius put to death without warning, suddenly sending a tribune of the soldiers to do the deed; besides driving his father-in-law Silanus to end his life by cutting his throat with a razor. His charge against the latter was that Silanus had not followed him when he put to sea in stormy weather, but had remained behind in the hope of taking possession of the city in case he should be lost in the storm; against Tiberius, that his breath smelled of an antidote, which he had taken to guard against being poisoned at his hand. Now as a matter of fact, Silanus was subject to sea-sickness and wished to avoid the discomforts of the voyage, while Tiberius had taken medicine for a chronic cough, which was growing worse. As for his uncle Claudius, he spared him merely as a laughingstock.

XXIV. He lived in habitual incest with all his sisters, and at a large banquet he placed each of them in turn below him, while his wife reclined above. Of these he is believed to have violated Drusilla when he was still a minor, and even to have been caught lying with her by his grandmother Antonia, at whose house they were brought up in company. Afterwards, when she was the wife of Lucius Cassius Longinus, an ex-consul, he took her from him and openly treated her as his lawful wife; and when ill, he made her heir to his property and the throne. When she died, he appointed a season of public mourning, during which it was a capital offence to laugh, bathe, or dine in company with one's parents, wife, or children. He was so beside himself with grief that suddenly fleeing the city by night and traversing Campania, he went to Syracuse and hurriedly returned from there without cutting his hair or shaving his beard. And he never afterwards took oath about matters of the highest moment, even before the assembly of the people or in the presence of the soldiers, except by the godhead of Drusilla. The rest of his sisters he did not love with so great affection, nor honour so highly, but often prostituted them to his favourites; so that he was the readier at the trial of Aemilius Lepidus to condemn them, as adulteresses and privy to the conspiracies against him; and he not only made public letters in the handwriting of all of them, procured by fraud and seduction, but also dedicated to Mars the Avenger, with an explanatory inscription, three swords designed to take his life.

XXV. It is not easy to decide whether he acted more basely in contracting his marriages, in annulling them, or as a husband. At the marriage of Livia Orestilla to Gaius Piso, he attended the ceremony himself, gave orders that the bride be taken to his own house, and within a few days divorced her; two years later he banished her, because of a suspicion that in the meantime she had gone back to her former husband. Others write that being invited to the wedding banquet, he sent word to Piso, who reclined opposite to him: "Don't take liberties with my wife," and at once carried her off with him from the table, the next day issuing a proclamation that he had got himself a wife in the manner of Romulus and Augustus. When the statement was made that the grandmother of Lollia Paulina, who was married to Gaius Memmius, an ex-consul commanding armies, had once been a remarkably beautiful woman, he suddenly called Lollia from the province, separated her from her husband, and married her; then in a short time he put her away, with the command never to have intercourse with anyone. Though Caesonia was neither beautiful nor young, and was already mother of three daughters by another, besides being a woman of reckless extravagance and wantonness, he loved her not only more passionately but more faithfully, often exhibiting her to the soldiers riding by his side, decked with cloak, helmet and shield, and to his friends even in a state of nudity. He did not honour her with the title of wife until she had borne him a child, announcing on the selfsame day that he had married her and that he was the father of her babe. This babe, whom he named Julia Drusilla, he carried to the temples of all the goddesses, finally placing her in the lap of Minerva and commending to her the child's nurture and training. And no evidence convinced him so positively that she was sprung from his own loins as her savage temper, which was even then so violent that she would try to scratch the faces and eyes of the little children who played with her.

XXVI. It would be trivial and pointless to add to this an account of his treatment of his relatives and friends, Ptolemy, son of king Juba, his cousin (for he was the grandson of Mark Antony by Antony's daughter Selene), and in particular Macro himself and even Ennia, who helped him to the throne; all these were rewarded for their kinship and their faithful services by a bloody death.

He was no whit more respectful or mild towards the senate, allowing some who had held the highest offices to run in their togas for several miles beside his chariot and to wait on him at table, standing napkin in hand[43] either at the head of his couch, or at his feet. Others he secretly put to death, yet continued to send for them as if they were alive, after a few days falsely asserting that they had committed suicide. When the consuls forgot to make proclamation of his birthday, he deposed them, and left the state for three days without its highest magistrates.[44] He flogged his quaestor, who was charged with conspiracy, stripping off the man's clothes and spreading them under the soldiers' feet, to give them a firm footing as they beat him.

He treated the other orders with like insolence and cruelty. Being disturbed by the noise made by those who came in the middle of the night to secure the free seats in the Circus, he drove them all out with cudgels; in the confusion more than twenty Roman knights were crushed to death, with as many matrons and a countless number of others. At the plays in the theatre, sowing discord between the commons and the knights, he scattered the gift tickets[45] ahead of time, to induce the rabble to take the seats reserved for the equestrian order. At a gladiatorial show he would sometimes draw back the awnings when the sun was hottest and give orders that no one be allowed to leave; then removing the usual equipment, he would match worthless and decrepit gladiators against mangy wild beasts, and have sham fights[46] between householders who were of good repute, but conspicuous for some bodily infirmity. Sometimes too he would shut up the granaries and condemn the people to hunger.

XXVII. The following are special instances of his innate brutality. When cattle to feed the wild beasts which he had provided for a gladiatorial show were rather costly, he selected criminals to be devoured, and reviewing the line of prisoners without examining the charges,[47] but merely taking his place in the middle of a colonnade, he bade them be led away "from baldhead to baldhead."[48] A man who had made a vow to fight in the arena,[49] if the emperor recovered, he compelled to keep his word, watched him as he fought sword in hand, and would not let him go until he was victorious, and then only after many entreaties. Another who had offered his life for the same reason, but delayed to kill himself, he turned over to his slaves, with orders to drive him through the streets decked with sacred boughs and fillets, calling for the fulfilment of his vow, and finally hurl him from the embankment. Many men of honourable rank were first disfigured with the marks of branding-irons and then condemned to the mines, to work at building roads, or to be thrown to the wild beasts; or else he shut them up in cages on all fours, like animals, or had them sawn asunder. Not all these punishments were for serious offences, but merely for criticising one of his shows, or for never having sworn by his Genius.[50] He forced parents to attend the executions of their sons, sending a litter for one man who pleaded ill health, and inviting another to dinner immediately after witnessing the death, and trying to rouse him to gaiety and jesting by a great show of affability. He had the manager of his gladiatorial shows and beast-baitings beaten with chains in his presence for several successive days, and would not kill him until he was disgusted at the stench of his putrefied brain. He burned a writer of Atellan farces alive in the middle of the arena of the amphitheatre, because of a humorous line of double meaning. When a Roman knight on being thrown to the wild beasts loudly protested his innocence, he took him out, cut off his tongue, and put him back again.

XXVIII. Having asked a man who had been recalled from an exile of long standing, how in the world he spent his time there, the man replied by way of flattery: "I constantly prayed the gods for what has come to pass, that Tiberius might die and you become emperor." Thereupon Caligula, thinking that his exiles were likewise praying for his death, sent emissaries from island to island to butcher them all. Wishing to have one of the senators torn to pieces, he induced some of the members to assail him suddenly, on his entrance into the House, with the charge of being a public enemy, to stab him with their styles, and turn him over to the rest to be mangled; and his cruelty was not sated until he saw the man's limbs, members, and bowels dragged through the streets and heaped up before him.

XXIX. He added to the enormity of his crimes by the brutality of his language. He used to say that there was nothing in his own character which he admired and approved more highly than what he called his *αδιατρεψὶα*,[51] that is to say, his shameless impudence. When his grandmother Antonia gave him some advice, he was not satisfied merely not to listen but replied: "Remember that I have the right to do anything to anybody." When he was on the point of killing his brother, and suspected that he had taken drugs as a precaution against poison, he cried: "What! an antidote against

Caesar?" After banishing his sisters, he made the threat that he not only had islands, but swords as well. An ex-praetor who had retired to Anticyra for his health, sent frequent requests for an extension of his leave, but Caligula had him put to death, adding that a man who had not been helped by so long a course of hellebore needed to be bled. On signing the list of prisoners who were to be put to death every ten days, he said that he was clearing his accounts. Having condemned several Gauls and Greeks to death in a body, he boasted that he had subdued Gallograecia.

XXX. He seldom had anyone put to death except by numerous slight wounds, his constant order, which soon became well-known, being: "Strike so that he may feel that he is dying." When a different man than he had intended had been killed, through a mistake in the names, he said that the victim too had deserved the same fate. He often uttered the familiar line of the tragic poet[52]:

"Let them hate me, so they but fear me."

He often inveighed against all the senators alike, as adherents of Sejanus and informers against his mother and brothers, producing the documents which he pretended to have burned,[53] and upholding the cruelty of Tiberius as forced upon him, since he could not but believe so many accusers. He constantly tongue-lashed the equestrian order as devotees of the stage and the arena. Angered at the rabble for applauding a faction which he opposed, he cried: "I wish the Roman people had but a single neck," and when the brigand Tetrinius was demanded,[54] he said that those who asked for him were Tetriniuses also. Once a band of five *retiarii*[55] in tunics, matched against the same number of *secutores*,[55] yielded without a struggle; but when their death was ordered, one of them caught up his trident and slew all the victors. Caligula bewailed this in a public proclamation as a most cruel murder, and expressed his horror of those who had had the heart to witness it.

XXXI. He even used openly to deplore the state of his times, because they had been marked by no public disasters, saying that the rule of Augustus had been made famous by the Varus massacre,[56] and that of Tiberius by the collapse of the amphitheatre at

Fidenae,[57] while his own was threatened with oblivion because of its prosperity; and every now and then he wished for the destruction of his armies, for famine, pestilence, fires, or a great earthquake.

XXXII. His acts and words were equally cruel, even when he was indulging in relaxation and given up to amusement and feasting. While he was lunching or revelling capital examinations by torture were often made in his presence, and a soldier who was an adept at decapitation cut off the heads of those who were brought from prison. At Puteoli, at the dedication of the bridge that he contrived,[58] as has been said, after inviting a number to come to him from the shore, on a sudden he had them all thrown overboard; and when some caught hold of the rudders of the ships, he pushed them off into the sea with boathooks and oars. At a public banquet in Rome he immediately handed a slave over to the executioners for stealing a strip of silver from the couches, with orders that his hands be cut off and hung from his neck upon his breast, and that he then be led about among the guests, preceded by a placard giving the reason for his punishment. When a *murmillo*[59] from the gladiatorial school fought with him with wooden swords and fell on purpose, he stabbed him with a real dagger and then ran about with a palm-branch, as victors do. Once when he stood by the altar dressed as a *popa*,[60] and a victim was brought up, he raised his mallet on high and slew the *cultrarius*. At one of his more sumptuous banquets he suddenly burst into a fit of laughter, and when the consuls, who were reclining next him, politely inquired at what he was laughing, he replied: "What do you suppose, except that at a single nod of mine both of you could have your throats cut on the spot?"

XXXIII. As a sample of his humour, he took his place beside a statue of Jupiter, and asked the tragic actor Apelles which of the two seemed to him the greater, and when he hesitated, Caligula had him flayed with whips, extolling his voice from time to time, when the wretch begged for mercy, as passing sweet even in his groans. Whenever he kissed the neck of his wife or sweetheart, he would say: "Off comes this beautiful head whenever I give the word." He even used to threaten now and then that he would resort to torture[61] if necessary, to find out from his dear Caesonia why he loved her so passionately.

XXXIV. He assailed mankind of almost every epoch with no less envy and malice than insolence and cruelty. He threw down the statues of famous men, which for lack of room Augustus had moved from the court of the Capitol to the Campus Martius, and so utterly demolished them that they could not be set up again with their inscriptions entire; and thereafter he forbade the erection of the statue of any living man anywhere, without his knowledge and consent. He even thought of destroying the poems of Homer, asking why he should not have the same privilege as Plato, who excluded Homer from his ideal commonwealth. More than that, he all but removed the writings and the busts of Vergil and of Titus Livius from all the libraries, railing at the former as a man of no talent and very little learning, and the latter as a verbose and careless historian. With regard to lawyers too, as if intending to do away with any practice of their profession, he often threatened that he would see to it, by Heaven, that they could give no advice contrary to his wish.

XXXV. He took from all the noblest of the city the ancient devices of their families, from Torquatus his collar, from Cincinnatus his lock of hair, from Gnaeus Pompeius the surname Great belonging to his ancient race. After inviting Ptolemy, whom I have mentioned before,[62] to come from his kingdom and receiving him with honour, he suddenly had him executed for no other reason than that when giving a gladiatorial show, he noticed that Ptolemy on entering the theatre attracted general attention by the splendour of his purple cloak. Whenever he ran across handsome men with fine heads of hair,[63] he disfigured them by having the backs of their heads shaved. There was a certain Aesius Proculus, son of a chief centurion, called Colosseros[64] because of his remarkable size and handsome appearance; this man Caligula ordered to be suddenly dragged from his seat in the amphitheatre and led into the arena, where he matched him first against a Thracian and then against a heavy-armed gladiator; when Proculus was victor in both contests, Caligula gave orders that he be bound at once, clad in rags, and then put to death, after first being led about the streets and exhibited to the women. In short, there was no one of such low condition or such abject fortune that he did not envy him such advantages as he possessed. Since the king of Nemi[65] had now held his priesthood for many years, he hired a stronger adversary to attack him. When an *essedarius*[66] called Porius was vigorously applauded on the day of one of the games for setting his slave free after a victory, Caligula rushed from the amphitheatre in such haste that he trod on the fringe of his toga and went headlong down the steps, fuming and shouting: "The people that rule the world give more honour to a gladiator for a trifling act than to their deified emperors or to the one still present with them."

XXXVI. He respected neither his own chastity nor that of anyone else. He is said to have had unnatural relations with Marcus Lepidus, the pantomimic actor Mnester, and certain hostages. Valerius Catullus, a young man of a consular family, publicly proclaimed that he had violated the emperor and worn himself out in commerce with him. To say nothing of his incest with his sisters and his notorious passion for the concubine Pyrallis, there was scarcely any woman of rank whom he did not approach. These as a rule he invited to dinner with their husbands, and as they passed by the foot of his couch, he would inspect them critically and deliberately, as if buying slaves, even putting out his hand and lifting up the face of anyone who looked down in modesty; then as often as the fancy took him he would leave the room, sending for the one who pleased him best, and returning soon afterward with evident signs of what had occurred, he would openly commend or criticise his partner, recounting her charms or defects and commenting on her conduct. To some he personally sent a bill of divorce in the name of their absent husbands, and had it entered in the public records.

XXXVII. In reckless extravagance he outdid the prodigals of all times in ingenuity, inventing a new sort of baths and unnatural varieties of food and feasts; for he would bathe in hot or cold perfumed oils, drink pearls of great price dissolved in vinegar, and set before his guests loaves and meats of gold, declaring that a man ought either to be frugal or Caesar. He even scattered large sums of money among the commons from the roof of the basilica Julia for several days in succession. He also built Liburnian galleys[67] with ten banks of oars, with sterns set with gems, particoloured sails, huge spacious baths, colonnades, and banquet-halls, and even a great variety of vines and fruit trees; that on board of them he might recline at table from an early hour, and coast along the shores of Campania amid songs and choruses. He built villas and country houses with utter disregard of expense, caring for nothing so much as to do what men said was impossible. So he built moles out into the deep and stormy sea, tunnelled rocks of hardest flint, built up plains to the height of mountains and razed mountains to the level of the plain; all with incredible dispatch, since the penalty for delay was death. To make a long story short, vast sums of money, including the 2,700,000,000 sesterces which Tiberius Caesar had amassed, were squandered by him in less than the revolution of a year.

XXXVIII. Having thus impoverished himself, from very need he turned his attention to pillage through a complicated and cunningly devised system of false accusations, auction sales, and imposts. He ruled that Roman citizenship could not lawfully be enjoyed by those whose forefathers had obtained it for themselves and their descendants, except in the case of sons, since "descendants" ought not to be understood as going beyond that degree; and when certificates of the deified Julius and Augustus were presented to him, he waved them aside as old and out of date. He also charged that those estates had been falsely returned, to which any addition had later been made from any cause whatever.[68] If any chief centurions since the beginning of Tiberius' reign had not named that emperor or himself among their heirs, he set aside their wills on the ground of ingratitude; also the testaments of all others, as null and void, if anyone said that they had intended to make Caesar their heir when they died. When he had roused such fear in this way that he came to be named openly as heir by strangers among their intimates and by parents among their children, he accused them of making game of him by continuing to live after such a declaration, and to many of them he sent poisoned dainties. He used further to conduct the trial of such cases in person, naming in advance the sum which he proposed to raise at each sitting, and not rising until it was made up. Impatient of the slightest delay, he once condemned in a single sentence more than forty who were accused on different counts, boasting to Caesonia, when she woke after a nap, of the great amount of business he had done while she was taking her siesta.

Appointing an auction, he put up and sold what was left from all the shows, personally soliciting bids and running them up so high, that some who were forced to buy articles at an enormous price and were thus stripped of their possessions, opened their veins. A well-known incident is that of Aponius Saturninus; he fell asleep on one of the benches, and as the auctioneer was warned by Gaius not to overlook the praetorian gentleman who kept nodding to him, the bidding was not stopped until thirteen gladiators were knocked down to the unconscious sleeper at nine million sesterces.

XXXIX. When he was in Gaul and had sold at immense figures the jewels, furniture, slaves, and even the freedmen of his sisters who had been condemned to death, finding the business so profitable, he sent to the city for all the paraphernalia of the old palace,[69] seizing for its transportation even public carriages and animals from the bakeries; with the result that bread was often scarce at Rome and many who had cases in court lost them from inability to appear and meet their bail. To get rid of this furniture, he resorted to every kind of trickery and wheedling, now railing at the bidders for avarice and because they were not ashamed to be richer than he, and now feigning regret for allowing common men to acquire the property of princes. Having learned that a rich provincial had paid those who issued the emperor's invitations two hundred thousand sesterces, to be smuggled in among the guests at one of his dinner-parties, he was not in the least displeased that the honour of dining with him was rated so high; but when next day the man appeared at his auction, he sent a messenger to hand him some trifle or other at the price of two hundred thousand sesterces and say that he should dine with Caesar on his personal invitation.

XL. He levied new and unheard of taxes, at first through the publicans and then, because their profit was so great, through the centurions and tribunes of the praetorian guard; and there was no class of commodities or men on which he did not impose some form of tariff. On all eatables sold in any part of the city he levied a fixed and definite charge; on lawsuits and legal processes begun anywhere, a fortieth part of the sum involved, providing a penalty in case anyone was found guilty of compromising or abandoning a suit; on the daily wages of porters, an eighth; on the earnings of prostitutes, as much as each received for one embrace; and a clause was added to this chapter of the law, providing that those who had ever been prostitutes or acted as panders should be liable to this public tax, and that even matrimony should not be exempt.

XLI. When taxes of this kind had been proclaimed, but not published in writing, inasmuch as many offences were committed through ignorance of the letter of the law, he at last, on the urgent demand of the people, had the law posted up, but in a very narrow place and in excessively small letters, to prevent the making of a copy. To leave no kind of plunder untried, he opened a brothel in his palace, setting apart a number of rooms and furnishing them to suit the grandeur of the place, where matrons and freeborn youths should stand exposed. Then he sent his pages[70] about the fora and basilicas, to invite young men and old to enjoy themselves, lending money on interest to those who came and having clerks openly take down their names, as contributors to Caesar's revenues. He did not even disdain to make money from play, and to increase his gains by falsehood and even by perjury. Having on one occasion given up his place to the player next him and gone into the courtyard, he spied two wealthy Roman knights passing by; he ordered them to be seized at once and their property confiscated and came back exultant, boasting that he had never played in better luck.

XLII. But when his daughter was born, complaining of his narrow means, and no longer merely of the burdens of a ruler but of those of a father as well, he took up contributions for the girl's maintenance and dowry. He also made proclamation that he would receive New Year's gifts,[71] and on the Kalends of January took his place in the entrance to the Palace, to clutch the coins which a throng of people of all classes showered on him by handfuls and lapfuls.[72] Finally, seized with a mania for feeling the touch of money, he would often pour out huge piles of goldpieces in some open place, walk over them barefooted, and wallow in them for a long time with his whole body.

XLIII. He had but one experience with military affairs or war, and then on a sudden impulse; for having gone to Mevania to visit the river Clitumnus[73] and its grove, he was reminded of the necessity of recruiting his body-guard of Batavians and was seized with the idea of an expedition to Germany. So without delay he assembled legions and auxiliaries from all quarters, holding levies everywhere with the utmost strictness, and collecting provisions of every kind on an unheard of scale. Then he began his march and made it now so hurriedly and rapidly, that the praetorian cohorts were forced, contrary to all precedent, to lay their standards on the pack-animals and thus to follow him; again he was so lazy and luxurious that he was carried in a litter by eight bearers, requiring the inhabitants of the towns through which he passed to sweep the roads for him and sprinkle them to lay the dust.

XLIV. On reaching his camp, to show his vigilance and strictness as a commander, he dismissed in disgrace the generals who were late in bringing in the auxiliaries from various places, and in reviewing his troops he deprived many of the chief centurions who were well on in years of their rank, in some cases only a few days before they would have served their time, giving as a reason their age and infirmity; then railing at the rest for their avarice, he reduced the rewards given on completion of full military service to six thousand sesterces.[74]

All that he accomplished was to receive the surrender of Adminius, son of Cynobellinus king of the Britons, who had been banished by his father and had deserted to the Romans with a small force; yet as if the entire island had submitted to him, he sent a grandiloquent letter to Rome, commanding the couriers who carried it to ride in their post-chaise[75] all the way to the Forum and the House, and not to deliver it to anyone except the consuls, in the temple of Mars the Avenger,[76] before a full meeting of the senate.

XLV. Presently, finding no one to fight with, he had a few Germans of his body-guard taken across the river and concealed there, and word brought him after luncheon with great bustle and confusion that the enemy were close at hand. Upon this he rushed out with his friends and a part of the praetorian cavalry to the woods close by, and after cutting the branches from some trees and adorning them like trophies, he returned by torchlight, taunting those who had not followed him as timorous and cowardly, and presenting his companions and the partners in his victory with crowns of a new kind and of a new name, ornamented with figures of the sun, moon and stars, and called *exploratoriae*.[77] Another time some hostages were taken from a common school and secretly sent on ahead of him, when he suddenly left a banquet and pursued them with the cavalry as if they were runaways, caught them, and brought them back in fetters, in this farce too showing immoderate extravagance. On coming back to the table, when some announced that the army was assembled, he urged them to take their places just as they were, in their coats of mail. He also admonished them in the familiar line of Vergil to "bear up and save themselves for better days."[78]

Meanwhile he rebuked the absent senate and people in a stern edict because "while Caesar was fighting and exposed to such dangers they were indulging in revels and frequenting the theatres and their pleasant villas."

XLVI. Finally, as if he intended to bring the war to an end, he drew up a line of battle on the shore of the Ocean, arranging his ballistas[79] and other artillery; and when no one knew or could imagine what he was going to do, he suddenly bade them gather shells and fill their helmets and the folds of their gowns, calling them "spoils from the Ocean, due to the Capitol and Palatine." As a monument of his victory he erected a lofty tower, from which lights were to shine at night to guide the course of ships, as from the Pharos.[80] Then promising the soldiers a gratuity of a hundred denarii each, as if he had shown unprecedented liberality, he said, "Go your way happy; go your way rich."

XLVII. Then turning his attention to his triumph, in addition to a few captives and deserters from the barbarians he chose all the tallest of the Gauls, and as he expressed it, those who were "worthy of a triumph," as well as some of the chiefs. These he reserved for his parade, compelling them not only to dye their hair red and to let it grow long, but also to learn the language of the Germans and assume barbarian names. He also had the triremes in which he had entered the Ocean carried overland to Rome for the greater part of the way. He wrote besides to his financial agents to prepare for a triumph at the smallest possible cost,[81] but on a grander scale than had ever before been known, since the goods of all were at their disposal.

XLVIII. Before leaving the province he formed a design of unspeakable cruelty, that of butchering the legions that had begun the mutiny years before just after the death of Augustus,[82] because they had beleagured his father Germanicus, their leader, and himself, at the time an infant; and though he was with difficulty turned from this mad purpose, he could by no means be prevented from persisting in his desire to decimate[83] them. Accordingly he summoned them to an assembly without their arms, not even wearing their swords, and surrounded them with armed horsemen. But seeing that some of the legionaries, suspecting his purpose, were stealing off to resume their arms, in case any violence should be offered them, he fled from the assembly and set out for the city in a hurry, turning all his ferocity upon the senate, against which he uttered open threats, in order to divert the gossip about his own dishonour. He complained among other things that he had been cheated of his fairly earned triumph; whereas a short time before he had himself given orders that on pain of death no action should be taken about his honours.

XLIX. Therefore when he was met on the road by envoys from that distinguished body, begging him to hasten his return, he roared, "I will come, and this will be with me," frequently smiting the hilt of the sword which he wore at his side. He also made proclamation that he was returning, but only to those who desired his presence, the equestrian order and the people, for to the senate he would never more be fellow-citizen nor prince. He even forbade anyone of the senators to meet him. Then giving up or postponing his triumph, he entered the city on his birthday in an ovation;[84] and within four months he perished, having dared great crimes and meditating still greater ones. For he had made up his mind to move to Antium, and later to Alexandria, after first slaying the noblest members of the two orders. That no one may doubt this, let me say that among his private papers two notebooks were found with different titles, one called "The Sword" and the other "The Dagger," and both containing the names and marks of identification of those whom he had doomed to death. There was found besides a great chest full of divers kinds of poisons, which they say were later thrown into the sea by Claudius and so infected it as to kill the fish, which were thrown up by the tide upon the neighbouring shores.

L. He was very tall and extremely pale, with a huge body, but very thin neck and legs.[85] His eyes and temples were hollow, his forehead broad and grim, his hair thin and entirely gone on the top of his head, though his body was hairy. Because of this to look upon him from a higher place as he passed by, or for any reason whatever to mention a goat, was treated as a capital offence. While his face was naturally forbidding and ugly, he purposely made it even more savage, practising all kinds of terrible and fearsome expressions before a mirror.

He was sound neither of body nor mind. As a boy he was troubled with the falling sickness,[86] and while in his youth he had some endurance, yet at times because of sudden faintness he was hardly able to walk, to stand up, to collect his thoughts, or to hold up his head. He himself realised his mental infirmity, and thought at times of going into retirement and clearing his brain. It is thought that his wife Caesonia gave him a drug intended for a love potion, which however had the effect of driving him mad. He was especially tormented with sleeplessness; for he never rested more than three hours at night, and even for that length of time he did not sleep quietly, but was terrified by strange apparitions, once for example dreaming that the spirit of the Ocean talked with him. Therefore weary of lying in bed wide awake during the greater part of the night, he would now sit upon his couch, and now wander through the long colonnades, crying out from time to time for daylight and longing for its coming.

LI. I think I may fairly attribute to mental weakness the existence of two exactly opposite faults in the same person, extreme assurance and, on the other hand, excessive timorousness. For this man, who so utterly despised the gods, was wont at the slightest thunder and lightning to shut his eyes, to muffle up his head, and if they increased, to leap from his bed and hide under it. In his journey through Sicily, though he made all manner of fun of the miracles in various places, he suddenly fled from Messana by night, panic-stricken by the smoke and roaring from Aetna's crater. Full of threats as he was also against the barbarians, when he was riding in a chariot through a narrow defile on the far side of the Rhine, and someone said that there would be no slight panic if the enemy should appear anywhere, he immediately mounted a horse and hastily returned to the bridges. Finding them crowded with camp servants and baggage, in his impatience of any delay he was passed along from hand to hand over the men's heads. Soon after, hearing of an uprising in Germany, he made preparations to flee from the city and equipped fleets for the purpose, finding comfort only in the thought that the provinces across the sea would at any rate be left him, in case the enemy should be victorious and take possession of the summits of the Alps, as the Cimbri, or even of the city, as the Senones had once done. And it was this, I think, that later inspired his assassins with the idea of pretending to the riotous soldiers[87] that he had laid hands on himself in terror at the report of a defeat.

LII. In his clothing, his shoes, and the vest of his attire he did not follow the usage of his country and his fellow-citizens; not always even that of his sex; or in fact, that of an ordinary mortal. He often appeared in public in embroidered cloaks covered with precious stones, with a long-sleeved tunic and bracelets; sometimes in silk[88] and in a woman's robe[89]; now in slippers or buskins, again in boots, such as the emperor's body-guard wear, and at times in the low slices which are used by females. But oftentimes he exhibited himself with a golden beard, holding in his hand a thunderbolt, a trident, or a caduceus, emblems of the gods, and even in the garb of Venus. He frequently wore the dress of a triumphing general, even before his campaign, and sometimes the breastplate of Alexander the Great, which he had taken from his sarcophagus.[90]

LIII. As regards liberal studies, he gave little attention to literature but a great deal to oratory, and he was as ready of speech and eloquent as you please, especially if he had occasion to make a charge against anyone. For when he was angry, he had an abundant flow of words and thoughts, and his voice and delivery were such that for very excitement he could not stand still and he was clearly heard by those at a distance. When about to begin an harangue, he threatened to draw the sword of his nightly labours, and he had such scorn of a polished and elegant style that he used to say that Seneca, who was very popular just then, composed "mere school exercises," and that he was "sand without lime." He had the habit too of writing replies to the successful pleas of orators and composing accusations and defences of important personages who were brought to trial before the senate; and according as his pen had run most easily, he brought ruin or relief to each of them by his speech,[91] while he would also invite the equestrian order by proclamation to come in and hear him.

LIV. Moreover he devoted himself with much enthusiasm to arts of other kinds and of great variety, appearing as a Thracian gladiator, as a charioteer, and even as a singer and dancer, fighting with the weapons of actual warfare,[92] and driving in circuses built in various places; so carried away by his interest in singing and dancing that even at the public performances he could not refrain from singing with the tragic actor as he delivered his lines, or from openly imitating his gestures by way of praise or correction. Indeed, on the day when he was slain he seems to have ordered an all-night vigil[93] for the sole purpose of taking advantage of the licence of the occasion to make his first appearance on the stage. Sometimes he danced even at night, and once he summoned three consulars to the Palace at the close of the second watch,[94] and when they arrived in great and deathly fear, he seated them on a stage and then on a sudden burst out with a great din of flutes and clogs,[95] dressed in a cloak and a tunic reaching to his heels, and after dancing a number went off again. And yet varied as were his accomplishments, the man could not swim.

LV. Toward those to whom he was devoted his partiality became madness. He used to kiss Mnester, an actor of pantomimes, even in the theatre, and if anyone made even the slightest sound while his favourite was dancing, he had him dragged from his seat and scourged him with his own hand. When a Roman knight created a disturbance, he sent a centurion to bid him go without delay to Ostia and carry a message for him to king Ptolemy in Mauretania; and its purport was this: "Do neither good nor ill to the man whom I have sent you." He gave some Thracian gladiators command of his German body-guard. He reduced the amount of armour of the *murmillones*.[96] When one Columbus had won a victory, but had suffered a slight wound, he had the place rubbed with a poison which he henceforth called "Columbinum"; at least that name was found included in his list of poisons. He was so passionately devoted to the green faction[97] that he constantly dined and spent the night in their stable,[98] and in one of his revels with them he gave the driver Eutychus two million sesterces in gifts.[99]

He used to send his soldiers on the day before the games and order silence in the neighbourhood, to prevent the horse Incitatus[100] from being disturbed. Besides a stall of marble, a manger of ivory, purple blankets and a collar of precious stones, he even gave this horse a house, a troop of slaves and furniture, for the more elegant entertainment of the guests invited in his name; and it is also said that he planned to make him consul.

LVI. During this frantic and riotous career several thought of attempting his life. But when one or two conspiracies had been detected and the rest were waiting for a favourable opportunity, two men made common cause and succeeded, with the connivance of his most influential freedmen and the officers of the praetorian guard; for although the charge that these last were privy to one of the former conspiracies was false, they realised that Caligula hated and feared them. In fact, he exposed them to great odium by at once taking them aside and declaring, drawn sword in hand, that he would kill himself, if they too thought he deserved death; and from that time on he never ceased accusing them one to the other and setting them all at odds.

When they had decided to attempt his life at the exhibition of the Palatine games, as he went out at noon, Cassius Chaerea, tribune of a cohort of the praetorian guard, claimed for himself the principal part; for Gaius used to taunt him, a man already well on in years, with voluptuousness and effeminacy by every form of insult. When he asked for the watchword Gaius would give him "Priapus" or "Venus," and when Chaerea had occasion to thank him for anything, he would hold out his hand to kiss, forming and moving it in an obscene fashion.[101]

LVII. His approaching murder was foretold by many prodigies. The statue of Jupiter at Olympia, which he had ordered to be taken to pieces and moved to Rome, suddenly uttered such a peal of laughter that the scaffoldings collapsed and the workmen took to their heels; and at once a man called Cassius turned up, who declared that he had been bidden in a dream to sacrifice a bull to Jupiter. The Capitol at Capua was struck by lightning on the Ides of March, and also the room of the doorkeeper of the Palace at Rome. Some inferred from the latter omen that danger was threatened to the owner at the hands of his guards; and from the former, the murder of a second distinguished personage, such as had taken place long before on that same day.[102] The soothsayer Sulla too, when Gaius consulted him about his horoscope, declared that inevitable death was close at hand. The lots of Fortune at Antium warned him to beware of Cassius, and he accordingly ordered the death of Cassius Longinus, who was at the time proconsul of Asia, forgetting that the family name of Chacrea was Cassius. The day before he was killed he dreamt that he stood in heaven beside the throne of Jupiter and that the god struck him with the toe of his right foot and hurled him to earth. Some things which had happened on that very day shortly before he was killed were also regarded as portents. As he was sacrificing, he was sprinkled with the blood of a flamingo,[103] and the pantomimic actor Mnester danced a tragedy[104] which the tragedian Neoptolemus had acted years before during the games at which Philip king of the Macedonians was assassinated. In a farce called "Laureolus,"[105] in which the chief actor falls as he is making his escape and vomits blood, several understudies[106] so vied with one another in giving evidence of their proficiency that the stage swam in blood. A nocturnal performance besides was rehearsing, in which scenes from the lower world were represented by Egyptians and Aethiopians. Mar. 15.

LVIII. On the ninth day before the Kalends of February at about the seventh hour he hesitated whether or not to get up for luncheon, since his stomach was still disordered from excess of food on the day before, but at length he came out at the persuasion of his friends. In the covered passage through which he had to pass, some boys of good birth, who had been summoned from Asia to appear on the stage, were rehearsing their parts, and he stopped to watch and encourage them; and had not the leader of the troop complained that he had a chill, he would have returned and had the performance given at once. From this point there are two versions of the story: some say that as he was Jan. 24, 41 A.D.

talking with the boys, Chaerea came up behind, and gave him a deep cut in the neck, having first cried, "Take that," and that then the tribune Cornelius Sabinus, who was the other conspirator and faced Gaius, stabbed him in the breast. Others say that Sabinus, after getting rid of the crowd through centurions who were in the plot, asked for the watchword, as soldiers do, and that when Gaius gave him "Jupiter," he cried "So be it,"[108] and as Gaius looked around, he split his jawbone with a blow of his sword. As he lay upon the ground and with writhing limbs called out that he still lived, the others dispatched him with thirty wounds; for the general signal was "Strike again." Some even thrust their swords through his privates. At the beginning of the disturbance his bearers ran to his aid with their poles,[109] and presently the Germans of his body-guard, and they slew several of his assassins, as well as some inoffensive senators.

LIX. He lived twenty-nine years and ruled three years, ten months and eight days. His body was conveyed secretly to the gardens of the Lamian family, where it was partly consumed on a hastily erected pyre and buried beneath a light covering of turf; later his sisters on their return from exile dug it up, cremated it, and consigned it to the tomb. Before this was done, it is well known that the caretakers of the gardens were disturbed by ghosts, and that in the house where he was slain not a night passed without some fearsome apparition, until at last the house itself was destroyed by fire. With him died his wife Caesonia, stabbed with a sword by a centurion, while his daughter's brains were dashed out against a wall.

LX. One may form an idea of the state of those times by what followed. Not even after the murder was made known was it at once believed that he was dead, but it was suspected that Gaius himself had made up and circulated the report, to find out by that means how men felt towards him. The conspirators too had not agreed on a successor, and the senate was so unanimously in favour of re-establishing the republic that the consuls called the first meeting, not in the senate house, because it had the name

Julia, but in the Capitol; while some in expressing their views proposed that the memory of the Caesars be done away with and their temples destroyed. Men further observed and commented on the fact that all the Caesars whose forename was Gaius perished by the sword, beginning with the one who was slain in the times of Cinna.[110]

STEMMA OF THE JULIO-CLAUDIAN FAMILY

A

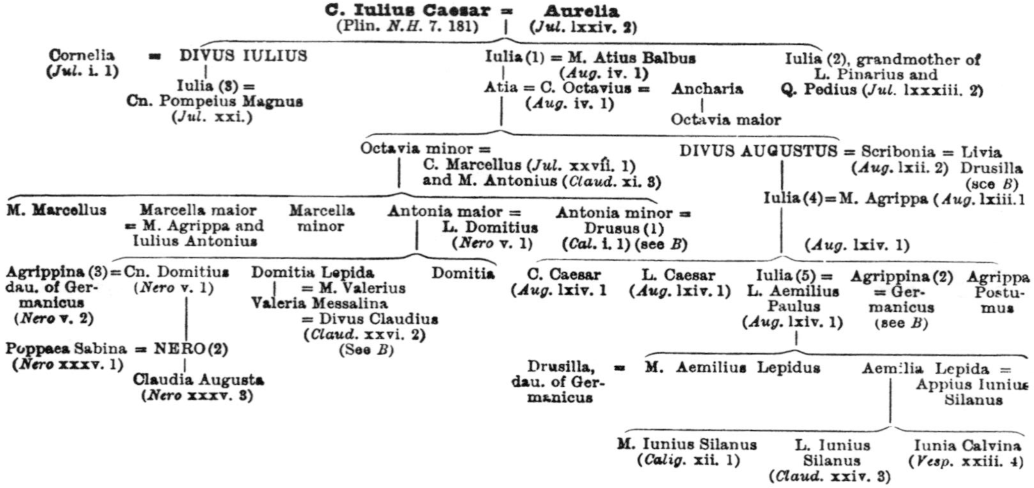

B

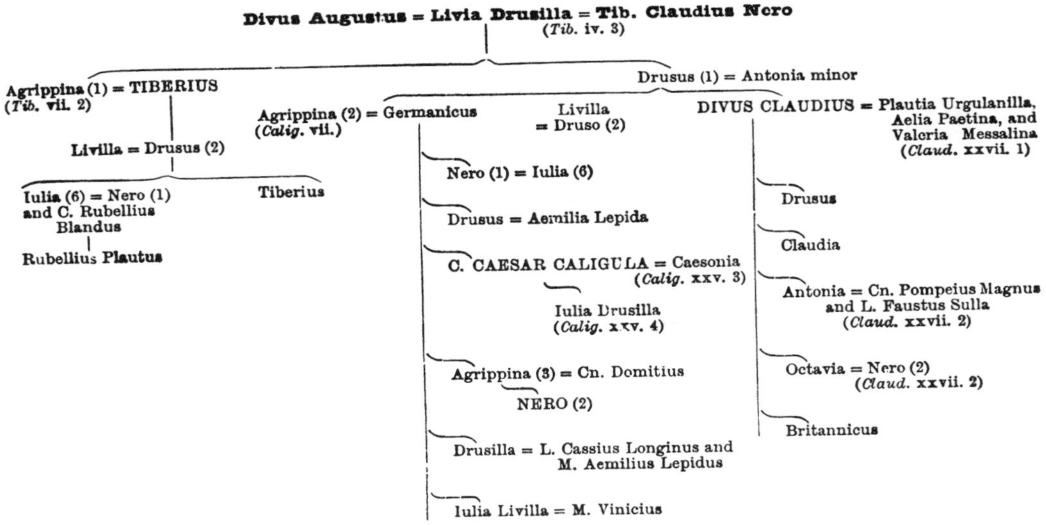

Divus Augustus = Livia Drusilla = Tib. Claudius Nero
(Tib. iv. 3)
Agrippina (1) = TIBERIUS
(Tib. vii. 2)
Livilla = Drusus (2)
Iulia (6) = Nero (1) and C. Rubellius Blandus
Rubellius Plautus
Tiberius
Drusus (1) = Antonia minor
Agrippina (2) = Germanicus
(Calig. vii.)
Livilla = Druso (2)
Nero (1) = Iulia (6)
Drusus = Aemilia Lepida
C. CAESAR CALIGULA = Caesonia
(Calig. xxv. 3)
Iulia Drusilla
(Calig. xxv. 4)
Agrippina (3) = Cn. Domitius
NERO (2)
Drusilla = L. Cassius Longinus and M. Aemilius Lepidus
Iulia Livilla = M. Vinicius
DIVUS CLAUDIUS = Plautia Urgulanilla, Aelia Paetina, and Valeria Messalina
(Claud. xxvii. 1)
Drusus
Claudia
Antonia = Cn. Pompeius Magnus and L. Faustus Sulla
(Claud. xxvii. 2)
Octavia = Nero (2)
(Claud. xxvii. 2)
Britannicus

BOOK V

THE DEIFIED CLAUDIUS

I. The father of Claudius Caesar, Drusus, who at first had the forename Decimus and later that of Nero, was born of Livia within three months after her marriage to Augustus[1] (for she was with child at the time) and there was a suspicion that he was begotten by his stepfather in adulterous intercourse. Certain it is that this verse at once became current: 38 B.C.

"In three months' time come children to the great."[2]

This Drusus, while holding the offices of quaestor and praetor, was in charge of the war in Raetia and later of that in Germany. He was the first of Roman generals to sail the northern Ocean, and beyond the Rhine with prodigious labour he constructed the huge canals which to this very day are called by his name.[3] Even after he had defeated the enemy in many battles and driven them far into the wilds of the interior, he did not cease his pursuit until the apparition of a barbarian woman of greater than human size, speaking in the Latin tongue, forbade him to push his victory further. For these exploits he received the honour of an ovation[4] with the triumphal regalia; and immediately after his praetorship he became consul and resumed his campaign, but died in his summer camp, which for that reason was given the name of "Accursed." The body was carried by the leading men of the free

15 B.C.
12-11 B.C.
9 B.C.

towns and colonies to Rome,[5] where it was met and received by the decuries of scribes,[6] and buried in the campus Martius. But the army reared a monument in his honour, about which the soldiers should make a ceremonial run[7] each year thereafter on a stated day, which the cities of Gaul were to observe with prayers and sacrifices. The senate, in addition to many other honours, voted him a marble arch adorned with trophies on the Appian Way, and the surname Germanicus for himself and his descendants. It is the general belief that he was as eager for glory as he was democratic[8] by nature; for in addition to victories over the enemy he greatly desired to win the "noble trophies,"[9] often pursuing the leaders of the Germans all over the field at great personal risk; and he made no secret of his intention of restoring the old-time form of government, whenever he should have the power. It is because of this, I think, that some have made bold to write that he was an object of suspicion to Augustus; that the emperor recalled him from his province, and when he did not obey at once, took him off by poison. This I have mentioned, rather not to pass it by, than that I think it true or even probable; for as a matter of fact Augustus loved him so dearly while he lived that he always named him joint-heir along with his sons, as he once declared in the senate; and when he was dead, he eulogized him warmly before the people, praying the gods to make his Caesars[10] like Drusus, and to grant him, when his time came, as glorious a death as they had given that hero. And not content with carving a laudatory inscription on his tomb in verses of his own composition, Augustus also wrote a memoir of his life in prose.

Drusus had several children by the younger Antonia, but was survived by only three, Germanicus, Livilla, and Claudius.

Aug, 1, 10 B.C. II. Claudius was born at Lugdunum on the Kalends of August in the consulship of Iullus Antonius and Fabius Africanus, the very day when an altar was first dedicated to Augustus in that town,[11] and he received the name of Tiberius Claudius Drusus. Later, on the adoption of his elder brother into the Julian family, he took the surname Germanicus. He lost his father when he was still an infant, and throughout almost the whole course of his childhood and youth he suffered so severely from various obstinate disorders that the vigour of both his mind and his body was dulled, and even when he reached the proper age he was not thought capable of any public or private business. For a long time, even after he reached the age of independence,[12] he was in a state of pupillage and under a guardian, of whom he himself makes complaint in a book of his, saying that he was a barbarian and a former chief of muleteers, put in charge of him for the express purpose of punishing him with all possible severity for any cause whatever. It was also because of his weak health that contrary to all precedent he wore a cloak when he presided at the gladiatorial games which he and his brother gave in honour of their father; and on the day when he assumed the gown of manhood he was taken in a litter to the Capitol about midnight without the usual escort.[13]

III. Yet he gave no slight attention to liberal studies from his earliest youth, and even published frequent specimens of his attainments in each line. But even so he could not attain any public position or inspire more favourable hopes of his future.

His mother Antonia often called him "a monster of a man, not finished but merely begun by Dame Nature"; and if she accused anyone of dulness, she used to say that he was "a bigger fool than her son Claudius." His grandmother Augusta always treated him with the utmost contempt, very rarely speaking to him; and when she admonished him, she did so in short, harsh letters, or through messengers. When his sister Livilla heard that he would one day be emperor, she openly and loudly prayed that the Roman people might be spared so cruel and undeserved a fortune. Finally to make it clearer what opinions, favourable and otherwise, his great uncle Augustus had of him, I have appended extracts from his own letters:

IV. "I have talked with Tiberius,[14] my dear Livia, as you requested, with regard to what is to be done with your grandson Tiberius[15] at the games of Mars.[16] Now we are both agreed that we must decide once for all what plan we are to adopt in his case. For if he be sound[17] and so to say complete,[17] what reason have we for doubting that he ought to be advanced through the same grades and steps through which his brother has been advanced? But if we realize that he is wanting and defective in soundness of body and mind, we must not furnish the means of ridiculing both him and us to a public which is wont to scoff at and deride such things. Surely we shall always be in a stew, if we deliberate about each separate occasion and do not make up our minds in advance whether we think he can hold public offices or not. However, as to the matters about which you ask my present advice, I do not object to his having charge of the banquet of the priests at the games of Mars, if he will allow himself to be advised by his kinsman the son of Silvanus, so as not to do anything to make himself conspicuous or ridiculous. That he should view the games in the Circus from the Imperial box[18] does not meet with my approval; for he will be conspicuous if exposed to full view in the front of the auditorium. I am opposed to his going to the Alban Mount or being in Rome on the days of the Latin festival; for why should he not be made prefect of the city, if he is able to attend his brother to the Mount? You have my views, my dear Livia, to wit that I desire that something be decided once for all about the whole matter, to save us from constantly wavering between hope and fear. Moreover, you may, if you wish, give this part of my letter to our kinswoman Antonia also to read." Again in another letter:

"I certainly shall invite the young Tiberius to dinner every day during your absence, to keep him from dining alone with his friends Sulpicius and Athenodorus. I do wish that he would choose more carefully and in a less scatter-brained fashion someone to imitate in his movements, bearing, and gait. The poor fellow is unlucky; for in important matters, where his mind does not wander, the nobility of his character is apparent enough." Also in a third letter:

"Confound me, dear Livia, if I am not surprised that your grandson Tiberius could please me with his declaiming. How in the world anyone who is so unclear in his conversation can speak with clearness and propriety when he declaims, is more than I can see."

There is no doubt at all what Augustus later decided, and that he left him invested with no office other than the augural priesthood, not even naming him as one of his heirs, save in the third degree[19] and to a sixth part of his estate, among those who were all but strangers; while the legacy that he left him was not more than eight hundred thousand sesterces.

V. His paternal uncle Tiberius gave him the consular regalia, when he asked for office; but when he urgently requested the actual position, Tiberius merely replied by a note in these words: "I have sent you forty gold-pieces for the Saturnalia and the Sigillaria."[20] Then at last Claudius abandoned all hope of advancement and gave himself up to idleness, living in obscurity now in his house and gardens in the suburbs, and sometimes at a villa in Campania; moreover from his intimacy with the lowest of men he incurred the reproach of drunkenness and gambling, in addition to his former reputation for dulness. Yet all this time, despite his conduct, he never lacked attention from individuals or respect from the public.

VI. The equestrian order twice chose him as their patron, to head a deputation on their behalf: once when they asked from the consuls the privilege of carrying the body of Augustus to Rome on their shoulders, and again when they offered them their congratulations on the downfall of Sejanus. They even used to rise when he appeared at the public shows and put off their cloaks. The senate too voted that he be made a special member of the priests of Augustus,[21] who were usually chosen by lot; when he later lost his house by fire, that it should be rebuilt at the public expense, and that he should have the honour of giving his opinion among the consulars. This second decree was however repealed, since Tiberius urged Claudius's infirmity as a reason, and promised that he would make the loss[22] good through his own generosity. Yet when Tiberius died, he named Claudius only among his heirs in the third degree, to a third part of his estate, although he gave him in addition a legacy of about two million sesterces, and expressly commended him besides to the armies and to the senate and people of Rome with the rest of his kinsfolk.

VII. It was only under his nephew Gaius, who in the early part of his reign tried to gain popularity by every device, that he at last began his official career, holding the consulship as his colleague for two months; and it chanced that as he entered the Forum for the first time with the fasces, an eagle that was flying by lit upon his shoulder. He was also allotted a second consulship, to be held four years later,[23] and several times he presided at the shows in place of Gaius, and was greeted by the people now with "Success to the emperor's uncle!" and now with "All hail to the brother of Germanicus!"

VIII. But all this did not save him from constant insults; for if he came to dinner a little after the appointed time, he took his place with difficulty and only after making the round of the dining-room. Whenever he went to sleep after dinner, which was a habit of his, he was pelted with the stones of olives and dates, and sometimes he was awakened by the jesters with a whip or cane, in pretended sport. They used also to put slippers on his hands as he lay snoring, so that when he was suddenly aroused he might rub his face with them.

IX. But he was exposed also to actual dangers. First in his very consulship, when he was all but deposed, because he had been somewhat slow in contracting for and setting up the statues of Nero and Drusus, the emperor's brothers. Afterwards he was continually harassed by all kinds of accusations, brought against him by strangers or even by the members of his household. Finally, when the conspiracy of Lepidus and Gaetulicus[24] was detected and he was sent to Germany as one of the envoys to congratulate the emperor, he was really in peril of his life, since Gaius raged and fumed because his uncle of all men had been sent to him, as if to a child in need of a guardian. So great, indeed, was his wrath that some have written that Claudius was even thrown into the river[25] clothes and all, just as he had come. Moreover, from that time on he always gave his opinion in the senate last among the consulars, having the question put to him after all the rest by way of humiliation. A case involving the forgery of a will was even admitted, in which Claudius himself was one of the signers. At last he was forced to pay eight million sesterces to enter a new priesthood,[26] which reduced him to such straitened circumstances that he was unable to meet the obligation incurred to the treasury[27]; whereupon by edict of the prefects[28] his property was advertised for sale to meet the deficiency,[29] in accordance with the law regulating confiscations.

X. Having spent the greater part of his life under these and like circumstances, he became emperor in his fiftieth year by a remarkable freak of fortune. When the assassins of Gaius shut out the crowd under pretence that the emperor wished to be alone, Claudius was ousted with the rest and withdrew to an apartment called the Hermaeum; and a little later, in great terror at the news of the murder, he stole away to a balcony hard by and hid among the curtains which hung before the door. As he cowered there, a common soldier, who was prowling about at random, saw his feet, and intending to ask who he was, pulled him out and recognized him; and when Claudius fell at his feet in terror, he hailed him as emperor. Then he took him to the rest of his comrades, who were as yet in a condition of uncertainty and purposeless rage. These placed him in a litter, took turns in carrying it, since his own bearers had made off, and bore him to the Camp in a state of despair and terror, while the throng that met him pitied him, as an innocent man who was being hurried off to execution. Received within the rampart, he spent the night among the sentries with much less hope than confidence;[30] for the consuls with the senate and the city cohorts had taken possession of the Forum and the Capitol, resolved on maintaining the public liberty.[31] When he too was summoned to the House by the tribunes of the commons, to give his advice on the situation, he sent word that "he was detained by force and compulsion." But the next day, since the senate was dilatory in putting through its plans because of the tiresome bickering of those who held divergent views, while the populace, who stood about the hall, called for one ruler and expressly named Claudius, he allowed the armed assembly of the soldiers to swear allegiance to him, and promised each man fifteen thousand sesterces; being the first of the Caesars who resorted to bribery to secure the fidelity of the troops.

41 A.D.

XI. As soon as his power was firmly established, he considered it of foremost importance to obliterate the memory of the two days when men had thought of changing the form of government. Accordingly he made a decree that all that had been done and said during that period should be pardoned and forever forgotten; he kept his word too, save only that a few of the tribunes and centurions who had conspired against Gaius were put to death, both to make an example of them and because he knew that they had also demanded his own death. Then turning to the duties of family loyalty, he adopted as his most sacred and frequent oath "By Augustus." He had divine honours voted his grandmother Livia and a chariot drawn by elephants in the procession at the Circus,[32] like that of Augustus; also public offerings to the shades of his parents and in addition annual games in the Circus on his father's birthday and for his mother a carriage to bear her image through the Circus and the surname of Augusta, which she had declined during her lifetime. In memory of his brother,[33] whom he took every opportunity of honouring, he brought out a Greek comedy in the contest at Naples[34] and awarded it the crown in accordance with the decision of the judges. He did not leave even Mark Antony unhonoured or without grateful mention, declaring once in a proclamation that he requested the more earnestly that the birthday of his father Drusus be celebrated because it was the same as that of his grandfather Antony. He completed the marble arch to Tiberius near Pompey's theatre, which had been voted some time before by the senate, but left unfinished. Even in the case of Gaius, while he annulled all his acts, yet he would not allow the day of his death to be added to the festivals, although it was also the beginning of his own reign.

XII. But in adding to his own dignity he was modest and unassuming, refraining from taking the forename Imperator,[35] refusing excessive honours, and passing over the betrothal of his daughter and the birthday of a grandson in silence and with merely private ceremonies. He recalled no one from exile except with the approval of the senate. He obtained from the members as a favour the privilege of bringing into the House with him the prefect of the praetorian guard and the tribunes of the soldiers, and the ratification of the judicial acts of his agents in the provinces. He asked the consuls for permission to hold fairs on his private estates. He often appeared as one of the advisers at cases tried before the magistrates; and when they gave games, he also arose with the rest of the audience and showed his respect by acclamations and applause. When the tribunes of the commons appeared before him as he sat upon the tribunal, he apologised to them because for lack of room he could not hear them unless they stood up.

By such conduct he won so much love and devotion in a short time, that when it was reported that he had been waylaid and killed on a journey to Ostia, the people were horror stricken and with dreadful execrations continued to assail the soldiers as traitors, and the senate as murderers, until finally one or two men, and later several, were brought forward upon the rostra by the magistrates and assured the people that Claudius was safe and on his way to the city.

XIII. Yet he did not remain throughout without experience of treachery, but he was attacked by individuals, by a conspiracy, and finally by a civil war. A man of the commons was caught near his bed-chamber in the middle of the night, dagger in hand; and two members of the equestrian order were found lying in wait for him in public places, one ready to attack him with a sword-cane as he came out of the theatre, the other with a hunting knife as he was sacrificing in the temple of Mars. Asinius Gallus and Statilius Corvinus, grandsons of the orators Pollio and Messala, conspired to overthrow him, aided by a number of his own freedmen and slaves. The civil war was set on foot by Furius Camillus Scribonianus, governor of Dalmatia; but his rebellion was put down within five days, since the legions which had changed their allegiance were turned from their purpose by superstitious fear; for when the order was given to march to their new commander, by some providential chance the eagles could not be adorned[36] nor the standards pulled up and moved.[37]

42, 43, 47, 51 A.D. XIV. He held four consulships in addition to his original one. Of these the first two were in successive years, while the other two followed at intervals of four years each, the last for six months, the others for two; and in his third he was substituted for one of the consuls who had died, a thing which was without precedent in the case of an emperor. He administered justice most conscientiously both as consul and when out of office, even on his own anniversaries and those of his family, and sometimes even on festivals of ancient date and days of ill-omen. He did not always follow the letter of the laws, but modified their severity or lenity in many cases according to his own notions of equity and justice; for he allowed a new trial to those who had lost their cases before private judges by demanding more than the law prescribed, while, overstepping the lawful penalty, he condemned to the wild beasts those who were convicted of especially heinous crimes.

XV. But in hearing and deciding cases[38] he showed strange inconsistency of temper, for he was now careful and shrewd, sometimes hasty and inconsiderate, occasionally silly and like a crazy man. In revising the lists of the divisions of jurors[39] he disqualified a man who had presented himself without mentioning that he was immune because of the number of his children,[40] on the ground that he had a passion for jury-duty. Another, who was challenged by his opponents about a suit of his own, said that it did not come before Caesar's tribunal, but the ordinary courts; whereupon Claudius compelled him at once to bring the case before him, saying that the man would show in a case affecting his own interests how just a juror he would be in the affairs of others. When a woman refused to recognise her son, and the evidence on both sides was conflicting, he forced her to admit the truth by ordering her to marry the young man. Whenever one party to a suit was absent, he was prone to decide in favour of the one who was present, without considering whether his opponent had failed to appear through his own fault or from a necessary cause.[41] On a man's being convicted of forgery, some one cried out that his hands ought to be cut off; whereupon Claudius insisted that an executioner be summoned at once with knife and block. In a case involving citizenship a fruitless dispute arose among the advocates as to whether the defendant ought to make his appearance in the toga[42] or in a Greek mantle, and the emperor, with the idea of showing absolute impartiality, made him change his garb several times, according as he was accused or defended. In one case he is credited with having rendered the following decision, which he had actually written out beforehand: "I decide in favour of those who have told the truth." By such acts as these he so discredited himself that he was held in general and open contempt. One man in making excuses for a witness that the emperor had summoned from one of the provinces, said that he could not appear, but for a long time would give no reason; at last, after a long series of questions, he said: "He's dead; I think the excuse is a lawful one." Another in thanking the emperor for allowing him to defend his client added "After all, it is usual." I myself used to hear older men say that the pleaders took such advantage of his good-nature, that they would not only call him back when he left the tribunal, but would catch hold of the fringe of his robe, and sometimes of his foot, and thus detain him. To prevent any surprise at this, I may add that a common Greek pettifogger let slip this remark in a hot debate: "You are both an old man and a fool." All the world knows that a Roman knight who was tried for improper conduct towards women, but on a false charge trumped up by unscrupulous enemies, seeing common strumpets called as witnesses against him and their testimony admitted, hurled the stylus and tablets which he held in his hand into the emperor's face with such force as to badly cut his cheek, at the same time loudly reviling his cruelty and stupidity.

XVI. He also assumed the censorship, which had long been dis- 48 A.D.
continued, ever since the term of Plancus and Paulus, but in this
office too he was variable, and both his theory and his practice 22 B.C.
were inconsistent. In his review of the knights he let off a young man of evil character, whose father said that he was perfectly satisfied with him, without any public censure,[43] saying "He has a censor of his own." Another who was notorious for corruption and

adultery he merely admonished to be more restrained in his indulgence, or at any rate more circumspect, adding, "For why should I know what mistress you keep?" When he had removed the mark of censure affixed to one man's name, yielding to the entreaties of the latter's friends, he said: "But let the erasure be seen." He not only struck from the list of jurors a man of high birth, a leading citizen of the province of Greece, because he did not know Latin, but even deprived him of the rights of citizenship; and he would not allow anyone to render an account of his life save in his own words, as well as he could, without the help of an advocate. And he degraded[44] many, some contrary to their expectation and on the novel charge that they had left Italy without consulting him and obtaining leave of absence; one man merely because he had been companion to a king in his province, citing the case of Rabirius Postumus, who in bygone days had been tried for treason because he had followed Ptolemy to Alexandria, to recover a loan. When he attempted to degrade still more, he found them in most cases blameless; for owing to the great carelessness of his agents, but to his own greater shame, those whom he accused of celibacy, childlessness, or lack of means proved that they were married, or fathers, or well-to-do. In fact, one man, who was charged with having stabbed himself, stripped off his clothing and showed a body without a scar. Other noteworthy acts of his censorship were the following: he had a silver chariot of costly workmanship, which was offered for sale in the Sigillaria,[45] bought and cut to pieces in his presence; in one single day he made twenty proclamations, including these two: "As the yield of the vineyards is bountiful, the wine jars should be well pitched"; and "Nothing is so effective a cure for snake-bite as the juice of the yew tree."

XVII. He made but one campaign and that of little importance. When the senate voted him the triumphal regalia, thinking the honour beneath the imperial dignity and desiring the glory of a legitimate triumph, he chose Britain as the best place for gaining it, a land that had been attempted by no one since the Deified Julius and was just at that time in a state of rebellion because of the

refusal to return certain deserters.[46] On the voyage thither from Ostia he was nearly cast away twice in furious north-westers, off Liguria and near the Stoechades islands. Therefore he made the journey from Massilia all the way to Gesoriacum by land, crossed from there, and without any battle or bloodshed received the sub- 44 A.D.
mission of a part of the island, returned to Rome within six months after leaving the city, and celebrated a triumph of great splendour. To witness the sight he allowed not only the governors of the provinces to come to Rome, but even some of the exiles; and among the tokens of his victory he set a naval crown on the gable of the Palace beside the civic crown, as a sign that he had crossed and, as it were, subdued the Ocean. His wife Messalina followed his chariot in a carriage, as did also those who had won the triumphal regalia in the same war; the rest marched on foot in fringed togas, except Marcus Crassus Frugi, who rode a caparisoned horse and wore a tunic embroidered with palms, because he was receiving the honour for the second time.

XVIII. He always gave scrupulous attention to the care of the city and the supply of grain. On the occasion of a stubborn fire in the Aemiliana[47] he remained in the Diribitorium[48] for two nights, and when a body of soldiers and of his own slaves could not give sufficient help, he summoned the commons from all parts of the city through the magistrates, and placing bags full of money before them, urged them to the rescue, paying each man on the spot a suitable reward for his services. When there was a scarcity of grain because of long-continued droughts, he was once stopped in the middle of the Forum by a mob and so pelted with abuse and at the same time with pieces of bread, that he was barely able to make his escape to the Palace by a back door; and after this experience he resorted to every possible means to bring grain to Rome, even in the winter season.

XIX. To the merchants he held out the certainty of profit by assuming the expense of any loss that they might suffer from storms, and offered to those who would build merchant ships large bounties, adapted to the condition of each: to a citizen exemption from the *lex Papia Poppaea*[49]; to a Latin[50] the rights of Roman citizenship; to women the privileges allowed the mothers of four children.[51] And all these provisions are in force to-day.

XX. The public works which he completed were great and essential rather than numerous; they were in particular the following: an aqueduct begun by Gaius; also the outlet of Lake Fucinus and the harbour at Ostia, although in the case of the last two he knew that Augustus had refused the former to the Marsians in spite of their frequent requests, and that the latter had often been thought of by the Deified Julius, but given up because of its difficulty. He brought to the city on stone arches the cool and abundant founts of the Claudian aqueduct, one of which is called Caeruleus and the other Curtius and Albudignus, and at the same time the spring of the new Anio, distributing them into many beautifully ornamented pools. He made the attempt on the Fucine Lake as much in the hope of gain as of glory, inasmuch as there were some who agreed to drain it at their own cost, provided the land that was uncovered be given to them. He finished the outlet, which was three miles in length, partly by levelling and partly by tunnelling a mountain, a work of great difficulty and requiring eleven years, although he had thirty thousand men at work all the time without interruption. He constructed the harbour at Ostia by building curving breakwaters on the right and left, while before the entrance he placed a mole in deep water. To give this mole a firmer foundation, he first sank the ship in which the great obelisk[52] had been brought from Egypt, and then securing it by piles, built upon it a very lofty tower after the model of the Pharos at Alexandria, to be lighted at night and guide the course of ships.

XXI. He very often distributed largesses to the people. He also gave several splendid shows, not merely the usual ones in the customary places, but some of a new kind and some revived from ancient times, and in places where no one had ever given them before. He opened the games at the dedication of Pompey's theatre, which he had restored when it was damaged by a fire, from a raised seat in the orchestra, after first offering sacrifice at the temples[53] in the upper part of the auditorium and coming down through the tiers of seats while all sat in silence. He also celebrated secular games,[54] alleging that they had been given too early by Augustus and not reserved for the regular time; although he himself writes in his own History that when they had been discontinued for a long time, Augustus restored them to their proper place after a very careful calculation of the intervals. Therefore the herald's proclamation was greeted with laughter, when he invited the people in the usual formula to games "which no one had ever seen or would ever see again"; for some were still living who had seen them before, and some actors who had appeared at the former performance appeared at that time as well. He often gave games in the Vatican Circus[55] also, at times with a beast-baiting between every five races. But the Great Circus he adorned with barriers of marble and gilded goals,[56] whereas before they had been of tufa and wood, and assigned special seats to the senators, who had been in the habit of viewing the games with the rest of the people. In addition to the chariot races he exhibited the game called Troy and also panthers, which were hunted down by a squadron of the praetorian cavalry under the lead of the tribunes and the prefect himself; likewise Thessalian horseman, who drive wild bulls all over the arena, leaping upon them when they are tired out and throwing them to the ground by the horns.

He gave many gladiatorial shows and in many places: one in yearly celebration of his accession, in the Praetorian Camp without wild beasts and fine equipment, and one in the Saepta of the regular and usual kind; another in the same place not in the regular list, short and lasting but a few days, to which he was the first to apply the name of *sportula*,[57] because before giving it for the first time he made proclamation that he invited the people "as it were to an extempore meal, hastily prepared" Now there was no form of entertainment at which he was more familiar and free, even thrusting out his left hand,[58] as the commons did, and counting aloud on his fingers the gold pieces which were paid to the victors; and ever and anon he would address the audience, and invite and urge them to merriment, calling them "masters" from time to time, and interspersing feeble and far-fetched jokes. For example, when they called for Palumbus[59] he promised that they should have him, "if he could be caught." The following, however, was both exceedingly timely and salutary; when he had granted the wooden sword[60] to an *essedarius*,[61] for whose discharge four sons begged, and the act was received with loud and general applause, he at once circulated a note, pointing out to the people how greatly they ought to desire children, since they saw that they brought favour and protection even to a gladiator. He gave representations in the Campus Martius of the storming and sacking of a town in the manner of real warfare, as well as of the surrender of the kings of the Britons, and presided clad in a general's cloak. Even when he was on the point of letting out the water from Lake Fucinus he gave a sham sea-fight first. But when the combatants cried out: "Hail, emperor, they who are about to die salute thee," he replied, "Or not,"[62] and after that all of them refused to fight, maintaining that they had been pardoned. Upon this he hesitated for some time about destroying them all with fire and sword, but at last leaping from his throne and running along the edge of the lake with his ridiculous tottering gait,[63] he induced them to fight, partly by threats and partly by promises. At this performance a Sicilian and a Rhodian fleet engaged, each numbering twelve triremes, and the signal was sounded on a horn by a silver Triton, which was raised from the middle of the lake by a mechanical device.

XXII. Touching religious ceremonies and civil and military customs, as well as the condition of all classes at home and abroad, he corrected various abuses, revived some old customs or even established new ones. In admitting priests into the various colleges he never named anyone until he had first taken oath,[64] and he scrupulously observed the custom of having the praetor call an assembly and proclaim a holiday, whenever there was an earthquake within the city; as well as that of offering up a supplication whenever a bird of ill-omen was seen on the Capitol. This last he himself conducted in his capacity of chief priest, first reciting the form of words to the people from the rostra, after all mechanics and slaves had been ordered to withdraw.

XXIII. The season for holding court, formerly divided into a winter and a summer term, he made continuous.[65] Jurisdiction in cases of trust, which it had been usual to assign each year and only to magistrates in the city, he delegated for all time and extended to the governors of the provinces. He annulled a clause added to the *lex Papia Poppaea* by Tiberius, implying that men of sixty could not beget children. He made a law that guardians might be appointed for orphans by the consuls, contrary to the usual procedure, and that those who were banished from a province by its magistrates should also be debarred from the city and from Italy. He himself imposed upon some a new kind of punishment,[66] by forbidding them to go more than three miles outside of the city.

When about to conduct business of special importance in the House, he took his seat between the two consuls or on the tribunes' bench. He reserved to himself the granting of permission to travel, which had formerly been requested of the senate.

XXIV. He gave the consular regalia even to the second grade of stewards.[67] If any refused senatorial rank,[68] he took from them that of knight also. Though he had declared at the beginning of his reign that he would choose no one as a senator who did not have a Roman citizen for a great-great-grandfather, he gave the broad stripe even to a freedman's son, but only on condition that he should first be adopted by a Roman knight. Even then, fearful of criticism, he declared that the censor Appius Caecus, the ancient founder of his family, had chosen the sons of freedmen into the senate; but he did not know that in the days of Appius and for some time afterwards the term *libertini* designated, not those who were themselves manumitted, but their freeborn sons. He obliged the college of quaestors to give a gladiatorial show in place of paving the roads; then depriving them of their official duties at Ostia and in Gaul, he restored to them the charge of the treasury of Saturn,[69] which had in the meantime been administered by praetors, or by ex-praetors, as in our time.

He gave the triumphal regalia to Silanus, his daughter's affianced husband, who was still a boy, and conferred them on older men so often and so readily, that a joint petition was circulated in the name of the legions,[70] praying that those emblems be given the consular governors at the same time with their armies, to prevent their seeking all sorts of pretexts for war. To Aulus Plautius he also granted an ovation, going out to meet him when he entered the city, and walking on his left as he went to the Capitol and returned again. He allowed Gabinius Secundus to assume the surname of Cauchius because of his conquest of the Cauchi, a German nation.

XXV. He rearranged the military career of the knights, assigning a division of cavalry after a cohort, and next the tribunate of a legion. He also instituted a fictitious kind of paid military career, which is called "supernumerary" and could be performed *in absentia* and in name only. He even had the Fathers pass a decree forbidding soldiers to enter the houses of senators to pay their respects. He confiscated the property of those freedmen who passed as Roman knights, and reduced to slavery again such as were ungrateful and a cause of complaint to their patrons, declaring to their advocates that he would not entertain a suit against their own freedmen.[71] When certain men were exposing their sick and worn out slaves on the Island of Aesculapius[72] because of the trouble of treating them, Claudius decreed that all such slaves were free, and that if they recovered, they should not return to the control of their master; but if anyone preferred to kill such a slave rather than to abandon him, he was liable to the charge of murder. He provided by an edict that travellers should not pass through the towns of Italy except on foot, or in a chair or litter. He stationed a cohort at Puteoli and one at Ostia, to guard against the danger of fires.

He forbade men of foreign birth to use the Roman names so far as those of the clans[73] were concerned. Those who usurped the privileges of Roman citizenship he executed in the Esquiline field.[74] He restored to the senate the provinces of Achaia and Macedonia, which Tiberius had taken into his own charge. He deprived the Lycians of their independence because of deadly intestine feuds, and restored theirs to the Rhodians, since they had given up their former faults. He allowed the people of Ilium perpetual exemption from tribute, on the ground that they were the founders of the Roman race, reading an ancient letter of the senate and people of Rome written in Greek to king Seleucus,in which they promised him their friendship and alliance only on condition that he should keep their kinsfolk of Ilium free from every burden. Since the Jews constantly made disturbances at the instigation of Chrestus,[75] he expelled them from Rome. He allowed the envoys of the Germans to sit in the orchestra, led by their naïve self-confidence; for when they had been taken to the seats occupied by the common people and saw the Parthian and Armenian envoys sitting with the senate, they moved of their own accord to the same part of the theatre, protesting that their merits and rank were no whit inferior. He utterly abolished the cruel and inhuman religion of the Druids among the Gauls, which under Augustus had merely been prohibited to Roman citizens; on the other hand he even attempted to transfer the Eleusinian rites from Attica to Rome, and had the temple of Venus Erycina in Sicily, which had fallen to ruin through age, restored at the expense of the treasury of the Roman people. He struck his treaties with foreign princes in the Forum, sacrificing a pig[76] and reciting the ancient formula of the fetial priests.[77] But these and other acts, and in fact almost the whole conduct of his reign, were dictated not so much by his own judgment as that of his wives and freedmen, since he nearly always acted in accordance with their interests and desires.

XXVI. He was betrothed twice at an early age: to Aemilia Lepida, great-granddaughter of Augustus, and to Livia Medullina, who also had the surname of Camilla and was descended from the ancient family of Camillus the dictator. He put away the former before their marriage, because her parents had offended Augustus;

the latter was taken ill and died on the very day which had been set for the wedding. He then married Plautia Urgulanilla, whose father had been honoured with a triumph, and later Aelia Paetina, daughter of an ex-consul. He divorced both these, Paetina for trivial offences, but Urgulanilla because of scandalous lewdness and the suspicion of murder. Then he married Valeria Messalina, daughter of his cousin Messala Barbatus. But when he learned that besides other shameful and wicked deeds she had actually married Gaius Silius, and that a formal contract had been signed in the presence of witnesses, he put her to death and declared before the assembled praetorian guard that inasmuch as his marriages did not turn out well, he would remain a widower, and if he did not keep his word, he would not refuse death at their hands. Yet he could not refrain from at once planning another match, even with Paetina, whom he had formerly discarded, and with Lollia Paulina, who had been the wife of Gaius Caesar. But his affections were ensnared by the wiles of Agrippina, daughter of his brother Germanicus, aided by the right of exchanging kisses and the opportunities for endearments offered by their relationship; and at the next meeting of the senate he induced some of the members to propose that he be compelled to marry Agrippina, on the ground that it was for the interest of the State; also that others be allowed to contract similar marriages, which up to that time had been regarded as incestuous. And he married her with hardly a single day's delay; but none were found to follow his example save a freedman and a chief centurion, whose marriage ceremony he himself attended with Agrippina.

XXVII. He had children by three of his wives: by Urgulanilla, Drusus, and Claudia; by Paetina, Antonia; by Messalina, Octavia and a son, at first called Germanicus and later Britannicus. He lost Drusus just before he came to manhood, for he was strangled by a pear which he had thrown in the air in play and caught in his open mouth. A few days before this he had betrothed him to the daughter of Sejanus, which makes me wonder all the more that
20 A.D. some say that Drusus was treacherously slain by Sejanus. Claudia

was the offspring of his freedman Boter, and although she was born within five months after the divorce[78] and he had begun to rear her, yet he ordered her to be cast out naked at her mother's door and disowned. He gave Antonia in marriage to Gnaeus Pompeius Magnus, and later to Faustus Sulla, both young men of high birth, and Octavia to his stepson Nero, after she had previously been betrothed to Silanus. Britannicus was born on the twenty-second day of his reign and in his second consulship.[79] 42 A.D.
When he was still very small, Claudius would often take him in his arms and commend him to the assembled soldiers, and to the people at the games, holding him in his lap or in his outstretched hands, and he would wish him happy auspices, joined by the applauding throng. Of his sons-in-law he adopted Nero; Pompeius and Silanus he not only declined to adopt, but even put to death.

XXVIII. Of his freedmen he had special regard for the eunuch Posides, whom he even presented with the headless spear[80] at his British triumph, along with those who had served as soldiers. He was equally fond of Felix, giving him the command of cohorts and of troops of horse, as well as of the province of Judaea; and he became the husband of three queens.[81] Also of Harpocras, to whom he granted the privilege of riding through the city in a litter and of giving public entertaiments.[82] Still higher was his regard for Polybius, his literary adviser, who often walked between the two consuls. But most of all he was devoted to his secretary Narcissus and his treasurer Pallas, and he gladly allowed them to be honoured in addition by a decree of the senate, not only with immense gifts, but even with the insignia of quaestors and praetors. Besides this he permitted them to amass such wealth by plunder, that when he once complained of the low state of his funds, the witty answer was made that he would have enough and to spare, if he were taken into partnership by his two freedmen.

XXIX. Wholly under the control of these and of his wives, as I have said,[83] he played the part, not of a prince, but of a servant, lavishing honours, the command of armies, pardons or punishments, according to the interests of each of them, or even their wish or whim; and that too for the most part in ignorance and blindly. Not to go into details about less important matters (such as revoking his grants, rescinding his decisions, substituting false letters patent, or even openly changing those which he had issued), he put to death his father-in-law Appius Silanus and the two Julias, daughters of Drusus and Germanicus, on an unsupported charge and giving them no opportunity for defence; also Gnaeus Pompeius, the husband of his elder daughter, and Lucius Silanus who was betrothed to his younger one. Of these Pompey was stabbed in the embraces of a favourite youth, while Silanus was compelled to abdicate his praetorship four days before the Kalends of January and to take his own life at the beginning of the year, the very day of the marriage of Claudius and Agrippina. He inflicted the death penalty on thirty-five senators and more than three hundred Roman knights with such easy indifference, that when a centurion in reporting the death of an ex-consul said that his order had been carried out, he replied that he had given no order; but he nevertheless approved the act, since his freedmen declared that the soldiers had done their duty in hastening to avenge their emperor without instructions. But it is beyond all belief, that at the marriage which Messalina had contracted with her paramour Silius he signed the contract for the dowry with his own hand, being induced to do so on the ground that the marriage was a feigned one, designed to avert and turn upon another a danger which was inferred from certain portents to threaten the emperor himself.

XXX. He possessed majesty and dignity of appearance, but only when he was standing still or sitting, and especially when he was lying down; for he was tall but not slender, with an attractive face, becoming white hair, and a full neck. But when he walked, his weak knees gave way under him and he had many disagreeable traits both in his lighter moments and when he was engaged in business; his laughter was unseemly and his anger still more disgusting, for he would foam at the mouth and trickle at the nose; he stammered besides and his head was very shaky at all times, but especially when he made the least exertion.

XXXI. Though previously his health was bad, it was excellent while he was emperor except for attacks of heartburn, which he said all but drove him to suicide.

XXXII. He gave frequent and grand dinner parties, as a rule in spacious places, where six hundred guests were often entertained at one time. He even gave a banquet close to the outlet of the Fucine Lake and was well-nigh drowned, when the water was let out with a rush and deluged the place. He always invited his own children to dinner along with the sons and daughters of distinguished men, having them sit at the arms[84] of the couches as they ate, after the old time custom.[85] When a guest was suspected of having stolen a golden bowl the day before, he invited him again the next day, but set before him an earthenware cup. He is even said to have thought of an edict allowing the privilege of breaking wind quietly or noisily at table, having learned of a man who ran some risk by restraining himself through modesty.

XXXIII. He was eager for food and drink at all times and in all places. Once when he was holding court in the forum of Augustus and had caught the savour of a meal which was preparing for the Salii[86] in the temple of Mars hard by, he left the tribunal, went up where the priests were, and took his place at their table. He hardly ever left the dining-room until he was stuffed and soaked; then he went to sleep at once, lying on his back with his mouth open, and a feather was put down his throat to relieve his stomach. He slept but little at a time, for he was usually awake before midnight; but he would sometimes drop off in the daytime while holding court and could hardly be roused when the advocates raised their voices for the purpose. He was immoderate in his passion for women, but wholly free from unnatural vice. He was greatly devoted to gaming, even publishing a book on the art, and he actually used to play while driving, having the board so fitted to his carriage as to prevent his game from being disturbed.

XXXIV. That he was of a cruel and bloodthirsty disposition was shown in matters great and small. He always exacted examination by torture and the punishment of parricides[87] at once and in his presence. When he was at Tibur and wished to see an execution in the ancient fashion,[88] no executioner could be found after the criminals were bound to the stake. Whereupon he sent to fetch one from the city and continued to wait for him until nightfall. At any gladiatorial show, either his own or another's, he gave orders that even those who fell accidentally should be slain, in particularly the net-fighters,[89] so that he could watch their faces as they died. When a pair of gladiators had fallen by mutually inflicted wounds, he at once had some little knives made from both their swords for his use.[90] He took such pleasure in the combats with wild beasts and of those that fought at noonday,[91] that he would go down to the arena at daybreak and after dismissing the people for luncheon at midday, he would keep his seat and in addition to the appointed combatants, he would for trivial and hasty reasons match others, even of the carpenters, the assistants, and men of that class, if any automatic device, or pageant,[92] or anything else of the kind, had not worked well. He even forced one of his pages[93] to enter the arena just as he was, in his toga.

XXXV. But there was nothing for which he was so notorious as timidity and suspicion. Although in the early days of his reign, as we have said,[94] he made a display of simplicity, he never ventured to go to a banquet without being surrounded by guards with lances and having his soldiers wait upon him in place of the servants; and he never visited a man who was ill without having the patient's room examined beforehand and his pillows and bed-clothing felt over and shaken out. Afterwards he even subjected those who came to pay their morning calls to search, sparing none the strictest examination. Indeed, it was not until late, and then reluctantly, that he gave up having women and young boys and girls grossly mishandled, and the cases for pens and styles taken from every man's attendant or scribe. When Camillus began his revolution, he felt sure that Claudius could be intimidated without resorting to war; and in fact when he ordered the emperor in an insulting, threatening, and impudent letter to give up his throne and betake himself to a life of privacy and retirement, Claudius called together the leading men and asked their advice about complying.

XXXVI. He was so terror-stricken by unfounded reports of conspiracies that he had tried to abdicate. When, as I have mentioned before,[95] a man with a dagger was caught near him as he was sacrificing, he summoned the senate in haste by criers and loudly and tearfully bewailed his lot, saying that there was no safety for him anywhere; and for a long time he would not appear in public. His ardent love for Messalina too was cooled, not so much by her unseemly and insulting conduct, as through fear of danger, since he believed that her paramour Silius aspired to the throne. On that occasion he made a shameful and cowardly flight to the camp,[96] doing nothing all the way but ask whether his throne was secure.

XXXVII. No suspicion was too trivial, nor the inspirer of it too insignificant, to drive him on to precaution and vengeance, once a slight uneasiness entered his mind. One of two parties to a suit, when he made his morning call, took Claudius aside, and said that he had dreamed that he was murdered by someone; then a little later pretending to recognize the assassin, he pointed out his opponent, as he was handing in his petition. The latter was immediately seized, as if caught red-handed, and hurried off to execution. It was in a similar way, they say, that Appius Silanus met his downfall. When Messalina and Narcissus had put their heads together to destroy him, they agreed on their parts and the latter rushed into his patron's bed-chamber before daybreak in pretended consternation, declaring that he had dreamed that Appius had made an attack on the emperor. Then Messalina, with assumed surprise, declared that she had had the same dream for several successive nights. A little later, as had been arranged, Appius, who had received orders the day before to come at that time, was reported to be forcing his way in, and as if this were proof positive of the truth of the dream, his immediate accusation and death were ordered. And Claudius did not hesitate to recount the whole affair to the senate next day and to thank the freedman[97] for watching over his emperor's safety even in his sleep.

XXXVIII. He was conscious of his tendency to wrath and resentment and excused both in an edict; he also drew a distinction between them, promising that the former would be short and harmless and the latter not without cause. After sharply rebuking the people of Ostia, because they had sent no boats to meet him when he entered the Tiber, and in such bitter terms that he wrote that they had reduced him to the rank of a commoner, he suddenly forgave them and all but apologised. He repulsed with his own hand men who approached him in public at unseasonable times. He also banished[98] a quaestor's clerk without a hearing, as well as a senator of praetorian rank, although they were blameless: the former for going too far in pleading a suit against him before he became emperor; the latter, because he had fined the tenants of Claudius's estates for violating the law forbidding the selling of cooked victuals, and had whipped his bailiff when he remonstrated. And with the same motive he took from the aediles the regulation of the cook-shops.[99]

He did not even keep quiet about his own stupidity, but in certain brief speeches he declared that he had purposely feigned it under Gaius, because otherwise he could not have escaped alive and attained his present station. But he convinced no one, and within a short time a book was published, the title of which was "The Elevation of Fools" and its thesis, that no one feigned folly.

XXXIX. Among other things men have marvelled at his absentmindedness and blindness, or to use the Greek terms, his *μετεωρια* and *ἀβλεία*. When he had put Messalina to death, he asked shortly after taking his place at the table why the empress did not come. He caused many of those whom he had condemned to death to be summoned the very next day to consult with him or game with him, and sent a messenger to upbraid them for sleepy-heads when they delayed to appear. When he was planning his unlawful marriage with Agrippina, in every speech that he made he constantly called her his daughter and nursling, born and brought up in his arms. Just before his adoption of Nero, as if it were not bad enough to adopt a stepson when he had a grown-up son of his own, he publicly declared more than once that no one had ever been taken into the Claudian family by adoption.

XL. In short, he often showed such heedlessness in word and act that one would suppose that he did not know or care to whom, with whom, when, or where he was speaking. When a debate was going on about the butchers and vintners, he cried out in the House: "Now, pray, who can live without a snack," and then went on to describe the abundance of the old taverns to which he himself used to go for wine in earlier days. He gave us one of his reasons for supporting a candidate for the quaestorship, that the man's father had once given him cold water when he was ill and needed it. Once when a witness had been brought before the senate, he said: "This woman was my mother's freedwoman and tirewoman, but she always regarded me as her patron; I mention this because there are still some in my household now who do not look on me as patron." When the people of Ostia made a public petition to him, he flew into a rage on the very tribunal and bawled out that he had no reason for obliging them; that he was surely free if anyone was. In fact every day, and almost every hour and minute, he would make such remarks as these; "What! do you take me for a Telegenius?"[100] "Scold me, but hands off!" and many others of the same kind which would be unbecoming even in private citizens, not to mention a prince who lacked neither eloquence nor culture, but on the contrary constantly devoted himself to liberal pursuits.

XLI. He began to write a history in his youth with the encouragement of Titus Livius[101] and the direct help of Sulpicius Flavus. But when he gave his first reading to a large audience, he had difficulty in finishing, since he more than once threw cold water on his own performance. For at the beginning or the reading the breaking down of several benches by a fat man raised a laugh, and even after the disturbance was quieted, Claudius could not keep from recalling the incident and renewing his guffaws. Even while he was emperor he wrote a good deal and gave constant recitals through a professional reader.[102] He began his history with the death of the dictator Caesar, but passed to a later period and took a fresh start at the end of the civil war, realising that he was not allowed to give a frank or true account of the earlier times, since he was often taken to task both by his mother and his grandmother.[103] He left two books of the earlier history, but forty-one of the later. He also composed an autobiography in eight books, lacking rather in good taste than in style, as well as a "Defence of Cicero against the Writings of Asinius Gallus," a work of no little learning. Besides this he invented three new letters and added them to the alphabet, maintaining that they were greatly needed;[104] he published a book on their theory when he was still in private life, and when he became emperor had no difficulty in bringing about their general use. These characters may still be seen in numerous books, in the daily gazette,[105] and in inscriptions on public buildings.

XLII. He gave no less attention to Greek studies, taking every occasion to declare his regard for that language and its superiority. To a foreigner who held forth both in Greek and in Latin he said: "Since you are ready with both our tongues"; and in commending Achaia to the senators he declared that it was a province dear to him through the association of kindred studies; while he often replied to Greek envoys in the senate in a set speech.[106] Indeed he quoted many Homeric lines from the tribunal, and whenever he had punished an enemy or a conspirator, he commonly gave the tribune of the guard[107] this verse when he asked for the usual watchword:

"Ward off stoutly the man whosoever is first to assail you."[108]

At last he even wrote historical works in Greek, twenty books of Etruscan History and eight of Carthaginian. Because of these works there was added to the old Museum at Alexandria a new one called after his name, and it was provided that in the one his Etruscan History should be read each year from beginning to end, and in the other his Carthaginian, by various readers in turn, in the manner of public recitations.

XLIII. Towards the end of his life he had shown some plain signs of repentance for his marriage with Agrippina and his adoption of Nero; for when his freedmen expressed their approval of a trial in which he had the day before condemned a woman for adultery, he declared that it had been his destiny also to have wives who were all unchaste, but not unpunished; and shortly afterwards meeting Britannicus, he hugged him close and urged him to grow up and receive from his father an account of all that he had done, adding in Greek, "He who dealt the wound will heal it."[109] When he expressed his intention of giving Britannicus the gown of manhood, since his stature justified it though he was still young and immature, he added: "That the Roman people may at last have a genuine Caesar."[110]

XLIV. Not long afterwards he also made his will and sealed it with the seals of all the magistrates. But before he could go any farther, he was cut short by Agrippina, who was being accused besides of many other crimes both by her own conscience and by informers.

That Claudius was poisoned is the general belief, but when it was done and by whom is disputed. Some say that it was his taster, the eunuch Halotus, as he was banqueting on the Citadel[111] with the priests; others that at a family dinner Agrippina served the drug to him with her own hand in mushrooms, a dish of which he was extravagantly fond. Reports also differ as to what followed. Many say that as soon as he swallowed the poison he became speechless, and after suffering excruciating pain all night, died just before dawn. Some say that he first fell into a stupor, then vomited up the whole contents of his overloaded stomach, and was given a second dose, perhaps in a gruel, under pretence that he must be refreshed with food after his exhaustion, or administered in a syringe, as if he were suffering from a surfeit and required relief by that form of evacuation as well.

XLV. His death was kept quiet until all the arrangements were made about the succession. Accordingly vows were offered for his safety, as if he were still ill, and the farce was kept up by bringing in comic actors, under pretence that he had asked to be entertained in that way. He died on the third day before the Ides of October in the consulship of Asinius Marcellus and Acilius Aviola, in the sixty-fourth year of his age and the fourteenth of his reign. He was buried with regal pomp and enrolled among the gods, an honour neglected and finally annulled by Nero, but later restored to him by Vespasian.

Oct. 13, 54 A.D.

XLVI. The principal omens of his death were the following: the rise of a long-haired star, commonly called a comet; the striking of his father Drusus's tomb by lightning; and the fact that many magistrates of all ranks had died that same year. There are besides some indications that he himself was not unaware of of his approaching end, and that he made no secret it; for when he was appointing the consuls, he made no appointment beyond the month when he died, and on his last appearance in the senate, after earnestly exhorting his children to harmony, he begged the members to watch over the tender years of both; and in his last sitting on the tribunal he declared more than once that he had reached the end of a mortal career, although all who heard him prayed that the omen might be averted.[112]

BOOK VI

NERO

I. Of the Domitian family two branches have acquired distinction, the Calvini and the Ahenobarbi. The latter have as the founder of their race and the origin of their surname Lucius Domitius, to whom, as he was returning from the country, there once appeared twin youths of more than mortal majesty, so it is said, and bade him carry to the senate and people the news of a victory,[1] which was as yet unknown. And as a token of their divinity it is said that they stroked his cheeks and turned his black beard to a ruddy hue, like that of bronze. This sign was perpetuated in his descendants, a great part of whom had red beards. After they had attained seven consulships, a triumph, and two censorships, and were enrolled among the patricians, they all continued to use the same surname. They confined their forenames to Gnaeus and Lucius, and used even these with a noteworthy variation, now conferring each one on three members of the family in succession, and now giving them to individual members in turn. Thus the first, second, and third of the Ahenobarbi, we are told, were called Lucius, the next three in order Gnaeus, while all those that followed were called in turn first Lucius and then Gnaeus. It seems to me worth while to give an account of several members of this family, to show more clearly that though Nero degenerated from the good qualities of his ancestors, he yet reproduced the vices of each of them, as if transmitted to him by natural inheritance.

261, 122, 96, 94, 54, 32 B.C.
32 A.D.
122 B.C.
115, 92 B.C.

II. To begin then somewhat far back, his greatgrandfather's grandfather, Gnaeus Domitius, when tribune of the commons, was enraged at the pontiffs for choosing another than himself in his father's place among them, and transferred the right of filling vacancies in the priesthoods from the colleges themselves to the 122 B.C. senate. Then having vanquished the Allobroges and the Arverni in his consulship, he rode through the province on an elephant, attended by a throng of soldiers, in a kind of triumphal procession.[2] He it was of whom the orator Licinius Crassus said that it was not surprising that he had a brazen beard, since he had a face[3] of iron and a heart of lead. His son, who was praetor at the time, summoned Gaius Caesar to an investigation before the senate at the close of his consulship, because it was thought that his administration had been in violation of the auspices and the laws. 54 B.C. Afterwards in his own consulship he tried to deprive Caesar of the command of the armies in Gaul, and being named Caesar's successor by his party, was taken prisoner at Corfinium at the beginning of the civil war.[4] Granted his freedom, he at first gave courage by his presence to the people of Massilia, who were hard pressed by their besiegers, but suddenly abandoned them and at last fell in the battle at Pharsalus. He was a man of no great resolution, though he had a violent temper, and when he once attempted to kill himself in a fit of despair and terror, he so shrank from the thought of death that he changed his mind and vomited up the poison, conferring freedom on his physician, since, knowing his master, he had purposely given him what was not a fatal dose. When Gnaeus Pompeius brought forward the question of the treatment of those who were neutral and sided with neither party, he alone was for regarding them as hostile.

III. He left a son, who was beyond all question better than the rest of the family. He was condemned to death by the Pedian law[5] among those implicated in Caesar's death, though he was guiltless, and accordingly joined Brutus and Cassius, who were his near relatives. After the death of both leaders he retained the fleet of which he had previously been made commander, and even added to it, and it was not until his party had been everywhere routed that he surrendered it to Mark Antony, of his own free will and as if it were a great favour. He too was the only one of those who were condemned by that same law[6] who was allowed to return to his native land, where he successively held all the highest offices. When the civil strife was subsequently renewed, and he was appointed one of Antony's lieutenants, he did not venture, owing to a sudden attack of illness, to accept the chief command when it was offered him by those who were ashamed of Cleopatra, nor yet positively to decline it; but he went over to Augustus and a few 31 B.C. days later died. Even he did not escape with an unblemished reputation, for Antony openly declared that he had changed sides from desire for the company of his mistress, Servilia Nais.

IV. He was the father of the Domitius who was later well known from being named in Augustus' will as the purchaser of his goods and chattels,[7] a man no less famous in his youth for his skill in driving than he was later for winning the insignia,of a triumph in the war in Germany. But he was haughty, extravagant, and cruel, and when he was only an aedile, forced the censor Lucius Plancus to make way for him on the street. While holding the offices of praetor and consul, he brought Roman knights and matrons on the stage to act a farce. He gave beast-baitings both in the Circus and in all the regions of the city; also a gladiatorial show, but with such inhuman cruelty that Augustus, after his private warning was disregarded, was forced to restrain him by an edict.

V. He had by the elder Antonia a son Domitius who became the father of Nero, a man hateful in every walk of life; for when he had gone to the East on the staff of the young Gaius Caesar,[8] he slew one of his own freedmen for refusing to drink as much as he was ordered, and when he was in consequence dismissed from the number of Gaius' friends, he lived not a whit less lawlessly. On the contrary, in a village on the Appian Way, suddenly whipping up his team, he purposely ran over and killed a boy; and right in the Roman Forum he gouged out the eye[9] of a Roman knight for being too outspoken in chiding him. He was moreover so dishonest that he not only cheated some bankers of the prices of wares which he had bought,[10] but in his praetorship he even defrauded the victors in the chariot races of the amount of their prizes. When for this reason he was held up to scorn by the jests of his own sister, and the managers of the troupes made complaint, he issued an edict[11] that the prizes should thereafter be paid on the spot. Just before the death of Tiberius he was also charged with treason, as well as with acts of adultery and with incest with his sister Lepida, but escaped owing to the change of rulers and died of dropsy at Pyrgi, after acknowledging[12] Nero son of Agrippina, the daughter of Germanicus.

Dec. 15, 37 A.D. VI. Nero was born at Antium nine months after the death of Tiberius, on the eighteenth day before the Kalends of January, just as the sun rose, so that he was touched by its rays almost before he could be laid upon the ground.[13] Many people at once made many direful predictions from his horoscope, and a remark of his father Domitius was also regarded as an omen; for while receiving the congratulations of his friends, he said that "nothing that was not abominable and a public bane could be born of Agrippina and himself." Another manifest indication of Nero's future unhappiness occurred on the day of his purification;[14] for when Gaius Caesar was asked by his sister to give the child whatever name he liked, he looked at his uncle Claudius, who later became emperor and adopted Nero, and said that he gave him his name. This he did, not seriously, but in jest, and Agrippina scorned the proposal, because at that time Claudius was one of the laughing-stocks of the court.

At the age of three he lost his father, being left heir to a third of his estate; but even this he did not receive in full, since his fellow heir Gaius seized all the property. Then his mother was banished too, and he was brought up at the house of his aunt Lepida almost in actual want, under two tutors, a dancer and a barber. But when Claudius became emperor, Nero not only recovered his father's property, but was also enriched by an inheritance from his stepfather, Passienus Crispus. When his mother was recalled from banishment and reinstated, he became so prominent through her influence that it leaked out that Messalina, wife of Claudius, had sent emissaries to strangle him as he was taking his noonday nap, regarding him as a rival of Britannicus. An addition to this bit of gossip is, that the would-be assassins were frightened away by a snake which darted out from under his pillow. The only foundation for this tale was, that there was found in his bed near the pillow the slough of a serpent; but nevertheless[15] at his mother's desire he had the skin enclosed in a golden bracelet, and wore it for a long time on his left arm. But when at last the memory of his mother grew hateful to him, he threw it away, and afterwards in the time of his extremity sought it again in vain.

VII. While he was still a young, half-grown boy he took part in the game of Troy at a performance in the Circus with great self-possession and success. In the eleventh[16] year of his age he 50 A.D. was adopted by Claudius and consigned to the training of Annaeus Seneca, who was then already a senator. They say that on the following night Seneca dreamed that he was teaching Gaius Caesar, and Nero soon proved the dream prophetic by revealing the cruelty of his disposition at the earliest possible opportunity. For merely because his brother Britannicus had, after his adoption, greeted him as usual as Ahenobarbus, he tried to convince his father[17] that Britannicus was a changeling. Also when his aunt Lepida was accused, he publicly gave testimony against her, to gratify his mother, who was using every effort to ruin Lepida.

At his formal introduction into public life he announced a largess to the people and a gift of money to the soldiers, ordered a drill[18] of the praetorians and headed them shield in hand; and thereafter returned thanks to his father in the senate. In the latter's consulship he pleaded the cause of the people of Bononia before him in Latin, and of those of Rhodes and Ilium in Greek. His first appearance as judge was when he was prefect of the city during the Latin Festival, when the most celebrated pleaders vied with one another in bringing before him, not trifling and brief cases according to the usual custom, but many of the highest importance, though this had been forbidden by Claudius. Shortly afterwards he took Octavia to wife and gave games and a beast-baiting in the Circus, that health might be vouchsafed Claudius.

54 A.D. VIII. When the death of Claudius was made public, Nero, who was seventeen years old, went forth to the watch[19] between the sixth and seventh hour, since no earlier time for the formal beginning of his reign seemed suitable because of bad omens throughout the day.[20] Hailed emperor on the steps of the Palace, he was carried in a litter to the praetorian camp, and after a brief address to the soldiers was taken from there to the House, which he did not leave until evening, of the unbounded honours that were heaped upon him refusing but one, the title of father of his country, and that because of his youth.

IX, Then beginning with a display of filial piety, he gave Claudius a magnificent funeral, spoke his eulogy, and deified him. He paid the highest honours to the memory of his father Domitius. He left to his mother the management of all public and private business. Indeed, on the first day of his rule he gave to the tribune on guard the watchword "The Best of Mothers," and afterwards he often rode with her through the streets in her litter. He
61 A.D. established a colony at Antium, enrolling the veterans of the praetorian guard and joining with them the wealthiest of the chief centurions, whom he compelled to change their residence; and he also made a harbour there at great expense.

X. To make his good intentions still more evident, he declared that he would rule according to the principles of Augustus, and he let slip no opportunity for acts of generosity and mercy, or even for displaying his affability. The more oppressive sources of revenue he either abolished or moderated. He reduced the rewards paid to informers against violators of the Papian law[21] to one fourth of the former amount. He distributed four hundred sesterces to each man of the people, and granted to the most distinguished of the senators who were without means an annual salary,[22] to some as much as five hundred thousand sesterces; and to the praetorian cohorts he gave a monthly allowance of grain free of cost. When he was asked according to custom to sign the warrant for the execution of a man who had been condemned to death, he said: "How I wish I had never learned to write!" He greeted men of all orders off-hand and from memory.[23] When the senate returned thanks to him, he replied, "When I shall have deserved them." He admitted even the commons to witness his exercises in the Campus, and often declaimed in public. He read his poems too, not only at home but in the theatre as well, so greatly to the delight of all that a thanksgiving[24] was voted because of his recital, while that part[25] of his poems was inscribed in letters of gold and dedicated to Jupiter of the Capitol.

XI. He gave many entertainments of different kinds: the *Juvenales*,[26] chariot races in the Circus, stage-plays, and a gladiatorial show. At the first mentioned he had even old men of consular rank and aged matrons take part. For the games in the Circus he assigned places to the knights apart from the rest,[27] and even matched chariots drawn by four camels. At the plays which he gave for the "Eternity of the Empire," which by his order were called the *Ludi Maximi*, parts were taken by several men and women of both the orders; a well known Roman knight mounted an elephant and rode down a rope;[28] a Roman play of Afranius, too, was staged, entitled "The Fire," and the actors were allowed to carry off the furniture of the burning house and keep it. Every day all kinds of presents were thrown to the people; these included a thousand birds of every kind each day, various kinds of food, tickets for grain, clothing, gold, silver, precious stones, pearls, paintings, slaves, beasts of burden, and even trained wild animals; finally, ships, blocks of houses, and farms.

XII. These plays he viewed from the top of the proscenium. At the gladiatorial show, which he gave in a wooden amphitheatre, erected in the district of the Campus Martius within the space of a 58 A.D.
single year, he had no one put to death, not even criminals. But he compelled four hundred senators and six hundred Roman knights, some of whom were well to do and of unblemished reputation, to fight in the arena. Even those who fought with the wild

beasts and performed the various services in the arena[29] were of the same orders. He also exhibited a naval battle in salt water with sea monsters swimming about in it; besides pyrrhic dances[30] by some Greek youths,[31] handing each of them certificates of Roman citizenship at the close of his performance. The pyrrhic dances represented various scenes. In one a bull mounted Pasiphae, who was concealed in a wooden image of a heifer; at least many of the spectators thought so. Icarus at his very first attempt fell close by the imperial couch and bespattered the emperor with his blood; for Nero very seldom presided at the games, but used to view them while reclining on a couch, at first through small openings, and then with the entire balcony[32] uncovered.

60 A.D. He was likewise the first to establish at Rome a quinquennial contest in three parts, after the Greek fashion, that is in music,[33] gymnastics, and riding, which he called the *Neronia;* at the same time he dedicated his baths and gymnasium,[34] supplying every member of the senatorial and equestrian orders with oil. To preside over[35] the whole contest he appointed ex-consuls, chosen by lot, who occupied the seats of the praetors. Then he went down into the orchestra among the senators and accepted the prize for Latin oratory and verse, for which all the most eminent men had contended but which was given to him with their unanimous consent; but when that for lyre-playing was also offered him by the judges, he knelt before it and ordered that it be laid at the feet of Augustus' statue. At the gymnastic contest, which he gave in the Saepta, he shaved his first beard to the accompaniment of a splendid sacrifice of bullocks, put it in a golden box adorned with pearls of great price, and dedicated it in the Capitol. He invited the Vestal virgins also to witness the contests of the athletes,[36] because at Olympia the priestesses of Ceres were allowed the same privilege.

XIII. I may fairly include among his shows the entrance of Tiridates into the city. He was a king of Armenia, whom Nero induced by great promises to come to Rome; and since he was prevented by bad weather from exhibiting him to the people on the day appointed by proclamation, he produced him at the first favourable opportunity, with the praetorian cohorts drawn up in full armour about the temples in the Forum, while he himself sat in a curule chair on the rostra in the attire of a triumphing general, surrounded by military ensigns and standards. As the king approached along a sloping platform, the emperor at first let him fall at his feet, but raised him with his right hand and kissed him. Then, while the king made supplication, Nero took the turban from his head and replaced it with a diadem, while a man of praetorian rank translated the words of the suppliant and proclaimed them to the throng. From there the king was taken to the theatre,[37] and when he had again done obeisance, Nero gave him a seat at his right hand. Because of all this Nero was hailed as Imperator,[38] and after depositing a laurel wreath in the Capitol,[39] he closed the two doors of the temple of Janus,[40] as a sign that no war was left anywhere.

XIV. He held four consulships, the first for two months, the second and the last for six months each, the third for four months. The second and third were in successive years, while a year intervened between these and each of the others.[41] 55, 57, 58, 60 A.D.

XV. In the administration of justice he was reluctant to render a decision to those who presented cases, except on the following day and in writing. The procedure was, instead of continuous pleadings, to have each point presented separately by the parties in turn. Furthermore, whenever he withdrew for consultation, he did not discuss any matter with all his advisers in a body, but had each of them give his opinion in written form; these he read silently and in private and then gave a verdict according to his own inclination, as if it were the view of the majority.

For a long time he would not admit the sons of freedmen to the senate and he refused office to those who had been admitted by his predecessors. Candidates who were in excess of the number of vacancies received the command of a legion as compensation for the postponement and delay. He commonly appointed consuls for a period of six months. When one of them died just before the Kalends of January, he appointed no one in his place, expressing his disapproval of the old-time case of Caninius Rebilus, the twenty-four hour consul.[42] He conferred the triumphal regalia even on men of the rank of quaestor, as well as on some of the knights, and sometimes for other than military services. As regards the speeches which he sent to the senate on various matters, he passed over the quaestors, whose duty it was to read them,[43] and usually had them presented by one of the consuls.

XVI. He devised a new form for the buildings of the city and in front of the houses and apartments he erected porches, from the flat roofs of which fires could be fought;[44] and these he put up at his own cost. He had also planned to extend the walls as far as Ostia and to bring the sea from there to Rome by a canal.

During his reign many abuses were severely punished and put down, and no fewer new laws were made: a limit was set to expenditures; the public banquets were confined to a distribution of food; the sale of any kind of cooked viands in the taverns was forbidden, with the exception of pulse and vegetables, whereas before every sort of dainty was exposed for sale.[45] Punishment was inflicted on the Christians, a class of men given to a new and mischievous superstition. He put an end to the diversions of the chariot drivers, who from immunity of long standing claimed the right of ranging at large and amusing themselves by cheating and robbing the people. The pantomimic actors and their partisans were banished from the city.[46]

XVII. It was in his reign that a protection against forgers was first devised, by having no tablets signed that were not bored with holes through which a cord was thrice passed.[47] In the case of wills it was provided that the first two leaves should be presented to the signatories[48] with only the name of the testator written upon them, and that no one who wrote a will for another should put down a legacy for himself; further, that clients should pay a fixed and reasonable fee for the services of their advocates,[49] but nothing at all for benches, which were to be furnished free of charge by the public treasury; finally as regarded the pleading of cases, that those connected with the treasury should be transferred to the Forum[50] and a board of arbiters, and that any appeal from the juries should be made to the senate.

XVIII. So far from being actuated by any wish or hope of increasing or extending the empire, he even thought of withdrawing the army from Britain and changed his purpose only because he was ashamed to seem to belittle the glory of his father.[51] He increased the provinces only by the realm of Pontus, when it was given up by Polemon, and that of Cottius in the Alps on the latter's death.

XIX. He planned but two foreign tours, to Alexandria and Achaia; and he gave up the former on the very day when he was to have started, disturbed by a threatening portent. For as he was making the round of the temples and had sat down in the shrine of Vesta, first the fringe of his garment caught when he attempted to get up, and then such darkness overspread his eyes that he could see nothing. In Achaia he attempted to cut through the Isthmus[52] and called together the praetorians and urged them to begin the work; then at a signal given on a trumpet he was first to break ground with a mattock and to carry off a basketful of earth upon his shoulders. He also prepared for an expedition to the Caspian Gates, after enrolling a new legion of raw recruits of Italian birth, each six feet tall,[53] which he called the "phalanx of Alexander the Great."

I have brought together these acts of his, some of which are beyond criticism, while others are even deserving of no slight praise, to separate them from his shameful and criminal deeds, of which I shall proceed now to give an account.

XX. Having gained some knowledge of music in addition to the rest of his early education, as soon as he became emperor he sent for Terpnus, the greatest master of the lyre in those days, and after listening to him sing after dinner for many successive days until late at night, he little by little began to practise himself, neglecting none of the exercises which artists of that kind are in the habit of following, to preserve or strengthen their voices. For he used to lie upon his back and hold a leaden plate on his chest, purge himself by the syringe and by vomiting, and deny himself fruits and all foods injurious to the voice. Finally encouraged by his progress, although his voice was weak and husky, he began to long to appear on the stage, and every now and then in the presence of his intimate friends he would quote a Greek proverb meaning "Hidden music counts for nothing."[54] And he made his debut at Naples, where he did not cease singing until he had finished the number which he had begun, even though the theatre was shaken by a sudden earthquake shock.[55] In the same city he sang frequently and for several successive days. Even when he took a short time to rest his voice, he could not keep out of sight but went to the theatre after bathing and dined in the orchestra with the people all about him, promising them in Greek, that when he had wetted his whistle a bit, he would ring out something good and loud.[56] He was greatly taken too with the rhythmic applause of some Alexandrians, who had flocked to Naples from a fleet that had lately arrived, and summoned more men from Alexandria. Not content with that, he selected some young men of the order of knights and more than five thousand sturdy young commoners, to be divided into groups and learn the Alexandrian styles of applause (they called them "the bees," "the roof-tiles," and "the bricks "),[57] and to ply them vigorously whenever he sang. These men were noticeable for their thick hair and fine apparel; their left hands were bare and without rings, and the leaders were paid four hundred thousand sesterces each.

XXI. Considering it of great importance to appear in Rome as well, he repeated the contest of the Neronia[58] before the appointed time, and when there was a general call for his "divine voice," he replied that if any wished to hear him, he would favour them in the gardens; but when the guard of soldiers which was then on duty seconded the entreaties of the people, he gladly agreed to appear at once. So without delay he had his name added to the list of the lyre-players who entered the contest, and casting his own lot into the urn with the rest, he came forward in his turn, attended by the prefects of the Guard carrying his lyre, and followed by the tribunes of the soldiers and his intimate friends. Having taken his place and finished his preliminary speech,[59] he announced through the ex-consul Cluvius Rufus that "he would sing Niobe"; and he kept at it until late in the afternoon, putting off the award of the prize for that event and postponing the rest of the contest to the next year, to have an excuse for singing oftener. But since even that seemed too long to wait, he did not cease to appear in public from time to time. He even thought of taking part in private performances[60] among the professional actors, when one of the praetors offered him a million sesterces. He also put on the mask and sang tragedies representing gods and heroes and even heroines and goddesses, having the masks fashioned in the likeness of his own features or those of the women of whom he chanced to be enamoured. Among other themes he sang "Canace in Labor," "Orestes the Matricide," "The Blinding of Oedipus" and the "Frenzy of Hercules." At the last named performance they say that a young recruit, seeing the emperor in mean attire and bound with chains, as the subject required, rushed forward to lend him aid.

XXII. From his earliest years he had a special passion for horses and talked constantly about the games in the Circus, though he was forbidden to do so.[61] Once when he was lamenting with his fellow pupils the fate of a charioteer of the "Greens,"[62] who was dragged by his horses, and his preceptor scolded him, he told a lie and pretended that he was talking of Hector. At the beginning of his reign he used to play every day with ivory chariots on a board, and he came from the country to all the games, even the most insignificant, at first secretly, and then so openly that no one doubted that he would be in Rome on that particular day. He made no secret of his wish to have the number of prizes increased, and in consequence more races were added and the performance was continued to a late hour, while the managers of the troupes no longer thought it worth while to produce their drivers at all except for a full day's racing. He soon longed to drive a chariot himself and even to show himself frequently in public; so after a trial exhibition in his gardens before his slaves and the dregs of the populace, he gave all an opportunity of seeing him in the Circus Maximus, one of his freedmen dropping the napkin[63] from the place usually occupied by the magistrates.

Not content with showing his proficiency in these arts at Rome, he went to Achaia, as I have said,[64] influenced especially by the following consideration. The cities in which it was the custom to hold contests in music had adopted the rule of sending all the lyric prizes to him. These he received with the greatest delight, not only giving audience before all others to the envoys who brought them, but even inviting them to his private table. When some of them begged him to sing after dinner and greeted his performance with extravagant applause, he declared that "the Greeks were the only ones who had an ear for music and that they alone were worthy of his efforts." So he took ship without delay and immediately on arriving at Cassiope made a preliminary appearance as a singer at the altar of Jupiter Cassius, and then went the round of all the contests.[65]

XXIII. To make this possible, he gave orders that even those which were widely separated in time should be brought together in a single year, so that some had even to be given twice, and he introduced a musical competition at Olympia also, contrary to custom. To avoid being distracted or hindered in any way while busy with these contests, he replied to his freedman Helius, who reminded him that the affairs of the city required his presence, in these words: "However much it may be your advice and your wish that I should return speedily, yet you ought rather to counsel me and to hope that I may return worthy of Nero."

While he was singing no one was allowed to leave the theatre even for the most urgent reasons. And so it is said that some women gave birth to children there, while many who were worn out with listening and applauding, secretly leaped from the wall,[66] since the gates at the entrance[67] were closed, or feigned death and were carried out as if for burial. The trepidation and anxiety with which he took part in the contests, his keen rivalry of his opponents and his awe of the judges, can hardly be credited. As if his rivals were of quite the same station as himself, he used to show respect to them and try to gain their favour, while he slandered them behind their backs, sometimes assailed them with abuse when he met them, and even bribed those who were especially proficient.

Before beginning, he would address the judges in the most deferential terms, saying that he had done all that could be done, but the issue was in the hands of Fortune; they however, being men of wisdom and experience, ought to exclude what was fortuitous. When they bade him take heart, he withdrew with greater confidence, but not even then without anxiety, interpreting the silence and modesty of some as sullenness and ill-nature, and declaring that he had his suspicions of them.

XXIV. In competition he observed the rules most scrupulously, never daring to clear his throat and even wiping the sweat from his brow with his arm.[68] Once indeed, during the performance of a tragedy, when he had dropped his sceptre but quickly recovered it, he was terribly afraid that he might be excluded from the competition because of his slip, and his confidence was restored only when his accompanist[69] swore that it had passed unnoticed amid the delight and applause of the people. When the victory was won, he made the announcement himself; and for that reason he always took part in the contests of the heralds.[70] To obliterate the memory of all other victors in the games[71] and leave no trace of them, their statues and busts were all thrown down by his order, dragged off with hooks, and cast into privies.

He also drove a chariot in many places, at Olympia even a ten-horse team, although in one of his own poems he had criticised Mithridates for just that thing. But after he had been thrown from the car and put back in it, he was unable to hold out and gave up before the end of the course; but he received the crown just the same. On his departure he presented the entire province with freedom[72] and at the same time gave the judges Roman citizenship and a large sum of money. These favours he announced in person on the day of the Isthmian Games, standing in the middle of the stadium.

XXV. Returning from Greece, since it was at Naples that he had made his first appearance, he entered that city with white horses through a part of the wall which had been thrown down, as is customary with victors in the sacred games.[73] In like manner he entered Antium, then Albanum, and finally Rome; but at Rome he rode in the chariot which Augustus had used in his triumphs in days gone by, and wore a purple robe and a Greek cloak adorned with stars of gold, bearing on his head the Olympic crown and in his right hand the Pythian, while the rest were carried before him with inscriptions telling where he had won them and against what competitors, and giving the titles of the songs or the subject of the plays. His car was followed by his claque[74] as by the escort of a triumphal procession, who shouted that they were the attendants of Augustus and the soldiers of his triumph. Then through the arch of the Circus Maximus, which was thrown down,[75] he made his way across the Velabrum and the Forum to the Palatine and the temple of Apollo. All along the route victims were slain, the streets were sprinkled from time to time with perfume, while birds,[76] ribbons, and sweetmeats were showered upon him. He placed the sacred crowns in his bed-chambers around his couches, as well as statues representing him in the guise of a lyre-player; and he had a coin too struck with the same device. So far from neglecting or relaxing his practice of the art after this, he never addressed the soldiers except by letter or in a speech delivered by another, to save his voice; and he never did anything for amusement or in earnest without an elocutionist[77] by his side, to warn him to spare his vocal organs and hold a handkerchief to his mouth. To many men he offered his friendship or announced his hostility, according as they had applauded him lavishly or grudgingly.

XXVI. Although at first his acts of wantonness, lust, extravagance, avarice and cruelty were gradual and secret, and might be condoned as follies of youth, yet even then their nature was such that no one doubted that they were defects of his character and not due to his time of life. No sooner was twilight over than he would catch up a cap or a wig and go to the taverns or range about the streets playing pranks, which however were very far from harmless; for he used to beat men as they came home from dinner, stabbing any who resisted him and throwing them into the sewers. He would even break into shops and rob them, setting up a market[78] in the Palace, where he divided the booty which he took, sold it at auction, and then squandered the proceeds. In the strife which resulted he often ran the risk of losing his eyes[79] or even his life, for he was beaten almost to death by a man of the senatorial order,[80] whose wife he had maltreated. Warned by this, he never afterwards ventured to appear in public at that hour without having tribunes follow him at a distance and unobserved. Even in the day-time he would be carried privately to the theatre in a sedan, and from the upper part of the proscenium would watch the brawls of the pantomimic actors[81] and egg them on; and when they came to blows and fought with stones and broken benches, he himself threw many missiles at the people and even broke a praetor's head.

XXVII. Little by little, however, as his vices grew stronger, he dropped jesting and secrecy and with no attempt at disguise openly broke out into worse crime. He prolonged his revels from midday to midnight, often livening himself by a warm plunge, or, if it were summer, into water cooled with snow. Sometimes too he closed the inlets and banqueted in public in the great tank[82] in the Campus Martius, or in the Circus Maximus, waited on by harlots and dancing girls from all over the city. Whenever he drifted down the Tiber to Ostia, or sailed about the Gulf of Baiae, booths were set up at intervals along the banks and shores, fitted out for debauchery, while bartering matrons played the part of inn-keepers and from every hand solicited him to come ashore. He also levied dinners on his friends, one of whom spent four million sesterces for a banquet at which turbans were distributed, and another a considerably larger sum for a rose dinner.[83]

XXVIII. Besides abusing freeborn boys and seducing married women, he debauched the vestal virgin Rubria. The freedwoman Acte he all but made his lawful wife, after bribing some ex-consuls to perjure themselves by swearing that she was of royal birth. He castrated the boy Sporus and actually tried to make a woman of him; and he married him with all the usual ceremonies, including a dowry and a bridal veil, took him to his house attended by a great throng, and treated him as his wife. And the witty jest that someone made is still current, that it would have been well for the world if Nero's father Domitius had had that kind of wife. This Sporus, decked out with the finery of the empresses and riding in a litter, he took with him to the assizes and marts of Greece, and later at Rome through the Street of the Images,[84] fondly kissing him from time to time. That he even desired illicit relations with his own mother, and was kept from it by her enemies, who feared that such a relationship might give the reckless and insolent woman too great influence, was notorious, especially after he added to his concubines a courtesan who was said to look very like Agrippina. Even before that, so they say, whenever he rode in a litter with his mother, he had incestuous relations with her, which were betrayed by the stains on his clothing.

XXIX. He so prostituted his own chastity that after defiling almost every part of his body, he at last devised a kind of game, in which, covered with the skin of some wild animal, he was let loose from a cage and attacked the private parts of men and women, who were bound to stakes, and when he had sated his mad lust, was dispatched[85] by his freedman Doryphorus; for he was even married to this man in the same way that he himself had married Sporus, going so far as to imitate the cries and lamentations of a maiden being deflowered. I have heard from some men that it was his unshaken conviction that no man was chaste or pure in any part of his body, but that most of them concealed their vices and cleverly drew a veil over them; and that therefore he pardoned all other faults in those who confessed to him their lewdness.

XXX. He thought that there was no other way of enjoying riches and money than by riotous extravagance, declaring that only stingy and niggardly fellows kept a correct account of what they spent,[86] while fine and genuinely magnificent gentlemen wasted and squandered. Nothing in his uncle Gaius so excited his envy and admiration as the fact that he had in so short a time run through the vast wealth which Tiberius had left him. Accordingly he made presents and wasted money without stint. On Tiridates,[87] though it would seem hardly within belief, he spent eight hundred thousand sesterces a day, and on his departure presented him with more than a hundred millions. He gave the lyre-player Menecrates and the gladiator Spiculus properties and residences equal to those of men who had celebrated triumphs. He enriched the monkey-faced usurer Panerotes with estates in the country and in the city and had him buried with almost regal splendour. He never wore the same garment twice. He played at dice for four hundred thousand sesterces a point.[88] He fished with a golden net drawn by cords woven of purple and scarlet threads. It is said that he never made a journey with less than a thousand carriages, his mules shod with silver and their drivers clad in wool of Canusium, attended by a train of Mazaces[89] and couriers with bracelets and trappings.[90]

XXXI. There was nothing however in which he was more ruinously prodigal than in building. He made a palace extending all the way from the Palatine to the Esquiline, which at first he called the House of Passage, but when it was burned shortly after its completion and rebuilt, the Golden House. Its size and splendour will be sufficiently indicated by the following details. Its vestibule was large enough to contain a colossal statue of the emperor a hundred and twenty feet high; and it was so extensive that it had a triple colonnade[91] a mile long. There was a pond too, like a sea, surrounded with buildings to represent cities,[92] besides tracts of country, varied by tilled fields, vineyards, pastures and woods, with great numbers of wild and domestic animals. In the rest of the house all parts were overlaid with gold and adorned with gems and mother-of-pearl. There were dining-rooms with fretted ceilings of ivory, whose panels could turn and shower down flowers and were fitted with pipes for sprinkling the guests with perfumes. The main banquet hall was circular and constantly revolved day and night, like the heavens.[93] He had baths supplied with sea water and sulphur water. When the edifice was finished in this style and he dedicated it, he deigned to say nothing more in the way of approval than that he was at last beginning to be housed like a human being.

He also began a pool, extending from Misenum to the lake of Avernus, roofed over and enclosed in colonnades, into which he planned to turn all the hot springs in every part of Baiae; a canal from Avernus all the way to Ostia, to enable the journey to be made by ship yet not by sea; its length was to be a hundred and sixty miles and its breadth sufficient to allow ships with five banks of oars to pass each other. For the execution of these projects he had given orders that the prisoners all over the empire should be transported to Italy, and that those who were convicted even of capital crimes should be punished in no other way than by sentence to this work.

He was led to such mad extravagance, in addition to his confidence in the resources of the empire, by the hope of a vast hidden treasure, suddenly inspired by the assurance of a Roman knight, who declared positively that the enormous wealth which queen Dido had taken with her of old in her flight from Tyre was hidden away in huge caves in Africa and could be recovered with but trifling labour.

XXXII. When this hope proved false, he resorted to false accusations and robbery, being at the end of his resources and so utterly impoverished that he was obliged to postpone and defer even the pay of the soldiers and the rewards due to the veterans.

First of all he made a law, that instead of one-half, five-sixths of the property of deceased freedmen should be made over to him, if without good and sufficient reason they bore the name of any family with which he himself was connected; further, that the estates of those who were ungrateful to their emperor[94] should belong to the privy purse, and that the advocates who had written or dictated such wills should not go unpunished. Finally, that any word or deed on which an informer could base an action should be liable to the law against lese-majesty. He demanded the return of the rewards[95] which he had given in recognition of the prizes conferred on him by any city in any competition. Having forbidden the use of amethystine or Tyrian purple dyes, he secretly sent a man to sell a few ounces on a market day and then closed the shops of all the dealers.[96] It is even said that when he saw a matron in the audience at one of his recitals clad in the forbidden colour he pointed her out to his agents, who dragged her out and stripped her on the spot, not only of her garment, but also of her property. He never appointed anyone to an office without adding: "You know what my needs are," and "Let us see to it that no one possess anything." At last he stripped many temples of their gifts and melted down the images of gold and silver, including those of the Penates, which however Galba soon afterwards restored.

XXXIII. He began his career of parricide and murder with Claudius, for even if he was not the instigator of the emperor's death, he was at least privy to it, as he openly admitted; for he used afterwards to laud mushrooms, the vehicle in which the poison was administered to Claudius, as "the food of the gods," as the Greek proverb has it.[97] At any rate, after Claudius's death he vented on him every kind of insult, in act and word,[98] charging him now with folly and now with cruelty; for it was a favourite joke of his to say that Claudius had ceased "to play the fool"[99] among mortals, lengthening the first syllable of the word *morari,* and he disregarded many of his decrees and acts as the work of a madman and a dotard. Finally, he neglected to enclose the place where his body was burned except with a low and mean wall.

He attempted the life of Britannicus by poison, not less from jealousy of his voice (for it was more agreeable than his own) than from fear that he might sometime win a higher place than himself in the people's regard because of the memory of his father. He procured the potion from an archpoisoner, one Locusta, and when the effect was slower than he anticipated, merely physicing Britannicus, he called the woman to him and flogged her with his own hand, charging that she had administered a medicine instead of a poison; and when she said in excuse that she had given a smaller dose to shield him from the odium of the crime, he replied: "It's likely that I am afraid of the Julian law[100];" and he forced her to mix as swift and instant a potion as she knew how in his own room before his very eyes. Then he tried it on a kid, and as the animal lingered for five hours, had the mixture steeped again and again and threw some of it before a pig. The beast instantly fell dead, whereupon he ordered that the poison be taken to the dining-room and given to Britannicus. The boy dropped dead at the very first taste, but Nero lied to his guests and declared that he was seized with the falling sickness, to which he was subject, and the next day had him hastily and unceremoniously buried in a pouring rain. He rewarded Locusta for her eminent services with a full pardon[101] and large estates in the country, and actually sent her pupils.[102]

XXXIV. His mother offended him by too strict surveillance and criticism of his words and acts, but at first he confined his resentment to frequent endeavours to bring upon her a burden of unpopularity by pretending that he would abdicate the throne and go off to Rhodes. Then depriving her of all her honours and of her guard of Roman and German soldiers, he even forbade her to live with him and drove her from the Palace. After that he passed all bounds in harrying her, bribing men to annoy her with lawsuits while she remained in the city, and after she had retired to the country, to pass her house by land and sea and break her rest with abuse and mockery. At last terrified by her violence and threats, he determined to have her life, and after thrice attempting it by poison and finding that she had made herself immune by antidotes, he tampered with the ceiling of her bedroom, contriving a mechanical device for loosening its panels and dropping them upon her while she slept. When this leaked out through some of those connected with the plot, he devised a collapsible boat,[103] to destroy her by shipwreck or by the falling in of its cabin. Then he pretended a reconciliation and invited her in a most cordial letter to come to Baiae and celebrate the feast of Minerva[104] with him. On her arrival, instructing his captains to wreck the galley in which she had come, by running into it as if by accident, he detained her at a banquet,[105] and when she would return to Bauli, offered her his contrivance in place of the craft which had been damaged, escorting her to it in high spirits and even kissing her breasts as they parted. The rest of the night he passed sleepless in intense anxiety, awaiting the outcome of his design. On learning that everything had gone wrong and that she had escaped by swimming, driven to desperation he secretly had a dagger thrown down beside her freedman Lucius Agermus, when he joyfully brought word that she was safe and sound, and then ordered that the freedman be seized and bound, on the charge of being hired to kill the emperor; that his mother be put to death, and the pretence made that she had escaped the consequences of her detected guilt by suicide. Trustworthy authorities[106] add still more gruesome details: that he hurried off to view the corpse, handled her limbs, criticising some and commending others, and that becoming thirsty meanwhile, he took a drink. Yet he could not either then or ever afterwards endure the stings of conscience, though soldiers, senate and people tried to hearten him with their congratulations; for he often owned that he was hounded by his mother's ghost and by the whips and blazing torches of the Furies. He even had rites performed by the Magi, in the effort to summon her shade and entreat it for forgiveness. Moreover, in his journey through Greece he did not venture to take part in the Eleusinian mysteries, since at the beginning the godless and wicked are warned by the herald's proclamation to go hence.

To matricide he added the murder of his aunt. When he once visited her as she was confined to her bed from costiveness, and she, as old ladies will, stroking his downy beard (for he was already well grown) happened to say fondly: "As soon as I receive this,[107] I shall gladly die," he turned to those with him and said as if in jest: "I'll take it off at once." Then he bade the doctors give the sick woman an overdose of physic and seized her property before she was cold, suppressing her will, that nothing might escape him.

XXXV. Besides Octavia he later took two wives, Poppaea Sabina, daughter of an ex-quaestor and previously married to a Roman knight, and then Statilia Messalina, daughter of the great-grand-daughter of Taurus, who had been twice consul and awarded a triumph. To possess the latter he slew her husband

Atticus Vestinus while he held the office of consul. He soon grew tired of living with Octavia, and when his friends took him to task, replied that "she ought to be content with the insignia of wifehood."[108] Presently after several vain attempts to strangle her, he divorced her on the ground of barrenness, and when the people took it ill and openly reproached him, he banished her besides; and finally he had her put to death on a charge of adultery that was so shameless and unfounded, that when all who were put to the torture maintained her innocence, he bribed his former preceptor Anicetus[109] to make a pretended confession that he had violated her chastity by a stratagem. He dearly loved Poppaea, whom he married twelve days after his divorce from Octavia, yet he caused her death too by kicking her when she was pregnant and ill, because she had scolded him for coming home late from the races. By her he had a daughter, Claudia Augusta, but lost her when she was still an infant.

Indeed there is no kind of relationship that he did not violate in his career of crime. He put to death Antonia, daughter of Claudius,[110] for refusing to marry him after Poppaea's death, charging her with an attempt at revolution; and he treated in the same way all others who were in any way connected with him by blood or by marriage. Among these was the young Aulus Plautius, whom he forcibly defiled before his death, saying "Let my mother come now and kiss my successor," openly charging that Agrippina had loved Plautius and that this had roused him to hopes of the throne. Rufrius Crispinus, a mere boy, his stepson and the child of Poppaea, he ordered to be drowned by the child's own slaves while he was fishing, because it was said that he used to play at being a general and an emperor. He banished his nurse's son Tuscus, because when procurator in Egypt, he had bathed in some baths which were built for a visit of Nero's. He drove his tutor Seneca to suicide, although when the old man often pleaded to be allowed to retire and offered to give up his estates,[111] he had sworn most solemnly that he did wrong to suspect him and that he would rather die than harm him. He sent poison to Burrus, prefect of the Guard, in place of a throat medicine which he had promised him. The old and wealthy freedmen who had helped him first to his adoption and later to the throne, and aided him by their advice,[112] he killed by poison, administered partly in their food and partly in their drink.

XXXVI. Those outside his family he assailed with no less cruelty. It chanced that a comet[113] had begun to appear on several successive nights, a thing which is commonly believed to portend the death of great rulers. Worried by this, and learning from the astrologer Balbillus that kings usually averted such omens by the death of some distinguished man, thus turning them from themselves upon the heads of the nobles, he resolved on the death of all the eminent men of the State; but the more firmly, and with some semblance of justice, after the discovery of two conspiracies. The earlier and more dangerous of these was that of Piso at Rome; the other was set on foot by Vinicius at Beneventum and detected there. 65 A.D.
The conspirators made their defence in triple sets of fetters, some voluntarily admitting their guilt, some even making a favour of it, saying that there was no way except by death that they could help a man disgraced by every kind of wickedness.[114] The children of those who were condemned were banished or put to death by poison or starvation; a number are known to have been slain all together at a single meal along with their preceptors and attendants,[115] while others were prevented from earning their daily bread.

XXXVII. After this he showed neither discrimination nor moderation in putting to death whomsoever he pleased on any pretext whatever. To mention but a few instances, Salvidienus Orfitus was charged with having let to certain states as headquarters three shops which formed part of his house near the Forum; Cassius Longinus, a blind jurist, with retaining in the old family tree of his house the mask of Gaius Cassius, the assassin of Julius Caesar; Paetus Thrasea with having a sullen mien, like that of a preceptor. To those who were bidden to die he never granted more than an hour's respite, and to avoid any delay, he brought physicians who were at once to "attend to" such as lingered; for that was the term he used for killing them by opening their veins. It is even believed that it was his wish to throw living men to be torn to pieces and devoured by a monster[116] of Egyptian birth, who would crunch raw flesh and anything else that was given him. Transported and puffed up with such successes, as he considered them, he boasted that no prince had ever known what power he really had, and he often threw out unmistakable hints that he would not spare even those of the senate who survived, but would one day blot out the whole order from the State and hand over the rule of the provinces and the command of the armies to the Roman knights and to his freedmen. Certain it is that neither on beginning a journey nor on returning did he kiss any member[117] or even return his greeting; and at the formal opening of the work at the Isthmus the prayer which he uttered in a loud voice before a great throng was, that the event might result favourably "for himself and the people of Rome," thus suppressing any mention of the senate.

XXXVIIII. But he showed no greater mercy to the people or the walls of his capital. When someone in a general conversation said:

"When I am dead, be earth consumed by fire,"[118]

he rejoined "Nay, rather while I live," and his action was wholly in accord. For under cover of displeasure at the ugliness of the old buildings and the narrow, crooked streets, he set fire to the city[119] so openly that several ex-consuls did not venture to lay hands on his chamberlains although they caught them on their estates with tow and firebrands, while some granaries near the Golden House, whose room he particularly desired, were demolished by engines of war and then set on fire, because their walls were of stone. For six days and seven nights destruction raged, while the people were driven for shelter to monuments and tombs. At that time, besides an immense number of dwellings,[120] the houses of leaders of old were burned, still adorned with trophies of victory, and the temples of the gods vowed and dedicated by the kings and later in the Punic and Gallic wars, and whatever else interesting and noteworthy had survived from antiquity. Viewing the conflagration from the tower of Maecenas[121] and exulting, as he said, in "the beauty of the flames," he sang the whole of the "Sack of Ilium,"[122] in his regular stage costume. Furthermore, to gain from this calamity too all the spoil and booty possible, while promising the removal of the debris and dead bodies free of cost he allowed no one to approach the ruins of his own property; and from the contributions which he not only received, but even demanded, he nearly bankrupted the provinces and exhausted the resources of individuals.

XXXIX. To all the disasters and abuses thus caused by the prince there were added certain accidents of fortune; a plague which in a single autumn entered thirty thousand deaths in the accounts of Libitina;[123] a disaster in Britain, where two important towns were sacked[124] and great numbers of citizens and allies were butchered; a shameful defeat in the Orient, in consequence of which the legions in Armenia were sent under the yoke and Syria was all but lost. It is surprising and of special note that all this time he bore nothing with more patience than the curses and abuse of the people, and was particularly lenient towards those who assailed him with gibes and lampoons. Of these many were posted or circulated both in Greek and Latin, for example the following;

"Nero, Orestes, Alcmeon their mothers slew."

"A calculation new. Nero his mother slew."[125]

"Who can deny the descent from Aeneas' great line of our Nero?

One his mother took off, the other one took off his sire."

"While our ruler his lyre doth twang and the Parthian his bowstring,

Paean-singer our prince shall be, and Far-darter our foe."

"Rome is becoming one house; off with you to Veii, Quirites!

If that house does not soon seize upon Veii as well."

He made no effort, however, to find the authors; in fact, when some of them were reported to the senate by an informer, he forbade their being very severely punished. As he was passing along a public street, the Cynic Isidorus loudly taunted him, "because he was a good singer of the ills of Nauplius, but made ill use of his own goods." Datus also, an actor of Atellan farces, in a song beginning:

"Farewell to thee, father; farewell to thee, mother,"

represented drinking and swimming in pantomime, referring of course to the death of Claudius and Agrippina; and in the final tag,

"Orcus guides your steps,"

he indicated the senate by a gesture.[126] Nero contented himself with banishing the actor and the philosopher from the city, either because he was impervious to all insults, or to avoid sharpening men's wits by showing his vexation.

XL. After the world had put up with such a ruler for nearly fourteen years, it at last cast him off, and the Gauls took the first step under the lead of Julius Vindex, who at that time governed their province as propraetor.

Astrologers had predicted to Nero that he would one day be repudiated, which was the occasion of that well known saying of his: "A humble art affords us daily bread,"[127] doubtless uttered to justify him in practising the art of lyre-playing, as an amusement while emperor, but a necessity for a private citizen. Some of them, however, had promised him the rule of the East, when he was cast off, a few expressly naming the sovereignty of Jerusalem, and several the restitution of all his former fortunes. Inclining rather to this last hope, after losing Armenia and Britain and recovering both, he began to think that he had suffered the misfortunes which fate had in store. And after consulting the oracle at Delphi and being told that he must look out for the seventy-third year, assuming that he would die only at that period, and taking no account of Galba's years, he felt so confident not only of old age, but also of unbroken and unusual good fortune, that when he had lost some articles of great value by shipwreck, he did not hesitate to say among his intimate friends that the fish would bring them back to him.

He was at Naples when he learned of the uprising of the Gallic provinces, on the anniversary of his mother's murder, and received the news with such calmness and indifference that he incurred the suspicion of actually rejoicing in it, because it gave him an excuse for pillaging those wealthy provinces according to the laws of war And he at once proceeded to the gymnasium, where he watched the contests of the athletes with rapt interest. At dinner too when interrupted by a more disturbing letter, he fired up only so far as to threaten vengeance on the rebels. In short for eight whole days making no attempt to write a reply to anyone, none to give any commission or command, he blotted out the affair with silence.

XLI. At last he was driven by numerous insulting edicts of Vindex, to urge the senate in a letter to avenge him and the state, alleging a throat trouble as his excuse for not appearing in person. Yet there was nothing which he so much resented as the taunt that he was a wretched lyre-player and that he was addressed as Ahenobarbus instead of Nero.[128] With regard to his family name, which was cast in his teeth as an insult, he declared that he would resume it and give up that of his adoption. He used no other arguments to show the falsity of the rest of the reproaches than that he was actually taunted with being unskilled in an art to which he had devoted so much attention and in which he had so perfected himself, and he asked various individuals from time to time whether they knew of any artist who was his superior. Finally, beset by message after message, he returned to Rome in a panic; but on the way, when but slightly encouraged by an insignificant omen, for he noticed a monument on which was sculptured the overthrow of a Gallic soldier by a Roman horseman, who was dragging him along by the hair, he leaped for joy at the sight and lifted up his hands to heaven.[129] Not even on his arrival did he personally address the senate or people, but called some of the leading men to his house and after a hasty consultation spent the rest of the day in exhibiting some water-organs of a new and hitherto unknown form, explaining their several features and lecturing on the theory and complexity of each of them; and he even declared that he would presently produce them all in the theatre "with the kind permission of Vindex."

XLII. Thereafter, having learned that Galba also and the Spanish provinces had revolted, he fainted and lay for a long time insensible, without a word and all but dead. When he came to himself, he rent his robe and beat his brow, declaring that it was all over with him; and when his old nurse tried to comfort him by reminding him that similar evils had befallen other princes before him, he declared that unlike all others he was suffering the unheard of and unparalleled fate of losing the supreme power while he still lived. Nevertheless he did not abandon or amend his slothful and luxurious habits; on the contrary, whenever any good news came from the provinces, he not only gave lavish feasts, but even ridiculed the leaders of the revolt in verses set to wanton music, which have since become public, and accompanied them with gestures; then secretly entering the audience room of the theatre, he sent word to an actor who was making a hit that he was taking advantage of the emperor's busy days.[130]

XLIII. At the very beginning of the revolt it is believed that he formed many plans of monstrous wickedness, but in no way inconsistent with his character: to depose and assassinate the commanders of the armies and the governors of the provinces, on the ground that they were all united in a conspiracy against him; to massacre all the exiles everywhere and all men of Gallic birth in the city: the former, to prevent them from joining the rebels; the latter, as sharing and abetting the designs of their countrymen; to turn over the Gallic provinces to his armies to ravage; to poison the entire senate at banquets; to set fire to the city, first letting the wild beasts loose, that it might be harder for the people to protect themselves. But he was deterred from these designs, not so much by any compunction, as because he despaired of being able to carry them out, and feeling obliged to take the field, he deposed the consuls before the end of their term and assumed the office alone in place of both of them, alleging that it was fated that the Gallic provinces could not be subdued except by a consul.[131] Having assumed the fasces, he declared as he was leaving the dining-room after a banquet, leaning on the shoulders of his comrades, that immediately on setting foot in the province he would go before the soldiers unarmed and do nothing but weep; and having thus led the rebels to change their purpose, he would next day rejoice among his rejoicing subjects and sing paeans of victory, which he ought at that very moment to be composing.

XLIV. In preparing for his campaign his first care was to select wagons to carry his theatrical instruments, to have the hair of his concubines, whom he planned to take with him, trimmed man-fashion, and to equip them with Amazonian axes and shields. Next he summoned the city tribes to enlist, and when no eligible person responded, he levied on their masters a stated number of slaves, accepting only the choicest from each household and not even exempting paymasters and secretaries. He also required all classes to contribute a part of their incomes, and all tenants of private houses and apartments to pay a year's rent at once to the privy purse.[132] With great fastidiousness and rigour he demanded newly minted coin, refined silver, and pure gold,[133] so that many openly refused to make any contribution at all, unanimously demanding that he should rather compel the informers to give up whatever rewards had been paid them.

XLV. The bitter feeling against him was increased because he also turned the high cost of grain to his profit;[134] for indeed, it so fell out that while the people were suffering from hunger it was reported that a ship had arrived from Alexandria, bringing sand for the court wrestlers.

When he had thus aroused the hatred of all, there was no form of insult to which he was not subjected. A curl[135] was placed on the head of his statue with the inscription in Greek: "Now there is a real contest[136] and you must at last surrender." To the neck of another statue a sack was tied and with it the words: "I have done what I could, but you have earned the sack."[137] People wrote on the columns that he had stirred up even the Gauls[138] by his singing. When night came on, many men pretended to be wrangling with their slaves and kept calling out for a defender.[139]

XLVI. In addition he was frightened by manifest portents from dreams, auspices and omens, both old and new. Although he had never before been in the habit of dreaming, after he had killed his mother it seemed to him that he was steering a ship in his sleep and that the helm was wrenched from his hands; that he was dragged by his wife Octavia into thickest darkness, and that he was now covered with a swarm of winged ants, and now was surrounded by the statues of the nations which had been dedicated in Pompey's theatre and stopped in his tracks. A Spanish steed of which he was very fond was changed into the form of an ape in the hinder parts of its body, and its head, which alone remained unaltered, gave forth tuneful neighs. The doors of the Mausoleum flew open of their own accord, and a voice was heard from within summoning him by name. After the Lares had been adorned on the Kalends of January, they fell to the ground in the midst of the preparations for the sacrifice. As he was taking the auspices, Sporus made him a present of a ring with a stone on which was engraved the rape of Proserpina. When the vows were to be taken[140] and a great throng of all classes had assembled, the keys of the Capitol could not be found for a long time. When a speech of his in which he assailed Vindex was being read in the senate, at the words "the wretches will suffer punishment and will shortly meet the end which they deserve," all who were present cried out with one voice: "You will do it, Augustus."[141] It also had not failed of notice that the last piece which he sang in public was "Oedipus in Exile," and that he ended with the line:

"Wife, father, mother drive me to my death."

XLVII. When meanwhile word came that the other armies had revolted, he tore to pieces the dispatches which were handed to him as he was dining, tipped over the table, and dashed to the ground two favourite drinking cups, which he called "Homeric," because they were carved with scenes from Homer's poems.[142] Then taking some poison from Locusta and putting it into a golden box, he crossed over into the Servilian gardens, where he tried to induce the tribunes and centurions of the Guard to accompany him in his flight, first sending his most trustworthy freedmen to Ostia, to get a fleet ready. But when some gave evasive answers and some openly refused, one even cried:

"Is it so dreadful a thing then to die?"[143]

Whereupon he turned over various plans in his mind, whether to go as a suppliant to the Parthians or Galba, or to appear to the people on the rostra, dressed in black, and beg as pathetically as he could for pardon for his past offences; and if he could not soften their hearts, to entreat them at least to allow him the prefecture of Egypt. Afterwards a speech composed for this purpose was found in his writing desk; but it is thought that he did not dare to deliver it for fear of being torn to pieces before he could reach the Forum.

Having therefore put off further consideration to the following day, he awoke about midnight and finding that the guard of soldiers had left, he sprang from his bed and sent for all his friends. Since no reply came back from anyone, he went himself to their rooms[144] with a few followers. But finding that all the doors were closed and that no one replied to him, he returned to his own chamber, from which now the very caretakers had fled, taking with them even the bedclothing and the box of poison. Then he at once called for the gladiator Spiculus[145] or any other adept[146] at whose hand he might find death, and when no one appeared, he cried "Have I then neither friend nor foe?" and ran out as if to throw himself into the Tiber.

XLVIII. Changing his purpose again, he sought for some retired place, where he could hide and collect his thoughts; and when his freedmen Phaon offered his villa in the suburbs between the Via Nomentana and the Via Salaria near the fourth milestone, just as he was, barefooted and in his tunic, he put on a faded cloak, covered his head, and holding a handkerchief before his face, mounted a horse with only four attendants, one of whom was Sporus. At once he was startled by a shock of earthquake and a flash of lightning full in his face, and he heard the shouts of the soldiers from the camp hard by, as they prophesied destruction for him and success for Galba. He also heard one of the wayfarers whom he met say: "These men are after Nero," and another ask: "Is there anything new in the city about Nero?" Then his horse took fright at the smell of a corpse which had been thrown out into the road, his face was exposed, and a retired soldier of the Guard recognised him and saluted him. When they came to a by-path leading to the villa, they turned the horses loose and he made his way amid bushes and brambles and along a path through a thicket of reeds to the back wall of the house, with great difficulty and only when a robe was thrown down for him to walk on. Here the aforesaid Phaon urged him to hide for a time in a pit, from which sand had been dug, but he declared that he would not go under ground while still alive, and after waiting for a while until a secret entrance into the villa could be made, he scooped up in his hand some water to drink from a pool close by, saying: "This is Nero's distilled water."[147] Then, as his cloak had been torn by the thorns, he pulled out the twigs which had pierced it, and crawling on all fours through a narrow passage that had been dug, he entered the villa and lay down in the first room[148] he came to, on a couch with a common mattress, over which an old cloak had been thrown. Though suffering from hunger and renewed thirst, he refused some coarse bread which was offered him, but drank a little lukewarm water.

XLIX. At last, while his companions one and all urged him to save himself as soon as possible from the indignities that threatened him, he bade them dig a grave in his presence, proportioned to the size of his own person, collect any bits of marble that could be found, and at the same time bring water and wood for presently disposing of his body.[149] As each of these things was done, he wept and said again and again: "What an artist the world is losing!"

While he hesitated, a letter was brought to Phaon by one of his couriers. Nero snatching it from his hand read that he had been pronounced a public enemy by the senate, and that they were seeking him to punish him in the ancient fashion;[150] and he asked what manner of punishment that was. When he learned that the criminal was stripped, fastened by the neck in a fork[151] and then beaten to death with rods, in mortal terror he seized two daggers which he had brought with him, and then, after trying the point of each, put them up again, pleading that the fated hour had not yet come. Now he would beg Sporus to begin to lament and wail, and now entreat someone to help him take his life by setting him the example; anon he reproached himself for his cowardice in such words as these: "To live is a scandal and shame—this does not become Nero, does not become him—one should be resolute at such times—come, rouse thyself!" And now the horsemen were at hand who had orders to take him off alive. When he heard them, he quavered:

> "Hark, now strikes on my ear the trampling of swift-footed coursers!"[152]

and drove a dagger into his throat, aided by Epaphroditus his private secretary.[153] He was all but dead when a centurion rushed in, and as he placed a cloak to the wound, pretending that he had come to aid him, Nero merely gasped: "Too late!" and "This is fidelity!" With these words he was gone, with eyes so set and starting from their sockets that all who saw him shuddered with horror. First and beyond all else he had forced from his companions a promise to let no one have his head, but to contrive in some way that he be buried unmutilated. And this was granted by

Icelus, Galba's freedman,[154] who had shortly before been released from the bondage to which he was consigned at the beginning of the revolt.

L. He was buried at a cost of two hundred thousand sesterces and laid out in white robes embroidered with gold, which he had worn on the Kalends of January. His ashes were deposited by his nurses, Egloge and Alexandria, accompanied by his mistress Acte, in the family tomb of the Domitii on the summit of the Hill of Gardens,[155] which is visible from the Campus Martius. In that monument his sarcophagus of porphyry, with an altar of Luna marble standing above it, is enclosed by a balustrade of Thasian stone.

LI. He was about the average height, his body marked with spots and malodorous, his hair light blond, his features regular rather than attractive, his eyes blue and somewhat weak, his neck over thick, his belly prominent, and his legs very slender. His health was good, for though indulging in every kind of riotous excess, he was ill but three times in all during the fourteen years of his reign, and even then not enough to give up wine or any of his usual habits. He was utterly shameless in the care of his person and in his dress, always having his hair arranged in tiers of curls, and during the trip to Greece also letting it grow long and hang down behind; and he often appeared in public in a dining-robe,[156] with a handkerchief bound about his neck, ungirt and unshod.[157]

LII. When a boy he took up almost all the liberal arts; but his mother turned him from philosophy, warning him that it was a drawback to one who was going to rule, while Seneca kept him from reading the early orators, to make his admiration for his teacher endure the longer. Turning therefore to poetry, he wrote verses with eagerness and without labour, and did not, as some think, publish the work of others as his own. I have had in my possession note-books and papers with some well-known verses of his, written with his own hand and in such wise that it was perfectly evident that they were not copied or taken down from dictation, but worked out exactly as one writes when thinking and creating;

so many instances were there of words erased or struck through and written above the lines. He likewise had no slight interest in painting and sculpture.

LIII. But above all he was carried away by a craze for popularity and he was jealous of all who in any way stirred the feeling of the mob. It was the general belief that after his victories on the stage he would at the next lustrum[158] have competed with the athletes at Olympia; for he practised wrestling constantly, and all over Greece he had always viewed the gymnastic contests after the fashion of the judges, sitting on the ground in the stadium; and if any pairs of contestants withdrew too far from their positions, he would force them forward with his own hand. Since he was acclaimed as the equal of Apollo in music and of the Sun in driving a chariot, he had planned to emulate the exploits of Hercules as well; and they say that a lion had been specially trained for him to kill naked in the arena of the amphitheatre before all the people, with a club or by the clasp of his arms.

LIV. Towards the end of his life, in fact, he had publicly vowed that if he retained his power, he would at the games in celebration of his victory give a performance on the water-organ, the flute, and the bagpipes, and that on the last day he would appear as an actor and dance "Vergil's Turnus." Some even assert that he put the actor Paris to death as a dangerous rival.

LV. He had a longing for immortality and undying fame, though it was ill-regulated. With this in view he took their former appellations from many things and numerous places and gave them new ones from his own name. He also called the month of April Neroneus and was minded to name Rome Neropolis.

LVI. He utterly despised all cults, with the sole exception of that of the Syrian Goddess,[159] and even acquired such a contempt for her that he made water on her image, after he was enamoured of another superstition, which was the only one to which he constantly clung. For he had received as a gift from some unknown man of the commons, as a protection against plots, a little image of a girl; and since a conspiracy at once came to light, he continued to venerate it as a powerful divinity and to offer three sacrifices to it every day, encouraging the belief that through its communication he had knowledge of the future. A few months before his death he did attend an inspection of victims, but could not get a favourable omen.

68 A.D. LVII. He met his death in the thirty-second year of his age, on the anniversary of the murder of Octavia, and such was the public rejoicing that the people put on liberty-caps[160] and ran about all over the city. Yet there were some who for a long time decorated his tomb with spring and summer flowers, and now produced his statues on the rostra in the fringed toga, and now his edicts, as if he were still alive and would shortly return and deal destruction to his enemies. Nay more, Vologaesus, king of the Parthians, when he sent envoys to the senate to renew his alliance, earnestly begged this too, that honour be paid to the memory of Nero. In fact, twenty years later, when I was a young man, a person of obscure origin appeared, who gave out that he was Nero,[161] and the name was still in such favour with the Parthians that they supported him vigorously and surrendered him with great reluctance.

BOOK VII

GALBA, OTHO, AND VITELLIUS

Galba

I. The race of the Caesars ended with Nero.[1] That this would be so was shown by many portents and especially by two very significant ones. Years before, as Livia was returning to her estate near Veii, immediately after her marriage with Augustus, an eagle which flew 38 B.C. by dropped into her lap a white hen, holding in its beak a sprig of laurel, just as the eagle had carried it off. Livia resolved to rear the fowl and plant the sprig, whereupon such a great brood of chickens was hatched that to this day the villa is called *Ad Gallinas,*[2] and such a grove of laurel sprang up, that the Caesars gathered their laurels from it when they were going to celebrate triumphs. Moreover it was the habit of those who triumphed to plant other branches[3] at once in that same place, and it was observed that just before the death of each of them the tree which he had planted withered. Now in Nero's last year the whole grove died from the root up, as well as all the hens. Furthermore, when shortly afterwards the temple of the Caesars[4] was struck by lightning, the heads fell from all the statues at the same time, and his sceptre, too, was dashed from the hand of Augustus.

II. Nero was succeeded by Galba, who was related in no degree 68 A.D. to the house of the Caesars, although unquestionably of noble origin and of an old and powerful family; for he always added to the inscriptions on his statues that he was the great-grandson of Quintus Catulus Capitolinus,[5] and when he became emperor he even displayed a family tree in his hall in which he carried back his ancestry on his father's side to Jupiter and on his mother's to Pasiphae, the wife of Minos.

III. It would be a long story to give in detail his illustrious ancestors and the honorary inscriptions of the entire race, but I shall give a brief account of his immediate family.[6] It is uncertain who was the first of the Sulpicii to bear the surname Galba, why he assumed it, and whence it was derived. Some think that it was because after having for a long time unsuccessfully besieged a town in Spain, he at last set fire to it by torches smeared with *galbanum*[7]*;* others because during a long illness he made constant use of *galbeum,* that is to say of remedies wrapped in wool; still others, because he was a very fat man, such as the Gauls term *galba,* or because he was, on the contrary, as slender as the insects called *galbae,* which breed in oak trees.

145 B.C. The family acquired distinction from Servius Galba, who became consul and was decidedly the most eloquent speaker of his time. This man, they say, was the cause of the war with
150–136 B.C. Viriathus, because while governing Spain as propraetor, he treacherously massacred thirty thousand of the Lusitanians. His grandson had been one of Caesar's lieutenants in Gaul, but angered because his commander caused his defeat for the consulship, he joined the conspiracy with Brutus and Cassius, and was consequently condemned to death by the Pedian law.[8] From him were descended the grandfather and the father of the emperor Galba. The former, who was more eminent for his learning than for his rank—for he did not advance beyond the grade of praetor—pub-
22 A.D. lished a voluminous and painstaking history. The father attained the consulship, and although he was short of stature and even hunchbacked, besides being only an indifferent speaker, was an industrious pleader at the bar. He married Mummia Achaica, the granddaughter of Catulus and great-granddaughter of Lucius Mummius who destroyed Corinth; and later Livia Ocellina, a very

rich and beautiful woman, who however is thought to have sought marriage with him because of his high rank, and the more eagerly when, in response to her frequent advances, he took off his robe in private and showed her his deformity, so as not to seem to deceive her by concealing it. By Achaica he had two sons, Gaius and Servius. Gaius, who was the elder, left Rome after squandering the greater part of his estate, and committed suicide because Tiberius would not allow him to take part in the allotment of the provinces in his year.[9]

IV. The emperor Servius Galba was born in the consulship of Marcus Valerius Messala and Gnaeus Lentulus, on the ninth day before the Kalends of January, in a country house situated on a hill near Tarracina, on the left as you go towards Fundi. Adopted by his stepmother Livia, he took her name and the surname Ocella, and also changed his forename; for he used Lucius, instead of Servius, from that time until he became emperor. It is well known that when he was still a boy and called to pay his respects to Augustus with others of his age, the emperor pinched his cheek and said in Greek: "Thou too, child, wilt have a nibble at this power of mine." Tiberius too, when he heard that Galba was destined to be emperor, but in his old age, said: "Well, let him live then, since that does not concern me." Again, when Galba's grandfather was busy with a sacrifice for a stroke of lightning,[10] and an eagle snatched the intestines from his hand and carried them to an oak full of acorns, the prediction was made that the highest dignity would come to the family, but late; whereupon he said with a laugh: "Very likely, when a mule has a foal.[11]" Afterwards when Galba was beginning his revolt, nothing gave him so much encouragement as the foaling of a mule, and while the rest were horrified and looked on it as an unfavourable omen, he alone regarded it as most propitious, remembering the sacrifice and his grandfather's saying.

Dec. 24, 3 B.C.

When he assumed the gown of manhood, he dreamt that Fortune said that she was tired of standing before his door, and that unless she were quickly admitted, she would fall a prey to the first comer. When he awoke, opening the door of the hall, he found close by the threshold a bronze statue of Fortune more than a cubit high. This he carried in his arms to Tusculum, where he usually spent the summer, and consecrated it in a room of his house; and from that time on he honoured it with monthly sacrifices and a yearly vigil.

Even before he reached middle life, he persisted in keeping up an old and forgotten custom of his country, which survived only in his own household, of having his freedmen and slaves appear before him twice a day in a body, greeting him in the morning and bidding him farewell at evening, one by one.

V. Among other liberal studies he applied himself to the law. He also assumed a husband's duties,[12] but after losing his wife Lepida and two sons whom he had by her, he remained a widower. And he could not be tempted afterwards by any match, not even with Agrippina, who no sooner lost Domitius by death, than she set her cap for Galba so obviously, even before the death of his wife, that Lepida's mother scolded her roundly before a company of matrons and went so far as to slap her.

He showed marked respect to Livia Augusta, to whose favour he owed great influence during her lifetime and by whose last will he almost became a rich man; for he had the largest bequest among her legatees, one of fifty million sesterces. But because the sum was designated in figures and not written out in words, Tiberius, who was her heir, reduced the bequest to five hundred thousand, and Galba never received even that amount.

VI. He began his career of office before the legal age, and in celebrating the games of the Floralia in his praetorship he gave a new kind of exhibition, namely of elephants walking the rope.[13] Then he governed the province of Aquitania for nearly a year and soon
33 A.D. afterwards held a regular consulship[14] for six months; and it chanced that in this office he succeeded Lucius[15] Domitius, the father of Nero, and was succeeded by Salvius Otho, the father of the emperor Otho, a kind of omen of what happened later, when he became emperor between the reigns of the sons of these two men.

Appointed governor of Upper Germany by Gaius Caesar in room of Gaetulicus, the day after he appeared before the legions he put a stop to their applause at a festival which chanced to fall at that time, by issuing a written order to keep their hands under their cloaks; and immediately this verse was bandied about the camp:

"Soldiers, learn to play the soldier; 'tis Galba,not Gaetulicus."

With equal strictness he put a stop to the requests for furloughs. He got both the veterans and the new recruits into condition by plenty of hard work, speedily checked the barbarians, who had already made inroads even into Gaul, and when Gaius arrived,[16] Galba and his army made such a good impression, that out of the great body of troops assembled from all the provinces none received greater commendation or richer rewards. Galba particularly distinguished himself, while directing the military manœuvres shield in hand, by actually running for twenty miles close beside the emperor's chariot.[17]

VII. When the murder of Gaius was announced, although many urged Galba to take advantage of the opportunity, he preferred quiet. Hence he was in high favour with Claudius, became one of his staff of intimate friends, and was treated with such consideration that the departure of the expedition to Britain was put off because Galba was taken with a sudden illness, of no great severity. He governed Africa for two years with the rank of proconsul, being specially chosen[18] to restore order in the province, which was disturbed both by internal strife and by a revolt of the barbarians. And he was successful, owing to his insistence on strict discipline and his observance of justice even in trifling matters. When provisions were very scarce during a foray and a soldier was accused of having sold for a hundred denarii a peck[19] of wheat which was left from his rations, Galba gave orders that when the man began to lack food, he should receive aid from no one; and he starved to death. On another occasion when he was holding court and the question of the ownership of a beast of burden was laid before him, as the evidence on both sides was slight and the witnesses unreliable, so that it was difficult to get at the truth, he ruled that the beast should be led with its head muffled up to the pool where it was usually watered, that it should then be unmuffled, and should belong to the man to whom it returned of its own accord after drinking.

VIII. His services in Africa at that time, and previously in Germany, were recognised by the triumphal regalia and three priesthoods, for he was chosen a member of the Fifteen,[20] of the brotherhood of Titius,[21] and of the priests of Augustus.[22] After that he lived for the most part in retirement until about the middle of Nero's reign, never going out even for recreation without taking a million sesterces in gold with him in a second carriage[23]; until at last, while 60 A.D. he was staying in the town of Fundi, Hispania Tarraconensis was offered him. And it fell out that as he was offering sacrifice in a public temple after his arrival in the province, the hair of a young attendant who was carrying an incense-box suddenly turned white all over his head, and there were some who did not hesitate to interpret this as a sign of a change of rulers and of the succession of an old man to a young one; that is to say, of Galba to Nero. Not long after this lightning struck a lake of Cantabria and twelve axes were found there, an unmistakable token of supreme power.

IX. For eight years he governed the province in a variable and inconsistent manner. At first he was vigorous and energetic and even over severe in punishing offences; for he cut off the hands of a money-lender who carried on his business dishonestly and nailed them to his counter; crucified a man for poisoning his ward, whose property he was to inherit in case of his death; and when the man invoked the law and declared that he was a Roman citizen, Galba, pretending to lighten his punishment by some consolation and honour, ordered that a cross much higher than the rest and painted white be set up, and the man transferred to it. But he gradually changed to sloth and inaction, not to give Nero any cause for jealousy, and as he used to say himself, because no one could be forced to render an account for doing nothing.

As he was holding the assizes at New Carthage, he learned of the rebellion of the Gallic provinces through an urgent appeal for help from the governor of Aquitania; then came letters from Vindex, calling upon him to make himself the liberator and leader of mankind. So without much hesitation he accepted the proposal, led by fear as well as by hope. For he had intercepted despatches ordering his own death, which had been secretly sent by Nero to his agents.[24] He was encouraged too, in addition to most favourable auspices and omens, by the prediction of a young girl of high birth, and the more so because the priest of Jupiter at Clunia, directed by a dream, had found in the inner shrine of his temple the very same prediction, likewise spoken by an inspired girl two hundred years before. And the purport of the verses[25] was that one day there would come forth from Spain the ruler and lord of the world.

X. Accordingly, pretending that he was going to attend to the manumitting of slaves, he mounted the tribunal, on the front of which he had set up as many images as he could find of those who had been condemned and put to death by Nero; and having by his side a boy of noble family, whom he had summoned for that very purpose from his place of exile hard by in the Balearic Isles, he deplored the state of the times; being thereupon hailed as emperor, he declared that he was their governor, representing the senate and people of Rome.[26] Then proclaiming a holiday, he enrolled from the people of the province legions and auxiliaries in addition to his former force of one legion, two divisions of cavalry, and three cohorts. But from the oldest and most experienced of the nobles he chose a kind of senate, to whom he might refer matters of special importance whenever it was necessary. He also chose young men of the order of knights, who were to have the title of volunteers[27] and keep guard before his bedchamber in place of the regular soldiers, without losing their right to wear the gold ring.[28] He also sent proclamations broadcast throughout the province, urging all men individually and collectively to join the revolution and aid the common cause in every possible way.

At about this same time, during the fortification of a town which he had chosen as the seat of war, a ring of ancient workmanship was found, containing a precious stone engraved with a Victory and a trophy. Immediately afterwards a ship from Alexandria loaded with arms arrived at Dertosa without a pilot, without a single sailor or passenger, removing all doubt in anyone's mind that the war was just and holy and undertaken with the approval of the gods. Then suddenly and unexpectedly the whole plan was almost brought to naught. One of the two divisions of cavalry,[29] repenting of its change of allegiance, attempted to desert Galba as he was approaching his camp and was with difficulty prevented. Some slaves too, whom one of Nero's freedmen had given Galba with treachery in view, all but slew him as he was going to the bath through a narrow passage-way. In fact they would have succeeded, had they not conjured one another not to miss the opportunity and so been questioned as to what the opportunity was to which they referred; for when they were put to the torture, a confession was wrung from them.

XI. To these great perils was added the death of Vindex, by which he was especially panic-stricken and came near taking his own life, in the belief that all was lost. But when some messengers came from the city, reporting that Nero was dead and that all the people had sworn allegiance to him, he laid aside the title of governor and assumed that of Caesar.[30] He then began his march to Rome in a general's cloak with a dagger hanging from his neck in front of his breast; and he did not resume the toga until he had overthrown those who were plotting against him, Nymphidius Sabinus, prefect of the praetorian guard at Rome, in Germany and Africa the governors Fonteius Capito and Clodius Macer.

XII. His double reputation for cruelty and avarice had gone before him; men said that he had punished the cities of the Spanish and Gallic provinces which had hesitated about taking sides with him by heavier taxes and some even by the razing of their walls, putting to death the governors and imperial deputies[31] along with their wives and children. Further, that he had melted down a golden crown of fifteen pounds weight, which the people of Tarraco had taken from their ancient temple of Jupiter and presented to him, with orders that the three ounces which were found lacking be exacted from them. This reputation was confirmed and even augmented immediately on his arrival in the city. For having compelled some marines whom Nero had made regular soldiers to return to their former position as rowers, upon their refusing and obstinately demanding an eagle and standards, he not only dispersed them by a cavalry charge, but even decimated[32] them. He also disbanded a cohort of Germans, whom the previous Caesars had made their body-guard[33] and had found absolutely faithful in many emergencies, and sent them back to their native country without any rewards, alleging that they were more favourably inclined towards Gnaeus Dolabella, near whose gardens they had their camp. The following tales too were told in mockery of him, whether truly or falsely:[34] that when an unusually elegant dinner was set before him, he groaned aloud; that when his duly appointed steward presented his expense account, he handed him a dish of beans in return for his industry and carefulness; and that when the flute player Canus greatly pleased him, he presented him with five denarii, which he took from his own purse with his own hand.[35]

XIII. Accordingly his coming was not so welcome as it might have been, and this was apparent at the first performance in the theatre; for when the actors of an Atellan farce began the familiar lines

"Here comes Onesimus from his farm"[36]

all the spectators at once finished the song in chorus and repeated it several times with appropriate gestures, beginning with that verse.

XIV. Thus his popularity and prestige were greater when he won, than while he ruled the empire,[37] though he gave many proofs of being an excellent prince; but he was by no means so much loved for those qualities as he was hated for his acts of the opposite character.

He was wholly under the control of three men, who were commonly known as his tutors because they lived with him in the palace and never left his side. They were Titus Vinius, one of his generals in Spain, a man of unbounded covetousness; Cornelius Laco, advanced from the position of judge's assistant to that of prefect of the Guard and intolerably haughty and indolent; and his own freedman Icelus, who had only just before received the honour of the gold ring[38] and the surname of Marcianus, yet already aspired to the highest office open to the equestrian order.[39] To these brigands, each with his different vice, he so entrusted and handed himself over as their tool, that his conduct was far from consistent; for now he was more exacting and niggardly, and now more extravagant and reckless than became a prince chosen by the people and of his time of life.

He condemned to death divers distinguished men of both orders on trivial suspicions without a trial. He rarely granted Roman citizenship, and the privileges of threefold paternity[40] to hardly one or two, and even to those only for a fixed and limited time. When the jurors petitioned that a sixth division be added to their number, he not only refused, but even deprived them of the privilege granted by Claudius,[41] of not being summoned for court duty in winter and at the beginning of the year.

XV. It was thought too that he intended to limit the offices open to senators and knights to a period of two years, and to give them only to such as did not wish them and declined them.[42] He had all the grants of Nero revoked, allowing only a tenth part to be retained; and he exacted repayment with the help of fifty Roman knights, stipulating that even if the actors and athletes had sold anything that had formerly been given them, it should be taken away from the purchasers, in case the recipient had spent the money and could not repay it. On the other hand, there was nothing that he did not allow his friends and freedmen to sell at a price or bestow as a favour, taxes and freedom from taxation, the punishment of the guiltless and impunity for the guilty. Nay more, when the Roman people called for the punishment of Halotus and Tigellinus, the most utterly abandoned of all Nero's creatures, not content with saving their lives, he honoured Halotus with a very important stewardship and in the case of Tigellinus even issued an edict rebuking the people for their cruelty.

XVI. Having thus incurred the hatred of almost all men of every class, he was especially detested by the soldiers; for although their officers[43] had promised them a larger gift than common when they swore allegiance to Galba in his absence, so far from keeping the promise, he declared more than once that it was his habit to levy troops, not buy them; and on this account he embittered the soldiers all over the empire. The praetorians he filled besides with both fear and indignation by discharging many of them from time to time as under suspicion of being partisans of Nymphidius.[44] But loudest of all was the grumbling of the army in Upper Germany, because it was defrauded of the reward for its services against the Gauls and Vindex. Hence they were the first to venture on mutiny, refusing on the Kalends of January to swear allegiance to anyone save the senate, and at once resolving to send a deputation to the praetorians with the following message: that the emperor created in Spain did not suit them and the Guard must choose one who would be acceptable to all the armies.

XVII. When this was reported to Galba, thinking that it was not so much his age as his lack of children that was criticised, he picked out Piso Frugi Licinianus from the midst of the throng at one of his morning receptions, a young man of noble birth and high character, who had long been one of his special favourites and always named in his will as heir to his property and his name. Calling him son, he led him to the praetorian camp and adopted him before the assembled soldiers. But even then he made no mention of largess, thus making it easier for Marcus Salvius Otho to accomplish his purpose within six days after the adoption.

XVIII. Many prodigies in rapid succession from the very beginning of his reign had foretold Galba's end exactly as it happened. When victims were being slain to right and left all along his route in every town,[45] an ox, maddened by the stroke of an axe, broke its bonds and charged the emperor's chariot, and as it raised its feet, deluged him with blood. And as Galba dismounted, one of his guards, pushed forward by the crowd, almost wounded him with his lance. Again, as he entered the city, and later the Palace, he was met by a shock of earthquake and a sound like the lowing of kine. There followed even clearer signs. He had set apart from all the treasure a necklace fashioned of pearls and precious stones, for the adornment of his image of Fortune at Tusculum.[46] This on a sudden impulse he consecrated to the Capitoline Venus, thinking it worthy of a more august position. The next night Fortune appeared to him in his dreams, complaining of being robbed of the gift intended for her and threatening in her turn to take away what she had bestowed. When Galba hastened in terror to Tusculum at daybreak, to offer expiatory sacrifices because of the dream, and sent on men to make preparations for the ceremony, he found on the altar nothing but warm ashes and beside it an old man dressed in black, holding the incense in a glass dish and the wine in an earthen cup.[47] It was also remarked that as he was sacrificing on the Kalends of January, the garland fell from his head, and that as he took the auspices, the sacred chickens flew away. As he was on the point of addressing the soldiers on the day of the adoption,[48] his camp chair, through the forgetfulness of his attendants, was not placed on the tribunal, as is customary, and in the senate his curule chair was set wrong side foremost.

XIX. As he was offering sacrifice on the morning before he was killed, a soothsayer warned him again and again to look out for danger, since assassins were not far off.

Not long after this he learned that Otho held possession of the Camp,[49] and when several advised him to proceed thither as soon as possible—for they said that he could win the day by his presence and prestige—he decided to do no more than hold his present position and strengthen it by getting together a guard of the legionaries, who were encamped in many different quarters of the city. He did however put on a linen cuirass, though he openly declared that it would afford little protection against so many swords. But he was lured out by false reports, circulated by the conspirators to induce him to appear in public; for when a few rashly assured him that the trouble was over, that the rebels had been overthrown, and that the rest were coming in a body to offer their congratulations, ready to submit to all his orders, he went out to meet them with so much confidence, that when one of the soldiers boasted that he had slain Otho, he asked him, "On whose authority?" and then he went on as far as the Forum. There the horsemen who had been bidden to slay him, spurring their horses through the streets and dispersing the crowd of civilians, caught sight of him from a distance and halted for a moment. Then they rushed upon him again and butchered him, abandoned by his followers.

XX. Some say that at the beginning of the disturbance he cried out, "What mean you, fellow soldiers? I am yours and you are mine," and that he even promised them largess.[50] But the more general account is, that he offered them his neck without resistance, urging them to do their duty[51] and strike, since it was their will. It was very surprising that none of those present tried to lend aid to their emperor, and that all who were sent for treated the summons with contempt except a company of German troops. These, because of his recent kindness in showing them great indulgence when they were weakened by illness, flew to his help, but through their unfamiliarity with the city took a roundabout way and arrived too late.

He was killed beside the Lake of Curtius[52] and was left lying just as he was, until a common soldier, returning from a distribution of grain, threw down his load and cut off the head. Then, since there was no hair by which to grasp it, he put it under his robe, but later thrust his thumb into the mouth and so carried it to Otho. He handed it over to his servants and camp-followers, who set it on a lance and paraded it about the camp with jeers, crying out from time to time, "Galba, thou Cupid, exult in thy vigour!" The special reason for this saucy jest was, that the report had gone abroad a few days before, that when someone had congratulated him on still looking young and vigorous, he replied:

"As yet my strength is unimpaired."[53]

From these it was bought by a freedman of Patrobius Neronianus for a hundred pieces of gold and thrown aside in the place where his patron had been executed by Galba's order. At last, however, his steward Argivus consigned it to the tomb with the rest of the body in Galba's private gardens on the Aurelian Road.

XXI. He was of average height, very bald, with blue eyes and a hooked nose. His hands and feet were so distorted by gout that he could not endure a shoe for long, unroll a book, or even hold one. The flesh on his left side too had grown out and hung down to such an extent, that it could with difficulty be held in place by a bandage.

XXII. It is said that he was a heavy eater and in winter time was in the habit of taking food even before daylight, while at dinner he helped himself so lavishly that he would have the leavings which remained in a heap before him passed along and distributed among the attendants who waited on him.[54] He was more inclined to unnatural desire, and in gratifying it preferred full-grown, strong men. They say that when Icelus, one of his old-time favourites, brought him news in Spain of Nero's death, he not only received him openly with the fondest kisses, but begged him to prepare himself without delay and took him one side.

69 A.D. XXIII. He met his end in the seventy-third year of his age and the seventh month of his reign. The senate, as soon as it was allowed to do so, voted him a statue standing upon a column adorned with the beaks of ships, in the part of the Forum where he was slain; but Vespasian annulled this decree, believing that Galba had sent assassins from Spain to Judaea, to take his life.

Otho

I. The ancestors of Otho came from an old and illustrious family in the town of Ferentium and were descended from the princes of Etruria.[55] His grandfather Marcus Salvius Otho, whose father was a Roman knight but whose mother was of lowly origin and perhaps not even free-born, became a senator through the influence of Livia Augusta, in whose house he was reared; but did not advance beyond the grade of praetor.

His father Lucius Otho was of a distinguished family on his mother's side, with many powerful connections, and was so beloved by Tiberius and so like him in appearance, that he was believed by many to be the emperor's son. In the regular offices at Rome, the proconsulate of Africa, and several special military commands he conducted himself with extreme severity. In Illyricum he even had the courage to punish some soldiers with death, because in the rebellion of Camillus,[56] repenting of their defection, they had killed their officers on the ground that they were the ringleaders in the revolt against Claudius; and they were executed in his presence before his headquarters, although he knew that they had been promoted to higher positions by Claudius because of that very act. By this deed, while he increased his reputation, he lost favour at court; but he speedily regained it by detecting the treachery of a Roman knight, whose slaves betrayed their master's design of killing the emperor.[57] For in consequence of this, the senate conferred a very unusual honour on him by setting up his statue in the Palace; and Claudius also enrolled him among the patricians, and after praising him in the highest terms, added these words: "a man of greater loyalty than I can even pray for in my own children." By Albia Terentia, a woman of an illustrious line, he had two sons, Lucius Titianus and a younger called Marcus, who had the same surname as himself; also a daughter, whom he betrothed to Drusus, son of Germanicus, almost before she was of marriageable age.

II. The emperor Otho was born on the fourth day before the Kalends of May in the consulate of Camillus Arruntius and Domitius Ahenobarbus. From earliest youth he was so extravagant Apr.28,
and wild that his father often flogged him; and they say that he 32 A.D.
used to rove about at night and lay hands on any one whom he met who was feeble or drunk and toss him in a blanket.[58]

After his father's death he pretended love for an influential freedwoman of the court, although she was an old woman and almost decrepit, that he might more effectually win her favour. Having through her wormed his way into Nero's good graces, he easily held the first place among the emperor's friends because of the similarity of their characters; but according to some, also through immoral relations. At any rate his influence was such, that when he had bargained for a huge sum of money to procure the pardon of an ex-consul who had been condemned for extortion, he had no hesitation in bringing him into the senate to give thanks, before he had fully secured his restoration.[59]

III. He was privy to all the emperor's plans and secrets, and on the day which Nero had chosen for the murder of his mother he gave both of them a most elaborate banquet,[60] in order to avert suspicion. Also when Poppaea Sabina, who up to that time had been Nero's mistress, was separated from her husband and turned over for the time being to Otho, he pretended marriage with her;[61] but not content with seducing her he became so devoted that he could not endure the thought of having Nero even as a rival. At all events it is believed that he not only would not admit those whom Nero sent to fetch her, but that on one occasion he even shut out the emperor himself, who stood before his door, vainly mingling threats and entreaties and demanding the return of his trust. Therefore Nero annulled the marriage[62] and under colour of an appointment as governor banished Otho to Lusitania, contenting himself with this through fear that by inflicting a severer punishment he would make the whole farce public; but even as it was, it was published abroad in this couplet:

> "Why, do you ask, in feigned honour does Otho in banishment
> languish?
> With his own wedded wife he had begun an intrigue."

With the rank of quaestor Otho governed the province for ten years with remarkable moderation and integrity.

IV. When at last an opportunity for revenge was given him, Otho was the first to espouse Galba's cause, at the same time conceiving on his own account high hopes of imperial power, because of the state of the times, but still more because of a declaration of the astrologer Seleucus.[63] For he had not only promised Otho some time before that he would survive Nero, but had at this time unexpectedly appeared unsought and made the further promise, that he would soon become emperor as well.

Accordingly Otho let slip no opportunity for flattery or attention to anyone. Whenever he entertained the prince at dinner, he gave a gold piece to each man of the cohort on guard, and put all the soldiers under obligation in one form or another. Chosen arbiter by a man who was at law with his neighbour about a part of his estate, he bought the whole property and presented it to him. As a result there was hardly anyone who did not both think and openly declare that he alone was worthy to succeed to the empire.

V. Now he had hoped to be adopted by Galba, and looked forward to it from day to day. But when Piso was preferred and he at last lost that hope, he resorted to force, spurred on not merely by feelings of resentment, but also by the greatness of his debts. For he flatly declared that he could not keep on his feet unless he became emperor, and that it made no difference whether he fell at the hands of the enemy in battle or at those of his creditors in the Forum.

He had extorted a million sesterces from one of the emperor's slaves a few days before for getting him a stewardship. This was the entire capital for his great undertaking. At first the enterprise was entrusted to five of his body-guard, then to ten others, two being chosen by each of the first five; to all of them ten thousand sesterces were paid at once and they were promised fifty thousand more. Through these others were won over, but not so very many, since he had full confidence that more would join him when the business was afoot.

VI. He had been inclined to seize the Camp immediately after the adoption, and set upon Galba as he was dining in the Palace, but had been prevented by consideration for the cohort which was on guard at the time, and a reluctance to increase its ill repute; for it was while that same cohort was at its post that both Galba had been slain and Nero had been forsaken. The intervening time[64] was lost owing to bad omens and the warnings of Seleucus.

Accordingly, when the day was set, after admonishing his confederates to await him in the Forum at the golden mile-post[65] hard by the temple of Saturn, he called upon Galba in the morning and was welcomed as usual with a kiss. He also attended the emperor as he was offering sacrifice, and heard the predictions of the soothsayer. Then a freedman announced that the architects had come, which was the signal agreed on, and going off as if to inspect a house which was for sale, he rushed from the Palace by a back door and hastened to the appointed place. Others say that he feigned an attack of fever and asked those who stood near him to give that excuse, in case he should be missed. Then hurriedly entering a closed sedan, such as women use, he hurried to the camp, but got out when the bearers' strength flagged, and started to run. His shoe came untied and he stopped, whereupon without delay he was at once taken up on the shoulders of his companions and hailed as emperor. In this way he arrived at headquarters, amid acclamations and drawn swords, while everyone whom he met fell in, just as though he were an accomplice and a participator in the plot. He then sent emissaries to kill Galba and Piso, and made no further promises in the assembly to win the loyalty of the soldiers than to declare that he would have that—and only that—which they should leave to him.

VII. Next, as the day was drawing to its close, he entered the senate and after giving a brief account of himself, alleging that he had been carried off in the streets and forced to undertake the rule, which he would exercise in accordance with the general will, he went to the Palace. When in the midst of the other adulations of those who congratulated and flattered him, he was hailed by the common herd as Nero, he made no sign of dissent; on the contrary, according to some writers, he even made use of that surname in his commissions and his first letters to some of the governors of the provinces. Certain it is that he suffered Nero's busts and statues to be set up again, and reinstated his procurators and freedmen in their former posts, while the first grant that he signed as emperor was one of fifty million sesterces for finishing the Golden House.

It is said that he had a fearful dream that night, uttered loud groans, and was found by those who ran to his aid lying on the ground beside his couch; that he tried by every kind of expiatory rite to propitiate the shade of Galba, by whom he dreamt that he was ousted and thrown out; and that next day, as he was taking the auspices, a great storm arose and he had a bad fall, whereat he muttered from time to time:

With long pipes what concern have I?[66]

VIII. Now at about this same time the armies in Germany swore allegiance to Vitellius. When Otho learned of this, he persuaded the senate to send a deputation, to say that an emperor had already been chosen and to counsel peace and harmony; but in spite of this he offered Vitellius by messengers and letters a share in the imperial dignity and proposed to become his son-in-law. But when it became clear that war was inevitable, and the generals and troops which Vitellius had sent in advance were already drawing near, he was given a proof of the affection and loyalty of the praetorians towards himself which almost resulted in the destruction of the senate. It had been resolved that some arms should be removed and carried back[67] on shipboard by the marines; but as these were being taken out[68] in the Camp towards nightfall, some suspected treachery and started a riot; then on a sudden all the soldiers hastened to the Palace without any particular leader, demanding the death of the senators. After putting to flight some of the tribunes who attempted to stop them, and killing others, just as they were, all blood-stained, they burst right into the dining-room, demanding to know where the emperor was; and they could not be quieted until they had seen him.[69]

He began his expedition with energy and in fact too hastily, without any regard even for the omens, and in spite of the fact that the sacred shields had been taken out,[70] but not yet put back, which for ages has been considered unlucky; on the very day, too, when the worshippers of the Mother of the Gods[71] begin their wailing and lamentation, and also with most unfavourable auspices. For having offered up a victim to father Dis, he had good omens, whereas in such a sacrifice adverse indications are more favourable; and when he first left the city, he was delayed by floods of the Tiber, while at the twentieth milestone he found the road blocked by fallen buildings.

IX. With like rashness, although no one doubted that the proper course was to protract the war, since the enemy were hard pressed by hunger and by the narrowness of their quarters, he decided to fight a decisive battle as soon as possible, either because he could not endure the continued worry and hoped that the war could be ended before the arrival of Vitellius, or from inability to resist the impetuosity of his soldiers, who clamoured for the fight. He himself did not take part in any of the battles, but remained behind at Brixellum.

He was victorious in three contests, but they were of little moment: in the Alps, near Placentia, and "at Castor's,"[72] as the place is called. In the final and decisive struggle at Betriacum he was defeated, but through treachery. For hope of a conference was offered, and when his soldiers were led out in the belief that they were to discuss terms of peace, a battle was forced upon them unexpectedly, just as they were exchanging greetings with the foe. After the defeat, Otho at once resolved to take his own life, rather from a feeling of shame, as many have thought with good reason, and an unwillingness to persist in a struggle for imperial power at the expense of such danger to life and property, than from any despair of success or distrust of his troops; for even then he had a fresh and strong force which he had held in reserve for a second attempt, while others were on their way from Dalmatia, Pannonia, and Moesia. Even the defeated troops were not so crushed as not to undergo any danger, and even without support undertake to avenge their disgrace.

X. My father Suetonius Laetus took part in that war, as a tribune of the equestrian order in the Thirteenth legion. He used often to declare afterwards that Otho, even when he was a private citizen, so loathed civil strife, that at the mere mention of the fate of Brutus and Cassius at a banquet he shuddered; that he would not have engaged with Galba, if he had not felt confident that the affair could be settled peacefully; further, that he was led to hold his life cheap at that time by the example of a common soldier. This man on bringing news of the defeat of the army was believed by no one, but was charged by the soldiers now with falsehood and now with cowardice, and accused of running away; whereupon he fell on his sword at the emperor's feet. My father used to say that at this sight Otho cried out that he would no longer endanger the lives of such brave men, who had deserved so well.

Having therefore advised his brother, his nephew, and his friends one by one to look out each for his own safety as best they could, he embraced and kissed them all and sent them off. Then going to a retired place he wrote two notes, one of consolation to his sister, and one to Nero's widow Messalina, whom he had intended to marry, commending to her his corpse and his memory. Then he burned all his letters, to prevent them from bringing danger or harm to anyone at the hands of the victor. He also distributed what money he had with him among his servants.

XI. When he had thus made his preparations and was now resolved upon death, learning from a disturbance which meantime arose that those who were beginning to depart and leave the camp were being seized and detained as deserters, he said "Let us add this one more night to our life" (these were his very words), and he forbade the offering of violence to anyone. Leaving the door of his bedroom open until a late hour, he gave the privilege of speaking with him to all who wished to come in. After that quenching his thirst with a draught of cold water, he caught up two daggers, and having tried the point of both of them, put one under his pillow. Then closing the doors, he slept very soundly. When he at last woke up at about daylight, he stabbed himself with a single stroke under the left breast; and now concealing the wound, and now showing it to those who rushed in at his first groan, he breathed his last and was hastily buried (for such were his orders) in the thirty-eighth year of his age and on the ninety-fifth day of his reign.

XII. Neither Otho's person nor his bearing suggested such great courage. He is said to have been of moderate height, splay-footed and bandy-legged, but almost feminine in his care of his person. He had the hair of his body plucked out, and because of the thinness of his locks wore a wig so carefully fashioned and fitted to his head, that no one suspected it. Moreover, they say that he used to shave every day and smear his face with moist bread, beginning the practice with the appearance of the first down, so as never to have a beard; also that he used to celebrate the rites of Isis publicly in the linen garment prescribed by the cult. I am inclined to think that it was because of these habits that a death so little in harmony with his life excited the greater marvel. Many of the soldiers who were present kissed his hands and feet as he lay dead, weeping bitterly and calling him the bravest of men and an incomparable emperor, and then at once slew themselves beside his bier. Many of those who were absent too, on receiving the news attacked and killed one another from sheer grief. In short the greater part of those who had hated him most bitterly while he lived lauded him to the skies when he was dead; and it was even commonly declared that he had put an end to Galba, not so much for the sake of ruling, as of restoring the republic and liberty.

Vitellius

I. Of the origin of the Vitellii different and widely varying accounts are given, some saying that the family was ancient and noble, others that it was new and obscure, if not of mean extraction. I should believe that these came respectively from the flatterers and detractors of the emperor, were it not for a difference of opinion about the standing of the family at a considerably earlier date. We have a book of Quintus Elogius addressed to Quintus Vitellius, quaestor of the

Deified Augustus, in which it is written that the Vitellii were sprung from Faunus, king of the Aborigines, and Vitellia, who was worshipped as a goddess in many places; and that they ruled in all Latium. That the surviving members of the family moved from the Sabine district to Rome and were enrolled among the patricians. That traces of this stock endured long afterwards in the Vitellian Road, running from the Janiculum all the way to the sea, as well as in a colony of the same name, which in ancient days the family had asked the privilege of defending against the Aequicoli with troops raised from their own line. That when afterwards a force was sent into Apulia at the time of the Samnite war, some of the Vitellii settled at Nuceria, and that after a long time their descendants returned to the city and resumed their place in the senatorial order.

II. On the other hand several have written that the founder of the family was a freedman, while Cassius Severus and others as well say further that he was a cobbler, and that his son, after making a considerable fortune from the sale of confiscated estates and the profession of informer, married a common strumpet, daughter of one Antiochus who kept a bakery, and became the father of a Roman knight. But this difference of opinion may be left unsettled.

In any event Publius Vitellius of Nuceria, whether of ancient stock or of parents and forefathers in whom he could take no pride, unquestionably a Roman knight and a steward of Augustus's property, left four sons of high rank with the same name and differing only in their forenames: Aulus, Quintus, Publius and Lucius. Aulus, who was given to luxury and especially notorious for the magnificence of his feasts, died a consul, appointed to the office with 32 A.D.
Domitius, father of the emperor Nero. Quintus lost his rank at the time when it was resolved, at the suggestion of Tiberius, to depose and get rid of undesirable senators.[73] Publius, a member of Germanicus' staff, arraigned Gnaeus Piso, the enemy and mur- 20 A.D.
derer of his commander, and secured his condemnation. Arrested among the accomplices of Sejanus, after holding the praetorship, and handed over to his own brother to be kept in confinement, he opened his veins with a penknife, but allowed 35 A.D.

himself to be bandaged and restored, not so much from unwillingness to die, as because of the entreaties of his friends; and he met a natural death while still in confinement. Lucius attained the consulate and then was made governor of Syria, where with supreme
34 A.D. diplomacy he not only induced Artabanus, king of the Parthians, to hold a conference with him,[74] but even to do obeisance to the standards of the legion. Later he held, with the emperor Claudius, two
43, 47, 50, 44 A.D. more regular consulships and the censorship. He also bore the charge of the empire while Claudius was away on his expedition to Britain. He was an honest and active man, but of very ill repute because of his passion for a freedwoman, which went so far that he used her spittle mixed with honey to rub on his throat and jaws as a medicine, not secretly nor seldom, but openly and every day. He had also a wonderful gift for flattery and was the first to begin to worship Gaius Caesar as a god; for on his return from Syria he did not presume to approach the emperor except with veiled head, turning himself about and then prostrating himself. To neglect no means of gaining the favour of Claudius, who was a slave to his wives and freedmen,[75] he begged of Messalina as the highest possible favour that she would allow him to take off her shoes; and when he had taken off her right slipper, he constantly carried it about between his toga and his tunic, and sometimes kissed it. Narcissus also and Pallas he honoured by cherishing their images among his household gods. It was he who made the famous remark, "May you often do it," when he was congratulating Claudius at the celebration of the Secular games.[76]

III. He died of a paralytic stroke on the second day after he was seized, leaving two sons, begotten of Sestilia, a most worthy woman and of no mean family, and having lived to see them consuls both in the same year, and for the whole year, since the younger succeeded the elder for six months. On his decease the senate honoured him with a public funeral and with a statue on the rostra with this inscription: "Of unwavering loyalty to his emperor."

The emperor Aulus Vitellius, son of Lucius, was born on the
Sept. 24, 15 A.D. eight day before the Kalends of October, or according to some, on the seventh day before the Ides of September, in the consulship of

Drusus Caesar and Norbanus Flaccus. His parents were so aghast at his horoscope as announced by the astrologers, that his father tried his utmost, while he lived, to prevent the assignment of any province to his son; and when he was sent to the legions and hailed as emperor, his mother immediately mourned over him as lost. He spent his boyhood and early youth at Capreae among the wantons of Tiberius, being branded for all time with the nickname Spintria[77] and suspected of having been the cause of his father's first advancement at the expense of his own chastity. Sept. 7

IV. Stained by every sort of baseness as he advanced in years, he held a prominent place at court, winning the intimacy of Gaius by his devotion to driving and of Claudius by his passion for dice. But he was still dearer to Nero, not only because of these same qualities, but because of a special service besides; for when he was presiding at the contests of the Neronia[78] and Nero wished to compete among the lyre-players, but did not venture to do so although there was a general demand for him and accordingly left the theatre, Vitellius called him back, alleging that he came as an envoy from the insistent people, and thus gave Nero a chance to yield to their entreaties.

V. Having in this way through the favour of three emperors been honoured not only with political positions but with distinguished priesthoods as well, he afterwards governed Africa as proconsul and served as curator of public works, but with varying purpose and reputation. In his province he showed exceptional integrity for two successive years, for he served as deputy to his brother, who succeeded him; but in his city offices he was said to have stolen some of the offerings and ornaments from the temples and changed others, substituting tin and brass for gold and silver. 60 A.D.

VI. He had to wife Petronia, daughter of an ex-consul, and by her a son Petronianus, who was blind in one eye. Since this son was named as his mother's heir on condition of being freed from his father's authority, he manumitted him, but shortly afterwards killed him, according to the general belief, charging him besides with attempted parricide, and alleging that his guilty conscience had led him to drink the poison which he had mixed for his intended crime. Soon afterwards he married Galeria Fundana, daughter of an ex-praetor, and from her too he had a son and a daughter, but the former stammered so, that he was all but dumb and tongue-tied.

VII. Galba surprised everyone by sending him to Lower Germany. Some think that it was due to Titus Vinius, who had great influence at the time, and whose friendship Vitellius had long since won through their common support of the Greens.[79] But since Galba openly declared that no men were less to be feared than those who thought of nothing but eating, and that Vitellius's bottomless gullet might be filled from the resources of the province, it is clear to anyone that he was chosen rather through contempt than favour. It is notorious that when he was about to start, he lacked means for his travelling expenses, and that his need of funds was such, that after consigning his wife and children, whom he left in Rome, to a hired garret, he let his house for the rest of the year; and that he took a valuable pearl from his mother's ear and pawned it, to defray the expenses of his journey. He had to resort to false accusation to get rid of the throng of creditors that lay in wait for him and tried to detain him, including the people of Sinuessa and of Formiae, whose public revenues he had embezzled; for he brought an action for damages against a freedman who was somewhat persistent in demanding what was due to him, alleging that he had been kicked by him, and would not let him off until he had squeezed him to the tune of fifty thousand sesterces.

On his arrival the army, which was disaffected towards the emperor and inclined to mutiny, received him gladly with open arms,[80] as if he had come to them as a gift from the gods; since he was the son of a man who had thrice been consul, in the prime of life, and of an easy-going and lavish disposition. This earlier good opinion Vitellius had also strengthened by recent acts, for throughout the march he kissed even the common soldiers whom he met, and at the posthouses and inns he was unusually affable to the mule drivers and travellers, asking each of them in the morning whether they had breakfasted and even showing by belching that he had done so.

VIII. As soon as he entered the camp, he granted every request that anyone made and even of his own accord freed those in disgrace from their penalties, defendants of suits from their mourning,[81] and the convicted from punishment. Therefore hardly a month had passed, when the soldiers, regardless of the hour, for it was already evening, hastily took him from his bedroom, just as he was, in his common house-clothes,[82] and hailed him as emperor. Then he was carried about the most populous villages, holding a drawn sword of the Deified Julius, which someone had taken from a shrine of Mars and handed him during the first congratulations. He did not return to headquarters until the dining-room caught fire from the stove and was ablaze; and then, when all were shocked and troubled at what seemed a bad omen, he said: "Be of good cheer; to us light is given"; and this was his only address to the soldiers. When he presently received the support of the army of the upper province too, which had previously transferred its allegiance from Galba to the senate, he eagerly accepted the surname of Germanicus, which was unanimously offered him, put off accepting the title of Augustus, and forever refused that of Caesar.

IX. Then hearing of the murder of Galba, he settled affairs in Germany and made two divisions of his forces, one to send on against Otho, and the other to lead in person. The former was greeted with a lucky omen at the start, for an eagle suddenly flew towards them from the right and after hovering about the standards, slowly preceded their line of march. But, on the contrary, when he himself began his advance, the equestrian statues which were being set up everywhere in his honour on a sudden all collapsed with broken legs, and the laurel crown which he had put on with due ceremony fell into a running stream. Later, as he was sitting in judgment on the tribunal at Vienna,[83] a cock perched on his shoulder and then on his head.[84] And the outcome corresponded with these omens; for he was not by his own efforts able to retain the power which his lieutenants secured for him.

X. He heard of the victory at Betriacum and of the death of Otho when he was still in Gaul, and without delay by a single edict he disbanded all the praetorian cohorts, as having set a pernicious example,[85] and bade them hand over their arms to their tribunes. Furthermore, he gave orders that one hundred and twenty of them should be hunted up and punished, having found petitions which they had written to Otho, asking for a reward for services rendered in connection with Galba's murder. These acts were altogether admirable and noble, and such as to give hope that he would be a great prince, had it not been that the rest of his conduct was more in harmony with his natural disposition and his former habits of life than with imperial dignity. For when he had begun his march, he rode through the middle of the cities like a triumphing general, and on the rivers he sailed in most exquisite craft wreathed with various kinds of garlands, amid lavish entertainments, with no discipline among his household or the soldiers, making a jest of the pillage and wantonness of all his followers. For not content with the banquets which were furnished them everywhere at public expense, they set free whatever slaves they pleased, promptly paying those who remonstrated with blows and stripes, often with wounds, and sometimes with death. When he came to the plains where the battle was fought and some shuddered with horror at the mouldering corpses, he had the audacity to encourage them by the abominable saying, that the odour of a dead enemy was sweet and that of a fellow-citizen sweeter still. But nevertheless, the better to bear the awful stench, he openly drained a great draught of unmixed wine and distributed some among the troops. With equal bad taste and arrogance, gazing upon the stone inscribed to the memory of Otho, he declared that he deserved such a Mausoleum, and sent the dagger with which his rival had killed himself to the Colony of Agrippina,[86] to be dedicated to Mars. He also held an all night festival[87] on the heights of the Apennines.

XI. Finally he entered the city to the sound of the trumpet, wearing a general's mantle and a sword at his side, amid standards and banners, with his staff in military cloaks and his troops with drawn swords.

Then showing greater and greater disregard for the laws of gods and men, he assumed the office of high priest on the day of Allia,[88] held elections for ten years to come, and made himself consul for life. And to leave no doubt in anyone's mind what model he chose for the government of the State, he made funerary offerings to Nero in the middle of the Campus Martius, attended by a great throng of the official priests; and when at the accompanying banquet a flute-player was received with applause, he openly urged him "to render something from the Master's Book[89] as well"; and when he began the songs of Nero, Vitellius was the first to applaud him and even jumped for joy.

XII. Beginning in this way, he regulated the greater part of his rule wholly according to the advice and whims of the commonest of actors and chariot-drivers, and in particular of his freedman Asiaticus. This fellow had immoral relations with Vitellius in his youth, but later grew weary of him and ran away. When Vitellius came upon him selling *posca*[90] at Puteoli, he put him in irons, but at once freed him again and made him his favourite. His vexation was renewed by the man's excessive insolence and thievishness, and he sold him to an itinerant keeper of gladiators. When, however, he was once reserved for the end of a gladiatorial show, Vitellius suddenly spirited him away, and finally on getting his province set him free. On the first day of his reign he presented him with the golden ring at a banquet, although in the morning, when there was a general demand that Asiaticus be given that honour, he had deprecated in the strongest terms such a blot on the equestrian order.

XIII. But his besetting sins were luxury and cruelty. He divided his feasts into three, sometimes into four a day, breakfast,[91] luncheon, dinner, and a drinking bout; and he was readily able to do justice to all of them through his habit of taking emetics.

Moreover, he had himself invited to each of these meals by different men on the same day, and the materials for any one of them never cost less than four hundred thousand sesterces. Most notorious of all was the dinner given by his brother to celebrate the emperor's arrival in Rome, at which two thousand of the choicest fishes and seven thousand birds are said to have been served. He himself eclipsed even this at the dedication of a platter, which on account of its enormous size he called the "Shield of Minerva, Defender of the City."[92] In this he mingled the livers of pike, the brains of pheasants and peacocks, the tongues of flamingoes and the milt of lampreys, brought by his captains and triremes from the whole empire, from Parthia to the Spanish strait.[93] Being besides a man of an appetite that was not only boundless, but also regardless of time or decency, he could never refrain, even when he was sacrificing or making a journey, from snatching bits of meat and cakes amid the altars, almost from the very fire, and devouring them on the spot; and in the cookshops along the road, viands smoking hot or even those left over from the day before and partly consumed.

XIV. He delighted in inflicting death and torture on anyone whatsoever and for any cause whatever, putting to death several men of rank, fellow students and comrades of his, whom he had solicited to come to court by every kind of deception, all but offering them a share in the rule. This he did in various treacherous ways, even giving poison to one of them with his own hand in a glass of cold water, for which the man had called when ill of a fever. Besides he spared hardly one of the money-lenders, contractors, and tax-gatherers who had ever demanded of him the payment of a debt at Rome or of a toll on a journey. When one of these had been handed over for execution just as he was paying his morning call and at once recalled, as all were praising the emperor's mercy, Vitellius gave orders to have him killed in his presence, saying that he wished to feast his eyes. In another case he had two sons who attempted to intercede for their father put to death with him. A Roman knight also, who cried as he was being taken off to execution, "You are my heir," he compelled to show his will; and reading that one of the man's freedmen was put down as joint-heir with himself, he ordered the death both of the knight and the freedman. He even killed some of the common people, merely because they had openly spoken ill of the Blue faction,[94] thinking that they had ventured to do this from contempt of himself and the anticipation of a change of rulers. But he was especially hostile to writers of lampoons[95] and to astrologers, and whenever any one of them was accused, he put him to death without trial, particularly incensed because after a proclamation of his in which he ordered the astrologers to leave the city and Italy before the Kalends of October, a placard was at once posted, reading: "By proclamation of the Chaldeans,[96] God bless the State[97]! Before the same day and date let Vitellius Germanicus have ceased to live." Moreover, when his mother died, he was suspected of having forbidden her being given food when she was ill, because a woman of the Chatti, in whom he believed as he would in an oracle, prophesied that he would rule securely and for a long time, but only if he should survive his parent. Others say that through weariness of present evils and fear of those which threatened, she asked poison of her son, and obtained it with no great difficulty.

XV. In the eighth month of his reign the armies of the Moesian provinces and Pannonia revolted from him, and also in the provinces beyond the seas those of Judaea and Syria, the former swearing allegiance to Vespasian in his absence and the latter in his presence. Therefore, to retain the devotion and favour of the rest of the people, there was nothing that he did not lavish publicly and privately, without any limit whatever. He also held a levy in the city, promising those who volunteered not only their discharge upon his victory but also the rewards and privileges given to veterans after their regular term of service. Later, when his enemies were pressing him hard by land and sea, he opposed to them in one quarter his brother with a fleet manned by raw recruits and a band of gladiators, and in another the forces and leaders who had fought at Betriacum. And after he was everywhere either worsted or betrayed, he made a bargain with Flavius Sabinus, the brother of Vespasian, that he should have his own life and a hundred million sesterces. Thereupon he immediately declared from the steps of the Palace before his assembled soldiers, that he withdrew from the rule which had been given him against his will; but when all cried out against this, he postponed the matter, and after a night had passed, went at daybreak to the rostra in mourning garb and with many tears made the same declaration, but from a written document. When the people and soldiers again interrupted him and besought him not to lose heart, vying with one another in promising him all their efforts in his behalf, he again took courage and by a sudden onslaught drove Sabinus and the rest of the Flavians, who no longer feared an attack, into the Capitol. Then he set fire to the temple of Jupiter Optimus Maximus and destroyed them, viewing the battle and the fire from the house of Tiberius, where he was feasting. Not long afterwards he repented of his action and throwing the blame upon others, called an assembly and took oath, compelling the rest to do the same, that there was nothing for which he would strive more earnestly than for the public peace. Then he took a dagger from his side and offered it first to the consul, and when he refused it, to the magistrates, and then to the senators, one by one.[98] When no one would take it, he went off as if he would place it in the temple of Concord; but when some cried out that he himself was Concord, he returned and declared that he would not only retain the steel but would also adopt the surname Concordia.

XVI. He also persuaded the senate to send envoys with the Vestal virgins, to sue for peace or at least to gain time for conference.

The following day, as he was waiting for a reply, word was brought by a scout that the enemy were drawing near. Then he was at once hurried into a sedan with only two companions, a baker and a cook, and secretly went to his father's house on the Aventine, intending to flee from there to Campania. Presently, on a slight and dubious rumour that peace had been granted, he allowed himself to be taken back to the Palace. Finding everything abandoned there, and that even those who were with him were making off, he put on a girdle filled with gold pieces and took refuge in the lodge of the door-keeper, tying a dog before the door and putting a couch and a mattress against it.

XVII. The foremost of the army had now forced their way in, and since no one opposed them, were ransacking everything in the usual way. They dragged Vitellius from his hiding-place and when they asked him his name (for they did not know him) and if he knew where Vitellius was, he attempted to escape them by a lie. Being soon recognised, he did not cease to beg that he be confined for a time, even in the prison, alleging that he had something to say of importance to the safety of Vespasian. But they bound his arms behind his back, put a noose about his neck, and dragged him with rent garments and half-naked to the Forum. All along the Sacred Way he was greeted with mockery and abuse, his head held back by the hair, as is common with criminals, and even the point of a sword placed under his chin, so that he could not look down but must let his face be seen. Some pelted him with dung and ordure, others called him incendiary and glutton, and some of the mob even taunted him with his bodily defects. He was in fact abnormally tall, with a face usually flushed from hard drinking, a huge belly, and one thigh crippled from being struck once upon a time by a four-horse chariot, when he was in attendance on Gaius as he was driving. At last on the Stairs of Wailing he was tortured for a long time and then despatched and dragged off with a hook to the Tiber.

XVIII. He met his death, along with his brother and his son, in the fifty-seventh year of his age, fulfilling the prediction of those who had declared from an omen which befell him at Vienna, as we have stated,[99] that he was destined to fall into the power of some man of Gaul. For he was slain by Antonius Primus, a leader of the opposing faction, who was born at Tolosa and in his youth bore the surname Becco, which means a rooster's beak.[100]

BOOK VIII

THE DEIFIED VESPASIAN, THE DEIFIED TITUS, DOMITIAN

The Deified Vespasian

I. The empire, which for a long time had been unsettled and, as it were, drifting, through the usurpation and violent death of three emperors, was at last taken in hand and given stability by the Flavian family. This house was, it is true, obscure and without family portraits, yet it was one of which our country had no reason whatever to be ashamed, even though it is the general opinion that the penalty which Domitian paid for his avarice and cruelty was fully merited.

Titus Flavius Petro, a burgher of Reate and during the civil war a centurion or a volunteer veteran[1] on Pompey's side, fled from the field of Pharsalus and went home, where after at last obtaining pardon and an honourable discharge, he carried on the business of a collector of moneys. His son, surnamed Sabinus (although some say that he was a centurion of the first grade, and others that while still in command of a cohort he was retired because of ill-health) took no part in military life, but farmed the public tax of a twentieth[2] in Asia. And there existed for some time statues erected in his honour by the cities of Asia, inscribed "To an honest tax-gatherer." Later he carried on a banking business in the Helvetian country and there he died, survived by his wife, Vespasia Polla, and by two of her children, of whom the elder, Sabinus, rose to the rank of prefect of

Rome, and the younger, Vespasian, even to that of emperor. Polla, who was born of an honourable family at Nursia, had for father Vespasius Pollio, thrice tribune of the soldiers and prefect of the camp,[3] while her brother became a senator with the rank of praetor. There is moreover on the top of a mountain, near the sixth milestone on the road from Nursia to Spoletium, a place called Vespasiae, where many monuments of the Vespasii are to be seen, affording strong proof of the renown and antiquity of the house. I ought to add that some have bandied about the report, that Petro's father came from the region beyond the Po and was a contractor for the day-labourers who come regularly every year from Umbria to the Sabine district, to till the fields; but that he settled in the town of Reate and there married. Personally I have found no evidence whatever of this, in spite of rather careful investigation.

II. Vespasian was born in the Sabine country, in a small village beyond Reate, called Falacrina, on the evening of the fifteenth day before the Kalends of December, in the consulate of Quintus Sulpicius Camerinus and Gaius Poppaeus Sabinus, five years before the death of Augustus. He was brought up under the care of his paternal grandmother Tertulla on her estates at Cosa. Therefore even after he became emperor he used constantly to visit the home of his infancy, where the manor house was kept in its original condition, since he did not wish to miss anything which he was wont to see there; and he was so devoted to his grandmother's memory, that on religous and festival days he always drank from a little silver cup that had belonged to her.

Nov. 14, 9 A.D.

After assuming the garb of manhood he for a long time made no attempt to win the broad stripe of senator, though his brother had gained it, and only his mother could finally induce him to sue for it. She at length drove him to it, but rather by sarcasm than by entreaties or parental authority, since she constantly taunted him with being his brother's footman.[4]

He served in Thrace as tribune of the soldiers; as quaestor was assigned by lot to the province of Crete and Cyrene; became a candidate for the aedileship and then for the praetorship, attaining

38 A.D. the former only after one defeat and then barely landing in the
39 A.D. sixth place, but the latter on his first canvass and among the foremost. In his praetorship, to lose no opportuity of winning the favour of Gaius, who was at odds with the senate,[5] he asked for special games because of the emperor's victory in Germany and recommended as an additional punishment of the conspirators[6] that they be cast out unburied. He also thanked the emperor before that illustrious body[7] because he had deigned to honour him with an invitation to dinner.

III. Meanwhile he took to wife Flavia Domitilla, formerly the mistress of Statilius Capella, a Roman knight of Sabrata in Africa, a woman originally only of Latin rank,[8] but afterwards declared a freeborn citizen of Rome in a suit before arbiters, brought by her father Flavius Liberalis, a native of Ferentum and merely a quaestor's clerk. By her he had three children, Titus, Domitian, and Domitilla. He outlived his wife and daughter; in fact lost them both before he became emperor. After the death of his wife he resumed his relations with Caenis, freedwoman and amanuensis of Antonia, and formerly his mistress; and even after he became emperor he treated her almost as a lawful wife.

IV. In the reign of Claudius he was sent in command of a legion to Germany, through the influence of Narcissus; from there he was transferred to Britain,[9] where he fought thirty battles with the enemy. He reduced to subjection two powerful nations, more than twenty towns, and the island of Vectis,[10] near Britain, partly under the leadership of Aulus Plautius, the consular governor, and partly under that of Claudius himself. For this he received the triumphal regalia, and shortly after two priesthoods, besides the consulship,
51 A.D. which he held for the last two months of the year. The rest of the time up to his proconsulate he spent in rest and retirement, through fear of Agrippina, who still had a strong influence over her son and hated any friend of Narcissus, even after the latter's death.

63 A.D. The chance of the lot then gave him Africa, which he governed with great justice and high honour, save that in a riot at Hadrumetum he was pelted with turnips. Certain it is that he

came back none the richer, for his credit was so nearly gone that he mortgaged all his estates to his brother, and had to resort to trading in mules[11] to keep up his position; whence he was commonly known as "the Muleteer." He is also said to have been found guilty of squeezing two hundred thousand sesterces out of a young man for whom he obtained the broad stripe against his father's wish, and to have been severely rebuked in consequence.

On the tour through Greece, among the companions of Nero,[12] he bitterly offended the emperor by either going out often while Nero was singing, or falling asleep, if he remained. Being in consequence banished, not only from intimacy with the emperor but even from his public receptions, he withdrew to a little out-of-the-way town, until a province and an army were offered him while he was in hiding and in fear of his life.

There had spread over all the Orient an old and established belief, that it was fated at that time for men coming from Judaea to rule the world. This prediction, referring to the emperor of Rome, as afterwards appeared from the event, the people of Judaea took to themselves; accordingly they revolted and after killing their governor, they routed the consular ruler of Syria as well, when he came to the rescue, and took one of his eagles. Since to put down this rebellion required a considerable army with a leader of no little enterprise, yet one to whom so great power could be entrusted without risk, Vespasian was chosen for the task, both as a man of tried energy and as one in no wise to be feared because of the obscurity of his family and name. Therefore there were added to the forces in Judaea two legions with eight divisions of cavalry and ten cohorts.[13] He took his elder son as one of his lieutenants, and as soon as he reached his province he attracted the attention of the neighbouring provinces also; for he at once reformed the discipline of the army and fought one or two battles with such daring, that in the storming of a fortress he was wounded in the knee with a stone and received several arrows in his shield.

V. While Otho and Vitellius were fighting for the throne after the death of Nero and Galba, he began to cherish the hope of imperial dignity, which he had long since conceived because of the following portents.

On the suburban estate of the Flavii an old oak tree, which was sacred to Mars, on each of the three occasions when Vespasia was delivered suddenly put forth a branch from its trunk, obvious indications of the destiny of each child. The first was slender and quickly withered, and so too the girl that was born died within the year; the second was very strong and long and portended great success, but the third was the image of a tree. Therefore their father Sabinus, so they say, being further encouraged by an inspection of victims, announced to his mother that a grandson had been born to her who would be a Caesar. But she only laughed, marvelling that her son should already be in his dotage, while she was still of strong mind.

Later, when Vespasian was aedile, Gaius Caesar, incensed at his neglect of his duty of cleaning the streets, ordered that he be covered with mud, which the soldiers accordingly heaped into the bosom of his fringed toga; this some interpreted as an omen that one day in some civil commotion his country, trampled under foot and forsaken, would come under his protection and as it were into his embrace.

Once when he was taking breakfast, a stray dog brought in a human hand from the cross-roads and dropped it under the table.[14] Again, when he was dining, an ox that was ploughing shook off its yoke, burst into the dining-room, and after scattering the servants, fell at the very feet of Vespasian as he reclined at table, and bowed its neck as if suddenly tired out. A cypress tree, also, on his grandfather's farm was torn up by the roots, without the agency of any violent storm, and thrown down, and on the following day rose again greener and stronger than before.

He dreamed in Greece that the beginning of good fortune for himself and his family would come as soon as Nero had a tooth extracted; and on the next day it came to pass that a physician walked into the hall[15] and showed him a tooth which he had just then taken out.

When he consulted the oracle of the god of Carmel in Judaea, the lots were highly encouraging, promising that whatever he planned or wished, however great it might be, would come to pass; and one of his high-born prisoners, Josephus by name, as he was being put in chains, declared most confidently that he would soon be released by the same man, who would then, however, be emperor. Omens were also reported from Rome: Nero in his latter days was admonished in a dream to take the sacred chariot of Jupiter Optimus Maximus from its shrine to the house of Vespasian and from there to the Circus. Not long after this, too, when Galba was on his way to the elections which gave him his second consulship, a statue of the Deified Julius of its own accord turned towards the East; and on the field of Betriacum, before the battle began, two eagles fought in the sight of all, and when one was vanquished, a third came from the direction of the rising sun and drove off the victor.

VI. Yet he made no move, although his followers were quite ready and even urgent, until he was roused to it by the accidental support of men unknown to him and at a distance. Two thousand soldiers of the three legions that made up the army in Moesia had been sent to help Otho. When word came to them after they had begun their march that he had been defeated and had taken his own life, they none the less kept on as far as Aquileia, because they did not believe the report. There, taking advantage of the lawless state of the times, they indulged in every kind of pillage; then, fearing that if they went back, they would have to give an account and suffer punishment, they took it into their heads to select and appoint an emperor, saying that they were just as good as the Spanish army which had appointed Galba, or the praetorian guard which had elected Otho, or the German army which had chosen Vitellius. Accordingly the names of all the consular governors who were serving anywhere were taken up, and since objection was made to the rest for one reason or another, while some members of the third legion, which had been transferred from Syria to Moesia just before the death of Nero, highly commended

Vespasian, they unanimously agreed on him and forthwith inscribed his name on all their banners. At the time, however, the movement was checked and the soldiers recalled to their allegiance for a season. But when their action became known, Tiberius Alexander, prefect of Egypt, was the first to compel his legions to take the oath for Vespasian on the Kalends of July, the day which was afterwards celebrated as that of his accession; then the army in Judaea swore allegiance to him personally on the fifth day before the Ides of July.[16]

The enterprise was greatly forwarded by the circulation of a copy of a letter of the late emperor Otho to Vespasian, whether genuine or forged, urging him with the utmost earnestness to vengeance and expressing the hope that he would come to the aid of his country; further, by a rumour which spread abroad that Vitellius had planned, after his victory, to change the winter quarters of the legions and to transfer those in Germany to the Orient, to a safer and milder service; and finally, among the governors of provinces, by the support of Licinius Mucianus,[17] and among the kings, by that of Vologaesus, the Parthian. The former, laying aside the hostility with which up to that time jealousy had obviously inspired him, promised the Syrian army; and the latter forty thousand bowmen.

VII. Therefore beginning a civil war and sending ahead generals with troops to Italy, he crossed meanwhile to Alexandria, to take possession of the key to Egypt.[18] There he dismissed all his attendants and entered the temple of Serapis alone, to consult the auspices as to the duration of his power. And when after many propitiary offerings to the god he at length turned about, it seemed to him that his freedman Basilides[19] offered him sacred boughs, garlands and loaves, as is the custom there; and yet he knew well that no one had let him in, and that for some time he had been hardly able to walk by reason of rheumatism, and was besides far away. And immediately letters came with the news that Vitellius had been routed at Cremona and the emperor himself slain at Rome.

Vespasian as yet lacked prestige and a certain divinity, so to speak, since he was an unexpected and still new-made emperor; but these also were given him. A man of the people who was blind, and another who was lame, came to him together as he sat on the tribunal, begging for the help for their disorders which Serapis had promised in a dream; for the god declared that Vespasian would restore the eyes, if he would spit upon them, and give strength to the leg, if he would deign to touch it with his heel. Though he had hardly any faith that this could possibly succeed, and therefore shrank even from making the attempt, he was at last prevailed upon by his friends and tried both things in public before a large crowd; and with success. At this same time, by the direction of certain soothsayers, some vases of antique workmanship were dug up in a consecrated spot at Tegea in Arcadia and on them was an image very like Vespasian.

VIII. Returning to Rome under such auspices and attended by so great renown, after celebrating a triumph over the Jews, he added eight consulships to his former one; he also assumed the censorship and during the whole period of his rule he considered nothing more essential than first to strengthen the State, which was tottering and almost overthrown, and then to embellish it as well. 70, 71, 72, 74, 75, 76, 77, 79 A.D.

The soldiery, some emboldened by their victory and some resenting their humiliating defeat, had abandoned themselves to every form of licence and recklessness; the provinces, too, and the free cities, as well as some of the kingdoms, were in a state of internal dissension. Therefore he discharged many of the soldiers of Vitellius and punished many; but so far from showing any special indulgence to those who had shared in his victory, he was even tardy in paying them their lawful rewards. To let slip no opportunity of improving military discipline, when a young man reeking with perfumes came to thank him for a commission which had been given him, Vespasian drew back his head in disgust, adding the stern reprimand: "I would rather you had smelt of garlic"; and he revoked the appointment. When the marines who march on foot by turns from Ostia and Puteoli to Rome,[20] asked that an allowance be made them under the head of shoe money, not content with sending them away without a reply, he ordered that in future they should make the run barefooted; and they have done so ever since.

He made provinces of Achaia, Lycia, Rhodes, Byzantium and Samos, taking away their freedom, and likewise of Trachian Cilicia and Commagene, which up to that time had been ruled by kings. He sent additional legions to Cappadocia because of the constant inroads of the barbarians, and gave it a consular governor in place of a Roman knight.

As the city was unsightly from fires and fallen buildings, he allowed anyone to take possession of vacant sites and build upon them, in case the owners failed to do so. He began the restoration of the Capitol in person, was the first to lend a hand in clearing away the debris, and carried some of it off on his own head.[21] He undertook to restore the three thousand bronze tablets which were destroyed with the temple, making a thorough search for copies: priceless and most ancient records of the empire, containing the decrees of the senate and the acts of the commons almost from the foundation of the city, regarding alliances, treaties, and special privileges granted to individuals.

IX. He also undertook new works, the temple of Peace hard by the Forum and one to the Deified Claudius on the Caelian mount, which was begun by Agrippina, but almost utterly destroyed by Nero; also an amphitheatre[22] in the heart of the city, a plan which he learned that Augustus had cherished.

He reformed the two great orders, reduced by a series of murders and sullied by long standing neglect, and added to their numbers, holding a review of the senate and the knights, expelling those who least deserved the honour and enrolling the most distinguished of the Italians and provincials. Furthermore, to let it be known that the two orders differed from each other not so much in their privileges as in their rank, in the case of an altercation between a senator and a Roman knight, he rendered this decision: "Unseemly language should not be used towards senators, but to return their insults in kind is proper and lawful."[23]

X. Lawsuit upon lawsuit had accumulated in all the courts to an excessive degree, since those of long standing were left unsettled though the interruption of court business[24] and new ones had arisen through the disorder of the times. He therefore chose commissioners by lot to restore what had been seized in time of war, and to make special decisions in the court of the Hundred,[25] reducing the cases to the smallest possible number, since it was clear that the lifetime of the litigants would not suffice for the regular proceedings.

XI. Licentiousness and extravagance had flourished without restraint; hence he induced the senate to vote that any woman who formed a connection with the slave of another person should herself be treated as a bond-woman; also that those who lend money to minors[26] should never have a legal right to enforce payment, that is to say, not even after the death of the fathers.

XII. In other matters he was unassuming and lenient from the very beginning of his reign until its end, never trying to conceal his former lowly condition, but often even parading it. Indeed, when certain men tried to trace the origin of the Flavian family to the founders of Reate and a companion of Hercules whose tomb still stands on the Via Salaria, he laughed at them for their pains. So far was he from a desire for pomp and show, that on the day of his triumph, exhausted by the slow and tiresome procession, he did not hesitate to say: "It serves me right for being such a fool as to want a triumph in my old age, as if it were due to my ancestors or had ever been among my own ambitions." He did not even assume the tribunician power at once nor the title of Father of his Country until late.[27] As for the custom of searching those who came to pay their morning calls,[28] he gave that up before the civil war was over.

XIII. He bore the frank language of his friends, the quips of pleaders, and the impudence of the philosophers with the greatest patience. Though Licinius Mucianus,[29] a man of notorious unchastity, presumed upon his services to treat Vespasian with scant respect, he never had the heart to criticise him except privately and then only to the extent of adding to a complaint made to a common friend, the significant words: "I at least am a man."[30] When Salvius Liberalis ventured to say while defending a rich client, "What is it to Caesar if Hipparchus has a hundred millions," he personally commended him. When the Cynic Demetrius met him abroad after being condemned to banishment, and without deigning to rise in his presence or to salute him, even snarled out some insult, he merely called him "cur."

XIV. He was not inclined to remember or to avenge affronts or enmities, but made a brilliant match for the daughter of his enemy Vitellius, and even provided her with a dowry and a house-keeping outfit. When he was in terror at being forbidden Nero's court, and asked what on earth he was to do or where he was to go, one of the ushers put him out and told him to "go to Morbovia[31]"; but when the man later begged for forgiveness, Vespasian confined his resentment to words, and those of about the same number and purport. Indeed, so far was he from being led by any suspicion or fear to cause anyone's death, that when his friends warned him that he must keep an eye on Mettius Pompusianus, since it was commonly believed that he had an imperial horoscope, he even made him consul, guaranteeing that he would one day be mindful of the favour.

XV. It cannot readily be shown that any innocent person was punished save in Vespasian's absence and without his knowledge, or at any rate against his will and by misleading him. Although Helvidius Priscus was the only one who greeted him on his return from Syria by his private name of "Vespasian," and moreover in his praetorship left the emperor unhonoured and unmentioned in all his edicts,[32] he did not show anger until by the extravagance of his railing Helvidius had all but degraded him.[33] But even in his case, though he did banish him and later order his death, he was most anxious for any means of saving him, and sent messengers to recall those who were to slay him; and he would have saved him, but for a false report that Helvidius had already been done to death. Certainly he never took pleasure in the death of anyone, but even wept and sighed over those who suffered merited punishment.

XVI. The only thing for which he can fairly be censured was his love of money. For not content with reviving the imposts which had been repealed under Galba, he added new and heavy burdens, increasing the amount of tribute paid by the provinces, in some cases actually doubling it, and quite openly carrying on traffic which would be shameful even for a man in private life; for he would buy up certain commodities merely in order to distribute them at a profit. He made no bones of selling offices to candidates and acquittals to men under prosecution, whether innocent or guilty. He is even believed to have had the habit of designedly advancing the most rapacious of his procurators to higher posts, that they might be the richer when he later condemned them; in fact, it was common talk that he used these men as sponges, because he, so to speak, soaked them when they were dry and squeezed them when they were wet.

Some say that he was naturally covetous and was taunted with it by an old herdsman of his, who on being forced to pay for the freedom for which he earnestly begged Vespasian when he became emperor, cried: "The fox changes his fur, but not his nature." Others on the contrary believe that he was driven by necessity to raise money by spoliation and robbery because of the desperate state of the treasury and the privy purse; to which he bore witness at the very beginning of his reign by declaring that forty thousand millions were needed to set the State upright. This latter view seems the more probable, since he made the best use of his gains, ill-gotten though they were.

XVII. He was most generous to all classes, making up the requisite estate[34] for senators, giving needy ex-consuls an annual stipend of five hundred thousand sesterces, restoring to a better condition many cities throughout the empire which had suffered from earthquakes or fires, and in particular encouraging men of talent and the arts.

XVIII. He was the first to establish a regular salary of a hundred thousand sesterces for Latin and Greek teachers of rhetoric, paid from the privy purse. He also presented eminent poets with princely largess[35] and great rewards, and artists, too, such as the restorer of the Venus of Cos[36] and of the Colossus.[37] To a mechanical engineer, who promised to transport some heavy columns to the Capitol at small expense, he gave no mean reward for his invention, but refused to make use of it, saying: "You must let me feed my poor commons."

XIX. At the plays with which he dedicated the new stage of the theatre of Marcellus he revived the old musical entertainments. To Apelles, the tragic actor, he gave four hundred thousand sesterces; to Terpnus and Diodorus, the lyre-players, two hundred thousand each; to several a hundred thousand; while those who received least were paid forty thousand, and numerous golden crowns were awarded besides. He gave constant dinner-parties, too, usually formally[38] and sumptuously, to help the marketmen. He gave gifts[39] to women on the Kalends of March,[40] as he did to the men on the Saturnalia.

Yet even so he could not be rid of his former ill-repute for covetousness. The Alexandrians persisted in calling him Cybiosactes,[41] the surname of one of their kings who was scandalously stingy. Even at his funeral, Favor, a leading actor of mimes, who wore his mask and, according to the usual custom, imitated the actions and words of the deceased during his lifetime, having asked the procurators in a loud voice how much his funeral procession would cost, and hearing the reply "Ten million sesterces," cried out: "Give me a hundred thousand and fling me even into the Tiber."

XX. He was well built,[42] with strong, sturdy limbs, and the expression of one who was straining. Apropos of which a witty fellow, when Vespasian asked him to make a joke on him also, replied rather cleverly: "I will, when you have finished relieving yourself." He enjoyed excellent health, though he did nothing to keep it up except to rub his throat and the other parts of his body a certain number of times in the tennis court, and to fast one day in every month.

XXI. This was in general his manner of life. While emperor, he always rose very early, in fact before daylight; then after reading his letters and the reports of all the officials, he admitted his friends, and while he was receiving their greetings, he put on his own shoes and dressed himself. After despatching any business that came up, he took time for a drive and then for a nap, lying with one of his concubines, of whom he had taken several after the death of Caenis. After his siesta he went to the bath and the dining-room; and it is said that at no time was he more good-natured or indulgent, so that the members of his household eagerly watched for these opportunities of making requests.

XXII. Not only at dinner but on all other occasions he was most affable, and he turned off many matters with a jest; for he was very ready with sharp sayings, albeit of a low and buffoonish kind, so that he did not even refrain from obscene expressions.[43] Yet many of his remarks are still remembered which are full of fine wit, and among them the following. When an ex-consul called Mestrius Florus called his attention to the fact that the proper pronunciation was *plaustra*[44] rather than *plostra,* he greeted him next day as "Flaurus." When he was importuned by a woman, who said that she was dying with love for him, he took her to his bed and gave her four hundred thousand sesterces for her favours. Being asked by his steward how he would have the sum entered in his accounts, he replied: "To a passion for Vespasian."

XXIII. He also quoted Greek verses with great timeliness, saying of a man of tall stature, and monstrous parts:

> "Striding along and waving a lance that casts a long shadow,"[45]

and of the freedman Cerylus, who was very rich, and to cheat the privy purse of its dues at his death had begun to give himself out as freeborn, changing his name to Laches:

> "O Laches, Laches,
> When you are dead, you'll change your name at once
> To Cerylus again."[46]

But he particularly resorted to witticisms about his unseemly means of gain, seeking to diminish their odium by some jocose saying and to turn them into a jest.

Having put off one of his favourite attendants, who asked for a stewardship for a pretended brother, he summoned the candidate himself, and after compelling him to pay him as much money as he had agreed to give his advocate, appointed him to the position without delay. On his attendant's taking up the matter again, he said: "Find yourself another brother; the man that you thought was yours is mine." On a journey, suspecting that his muleteer had got down to shoe the mules merely to make delay and give time for a man with a lawsuit to approach the emperor, he asked how much he was paid for shoeing the mules and insisted on a share of the money. When Titus found fault with him for contriving a tax upon public conveniences, he held a piece of money from the first payment to his son's nose, asking whether its odour was offensive to him. When Titus said "No," he replied, "Yet it comes from urine." On the report of a deputation that a colossal statue of great cost had been voted him at public expense, he demanded to have it set up at once, and holding out his open hand, said that the base was ready. He did not cease his jokes even when in apprehension of death and in extreme danger; for when among other portents the Mausoleum[47] opened on a sudden and a comet appeared in the heavens, he declared that the former applied to Junia Calvina of the family of Augustus, and the latter to the king of the Parthians, who wore his hair long;[48] and as death drew near, he said: "Woe's me. Methinks I'm turning into a god."

79 A.D. XXIV. In his ninth consulship he had a slight illness in Campania, and returning at once to the city, he left for Cutilae and the country about Reate, where he spent the summer every year. There, in addition to an increase in his illness, having contracted a bowel complaint by too free use of the cold waters, he nevertheless continued to perform his duties as emperor, even receiving embassies as he lay in bed. Taken on a sudden with such an attack of diarrhœa that he all but swooned, he said: "An emperor ought to die standing," and June 23, 79 A.D. while he was struggling to get on his feet, he died in the arms of those who tried to help him, on the ninth day before the Kalends of July, at the age of sixty-nine years, one month and seven days.

XXV. All agree that he had so much faith in his own horoscope and those of his family, that even after constant conspiracies were made against him he had the assurance to say to the senate that either his sons would succeed him or he would have no successor. It is also said that he once dreamed that he saw a balance with its beam on a level placed in the middle of the vestibule of the Palace, in one pan of which stood Claudius and Nero and in the other himself and his sons. And the dream came true, since both houses reigned for the same space of time and the same term of years.[49]

The Deified Titus

I. Titus, of the same surname as his father, was the delight and darling of the human race; such ability had he, by nature, art, or good fortune, to win the affections of all men, and that, too, which is no easy task, while he was emperor; for as a private citizen, and even during his father's rule, he did not escape hatred, much less public criticism.

He was born on the third day before the Kalends of January, in the year memorable for the death of Gaius, in a mean house near the Septizonium[50] and in a very small dark room besides; for it still remains and is on exhibition. Dec. 30, 41 A.D

II. He was brought up at court in company with Britannicus and taught the same subjects by the same masters. At that time, so they say, a physiognomist was brought in by Narcissus, the freedman of Claudius, to examine Britannicus and declared most positively that he would never become emperor; but that Titus, who was standing near by at the time, would surely rule. The boys were so intimate too, that it is believed that when Britannicus drained the fatal draught,[51] Titus, who was reclining at his side, also tasted of the potion and for a long time suffered from an obstinate disorder. Titus did not forget all this, but later set up a golden statue of his friend in the Palace, and dedicated another equestrian statue of ivory and attended it in the processions in the Circus, where it is still carried to this day.

III. Even in boyhood his bodily and mental gifts were conspicuous and they became more and more so as he advanced in years. He had a handsome person, in which there was no less dignity than grace, and was uncommonly strong, although he was not tall of stature and had a rather protruding belly. His memory was extraordinary and he had an aptitude for almost all the arts, both of war and of peace. Skilful in arms and horsemanship, he made speeches and wrote verses in Latin and Greek with ease and readiness, and even off-hand. He was besides not unacquainted with music, but sang and played the harp agreeably and skilfully. I have heard from many sources that he used also to write shorthand with great speed and would amuse himself by playful contests with his secretaries; also that he could imitate any handwriting that he had ever seen and often declared that he might have been the prince of forgers.

IV. He served as military tribune both in Germany and in Britain, winning a high reputation for energy and no less for integrity, as is evident from the great number of his statues and busts in both those provinces and from the inscriptions they bear.

After his military service he pleaded in the Forum, rather for glory than as a profession, and at the same time took to wife Arrecina Tertulla, whose father, though only a Roman knight, had once been prefect of the praetorian cohorts;[52] on her death he replaced her by Marcia Furnilla, a lady of a very distinguished family, but divorced her after he had acknowledged a daughter which she bore him.

67 A.D. Then, after holding the office of quaestor, as commander of a legion he subjugated the two strong cities of Tarichaeae and Gamala in Judaea, having his horse killed under him in one battle and mounting another, whose rider had fallen fighting by his side.

V. Presently he was sent to congratulate Galba on becoming ruler of the state, and attracted attention wherever he went, through the belief that he had been sent for to be adopted. But observing that everything was once more in a state of turmoil, he turned back, and visiting the oracle of the Paphian Venus, to consult it about his voyage, he was also encouraged to hope for imperial power. Soon realising his hope[53] and left behind to complete the conquest of Judaea, in the final attack on Jerusalem he slew twelve of the defenders with as many arrows; and he took the city on his daughter's birthday, so delighting the soldiers and winning their devotion that they hailed him as Imperator[54] and detained him from time to time, when he would leave the province, urging him with prayers and even with threats either to stay or to take them all with him. This aroused the suspicion that he had tried to revolt from his father and make himself king of the East; and he strengthened this suspicion on his way to Alexandria by wearing a diadem at the consecration of the bull Apis in Memphis, an act quite in accord with the usual ceremonial of that ancient religion, but unfavourably interpreted by some. Because of this he hastened to Italy, and putting in at Regium and then at Puteoli in a transport ship, he went with all speed from there to Rome, where as if to show that the reports about him were groundless, he surprised his father with the greeting, "I am here, father; I am here."

VI. From that time on he never ceased to act as the emperor's partner and even as his protector. He took part in his father's triumph and was censor with him. He was also his colleague in the tribunicial power and in seven consulships. He took upon himself the discharge of almost all duties, personally dictated letters and wrote edicts in his father's name, and even read his speeches in the senate in lieu of a quaestor.[55] He also assumed the command of the praetorian guard, which before that time had never been held except by a Roman knight, and in this office conducted himself in a somewhat arrogant and tyrannical fashion. For whenever he himself regarded anyone with suspicion, he would secretly send some of the Guard to the various theatres and camps, to demand their punishment as if by consent of all who were present; and then he would put them out of the way without delay. Among these was Aulus Caecina, an ex-consul, whom he invited to dinner and then ordered to be stabbed almost before he left the dining-room; but in this case he was led by a pressing danger, having got possession of an autograph copy of an harangue which

73 A.D.
70, 72,
74, 75,
76, 77,
79 A.D.

Caecina had prepared to deliver to the soldiers. Although by such conduct he provided for his safety in the future, he incurred such odium at the time that hardly anyone ever came to the throne with so evil a reputation or so much against the desires of all.

VII. Besides cruelty, he was also suspected of riotous living, since he protracted his revels until the middle of the night with the most prodigal of his friends; likewise of unchastity because of his troops of catamites and eunuchs, and his notorious passion for queen Berenice, to whom it was even said that he promised marriage. He was suspected of greed as well; for it was well known that in cases which came before his father he put a price on his influence and accepted bribes. In short, people not only thought, but openly declared, that he would be a second Nero. But this reputation turned out to his advantage and gave place to the highest praise, when no fault was discovered in him, but on the contrary the highest virtues.

His banquets were pleasant rather than extravagant. He chose as his friends men whom succeeding emperors also retained as indispensable alike to themselves and to the State, and of whose services they made special use. Berenice he sent from Rome at once, against her will and against his own. Some of his most beloved paramours, although they were such skilful dancers that they later became stage favourites, he not only ceased to cherish any longer, but even to witness their public performances.

He took away nothing from any citizen. He respected others' property, if anyone ever did; in fact, he would not accept even proper and customary presents. And yet he was second to none of his predecessors in munificence. At the dedication of the
80 A.D. amphitheatre[56] and of the baths which were hastily built near it he gave a most magnificent and costly gladiatorial show. He presented a sham sea-fight too in the old naumachia,[57] and in the same place a combat of gladiators,[58] exhibiting five thousand wild beasts of every kind in a single day.

VIII. He was most kindly by nature, and whereas in accordance with a custom established by Tiberius, all the Caesars who followed him refused to regard favours granted by previous emperors as valid, unless they had themselves conferred the same ones on the same individuals, Titus was the first to ratify them all in a single edict, without allowing himself to be asked. Moreover, in the case of other requests made of him, it was his fixed rule not to let anyone go away without hope. Even when his household officials warned him that he was promising more than he could perform, he said that it was not right for anyone to go away sorrowful from an interview with his emperor. On another occasion, remembering at dinner that he had done nothing for anybody all that day, he gave utterance to that memorable and praiseworthy remark: "Friends, I have lost a day."

The whole body of the people in particular he treated with such indulgence on all occasions, that once at a gladiatorial show he declared that he would give it, "not after his own inclinations, but those of the spectators"; and what is more, he kept his word. For he refused nothing which anyone asked, and even urged them to ask for what they wished. Furthermore, he openly displayed his partiality for Thracian gladiators and bantered the people about it by words and gestures,[59] always however preserving his dignity, as well as observing justice. Not to omit any act of condescension, he sometimes bathed in the baths which he had built, in company with the common people.

There were some dreadful disasters during his reign, such as the eruption of Mount Vesuvius in Campania, a fire at Rome which continued three days and as many nights, and a plague the 79 A.D.
like of which had hardly ever been known before. In these many 80 A.D.
great calamities he showed not merely the concern of an emperor, but even a father's surpassing love, now offering consolation in edicts, and now lending aid so far as his means allowed. He chose commissioners by lot from among the ex-consuls for the relief of Campania; and the property of those who lost their lives by Vesuvius and had no heirs left alive he applied to the rebuilding of the buried cities. During the fire in Rome he made no remark except "I am ruined,"[60] and he set aside all the ornaments of his villas for the public buildings and temples, and put several men of

the equestrian order in charge of the work, that everything might be done with the greater dispatch. For curing the plague and diminishing the force of the epidemic there was no aid, human or divine, which he did not employ, searching for every kind of sacrifice[61] and all kinds of medicines.

Among the evils of the times were the informers and their instigators, who had enjoyed a long standing licence. After these had been soundly beaten in the Forum with scourges and cudgels, and finally led in procession across the arena of the amphitheatre, he had some of them put up and sold, and others deported to the wildest of the islands. To further discourage for all time any who might think of venturing on similar practices, among other precautions he made it unlawful for anyone to be tried under several laws for the same offence, or for any inquiry to be made as to the legal status of any deceased person after a stated number of years.

IX. Having declared that he would accept the office of pontifex maximus[62] for the purpose of keeping his hands unstained, he was true to his promise; for after that he neither caused nor connived at the death of any man, although he sometimes had no lack of reasons for taking vengeance; but he swore that he would rather be killed than kill. When two men of patrician family were found guilty of aspiring to the throne, he satisfied himself with warning them to abandon their attempt, saying that imperial power was the gift of fate, and promising that if there was anything else they desired, he himself would bestow it. Then he sent his couriers with all speed to the mother of one of them, for she was some distance off, to relieve her anxiety by reporting that her son was safe; and he not only invited the men themselves to dinner among his friends, but on the following day at a gladiatorial show he purposely placed them near him, and when the swords of the contestants were offered him,[63] handed them over for their inspection. It is even said that inquiring into the horoscope of each of them, he declared that danger threatened them both, but at some future time and from another, as turned out to be the case.

Although his brother never ceased plotting against him, but almost openly stirred up the armies to revolt and meditated flight to them, he had not the heart to put him to death or banish him from the court, or even to hold him in less honour than before. On the contrary, as he had done from the very first day of his rule, he continued to declare that he was his partner and successor, and sometimes he privately begged him with tears and prayers to be willing at least to return his affection.

X. In the meantime he was cut off by death, to the loss of mankind rather than to his own. After finishing the public games, at the close of which he wept bitterly in the presence of the people, he went to the Sabine territory, somewhat cast down because a victim had escaped as he was sacrificing and because it had thundered from a clear sky. Then at the very first stopping place he was seized with a fever, and as he was being carried on from there in a litter, it is said that he pushed back the curtains, looked up to heaven, and lamented bitterly that his life was being taken from him contrary to his deserts; for he said that there was no act of his life of which he had cause to repent, save one only. What this was he did not himself disclose at the time, nor could anyone easily divine.[64] Some think that he recalled the intimacy which he had with his brother's wife; but Domitia swore most solemnly that this did not exist, although she would not have denied it if it had been in the least true, but on the contrary would have boasted of it, as she was most ready to do of all her scandalous actions.

XI. He died in the same farmhouse[65] as his father, on the Ides of September, two years two months and twenty days after succeeding Vespasian, in the forty-second year of his age. When his death was made known, the whole populace mourned as they would for a loss in their own families, the senate hastened to the House before it was summoned by proclamation, and with the doors still shut, and then with them open, rendered such thanks to him and heaped such praise on him after death as they had never done even when he was alive and present.

Sept. 13, 81 A.D.

Domitian

Oct. 24, 51 A.D. I. Domitian was born on the ninth day before the Kalends of November of the year when his father was consul elect and was about to enter on the office in the following month, in a street of the sixth region called "the Pomegranate,"[66] in a house which he afterwards converted into a temple of the Flavian family. He is said to have passed the period of his boyhood and his early youth in great poverty and infamy. For he did not possess a single piece of plate and it is a well known fact that Claudius Pollio, a man of praetorian rank, against whom Nero's poem entitled "The One-eyed Man" is directed, preserved a letter in Domitian's handwriting and sometimes exhibited it, in which the future emperor promised him an assignation; and there have not been wanting those who declared that Domitian was also debauched by Nerva, who succeeded him. In the war with Vitellius he took refuge in the Capitol with his paternal uncle Sabinus and a part of the forces under him. When the enemy forced an entrance and the temple was fired, he hid during the night with the guardian of the shrine, and in the morning, disguised in the garb of a follower of Isis[67] and mingling with the priests of that fickle superstition, he went across the Tiber with a single companion to the mother of one of his school-fellows. There he was so effectually concealed, that though he was closely followed, he could not be found, in spite of a thorough search. It was only after the victory that he ventured forth and after being hailed as Caesar,[68] he assumed the office of city praetor with consular powers, but only in name, turning over all the judicial business to his next colleague. But he exercised all the tyranny of his high position[69] so lawlessly, that it was even then apparent what sort of a man he was going to be. Not to mention all details, after making free with the wives of many men, he went so far as to marry Domitia Longina, who was the wife of Aelius Lamia, and in a single day he assigned more than twenty positions in the city and abroad,[70] which led Vespasian to say more than once that he was surprised that he did not appoint the emperor's successor with the rest.

II. He began an expedition against Gaul and the Germanies, which was uncalled for and from which his father's friends dissuaded him, merely that he might make himself equal to his brother in power and rank. For this he was reprimanded, and to give him a better realisation of his youth[71] and position, he had to live with his father, and when they appeared in public he followed the emperor's chair and that of his brother in a litter, while he also attended their triumph over Judaea riding on a white horse.[72] Moreover, of his six consulships only one was a regular one,[73] and he obtained that only because his brother gave place to him and recommended his appointment.

He himself too made a remarkable pretence of modesty and especially of an interest in poetry, an art which had previously been as unfamiliar to him as it was later despised and rejected, and he even gave readings in public. Yet in spite of all this, when Vologaesus, king of the Parthians, had asked for auxiliaries against the Alani and for one of Vespasian's sons as their leader, Domitian used every effort to have himself sent rather than Titus; and because the affair came to nothing, he tried by gifts and promises to induce other eastern kings to make the same request.

On the death of his father he hesitated for some time whether to offer a double largess[74] to the soldiers, and he never had any compunction about saying that he had been left a partner in the imperial power, but that the will had been tampered with.[75] And from that time on he never ceased to plot against his brother secretly and openly, until Titus was seized with a dangerous illness, when Domitian ordered that he be left for dead, before he had actually drawn his last breath. And after his death he bestowed no honour upon him, save that of deification, and he often assailed his memory in ambiguous phrases, both in his speeches and in his edicts.

III. At the beginning of his reign he used to spend hours in seclusion every day, doing nothing but catch flies and stab them with a keenly-sharpened stylus. Consequently when someone once asked whether anyone was in there with Caesar, Vibius Crispus made the witty reply: "Not even a fly." Then he saluted his wife Domitia as Augusta. He had had a son by her in his second consulship, whom he lost the next year; but he divorced her because of her infatuation for the actor Paris, though he could not bear the separation from her and took her back, alleging that the people demanded it.

In his administration of the government he for some time showed himself inconsistent, with about an equal number of virtues and vices, but finally he turned the virtues also into vices; for so far as one may guess, it was contrary to his natural disposition[76] that he was made rapacious through need and cruel through fear.

IV. He constantly gave grand and costly entertainments, both in the amphitheatre[77] and in the Circus, where in addition to the usual races between two-horse and four-horse chariots, he also exhibited two battles, one between forces of infantry and the other by horsemen; and he even gave a naval battle in the amphitheatre. Besides he gave hunts of wild beasts, gladiatorial shows at night by the light of torches, and not only combats between men but between women as well. He was always present too at the games given by the quaestors, which he revived after they had been abandoned for some time, and invariably granted the people the privilege of calling for two pairs of gladiators from his own school, and brought them in last in all the splendour of the court. During the whole of every gladiatorial show there always stood at his feet a small boy clad in scarlet, with an abnormally small head, with whom he used to talk a great deal, and sometimes seriously. At any rate, he was overheard to ask him if he knew why he had decided at the last appointment day to make Mettius Rufus praefect of Egypt. He often gave sea-fights almost with regular fleets, having dug a pool near the Tiber and surrounded it with seats; and he continued to witness the contests amid heavy rains.

He also celebrated Secular games,[78] reckoning the time, not according to the year when Claudius had last given them, but by the previous calculation of Augustus. In the course of these, to make it possible to finish a hundred races on the day of the contests in the Circus, he diminished the number of laps from seven to five.[79]

He also established a quinquennial contest in honour of Jupiter Capitolinus of a threefold character, comprising music, riding, and gymnastics, and with considerably more prizes than are awarded nowadays. For there were competitions in prose declamation[80] both in Greek and in Latin; and in addition to those of the lyre-players, between choruses of such players and in the lyre alone, without singing; while in the stadium there were races even between maidens. He presided at the competitions in half-boots, clad in a purple toga in the Greek fashion, and wearing upon his head a golden crown with figures of Jupiter, Juno, and Minerva, while by his side sat the priest of Jupiter and the college of the Flaviales,[81] similarly dressed, except that their crowns bore his image as well. He celebrated the Quinquatria[82] too every year in honour of Minerva at his Alban villa, and established for her a college of priests, from which men were chosen by lot to act as officers and give splendid shows of wild beasts and stage plays, besides holding contests in oratory and poetry.

He made a present to the people of three hundred sesterces each on three occasions, and in the course of one of his shows in celebration of the feast of the Seven Hills gave a plentiful banquet,[83] distributing large baskets of victuals to the senate and knights, and smaller ones to the commons; and he himself was the first to begin to eat. On the following day he scattered gifts of all sorts of things[84] to be scrambled for, and since the greater part of these fell where the people sat, he had five hundred tickets thrown into each section occupied by the senatorial and equestrian orders.

V. He restored many splendid buildings which had been destroyed by fire, among them the Capitolium, which had again 82 A.D. been burned,[85] but in all cases with the inscription of his own name only, and with no mention of the original builder. Furthermore, he built a new temple on the Capitoline hill in honour of Jupiter Custos and the forum which now bears the name of Nerva;[86] likewise a temple to the Flavian family, a stadium, an Odeum,[87] and a pool for sea-fights.[88] From the stone used in this last the Circus Maximus was afterwards rebuilt, when both sides of it had been destroyed by fire.

VI. His campaigns he undertook partly without provocation and partly of necessity. That against the Chatti was uncalled for, while the one against the Sarmatians was justified by the destruc-
84 A.D. tion of a legion with its commander. He made two against the Dacians, the first when Oppius Sabinus an ex-consul was defeated,
86 A.D. and the second on the overthrow of Cornelius Fuscus, prefect of the praetorian guard, to whom he had entrusted the conduct of the war. After several battles of varying success he celebrated a double triumph over the Chatti and the Dacians.[89] His victories over the Sarmatians he commemorated merely by the offering of a laurel crown to Jupiter of the Capitol.

A civil war which was set on foot by Lucius Antonius, governor of Upper Germany, was put down in the emperor's absence by a remarkable stroke of good fortune; for at the very hour of the battle the Rhine suddenly thawed and prevented his barbarian allies from crossing over to Antonius. Domitian learned of this victory through omens before he actually had news of it, for on the very day when the decisive battle was fought a magnificent eagle enfolded his statue at Rome with its wings, uttering exultant shrieks; and soon afterwards the report of Antony's death became so current, that several went so far as to assert positively that they had seen his head brought to Rome.

VII. He made many innovations also in common customs. He did away with the distribution of food to the people[90] and revived that of formal dinners.[91] He added two factions of drivers in the Circus, with gold and purple as their colours, to the four former ones.[92] He forbade the appearance of actors on the stage, but allowed the practice of their art in private houses. He prohibited the castration of males, and kept down the price of the eunuchs that remained in the hands of the slave dealers. Once upon the occasion of a plentiful wine crop, attended with a scarcity of grain, thinking that the fields were neglected through too much attention to the vineyards, he made an edict forbidding anyone to plant more vines in Italy and ordering that the vineyards in the provinces be cut down, or but half of them at most be left standing; but he did not persist in carrying out the measure.[93] He opened some of the most important offices of the court[94] to freedmen and Roman knights. He prohibited the uniting of two legions in one camp and the deposit of more than a thousand sesterces by any one soldier at headquarters,[95] because it was clear that Lucius Antonius had been especially led to attempt a revolution by the amount of such deposits in the combined winter quarters of two legions. He increased the pay of the soldiers one fourth, by the addition of three gold pieces each year.[96]

VIII. He administered justice scrupulously and conscientiously, frequently holding special sittings on the tribunal in the Forum. He rescinded such decisions of the Hundred Judges as were made from interested motives.[97] He often warned the arbiters[98] not to grant claims for freedom made under false pretences. He degraded jurors who accepted bribes, together with all their associates.[99] He also induced the tribunes of the commons to prosecute a corrupt aedile for extortion, and to ask the senate to appoint jurors in the case. He took such care to exercise restraint over the city officials and the governors of the provinces, that at no time were they more honest or just, whereas after his time we have seen many of them charged with all manner of offences. Having 83 A.D. undertaken the correction of public morals,[100] he put an end to the licence at the theatres, where the general public occupied the seats reserved for the knights; did away with the prevailing publication of scurrilous lampoons, in which distinguished men and women were attacked, and imposed ignominious penalties on their authors; expelled an ex-quaestor from the senate, because he was given to acting and dancing; deprived notorious women of the use of litters, as well as of the right to receive inheritances and legacies; struck the name of a Roman knight from the list of jurors, because he had taken back his wife after divorcing her and charging her with adultery; condemned several men of both orders, offenders against the Scantinian law;[101] and the incest of Vestal virgins, condoned even by his father and his brother, he punished severely in divers ways, at first by capital punishment, and afterwards in the ancient fashion. For while he allowed the sisters Oculata and also Varronilla free choice of the manner of their death, and banished their paramours, he later ordered that Cornelia, a chief-vestal who had been acquitted once but after a long interval again arraigned and found guilty, be buried alive; and her lovers were beaten to death with rods in the Comitium, with the exception of an ex-praetor, whom he allowed to go into exile, because he admitted his guilt while the case was still unsettled and the examination and torture of the witnesses had led to no result. To protect the gods from being dishonoured with impunity by any sacrilege, he caused a tomb which one of his freedmen had built for his son from stones intended for the temple of Jupiter of the Capitol to be destroyed by the soldiers and the bones and ashes contained in it thrown into the sea.

IX. In the earlier part of his reign he so shrank from any form of bloodshed, that while his father was still absent from the city, he planned to issue an edict that no oxen should be offered up, recalling the line of Vergil,

"E'er yet an impious race did slay and feast upon bullocks."[102]

He was equally free from any suspicion of love of gain or of avarice, both in private life and for some time after becoming emperor; on the contrary, he often gave strong proofs not merely of integrity, but even of liberality. He treated all his intimates most generously, and there was nothing which he urged them more frequently, or with greater insistence, than that they should be niggardly in none of their acts. He would not accept inheritances left him by those who had children. He even annulled a legacy in the will of Rustus Caepio, who had provided that his heir should yearly pay a specified sum to each of the senators on his entrance into the House.[103] He cancelled the suits against those who had been posted as debtors to the public treasury for more than five years, and would not allow a renewal except within a year and on the condition that an accuser who did not win his suit should be punished with exile. Scribes of the quaestors who carried on business, which had become usual although contrary to the Clodian law,[104] he pardoned for past offences. Parcels of land which were left unoccupied here and there after the assignment of lands to the veterans he granted to their former owners as by right of possession. He checked false accusations designed for the profit of the privy purse[105] and inflicted severe penalties on offenders; and a saying of his was current, that an emperor who does not punish informers hounds them on.

X. But he did not continue this course of mercy or integrity, although he turned to cruelty somewhat more speedily than to avarice. He put to death a pupil of the pantomimic actor Paris, who was still a beardless boy and ill at the time, because in his skill and his appearance he seemed not unlike his master;[106] also Hermogenes of Tarsus because of some allusions in his History, besides crucifying even the slaves who had written it out. A householder who said that a Thracian gladiator was a match for the *murmillo,* but not for the giver of the games,[107] he caused to be dragged from his seat and thrown into the arena to dogs, with this placard: "A favourer of the Thracians who spoke impiously."[108]

He put to death many senators, among them several ex-consuls, including Civica Cerealis, at the very time when he was proconsul in Asia, Salvidienus Orfitus, Acilius Glabrio while he was in exile—these on the ground of plotting revolution, the rest on any charge, however trivial. He slew Aelius Lamia for joking remarks, which were reflections on him, it is true, but made long before and harmless. For when Domitian had taken away Lamia's wife,[109] the latter replied to someone who praised his voice: "I practise continence";[110] and when Titus urged him to marry again, he replied: "Are you too looking for a wife?" He put to death Salvius Cocceianus, because he had kept the birthday of the emperor Otho, his paternal uncle; Mettius Pompusianus, because it was commonly reported that he had an imperial nativity and carried about a map of the world on parchment and speeches of the kings and generals from Titus Livius, besides giving two of his slaves the names of Mago and Hannibal; Sallustius Lucullus, governor of Britain, for allowing some lances of a new pattern to be called "Lucullean," after his own name; Junius Rusticus, because he had published eulogies of Paetus Thrasea and Helvidius Priscus and called them the most upright of men; and on the occasion of this charge he banished all the philosophers from the city and from Italy. He also executed the younger Helvidius, alleging that in a farce composed for the stage he had under the characters of Paris and Oenone censured Domitian's divorce from his wife; Flavinus Sabinus too, one of his cousins, because on the day of the consular elections the crier had inadvertently announced him to the people as emperor elect, instead of consul.

After his victory in the civil war he became even more cruel, and to discover any conspirators who were in hiding, tortured many of the opposite party by a new form of inquisition, inserting fire in their privates; and he cut off the hands of some of them. It is certain that of the more conspicuous only two were pardoned, a tribune of senatorial rank and a centurion, who the more clearly to prove their freedom from guilt, showed that they were of shameless unchastity and could therefore have had no influence with the general or with the soldiers.

XI. His savage cruelty was not only excessive, but also cunning and sudden. He invited one of his stewards to his bed-chamber the day before crucifying him, made him sit beside him on his couch, and dismissed him in a secure and gay frame of mind, even deigning to send him a share of his dinner. When he was on the point of condemning the ex-consul Arrecinius Clemens, one of his intimates and tools, he treated him with as great favour as before, if not greater, and finally, as he was taking a drive with him, catching sight of his accuser he said: "Pray, shall we hear this base slave to-morrow?"

To abuse men's patience the more insolently, he never pronounced an unusually dreadful sentence without a preliminary declaration of clemency, so that there came to be no more certain indication of a cruel death than the leniency of his preamble. He had brought some men charged with treason into the senate, and when he had introduced the matter by saying that he would find out that day how dear he was to the members, he had no difficulty in causing them to be condemned to suffer the ancient method of punishment.[111] Then appalled at the cruelty of the penalty, he interposed a veto, to lessen the odium, in these words (for it will be of interest to know his exact language): "Allow me, Fathers of the senate, to prevail on you by your love for me to grant a favour which I know I shall obtain with difficulty, namely that you grant the condemned free choice of the manner of their death; for thus you will spare your own eyes and all men will know that I was present at the meeting of the senate."

XII. Reduced to financial straits by the cost of his buildings and shows, as well as by the additions which he had made to the pay of the soldiers, he tried to lighten the military expenses by diminishing the number of his troops; but perceiving that in this way he exposed himself to the attacks of the barbarians, and nevertheless had difficulty in easing his burdens, he had no hesitation in resorting to every sort of robbery. The property of the living and the dead was seized everywhere on any charge brought by any accuser. It was enough to allege any action or word derogatory to the majesty of the prince. Estates of those in no way connected with him were confiscated, if but one man came forward to declare that he had heard from the deceased during his lifetime that Caesar was his heir. Besides other taxes, that on the Jews[112] was levied with the utmost rigour, and those were prosecuted who without publicly acknowledging that faith yet lived as Jews, as well as those who concealed their origin and did not pay the tribute levied upon their people.[113] I recall being present in my youth when the person of a man ninety years old was examined before the procurator and a very crowded court, to see whether he was circumcised.

From his youth he was far from being of an affable disposition, but was on the contrary presumptuous and unbridled both in act and in word. When his father's concubine Caenis[114] returned from Histria and offered to kiss him as usual, he held out his hand to her. He was vexed that his brother's son-in-law had attendants clad in white, as well as he, and uttered the words

"Not good is a number of rulers."[115]

XIII. When he became emperor, he did not hesitate to boast in the senate that he had conferred their power on both his father and his brother, and that they had but returned him his own; nor on taking back his wife after their divorce, that he had "recalled her to his divine couch."[116] He delighted to hear the people in the amphitheatre shout on his feast day:[117] "Good Fortune attend out Lord[118] and Mistress." Even more, in the Capitoline competition,[119] when all the people begged him with great unanimity to restore Palfurius Sura, who had been banished some time before from the senate, and on that occasion received the prize for oratory, he deigned no reply, but merely had a crier bid them be silent. With no less arrogance he began as follows in dictating a circular letter in the name of his procurators, "Our Master and our God bids that this be done." And so the custom arose of henceforth addressing him in no other way even in writing or in conversation. He suffered no statues to be set up in his honour in the Capitol, except of gold and silver and of a fixed weight. He erected so many and such huge vaulted passage-ways and arches in the various regions of the city, adorned with chariots and triumphal emblems, that on one of them someone wrote
71, 72, in Greek: "It is enough."[120] He held the consulship seventeen
77, (cos. v), times, more often than any of his predecessors. Of these the
80, seven middle ones were in successive years, but all of them he
82–88, 90, 92, filled in name only, continuing none beyond the first of May and
95 A.D. few after the Ides of January. Having assumed the surname Germanicus after his two triumphs, he renamed the months of September and October from his own names, calling them "Germanicus" and "Domitianus," because in the former he had come to the throne and was born in the latter.

XIV. In this way he became an object of terror and hatred to all, but he was overthrown at last by a conspiracy of his friends and favourite freedmen, to which his wife was also privy. He had long since had a premonition of the last year and day of his life, and even of the very hour and manner of his death. In his youth astrologers had predicted all this to him, and his father once even openly ridiculed him at dinner for refusing mushrooms, saying that he showed himself unaware of his destiny in not rather fearing the sword. Therefore he was at all times timorous and worried, and was disquieted beyond measure by even the slightest suspicions. It is thought that nothing had more effect in inducing him to ignore his proclamation about cutting down the vineyards[121] than the circulation of notes containing the following lines:

"Gnaw at my root, an you will; even then shall I have juice in plenty
To pour upon thee, O goat, when at the altar you stand."[122]

It was because of this same timorousness that although he was most eager for all such honours, he refused a new one which the senate had devised and offered to him, a decree, namely, that whenever he held the consulship Roman knights selected by lot should precede him among his lictors and attendants, clad in the trabea[123] and bearing lances.

As the time when he anticipated danger drew near, becoming still more anxious every day, he lined the walls of the colonnades in which he used to walk with phengite stone,[124] to be able to see in its brilliant surface the reflection of all that went on behind his back. And he did not give a hearing to any prisoners except in private and alone, even holding their chains in his hands. Further, to convince his household that one must not venture to kill a patron even on good grounds, he condemned Epaphroditus, his confidential secretary, to death, because it was believed that after Nero was abandoned[125] the freedman's hand had aided him in taking his life.[126]

XV. Finally he put to death his own cousin Flavius Clemens, suddenly and on a very slight suspicion, almost before the end of his consulship; and yet Flavius was a man of most contemptible laziness and Domitian had besides openly named his sons, who were then very young, as his successors, changing their former names and calling the one Vespasian and the other Domitian. And it was by this deed in particular that he hastened his own destruction.

For eight successive months so many strokes of lightning occurred and were reported, that at last he cried: "Well, let him now strike whom he will." The temple of Jupiter of the Capitol was struck and that of the Flavian family, as well as the Palace and the emperor's own bedroom. The inscription too on the base of a triumphal statue of his was torn off in a violent tempest and fell upon a neighbouring tomb.[127] The tree which had been overthrown when Vespasian was still a private citizen but had sprung up anew,[128] then on a sudden fell down again. Fortune of Praeneste[129] had throughout his whole reign, when he commended the new year to her protection, given him a favourable omen and always in the same words. Now at last she returned a most direful one, not without the mention of bloodshed.

He dreamed that Minerva, whom he worshipped with superstitious veneration, came forth from her shrine and declared that she could no longer protect him, since she had been disarmed by Jupiter. Yet there was nothing by which he was so much disturbed as a prediction of the astrologer Ascletarion and what befell him. When this man was accused before the emperor and did not deny that he had spoken of certain things which he had foreseen through his art, he was asked what his own end would be. When he replied that he would shortly be rent by dogs, Domitian ordered him killed at once; but to prove the fallibility of his art, he ordered besides that his funeral be attended to with the greatest care.[130] While this was being done, it chanced that the pyre was overset by a sudden storm and that the dogs mangled the corpse, which was only partly consumed;

and that an actor of farces called Latinus, who happened to pass by and see the incident, told it to Domitian at the dinner table, with the rest of the day's gossip.

XVI. The day before he was killed he gave orders to have some apples which were offered him kept until the following day, and added: "If only I am spared to eat them"; then turning to his companions, he declared that on the following day the moon would be stained with blood in Aquarius, and that a deed would be done of which men would talk all over the world. At about midnight he was so terrified that he leaped from his bed. The next morning he conducted the trial of a soothsayer sent from Germany, who when consulted about the lightning strokes had foretold a change of rulers, and condemned him to death. While he was vigorously scratching a festered wart on his forehead, and had drawn blood, he said: "May this be all." Then he asked the time, and by prearrangement the sixth hour was announced to him, instead of the fifth, which he feared. Filled with joy at this, and believing all danger now past, he was hastening to the bath, when his chamberlain Parthenius changed his purpose by announcing that someone had called about a matter of great moment and would not be put off. Then he dismissed all his attendants and went to his bedroom, where he was slain.

XVII. Concerning the nature of the plot and the manner of his death, this is about all that became known. As the conspirators were deliberating when and how to attack him, whether at the bath or at dinner, Stephanus, Domitilla's[131] steward, at the time under accusation for embezzlement, offered his aid and counsel. To avoid suspicion, he wrapped up his left arm in woollen bandages for some days, pretending that he had injured it, and concealed in them a dagger. Then pretending to betray a conspiracy and for that reason being given an audience, he stabbed the emperor in the groin as he was reading a paper which the assassin handed him, and stood in a state of amazement. As the wounded prince attempted to resist, he was slain with seven wounds by Clodianus, a subaltern, Maximus, a freedman of Parthenius, Satur, decurion of the chamberlains, and a gladiator from the imperial school. A boy who was engaged in his usual duty of attending to the Lares in the bedroom,[132] and so was a witness of the murder, gave this additional information. He was bidden by Domitian, immediately after he was dealt the first blow, to hand him the dagger hidden under his pillow and to call the servants; but he found nothing at the head of the bed save the hilt, and besides all the doors were closed. Meanwhile the emperor grappled with Stephanus and bore him to the ground, where they struggled for a long time, Domitian trying now to wrest the dagger from his assailant's hands and now to gouge out his eyes with his lacerated fingers.

Sept. 18, 96 A.D. He was slain on the fourteenth day before the Kalends of October in the forty-fifth year of his age and the fifteenth of his reign. His corpse was carried out on a common bier by those who bury the poor, and his nurse Phyllis cremated it at her suburban estate on the Via Latina; but his ashes she secretly carried to the temple of the Flavian family and mingled them with those of Julia, daughter of Titus, whom she had also reared.

XVIII. He was tall of stature, with a modest expression and a high colour.[133] His eyes were large, but his sight was somewhat dim. He was handsome and graceful too, especially when a young man, and indeed in his whole body with the exception of his feet, the toes of which were somewhat cramped. In later life he had the further disfigurement of baldness, a protruding belly, and spindling legs, though the latter had become thin from a long illness. He was so conscious that the modesty of his expression was in his favour, that he once made this boast in the senate: "So far, at any rate, you have approved my heart and my countenance." He was so sensitive about his baldness, that he regarded it as a personal insult if anyone else was twitted with that defect in jest or in earnest; though in a book "On the Care of the Hair," which he published and dedicated to a friend, he wrote the following by way of consolation to the man and himself:

"Do you not see that I too am tall and comely to look on?[134]

And yet the same fate awaits my hair, and I bear with resignation the ageing of my locks in youth. Be assured that nothing is more pleasing than beauty, but nothing shorter-lived."

XIX. He was incapable of exertion and seldom went about the city on foot, while on his campaigns and journeys he rarely rode on horseback, but was regularly carried in a litter. He took no interest in arms, but was particularly devoted to archery.[135] There are many who have more than once seen him slay a hundred wild beasts of different kinds on his Alban estate, and purposely kill some of them with two successive shots in such a way that the arrows gave the effect of horns. Sometimes he would have a slave stand at a distance and hold out the palm of his right hand for a mark, with the fingers spread; then he directed his arrows with such accuracy that they passed harmlessly between the fingers.

XX. At the beginning of his rule he neglected liberal studies,[136] although he provided for having the libraries, which were destroyed by fire,[137] renewed at very great expense, seeking everywhere for copies of the lost works, and sending scribes to Alexandria to transcribe and correct them. Yet he never took any pains to become acquainted with history or poetry, or even to acquiring an ordinarily good style. He read nothing except the memoirs and transactions of Tiberius Caesar; for his letters, speeches and proclamations he relied on others' talents. Yet his conversation was not inelegant, and some of his sayings were even noteworthy, "How I wish," said he "that I were as fine looking as Maecius thinks he is." He declared too that the head of a certain man, whose hair had changed colour in such a way that it was partly reddish and partly grey, was like "snow on which mead had been poured."

XXI. He used to say that the lot of princes was most unhappy, since when they discovered a conspiracy, no one believed them unless they had been killed.

Whenever he had leisure he amused himself with playing at dice, even on working days and in the morning hours. He went to the bath before the end of the forenoon and lunched to the point of satiety, so that at dinner he rarely took anything except a Matian apple[138] and a moderate amount of wine from a jug. He gave numerous and generous banquets, but usually ended them early; in no case did he protract them beyond sunset, or follow them by a drinking bout. In fact, he did nothing until the hour for retiring except walk alone in a retired place.

XXII. He was excessively lustful. His constant sexual intercourse he called bed-wrestling, as if it were a kind of exercise. It was reported that he depilated his concubines with his own hand and swam with common prostitutes. After persistently refusing his niece, who was offered him in marriage when she was still a maid, because he was entangled in an intrigue with Domitia, he seduced her shortly afterwards when she became the wife of another, and that too during the lifetime of Titus. Later, when she was bereft of father and husband, he loved her ardently and without disguise, and even became the cause of her death by compelling her to get rid of a child of his by abortion.[139]

XXIII. The people received the news of his death with indifference, but the soldiers were greatly grieved and at once attempted to call him the Deified Domitian; while they were prepared also to avenge him, had they not lacked leaders. This, however, they did accomplish a little later by most insistently demanding the execution of his murderers. The senators on the contrary were so overjoyed, that they raced to fill the House, where they did not refrain from assailing the dead emperor with the most insulting and stinging kind of outcries. They even had ladders brought and his shields[140] and images torn down before their eyes and dashed upon the ground; finally they passed a decree that his inscriptions should everywhere be erased, and all record of him obliterated.[141]

A few months before he was killed, a raven perched on the Capitolium and cried "All will be well," an omen which some interpreted as follows:

"High on the gable Tarpeian[142] a raven but lately alighting,
Could not say 'It is well,' only declared 'It will be.'"

Domitian himself, it is said, dreamed that a golden hump grew out on his back, and he regarded this as an infallible sign that the condition of the empire would be happier and more prosperous after his time; and this was shortly shown to be true through the uprightness and moderate rule of the succeeding emperors.

PART II

THE LIVES OF ILLUSTRIOUS MEN

PREFATORY NOTE

THE manuscripts of the *Dialogus* and *Agricola* of Tacitus contain also a treatise "On Grammarians and Rhetoricians," attributed to Suetonius. This work was used by Gellius (*Noct. Att.* 15. 11) and by Hieronymus, but after the latter's day was lost for many centuries.

About the middle of the fifteenth century,[1] in the course of a journey through Germany and Denmark, Enoc of Ascoli[2] found the two works of Tacitus and the treatise on Grammarians and Rhetoricians, apparently at Hersfeld and in a single codex, and brought them to Italy. This codex is now lost,[3] but some eighteen copies of the *De Grammaticis et Rhetoribus* are in existence, all belonging to the fifteenth century, which show remarkable differences in reading, considering that they are derived from a single archetype, and are separated from it by so short a time. These manuscripts, not all of which have been collated, fall into two classes, distinguished from each other by the presence or absence of the index of names at the beginning of the treatise. Roth in his edition of 1858 asserted the superiority of the former class, and Ihm is inclined to agree with him.[4] For a list of the better codices with their sigla see footnote on p. 395.

Owing to the late date of all the manuscripts, the early printed editions are of some value in the criticism of the text; see the Bibliographical Note, p. 394.

The work begins with an index, containing a list of the grammarians and rhetoricians who are to be discussed, which, as has been said, is omitted by some of the manuscripts. This is followed by an introduction on the origin and development of grammatical studies at Rome, and the connection of grammar with rhetoric, after which the individual representatives of the subject are treated. The part devoted to rhetoricians also begins with an introduction on the history of the study, but the work comes to an end after dealing with five of the fifteen persons named in the index.

It has been generally recognized that this treatise on "Grammarians and Rhetoricians" formed part of a larger work by Suetonius, entitled *De Viris Illustribus,* which treated of Romans who were eminent in the field of literature.[5] It seems to have consisted of five divisions, devoted respectively to Poets, Orators, Historians, Philosophers, and Grammarians and Rhetoricians under one head. The order of the various divisions, or books, cannot be determined.[6]

To judge from the personages treated by Suetonius and those whom he omits, the *De Viris Illustribus* appears to have been written between 106 and 113. It was therefore his earliest work, and is in all probability the one to which Pliny refers.[7] As was the case with the *Lives of the Caesars,* he apparently set as his limit the close of the reign of Domitian, so that Juvenal, Tacitus and the younger Pliny were not included.

While the greater part of the *De Viris Illustribus* has been lost, some passages of considerable length, in addition to the "Grammarians and Rhetoricians," have been recovered from various sources. These consist of Lives of various Roman writers, prefixed to their works by way of introduction.[8] None of these has come down to us in its original form, and they differ greatly in the amount of abridgment or of interpolation to which they have been subjected. Those which may properly be included in an edition of Suetonius are the following.

From the book on Poets (*De Poetis*), to which an index of thirty-three names has been compiled from the references in Hieronymus,[9] we have a Life of Terence, preserved in the

Commentary of Aelius Donatus, of the fourth century, and ascribed by him to Suetonius. A Life of Horace, which is found in some of the manuscripts, is not directly attributed to Suetonius, but is believed to be his because of the occurrence in it of certain statements which are credited to Suetonius by the scholiasts.[10] A very fragmentary Life of Lucan is assigned to Suetonius also on internal evidence.

With regard to the ultimate authorship of these three Lives there is little, if any, difference of opinion. With regard to three others the agreement is not so general, but they are assigned to Suetonius by some scholars. These are the Life of Vergil, in Donatus' Commentary, where it is followed by an introduction to the Bucolics from Donatus' own hand; a Life of Tibullus, greatly abridged; and a Life of Persius. The last is directly attributed to Valerius Probus, but in spite of this is believed by many to be Suetonian.[11]

The discussion of the varieties of poety, found in Diomedes, *Grammatici Latini,* i. 482. 14 ff. K., was assigned to Suetonius by Reifferscheid and printed in his edition of 1860. Schanz also includes this among the fragments of the *De Viris Illustribus*[12] but on insufficient grounds; see Teuffel, *Geschichte der römischen Literatur,* 6th ed., iii., p. 57 and the literature there cited.

From the Orators (*De Oratoribus*), with an index of fifteen names, only the brief abstract of the Life of Passienus Crispus has come down to us, preserved in the scholia Pithoeana on Juvenal 4. 81, where Passienus is confused with Vibius Crispus. Although his source is not given by the scholiast, the Life is generally attributed to Suetonius. Since in the excerpts from the *De Oratoribus* made by Hieronymus we find no orator earlier than Cicero, it has been inferred that Suetonius began his biographies with Cicero and treated the earlier orators in a general introduction.

From the Historians, with an index of six names, we have only the Life of Pliny the Elder, which is attributed to Suetonius in the manuscripts which contain it. Here Suetonius seems to have begun with Sallust, discussing the earlier historians in his introduction.

From the *De Philosophis* we have only an index of three names, Marcus Terentius Varro, Publius Nigidius Figulus, and Lucius Annaeus Seneca, which have been recovered from Hieronymus.

As in the *Lives of the Caesars,* Suetonius' sources for the *Lives of Illustrious Men* were in the main literary, in particular Varro, the previous writers of books of the same title (Nepos, Santra and Hyginus), Asconius and Fenestella. In part through these writers, and perhaps in part directly, his work goes back to the Greek authors Antigonus of Carystos, Aristoxenes, Satyros, and Hermippos. He also made some use of private letters, public documents, hearsay evidence and personal recollection.

The Text of the *De Grammaticis et Rhetoribus* is in a less satisfactory condition than that of the *Caesars.* Some manuscipts of the better class have not yet been collated, and Ihm's untimely death has prevented or indefinitely postponed the publication of the second volume of his edition with the text of the fragments. New recensions of the Lives have appeared in various editions of the authors in question and one of the Life of Vergil by E. Diehl in the *Kleine Texte für theologische und philologische Vorlesungen und Uebungen,* Bonn, 1911.

BIBLIOGRAPHICAL NOTE

THERE are three editions of the *De Grammaticis et Rhetoribus* that rank as *principes*: one of uncertain authorship and date, believed by some to have been published by Nicòlas Jensen at Venice in 1472, a Venetian edition of 1474, and one issued at Florence in 1478. Other early editions are the Aldine, 1508, based upon the three *principes*, and those of R. Stephanus, E. Vinetus, and Achilles Statius. In more recent times separate editions have been published by L. Tross, 1841, Fr. Osann, Giessen, 1854, L. Roth, Leipzig, 1858, and A. Reifferscheid, Leipzig, 1860. The last two are still the standard texts. The De *Viris Illustribus* was first published with the *Caesars* by Antonius Gryphius at Lyons in 1566 and Th. Pulmann at Antwerp, in 1574. They were followed by Casaubon, and his edition, as well as others of those mentioned on p. xxvii of Volume I, contains the fragments. In 1863 H. Doergens published an edition at Leipzig with a German translation and a commentary. The only translation into English, so far as I know, is that of T. Forester in the Bohn library; see Volume I, p. xxviii.

DE GRAMMATICIS ET RHETORIBUS

SEVERAL of the better manuscripts have before or after the title the following Index: Grammatici: [Aelius Praeconius],[1] Saevius Nicanor, Aurelius Opilius, M. Antonius Gnipho, M. Pompilius Andronicus, L. Orbilius (Pupillus), L. Ateius Philologus, P. Valerius Cato, Cornelius Epicadius, (Staberius Eros), Curtius Nicias, Lenaeus, Q. Caecilius (Epirota), M. Verrius Flaccus, L. Crassicius, Scribonius Aphrodisius, C. Iulius Hyginus, C. Melissus, M. Pomponius Marcellus, Q. Remmius Palaemon, (M.) Valerius Probus. Rhetores: (L.) Plotius Gallus, L. Voltacilius Plotus, M. Epidius, Sex. Clodius, C. Albucius Silus, L. Cestius Pius, M. Porcius Latro, Q. Curtius Rufus, L. Valerius Primanus, Verginius Flavus, L. Statius Ursulus, P. Clodius Quirinalis, M. Antonius Liberalis, Sex. Iulius Gabinianus, M. Fabius Quintilianus, [M. Tullius Tiro].[2]

The following Sigla are used: V = codex Vaticanus, 1862; L = codex Leidensis, formerly Perizonianus; N = codex Neapolitanus, formerly Farnesianus; O = codex Ottobonianus, 1455; G = codex Gudianus, 93; I = codex Vaticanus, 1518; W = codex Vindobonensis, 711 (see Ihm, *Rh. Mus.* 61. 543 ff.).

ON GRAMMARIANS[1]

I. The study of Grammar was not even pursued at Rome in early days, still less held in any esteem; and naturally enough, since the state was then still uncultivated and given to war, and had as yet little leisure for liberal pursuits. The beginnings of the subject, too, were humble, for the earliest teachers, who were also both poets and Italian[2] Greeks (I refer to Livius and Ennius, who gave instruction in both tongues at home and abroad, as is well known), did no more than interpret the Greeks or give readings from whatever they themselves had composed in the Latin language. For while some tell us that this same Ennius published a book "On Letters and Syllables" and another "On Metres," Lucius Cotta is right in maintaining that these were not the work of the poet, but of a later Ennius, who is also the author of the volumes "On the Science of Augury."

II. In my opinion then, the first to introduce the study of grammar into our city was Crates of Mallos, a contemporary of Aristarchus. He was sent to the senate by king Attalus between the second and third Punic wars, at about the time when Ennius died; 169 B.C.
and having fallen into the opening of a sewer in the Palatine quarter and broken his leg, he held numerous and frequent conferences during the whole time both of his embassy and of his convalescence, at which he constantly gave instruction, and thus set an example for our countrymen to imitate. Their imitation, however, was confined to a careful criticism of poems which had as yet but little circulation,

either those of deceased friends or others that met with their approval, and to making them known to the public by reading and commenting on them. For example, Gaius Octavius Lampadio thus treated the "Punic War" of Naevius, which was originally written in a single volume without a break, but was divided by Lampadio into seven books. At a later time Quintus Vargunteius took up the "Annals" of Ennius, which he expounded on set days to large audiences; and Laelius Archelaus and Vettius Philocomus the satires of their friend Lucilius, which Lenaeus Pompeius prides himself on having read with Archelaus, and Valerius Cato with Philocomus.

III. The foundations of the study were laid, and it was advanced in all directions, by Lucius Aelius of Lanuvium and his son-in-law Servius Clodius, both of whom were Roman knights and men of wide and varied experience in scholarship and statecraft.

Aelius had two surnames, for he was called Praeconinus because his father had followed the occupation of a crier,[3] and Stilo[4] because he used to write speeches for all the great men of the day; and he was so devoted to the aristocratic party, that he accompanied Metellus Numidicus into exile.

Servius stole one of his father-in-law's books before it was published, and being in consequence disowned, left the city through shame and remorse, and fell ill of the gout. Unable to endure the pain, he applied a poisonous drug to his feet, which finally killed him, after he had lived for a time with that part of his body as it were prematurely dead.

After this the science constantly grew in favour and popularity, so much so that even the most eminent men did not hesitate to make contributions to it, while at times there are said to have been more than twenty well-attended schools in the city. The grammarians too were so highly esteemed, and their compensation was so ample, that Lutatius Daphnis, whom Laevius Melissus, punning on his name, often called the "darling of Pan," [5] is known to have been bought for seven hundred thousand sesterces and soon afterwards set free, while Lucius Appuleius was hired for four hundred sesterces a year by Eficius Calvinus, a wealthy Roman knight, to teach a large school.[6]

In fact, Grammar even made its way into the provinces, and some of the most famous teachers gave instruction abroad, especially in Gallia Togata, including Octavius Teucer, Pescennius Iaccus and Oppius Chares; indeed the last named taught until the very end of his life, when he could no longer walk, or even see.

IV. The term *grammaticus* became prevalent through Greek influence, but at first such men were called *litterati*.[7] Cornelius Nepos, too, in a little book in which he explains the difference between *litteratus* and *eruditus*[8] says that the former is commonly applied to those who can speak or write on any subject accurately, cleverly and with authority; but that it should strictly be used of interpreters of the poets, whom the Greeks call *grammatici*. That these were also called *litteratores* is shown by Messala Corvinus in one of his letters, in which he says: "I am not concerned with Furius Bibaculus, nor with Ticidas either, or with the *litterator* Cato." For he unquestionably refers to Valerius Cato, who was famous both as a poet and as a grammarian. Some however make a distinction between *litteratus* and *litterator*, as the Greeks do between *grammaticus* and *grammatista*, using the former of a master of his subject, the latter of one moderately proficient. Orbilius too supports this view by examples, saying: "In the days of our forefathers, when anyone's slaves were offered for sale, it was not usual except in special cases to advertise any one of them as *litteratus* but rather as *litterator*, implying that he had a smattering of letters, but was not a finished scholar."

The grammarians of early days taught rhetoric as well, and we have treatises from many men on both subjects. It was this custom, I think, which led those of later times also, although the two professions had now become distinct, nevertheless either to retain or to introduce certain kinds of exercises suited to the training of orators, such as problems, paraphrases, addresses, character sketches and similar things; doubtless that they might not turn over their pupils to the rhetoricians wholly ignorant and unprepared.[9] But I observe that such instruction is now given up, because of the lack of application and the youth of some of the pupils; for I do not believe that it is because the subjects are underrated. I remember that at any rate when I was a young man, one of these teachers, Princeps by name, used to declaim and engage in discussion on alternate days; and that sometimes he would give instruction in the morning, and in the afternoon remove his desk and declaim. I used to hear, too, that within the memory of our forefathers some passed directly from the grammar school to the Forum and took their place among the most eminent advocates.

The following list includes about all the distinguished teachers of the subject, at least those of whose life I am able to give any account.

V. Saevius Nicanor was the first to attain to fame and recognition through his teaching, and besides his commentaries, the greater part of which, however, are said to be stolen, he wrote a satire, in which he shows by the following lines that he was a freedman and had two surnames;

"Saevius Nicanor, the freedman of Marcus, may deny this; but Saevius Postumius, who is the same man, and a Marcus as well, will prove it."[10]

Some write that because of some disgrace he retired to Sardinia and there died.

VI. Aurelius Opilius, freedman of an Epicurean, first taught philosophy, afterwards rhetoric, and finally grammar. But when Rutilius Rufus was banished, he gave up his school and followed him to Asia, where he lived with him in Smyrna to old age. He wrote several books on various learned topics, nine of which, so he tells us, forming a single work, he appropriately made to correspond with the number of the Muses, and called them by their names, because he considered writers and poets to be under the protection of those divinities. I observe that his surname is given in numerous catalogues and titles with a single L, but he himself writes it with two in an acrostic in a little book of his called "Pinax."[11]

VII. Marcus Antonius Gnipho was born in Gaul of free parents, but was disowned.[12] He was set free by his foster-father[13] and given an education, at Alexandria, according to some, and in intimate association with Dionysius Scytobrachion; but this I can hardly credit for chronological reasons. It is said that he was a man of great talent, of unexampled powers of memory, and well read not only in Latin but in Greek as well; that his disposition, too, was kindly and good-natured, and that he never made any stipulation about his fees, and therefore received more from the generosity of his pupils. He first gave instruction in the house of the Deified Julius, when the latter was still a boy, and then in his own home. He taught rhetoric too, giving daily instruction in speaking, but declaiming only once a week.[14] They say also that distinguished men attended his school, including Cicero even while he was praetor. Although he did not live beyond his fiftieth year, he wrote a great deal. Ateius Philologus, however, declares that he left but two volumes, "On the Latin Language," maintaining that the other works attributed to him were those of his pupils and not his own. Yet his own name is sometimes found in them, for example * * *

VIII. Marcus Pompilius Andronicus, a native of Syria, because of his devotion to the Epicurean sect was considered somewhat indolent in his work as a grammarian and not qualified to conduct a school. Therefore, realizing that he was held in less esteem at Rome, not only than Antonius Gnipho, but than others of even less ability, he moved to Cumae, where he led a quiet life and wrote many books. But he was so poor and needy that he was forced to sell that admirable little work of his, "Criticisms of the Annals of Ennius"[15] to someone or other for sixteen thousand sesterces. Orbilius tells us that he bought up these books after they had been suppressed, and caused them to be circulated under their author's name.

IX. Lucius Orbilius Pupillus of Beneventum, left alone in the world by the death of his parents, both of whom were slain on the selfsame day by treacherous enemies, at first earned a living as an

attendant on the magistrates. He then served as a subaltern in Macedonia, and later in the cavalry. After completing his military service, he resumed his studies, to which he had given no little attention from boyhood; and after teaching for a long time in his native place, he at last went to Rome in his fiftieth year, when
63 B.C. Cicero was consul, where he gave instruction with greater renown than profit. For in one of his books, written when he was well on in years, he admits that he was poor and lived under the tiles.[16] He also wrote a book called "Perialogos,"[17] full of complaints of the wrongs which teachers suffered from the indifference or selfishness of parents. Indeed he was sour-tempered, not only towards rival scholars,[18] whom he assailed at every opportunity, but also towards his pupils, as Horace implies when he calls him "the flogger,"[19] and Domitius Marsus in the line:

"Whomever Orbilius thrashed with rod or with whiplash of leather."

He did not even refrain from gibes at men of distinction; for when he was still obscure and was giving testimony in a crowded court-room, being asked by Varro, the advocate on the other side, what he did and what his profession was, he replied: "I remove hunchbacks from the sun into the shade." Now Murena[20] was hunchbacked. Orbilius lived to be nearly a hundred, having long since lost his memory, as is shown by the verse of Bibaculus:

"Where is Orbilius, pray, great learning's tomb?'

His marble statue may be seen at Beneventum, on the left side of the capitol, representing him seated and clad in a Greek mantle, with two book-boxes by his side. He left a son Orbilius, who was also a teacher of grammar.

X. Lucius Ateius Philologus was a freedman, born at Athens. The well-known jurist Ateius Capito says that he was "a rhetorician among grammarians and a grammarian among rhetoricians." Asinius Pollio, too, in the book in which he criticizes the writings of Sallust, as marred by an excessive effort for archaism, writes as follows: "He was especially abetted in this by Ateius Praetextatus, a famous Latin grammarian, afterwards a critic and teacher of declamation, and finally self-styled Philologus." Ateius himself wrote to Laelius Hermas that he had made great progress in Greek letters and some in Latin, had been a pupil of Antonius Gnipho * * *,[21] and afterwards a teacher; further, that he had given instruction to many eminent young men, including the brothers Appius and Claudius Pulcher, whom he had also accompanied to their province. He seems to have assumed the title Philologus, because like Eratosthenes, who was first to lay claim to that surname, he regarded himself as a man of wide and varied learning. And that he was such is evident from his commentaries, though very few of them survive; but he gives some idea of their number in a second letter to the aforesaid Hermas: "Remember to recommend my *Hyle*[22] to others; as you know, it consists of material of every kind, collected in eight hundred books." He was afterwards a close friend of Gaius Sallustius, and after Sallust's death, of Asinius Pollio; and when they set about writing history, he provided the one with an epitome of all Roman story, from which to select what he wished, and the other with rules on the art of composition. This makes me wonder all the more that Asinius believed that Ateius used to collect archaic words and expressions for Sallust; for he knows that the grammarian's strongest recommendation to him was to use familiar, unassuming, natural[23] language, especially avoiding Sallust's obscurity and his bold figures of speech.

XI. Publius Valerius Cato, according to some writers, was the freedman of a certain Bursenus from Gaul; but he himself, in a little work called "Indignation," declares that he was freeborn but was left an orphan; so that he was the more easily stripped of his patrimony in the lawless times of Sulla. He had many distinguished pupils and was regarded as a very competent teacher, especially of those who had a bent for poetry, as indeed is especially evident from these verses:

"Cato, teacher of letters, Siren Latin-born,

He, and none other, poets reads and makes."
Besides books of a grammatical character, he wrote poems also, of which the most highly esteemed are the "Lydia" and the "Diana." Ticidas says of the former:

"Lydia, a book most dear to cultured minds." And Cinna of the latter:

"For ages may our Cato's Dian[24] live."

He reached an advanced age, but in extreme poverty and almost in destitution, buried in a little hovel, after he had given up his villa at Tusculum to his creditors, as Bibaculus tells us:

"If haply one has seen my Cato's house,
His shingles stained with red,
His garden over which Priapus watched:
One can but wonder by what training he
To such a height of wisdom has attained
That three small cabbages, half a pound of meal,
And clusters twain of grapes beneath one roof
Suffice for him when well-nigh at life's end."

And again:
"Gallus, but now our Cato's creditor
His Tusculanum offered through the town.
We wondered that the master without peer,
The great grammarian, chief among our poets,
Could solve all questions, solvent[25] could not be.
Lo! Crates' heart, mind of Zenodotus."[26]

XII. Cornelius Epicadius was a freedman of Lucius Cornelius Sulla, the dictator, and one of his servants[27] in the augural priesthood, besides being a great favourite of his son Faustus.

Therefore he always declared that he was the freedman of both. He himself supplied the last book of Sulla's "Autobiography," which the dictator left unfinished.

XIII. Staberius Eros was purchased with his own savings at a public sale[28] and formally manumitted because of his devotion to literature. He numbered among his pupils Brutus and Cassius. Some say that he was so noble-minded that in the times of Sulla he admitted the children of the proscribed to his school free of charge and without any fee.

XIV. Curtius Nicias was an adherent of Gnaeus Pompeius and Gaius Memmius; but having brought a note from Memmius to Pompey's wife with an infamous proposal, he was betrayed by her, lost favour with Pompey, and was forbidden his house. He was an intimate friend of Marcus Cicero too, and in a letter of the orator's to Dolabella[29] we read these words about Nicias: "I think there is nothing going on in Rome which you are interested in knowing, unless perhaps you would like to know that I am acting as arbiter between our friend Nicias and Vidius. The one presents a note for payment, consisting of two lines, I believe. The other, like an Aristarchus, marks them with an obelus.[30] I, like a critic of old, am to decide whether they are the poet's, or a forgery." In another letter to Atticus[31]: "As to what you write of Nicias, if I were in a position to enjoy his learned society, I should particularly like to have him with me; but my province is solitude and retirement. Besides you know our friend Nicias' weakness, self-indulgence, and mode of life. Why then should I wish to bore him, when he can give me no pleasure? Nevertheless I appreciate his desire." Santra likewise commends his books "On Lucilius."

XV. Lenaeus, freedman of Pompey the Great and his companion in almost all his campaigns, on the death of his patron and his sons supported himself by a school, teaching in the Carinae,[32] near the temple of Tellus, the quarter of the city in which the house of the Pompeys was formerly situated. He was so devoted to his patron's memory, that because the historian Sallust wrote that

Pompey had "an honest face but a shameless character," he tore Sallust to pieces in a biting satire, calling him "a debauchee, a gourmandizer, a spendthrift, and a tippler, a man whose life and writings were monstrous, and who was besides an ignorant pilferer of the language of the ancients and of Cato in particular." It is further said that when Lenaeus was still a boy he was stolen from Athens, made his escape and returned to his native land, and after acquiring a liberal education, offered the price of his liberty to his former master, but received his freedom as a gift because of his ability and learning.

XVI. Quintus Caecilius Epirota, born at Tusculum, was a freedman of Atticus, a Roman knight, the correspondent of Cicero. While he was teaching his patron's daughter, who was the wife of Marcus Agrippa, he was suspected of improper conduct towards her and dismissed; whereupon he attached himself to Cornelius Gallus and lived with him on most intimate terms, a fact which Augustus made one of his heaviest charges against Gallus him-
25 B.C. self.[33] After the conviction and death of Gallus he opened a school, but took few pupils and only grown up young men, admitting none under age, except those to whose fathers he was unable to refuse that favour. He is said to have been the first to hold extempore discussions in Latin, and the first to begin the practice of reading Vergil and other recent poets, a fact also alluded to by Domitius Marsus in the verse:

"Epirota, fond nurse of fledgling bards."

XVII. Marcus Verrius Flaccus, a freedman, gained special fame by his method of teaching. For to stimulate the efforts of his pupils, he used to pit those of the same advancement against one another, not only setting the subject on which they were to write, but also offering a prize for the victor to carry off. This was some old book, either beautiful or rare. He was therefore chosen by Augustus as the tutor of his grandsons and he moved to the Palace with his whole school, but with the understanding that he should admit no more pupils. He gave instruction in the hall of the house of Catulus,[34] which at that time formed part of the Palace, and was paid a hundred thousand sesterces a year. He died at an advanced age under Tiberius. His statue stands at Praeneste in the upper part of the forum near the hemicycle,[35] on which he exhibited the calendar[36] which he had arranged and inscribed upon its marble walls.

XVIII. Lucius Crassicius, a Tarentine by birth and a freedman by position, had the surname Pasicles, which he afterwards changed to Pansa. He was at first connected with the stage, as an assistant to the writers of farces; then he gave instruction in a school,[37] until he became so famous through the publication of his commentary on the "Zmyrna," that the following verses were written about him:

"Zmyrna will trust her fate but to Crassicius;
Cease then to woo her, ye unlettered throng.
She has declared none other will she wed,
Since he alone her hidden charms doth know."

But when he had already attracted many pupils of high rank, including Iullus Antonius, the triumvir's son, so that he was a rival even of Verrius Flaccus, he suddenly disbanded his school and became a disciple of the philosopher Quintus Sextius.

XIX. Scribonius Aphrodisius, slave and pupil of Orbilius, afterwards bought and set free by Scribonia, daughter of Libo, who had formerly been the wife of Augustus,[38] taught at the same time as Verrius. He wrote a critique of Verrius's "Orthography," at the same time attacking the author's scholarship and character.

XX. Gaius Julius Hyginus, a freedman of Augustus and a Spaniard by birth (some think that he was a native of Alexandria and was brought to Rome when a boy by Caesar after his capture of the city), was a zealous pupil and imitator of the Greek grammarian Cornelius Alexander, whom many called "Polyhistor" because of his knowledge of the past, and some "History." Hyginus was in charge of the Palatine Library,[39] but nevertheless took many pupils. He was an intimate friend of the poet Ovid and of Clodius Licinus the ex-consul and historian, who tells us that Hyginus died very poor after being supported as long as he lived by the writer's generosity. He had a freedman Julius Modestus, who followed in his patron's footsteps as student and scholar.

XXI. Gaius Melissus, a native of Spoletium, was freeborn, but was disowned[40] owing to a disagreement between his parents. Nevertheless through the care and devotion of the man who reared him, he received a superior education, and was presented to Maecenas as a grammarian. Finding that Maecenas appreciated him and treated him as a friend, although his mother claimed his freedom, he yet remained in a condition of slavery, since he preferred his present lot to that of his actual origin. In consequence he was soon set free, and even won the favour of Augustus. At the emperor's appointment he undertook the task of arranging the library in the Colonnade of Octavia.[41] In his sixtieth year, as he himself writes, he began to compile his volumes of "Trifles," now entitled "Jests," of which he completed a hundred and fifty; and he later added other volumes of a different character. He likewise originated a new kind of *togatae*,[42] to which he gave the name of *trabeatae*.[43]

XXII. Marcus Pomponius Marcellus, a most pedantic critic of the Latin language, in one of his cases (for he sometimes acted as an advocate) was so persistent in criticizing an error in diction made by his opponent, that Cassius Severus appealed to the judges and asked for a postponement, to enable his client to employ a grammarian in his stead: "For," said he, "he thinks that the contest with his opponent will not be on points of law, but of diction." When this same Marcellus had criticized a word in one of Tiberius's speeches, and Ateius Capito declared that it was good Latin, or if not, that it would surely be so from that time on, Marcellus answered: "Capito lies; for you, Caesar, can confer citizenship upon men, but not upon a word." That he had formerly been a boxer is shown by this epigram which Asinius Pollio made upon him:

"He who learned 'Head to the left'[44] explains to us difficult
language;
Talent[45] indeed he has none, merely a pugilist's skill.

XXIII. Quintus Remmius Palaemon, of Vicetia, was the home-born slave of a woman. He first, they say, learned the weaver's trade, and then got an education by accompanying his master's son to school.[46] He was afterwards set free, and became a teacher at Rome, where he held a leading rank among the grammarians, in spite of the fact that he was notorious for every kind of vice, and that Tiberius and later Claudius openly declared that there was no one less fitted to be trusted with the education of boys or young men. But he caught men's fancy by his remarkable memory, as well as by his readiness of speech; for he even extemporized poems. He wrote too in various uncommon metres. He was so presumptuous that he called Marcus Varro "a hog"; declared that letters were born with him and would die with him; and that it was no accident that his name appeared in the "Bucolics,"[47] but because Vergil divined that one day a Palaemon would be judge of all poets and poems. He boasted too that brigands once spared him because of the celebrity of his name. He was so given to luxurious living that he went to the bath several times a day, and could not live within his income, although he received four hundred thousand sesterces a year from his school and almost as much from his private property. To the latter he gave great attention, keeping shops for the sale of ready made clothing and cultivating his fields with such care that it is common talk that a vine which he grafted himself yielded three hundred and sixty bunches of grapes. But he was especially notorious for acts of licentiousness with women, which he carried to the pitch of shameful indecency; and they say that he was held up to scorn by the witty remark of a man who met him in a crowd and being unable to escape his kiss, although he tried to avoid it, cried: "Master, do you wish to mouth everyone whom you see in a hurry?"

XXIV. Marcus Valerius Probus of Berytus for a long time sought an appointment as centurion, finally grew tired of waiting, and devoted himself to study. He had read some early writers with an elementary teacher in one of the provinces; for the memory of those writers still lingers there and is not wholly lost, as it is in Rome. When he took these up again with greater care, and sought to extend his acquaintance to others of the same period, although he perceived that they were all held in contempt and brought rather reproach to those who read them than honour and profit, he nevertheless persisted in his purpose. After getting together a large number of copies, he gave his attention to correcting and punctuating them, and furnishing them with critical notes, devoting himself to this branch of grammar to the exclusion of all others. He had a few followers, rather than pupils; for he never taught in such a way as to assume the rôle of a master. He used to receive one or two, or at most three or four, in the afternoon hours, when he would lie upon a couch and in the course of long and general conversations[48] would read some few things, though very rarely. He published a few slight works on divers minute points, and also left a good sized "Grove[49] of Observations on our Early Language."

ON RHETORICIANS[1]

I. THE study of rhetoric was introduced into our country in about the same way as that of grammar, but with somewhat greater difficulty, since, as is well known, its practice was at times actually prohibited. To remove any doubt on this point, I shall append an ancient decree of the senate, as well as an edict of the censors:

"In the consulship of Gaius Fannius Strabo and Marcus 161 B.C.
Valerius Messala the praetor Marcus Pomponius laid a proposition before the senate. As the result of a discussion about philosophers and rhetoricians, the senate decreed that Marcus Pomponius, the praetor, should take heed and provide, in whatever way seemed in accord with the interests of the State and his oath of office, that they be not allowed to live in Rome." Some time afterward the censors Gnaeus Domitius
Ahenobarbus and Lucius Licinius Crassus issued the following 92 B.C.
edict about the same class of men: "It has been reported to us that there be men who have introduced a new kind of training, and that our young men frequent their schools; that these men have assumed the title of Latin rhetoricians, and that young men spend whole days with them in idleness. Our forefathers determined what they wished their children to learn and what schools they desired them to attend. These innovations in the customs and principles of our forefathers do not please us nor seem proper. Therefore it appears necessary to

make our opinion known, both to those who have such schools and to those who are in the habit of attending them, that they are displeasing to us."

By degrees rhetoric itself came to seem useful and honourable, and many devoted themselves to it as a defence and for glory. Cicero continued to declaim in Greek as well as Latin up to the time of his praetorsip, and in Latin even when he was getting on in years; and that too in company with the future consuls Hirtius and Pansa, whom he calls "his pupils and his big boys."[2] Some historians assert that Gnaeus Pompeius resumed the practice of declaiming just before the civil war, that he might be the better able to argue against Gaius Curio, a young man of very ready tongue, who was espousing Caesar's cause; and that Marcus Antonius, and Augustus as well, did not give it up even during the war at Mutina.[3] The emperor Nero declaimed in the first year of his reign, and had also done so in public twice before. Furthermore, many even of the orators published declamations. In this way general enthusiasm was aroused, and a great number of masters and teachers flocked to Rome, where they were so well received that some advanced from the lowest estate to senatorial dignity and to the highest magistracies.

But they did not all follow the same method of teaching, and the individual teachers also varied in their practice, since each one trained his pupils in various ways. For they would explain fine speeches with regard to their figures, incidents and illustrations,[4] now in one way and now in another, and compose narratives sometimes in a condensed and brief form, again with greater detail and flow of words. Sometimes they would translate Greek works, and praise or censure distinguished men. They would show that some practices in everyday life were expedient and essential, others harmful and superfluous. Frequently they defended or assailed the credibility of myths, an exercise which the Greeks call "destructive" and "constructive" criticism. But finally all these exercises[5] went out of vogue and were succeeded by the debate.

The earlier debates were based either upon historical narrative, as indeed is sometimes the case at present, or upon some event of recent occurrence in real life. Accordingly they were usually presented with even the names of the localities included. At any rate that is the case with the published collections, from which it may be enlightening to give one or two specimens word for word.

"Some young men from the city went to Ostia in the summer season, and arriving at the shore, found some fishermen drawing in their nets. They made a bargain to give a certain sum for the haul. The money was paid and they waited for some time until the nets were drawn ashore. When they were at last hauled out, no fish was found in them, but a closed basket of gold. Then the purchasers said that the catch belonged to them, the fishermen that it was theirs."

"When some dealers were landing a cargo of slaves from a ship at Brundisium, they dressed a handsome and high-priced young slave in the amulet and fringed toga[6] for fear of the collectors of customs, and their fraud easily escaped detention. When they reached Rome, the case was taken to court and a claim was made for the slave's liberty, on the ground that his master had voluntarily freed him."

Such discussions they formerly called by their Greek name of "syntheses,"[7] but afterwards "debates"; but they might be either fictitious or legal.

The eminent teachers of the subject, of whom any account is to be found, are limited pretty closely to those whom I shall mention.

II. Of Lucius Plotius Gallus, Cicero gives the following account in a letter to Marcus Titinnius[8]: "I well remember that when we were boys, a certain Plotius first began to teach in Latin. When crowds flocked to him, for all the most diligent students of the subject were trained under him, I regretted not having the same privilege. But I was deterred by the advice of certain men of wide experience, who believed that one's mind could better be trained by exercises in Greek." Marcus Caelius, in a speech in which he defended himself against a charge of violence, implies that this same Plotius, for he lived to a great age, supplied Caelius's accuser,

Atratinus, with his plea[9]; and without mentioning him by name, Caelius calls him a "barley-bread rhetorician," mocking at him as "puffy, light, and coarse."

III. Lucius Voltacilius Plotus is said to have been a slave and even to have served as a doorkeeper in chains, according to the ancient custom, until he was set free because of his talent and interest in letters, and helped his patron prepare his accusations. Then becoming a teacher of rhetoric, he had Gnaeus Pompeius the Great for a pupil, and wrote a history of the exploits of Pompey's father, as well as those of the son, in several volumes. In the opinion of Cornelius Nepos, he was the first of all freedmen to take up the writing of history, which up to that time had been confined to men of the highest position.

IV. Marcus Epidius, notorious as a blackmailer, opened a school of oratory and numbered among his pupils Mark Antony and Augustus; and when they once jeered at Gaius Cannutius because he preferred to side with the political party of Isauricus, the ex-consul, Cannutius rejoined: "I would rather be a disciple of Isauricus than of a false accuser like Epidius." This Epidius claimed descent from Epidius of Nuceria, who, it is said, once threw himself into the source of the river Sarnus and came out shortly afterwards with bull's horns on his head; then he at once disappeared and was reckoned among the number of the gods.

V. Sextus Clodius of Sicily, a teacher of both Greek and Latin oratory and man with poor sight and a sharp tongue, used to say that he had worn out a pair of eyes[10] during his friendship with Mark Antony, the triumvir. He also said of the latter's wife, Fulvia, one of whose cheeks was somewhat swollen: "She tempts the point of my pen"[11]; and by this witticism he rather gained than lost favour with Antony. When Antony presently became consul, Clodius received from him an enormous gift,[12]" as Cicero charges against Antony in his "Philippics"[13]: "For the sake of his jokes you employ a schoolmaster, elected a rhetorician by your vote and those of your pot-companions, and you have allowed him to say anything he likes about you; a witty fellow, no doubt, but it is not a hard matter to say clever things of you and your mates. But what pay does this rhetorician receive? Listen, senators, listen, and know the wounds which our country suffers. You made over to this rhetorician, Sextus Clodius, two thousand acres[14] of the Leontine territory, and free of taxes too, that at so great a price you might learn to know nothing."

VI. Gaius Albucius Silus of Novara, while he was holding the office of aedile in his native town and chanced to be sitting in judgment, was dragged by the feet from the tribunal by those against whom he was rendering a decision. Indignant at this, he at once made for the gate and went off to Rome. There he was admitted to the house of the orator Plancus, who had the habit, when he was going to declaim, of calling upon someone to speak before him. Albucius undertook that rôle, and filled it so effectively, that he reduced Plancus to silence, since he did not venture to enter into competition. But when Albucius had thus become famous, he opened a lecture room of his own, where it was his habit after proposing a subject for a debate, to begin to speak from his seat, and then as he warmed up, to rise and make his peroration on his feet. He declaimed, too, in various manners, now in a brilliant and ornate style, and at another time, not to be thought invariably academic, speaking briefly, in everyday language and all but that of the streets. He also pleaded causes, but rather seldom, taking part only in those of greatest importance, and even then confining himself to summing them up. Later he withdrew from the Forum, partly through shame and partly through fear. For in a case before the Hundred[15] he had offered his opponent, whom he was inveighing against as undutiful towards his parents, the privilege of taking oath but merely as a figure of speech, using the following language: "Swear by the ashes of your father and mother, who lie unburied"; and made other remarks in the same vein. His opponent accepted the challenge; and since the judges made no objection, Albucius lost his case to his great humiliation.[16] Again, when he was defending a client in a murder trial at Mediolanum before the proconsul Lucius Piso, and the lictors tried to suppress the immoderate applause,[17] he grew so angry, that lamenting the condition of Italy and saying that "it was being reduced once more to the form of a province," he called besides upon Marcus Brutus, whose statue was in sight, as "the founder and defender of our laws and liberties"; and for that he narrowly escaped punishment. When already well on in years, he returned to Novara because he was suffering from a tumour, called the people together and explained in a long set speech the reasons which led him to take his life, and then starved himself to death.

DE POETIS

THE following Index has been compiled from Hieronymus: L. Livius Andronicus, Cn. Naevius, T. Maccius Plautus, Q. Ennius, Statius Caecilius, P. Terentius Afer, M. Pacuvius, L. Accius, Sex. Turpilius, C. Licilius, P. Quintius Atta, L. Afranius, L. Pomponius, T. Lucretius Carus, M. Furius Bibaculus, C. Valerius Catullus, P. Terentius Varro, D. Laberius, P. Publilius Lochius, Cornificius, M. Bavius, C. Cornelius Gallus, Aemilius Macer, Quintilius Varus, P. Vergilius Maro, Albius Tibullus, Sex. Propertius, Q. Horatius Flaccus, L. Varius Rufus, P. Ovidius Naso, Philistio, A. Persius Flaccus, M. Annaeus Lucanus.

The following Sigla are used:—

For Terence: A = cod. Parisinus, 7920, eleventh century; B = cod. Parisinus, 7921; C = cod. Leidensis Vossianus, 186; D = cod. Dresdensis Elect. 539^b, Reg. D. 101; E = cod. Urbinas, 354; F = cod. Reginensis, 1496; G, = cod. Neapolitanus Mus. Borbon. 411 (all of the fifteenth century); Z = editio princeps of Donatus, Rome, 1472; Ald. = Aldine ed. of 1517; St. = ed. of Stephanus, Paris, 1529; Dz. = Dziatzko; Reiff. = Reifferscheid.

For Vergil: B = cod. Bernensis, 172, ninth or tenth century; G = cod. Sangallensis, 862, tenth century; P = cod. Parisinus Lat. 11308 (formerly Suppl. Lat. 1011), ninth century; ζ = Edition of Vergil by Heyne-Wagener, i. pp. lxxxi. ff.

For Horace: V = cod. Blandinianus Vetustissimus; ϕ = cod. Parisinus, 7974, tenth century; ψ = cod. Parisinus, 7971, tenth century; F = ϕ and ψ ; λ = Parisinus, 7972, tenth century; ρ = Parisinus Lat. 8214, twelfth century; ζ = mss. which contain the Life in a abridged form; see note 6, p. 484.

For Tibulus: A = cod. Ambrosianus, R 26 sup., fourteenth century; V = cod. Vaticanus, 3270; g = cod. Guelferbytanus, Ms. Aug. 82, 6 fol., both of the fifteenth century; ψ = other mss. or the Itali.

For Aulus Persius Flaccus: A = cod. Montepessulanus, 212, tenth century; B = cod. Vaticanus, tab. basil. Vat., H. 36, ninth century; P = cod. Montepessulanus, 125, formerly Pithoeanus.

For Lucan: M = cod. Montepessulanus, H. 113; B = cod. Bernensis, 45; P = cod. Parisinus, 7502, formerly Colbertinus, all of the tenth century.

ON POETS

THE LIFE OF TERENCE

I. Publius Terentius Afer, born at Carthage, was the slave at Rome of Terentius Lucanus, a senator, who because of the young man's talent and good looks not only gave him a liberal education, but soon set him free. Some think that he was taken in war, but Fenestella shows that that could not possibly be, since Terence was born and died between the end of the second Punic war and the beginning of the third; and even if he had been taken by the 201–149 B.C. Numidians and Gaetulians, he could not have come into the hands of a Roman general, since commerce between the Italic and the African races did not begin until after the destruction of Carthage. He lived on intimate terms with many men of high 146 B.C. rank, in particular with Scipio Africanus and Gaius Laelius. It is even thought that he won the favour of these two men by his youthful beauty, but Fenestella denies this too, maintaining that he was older than either of them. Nepos, however, writes that they were all three of an age, and Porcius rouses a suspicion of too great intimacy in the following words:

"Though he courted the wantonness of great men and their counterfeit[1] praise, though with greedy ears he drank in the divine voice of Africanus, though he thought it fine to frequent the tables of Philus and Laelius, though he was often taken to the Alban villa because of his youthful charms, he later found himself stripped of his all and reduced to utmost want. So he withdrew from the sight of men to a remote part of Greece and died at Stymphalus, a town of Arcady. Naught availed him Publius Scipio, naught Laelius, naught Furius, the three wealthiest[2] nobles of that time. Their help did not give him even a rented house, to provide at least a place where his slave might announce his master's death."

II. He wrote six comedies, and when he offered the first of these, the "Andria," to the aediles, they bade him first read it to Caecilius. Having come to the poet's house when he was dining, and being meanly clad, Terence is said to have read the beginning of his play sitting on a bench near the great man's couch. But after a few lines he was invited to take his place at table, and after dining with Caecilius, he ran through the rest to his host's great admiration. Moreover, this play and the five others were equally pleasing to the people, although Vulcatius in enumerating them all, writes thus:

"The sixth play, the 'Hecyra,' will not be included."[3]

The "Eunuch" was even acted twice in the same day and earned more money than any previous comedy of any writer, namely eight thousand sesterces; and for this reason the sum is included in the title-page.[4] Indeed Varro rates the beginning of the "Adelphoe" above that of Menander.[5]

III. It is common gossip that Scipio and Laelius aided Terence in his writings, and he himself lent colour to this by never attempting to refute it, except in a half-hearted way, as in the prologue to the "Adelphoe":

"For as to what those malicious critics say, that men of rank aid your poet and constantly write in concert with him; what they regard as a grievous slander, he considers the highest praise, to please those who please you all and all the people, whose timely help everyone has used without shame in war, in leisure, in business."

Now he seems to have made but a lame defence, because he knew that the report did not displease Laelius and Scipio; and it gained ground in spite of all and came down even to later times. Gaius Memmius in a speech in his own defence says: "Publius Africanus, who borrowed a mask from Terence, and put upon the stage under his name what he had written himself for his own amusement at home." Nepos says that he learned from a trustworthy source that once at his villa at Puteoli Gaius Laelius was urged by his wife to come to dinner at an earlier hour than common on the Kalends of March,[6] but begged her not to interrupt him. When he at last entered the dining-room at a late hour, he said that he had seldom written more to his own satisfaction; and on being asked to read what he had written, he declaimed the lines of the "Heautontimorumenos," beginning:

> "Impudently enough, by Heaven, has Syrus lured me here by promises."

IV. Santra thinks that if Terence had really needed help in his writing, he would not have been so likely to resort to Scipio and Laelius, who were then mere youths, as to Gaius Sulpicius Gallus, a scholarly man, at whose consular games he brought out his first play, or to Quintus Fabius Labeo and Marcus Popillius, both of whom were ex-consuls and poets; and that it was for that reason that he spoke, not of "young men" who were said to help him, but "men whose mettle the people had tried in war, in leisure, in business."

After publishing these comedies before he had passed his twenty-fifth year, either to escape from the gossip about publishing the work of others as his own, or else to become versed in Greek manners and customs, which he felt that he had not been wholly successful in depicting in his plays, he left Rome and never returned. Of his death Vulcatius writes in these words:

"But when Afer had presented six comedies to the people, he journeyed from here to Asia, but from the time he embarked was never seen again; thus he vanished from life."

V. Quintus Cosconius writes that he was lost at sea as he was returning from Greece with one hundred and eight plays adapted from Menander; the rest of our authorities declare that he died at Stymphalus in Arcadia, or at Leucadia, in the consulship of
159 B.C. Gnaeus Cornelius Dolabella and Marcus Fulvius Nobilior, having fallen ill from grief and annoyance at the loss of his baggage, which he had sent on to the ship, and with it of the new plays which he had written.

He is said to have been of moderate height, slender and of dark complexion. He left a daughter, who afterwards became the wife of a Roman knight; also gardens twenty acres[7] in extent on the Appian Way, near the villa of Mars. This makes me feel the more surprised that Porcius should write:

"Naught availed him Scipio, naught Laelius, naught Furius, the three wealthiest nobles of that time. Their aid did not even give him a rented house, to provide at least a place where his slave might announce his master's death."

Afranius ranks Terence above all other writers of comedy, writing in his "Compitalia":

"Declaring that no one is the equal of Terence."
But Vulcatius[8] puts him not only below Naevius, Plautus, and Caecilius, but even below Licinius and Atilius. Cicero in his "Limo"[9] gives him this much praise:

"Thou, Terence, who alone dost reclothe Menander in choice speech, and rendering him into the Latin tongue, dost present him with thy quiet utterance[10] on our public stage, speaking with a certain graciousness and with sweetness in every word."

Also Gaius Caesar:[11]

"Thou too, even thou, art ranked among the highest, thou half-Menander, and justly, thou lover of language undefiled. But would that thy graceful verses had force as well, so that thy comic power might have equal honour with that of the Greeks, and thou mightest not be scorned in this regard and neglected. It hurts and pains me, my Terence, that thou lackest this one quality."

THE LIFE OF VERGIL

Publius Vergilius Maro, a native of Mantua, had parents of humble origin, especially his father, who according to some was a potter, although the general opinion is that he was at first the hired man of a certain Magus, an attendant on the magistrates, later became his son-in-law because of his diligence, and greatly increased his little property by buying up woodlands and raising bees. He was born in the first consulship of Gnaeus Pompeius the Great and Marcus Licinius Crassus, on the Ides of October, in a Oct. 15,
district called Andes, not far distant from Mantua. While he was 70 B.C.
in his mother's womb, she dreamt that she gave birth to a laurel-branch, which on touching the earth took root and grew at once to the size of a full-grown tree, covered with fruits and flowers of various kinds; and on the following day, when she was on the way to a neighbouring part of the country with her husband, she turned aside and gave birth to her child in a ditch beside the road. They say that the infant did not cry at its birth, and had such a gentle expression as even then to give assurance of an unusually happy destiny. There was added another omen; for a poplar branch, which, as was usual in that region on such occasions, was at once planted where the birth occurred, grew so fast in a short time that it equalled in size poplars planted long before. It was called from him "Vergil's tree" and was besides worshipped with great veneration by pregnant and newly delivered women, who made and paid vows beneath it.

Vergil spent his early life at Cremona until he assumed the gown of manhood, upon his fifteenth birthday, in the consulship 55 B.C.
of the same two men who had been consuls the year he was born; and it chanced that the poet Lucretius died that very same day. Vergil, however, moved from Cremona to Mediolanum, and

shortly afterwards from there to Rome. He was tall and of full habit, with a dark complexion and a rustic appearance. His health was variable; for he very often suffered from stomach and throat troubles, as well as with headache; and he also had frequent haemorrhages. He ate and drank but little. He was especially given to passions for boys, and his special favourites were Cebes and Alexander, whom he calls Alexis in the second poem of his "Bucolics." This boy was given him by Asinius Pollio, and both his favourites had some education, while Cebes was even a poet. It is common report that he also had an intrigue with Plotia Hieria. But Asconius Pedianus declares that she herself used to say afterwards, when she was getting old, that Vergil was invited by Varius to associate with her, but obstinately refused. Certain it is that for the rest of his life he was so modest in speech and thought, that at Naples he was commonly called "Parthenias,"[1] and that whenever he appeared in public in Rome, where he very rarely went, he would take refuge in the nearest house, to avoid those who followed and pointed him out. Moreover, when Augustus offered him the property of a man who had been exiled, he could not make up his mind to accept it. He possessed nearly ten million sesterces from the generous gifts of friends, and he had a house at Rome on the Esquiline, near the gardens of Maecenas, although he usually lived in retirement in Campania and in Sicily.

He was already grown up when he lost his parents, of whom his father previously went blind, and two own brothers: Silo, who died in childhood, and Flaccus, who lived to grow up, and whose death he laments under the name of Daphnis.[2]

Among other studies he gave attention also to medicine and in particular to mathematics. He pleaded one single case in court too, but no more; for, as Melissus has told us, he spoke very slowly and almost like an uneducated man.

He made his first attempt at poetry when he was still a boy, composing the following couplet on a schoolmaster called Ballista, who was stoned to death because of his evil reputation for brigandage:

"Under this mountain of stones Ballista is covered and buried;
Wayfarer, now night and day follow your course without fear."

Then he wrote the "Catalepton," "Priapea," "Epigrams" and the "Dirae," as well as the "Ciris" and the "Culex" when he was sixteen years old. The story of the "Culex" is this. When a shepherd, exhausted by the heat, had fallen asleep under a tree, and a snake was creeping upon him, a gnat flew from a marsh and stung the shepherd between his two temples; he at once crushed the gnat and killed the snake; then he made a tomb for the insect, inscribed with this couplet:

"Thee, tiny gnat, well deserving, the flock's grateful keeper now offers
For the gift of his life due funeral rites in requital."[3]

He also wrote the "Aetna," though its authorship is disputed. Presently he began to write of Roman story, but thinking himself unequal to the subject, turned to the "Bucolics," especially in order to sing the praises of Asinius Pollio, Alfenus Varus, and Cornelius Gallus, because at the time of the assignment of the lands beyond the Po, which were divided among the veterans by order of the triumvirs after the victory at Philippi, these men had saved him from ruin. Then he wrote the "Georgics" in honour of Maecenas, because he had rendered him aid, when the poet was 42 B.C.
still but little known, against the violence of one of the veterans, from whom Vergil narrowly escaped death in a quarrel about his farm. Last of all he began the "Aeneid," a varied and complicated theme, and as it were a mirror of both the poems of Homer; moreover it treated Greek and Latin personages and affairs in common, and contained at the same time an account of the origin of the city of Rome and of Augustus, which was the poet's special aim. When he was writing the "Georgics," it is said to have been his custom to dictate each day a large number of verses which he had composed in the morning, and then to spend the rest of the day in

reducing them to a very small number, wittily remarking that he fashioned his poem after the manner of a she-bear, and gradually licked it into shape. In the case of the "Aeneid," after writing a first draft in prose and dividing it into twelve books, he proceeded to turn into verse one part after another, taking them up just as he fancied, in no particular order. And that he might not check the flow of his thought, he left some things unfinished, and, so to speak, bolstered others up with very slight words, which, as he jocosely used to say, were put in like props, to support the structure until the solid columns should arrive.

The "Bucolics" he finished in three years, the "Georgics" in seven, the "Aeneid" in twelve. The success of the "Bucolics" on their first appearance was such, that they were even frequently rendered by singers on the stage. When Augustus was returning after his victory at Actium and lingered at Atella to treat his throat, Vergil read the "Georgics" to him for four days in succession, Maecenas taking his turn at the reading whenever the poet was interrupted by the failure of his voice. His own delivery, however, was sweet and wonderfully effective. In fact, Seneca has said that the poet Julius Montanus used to declare that he would have purloined some of Vergil's work, if he could also have stolen his voice, expression, and dramatic power; for the same verses sounded well when Vergil read them, which on another's lips were flat and toneless. Hardly was the "Aeneid" begun, when its repute became so great that Sextus Propertius[4] did not hesitate to declare:

> "Yield, ye Roman writers; yield, ye Greeks; A greater than the Iliad is born."

Augustus indeed (for it chanced that he was away on his Cantabrian campaign) demanded in entreating and even jocosely threatening letters that Vergil send him "something from the 'Aeneid'"; to use his own words, "either the first draft of the poem or any section of it that he pleased." But it was not until long afterwards, when the material was at last in shape, that Vergil read to him three books in all, the second, fourth, and sixth. The last of these produced a remarkable effect on Octavia, who was present at the reading; for it is said that when he reached the verses about her son, "Thou shalt be Marcellus,"[5] she fainted and was with difficulty revived. He gave readings also to various others, but never before a large company, selecting for the most part passages about which he was in doubt, in order to get the benefit of criticism. They say that Eros, his amanuensis and freedman, used to report, when he was an old man, that Vergil once completed two half-verses off-hand in the course of a reading. For having before him merely the words "Misenum Aeoliden," he added "quo non praestantior alter,"[6] and again to "aere ciere viros" he joined "Martemque accendere cantu,"[7] thrown off with like inspiration, and he immediately ordered Eros to add both half-lines to his manuscript.

In the fifty-second year of his age, wishing to give the final touch to the "Aeneid," he determined to go away to Greece and Asia, and after devoting three entire years to the sole work of improving his poem, to give up the rest of his life wholly to philosophy. But having begun his journey, and at Athens meeting Augustus, who was on his way back to Rome from the Orient, he resolved not to part from the emperor and even to return with him; but in the course of a visit to the neighbouring town of Megara in a very hot sun, he was taken with a fever, and added to his disorder by continuing his journey; hence on his arrival at Brundisium he was considerably worse, and died there on the eleventh day before the Kalends of October, in the consulship of Gnaeus Sentius and Quintus Lucretius. His ashes were taken to Naples and laid to rest on the via Puteolana less than two miles from the city, in a tomb for which he himself composed this couplet: Sept. 21, 19 B.C.

"Mantua gave me the light, Calabria slew me; now holds me
Parthenope. I have sung shepherds, the country, and wars."

He named as his heirs Valerius Proculus, his half-brother, to one-half of his estate, Augustus to one-fourth, Maecenas to one-twelfth; the rest he left to Lucius Varius and Plotius Tucca, who revised the "Aeneid" after his death by order of Augustus. With regard to this matter we have the following verses of Sulpicius of Carthage:

"Vergil had bidden these songs by swift flame be turned into ashes,
Songs which sang of thy fates, Phrygia's leader renowned.
Varius and Tucca forbade, and thou, too, greatest of Caesars,
Adding your veto to theirs, Latium's story preserved.
All but twice in the flames unhappy Pergamum perished
Troy on a second pyre narrowly failed of her doom."

He had arranged with Varius, before leaving Italy, that if anything befell him[8] his friend should burn the "Aeneid"; but Varius had emphatically declared that he would do no such thing. Therefore in his mortal illness Vergil constantly called for his book-boxes, intending to burn the poem himself; but when no one brought them to him, he made no specific request about the matter, but left his writings jointly to the above mentioned Varius and to Tucca, with the stipulation that they should publish nothing which he himself would not have given to the world. However, Varius published the "Aeneid" at Augustus' request, making only a few slight corrections, and even leaving the incomplete lines just as they were. These last many afterwards tried to finish, but failed owing to the difficulty that nearly all the half-lines in Vergil are complete in sense and meaning, the sole exception being "Quem tibi iam Troia."[9] The grammarian Nisus used to say that he had heard from older men that Varius changed the order of two of the books and made what was then the second book the third; also that he emended the beginning of the first book by striking out the lines:

"I who on slender reed once rustic numbers did render,
Parting then from the groves, commanded the neighbouring fallows
Tribute to pay to their lords, however much they exacted,

Task hailed with joy by the hind; but now dread deeds of the war-god,
Arms and the hero I sing."

Vergil never lacked detractors, which is not strange; for neither did Homer. When the "Bucolics" appeared, a certain Numitorius wrote "Anti-bucolics," consisting of but two poems, which were a very insipid parody. The first began as follows:

"Tityrus, if a warm toga you have, why then a beech mantle?"

The second:—

"Tell me, Damoetas, I pray, is 'cuium pecus' really good Latin?
Nay, but our Aegon's way, and thus men talk in the country."

Another man, when Vergil recited from his "Georgics," "nudus ara, sere nudus,"[10] added "habebis frigore febrem."[11] There is also a book in criticism of the "Aeneid" by Carvilius Pictor, called "Aeneomastix."[12] Marcus Vipsanius called Vergil a supposititious child of Maecenas, that inventor of a new kind of affected language,[13] neither bombastic nor of studied simplicity, but in ordinary words and hence less obvious. Herennius made selections confined to his defects, and Perellius Fausta to his pilferings. More than that, the eight volumes of Quintus Octavius Avitus, entitled "Resemblances," contain the verses which he borrowed, with their sources. Asconius Pedianus, in a book which he wrote "Against the Detractors of Vergil," sets forth a very few of the charges against him, and those for the most part dealing with history and with the accusation that he borrowed a great deal from Homer; but he says that Vergil used to meet this latter accusation with these word: "Why don't my critics also attempt the same thefts? If they do, they will realize that it is easier to filch his club from Hercules than a line from Homer." Yet Asconius says that Vergil had intended to go into retirement, in order to prune down everything to the satisfaction of carping critics.

LIFE OF HORACE

Quintus Horatius Flaccus of Venusia had for a father, as he himself writes, a freedman who was a collector of money at auctions; but it is believed that he was a dealer in salted provisions, for a certain man in a quarrel thus taunted Horace: "How often have I seen your father wiping his nose with his arm!" Horace served as tribune of the soldiers in the war of Philippi, at the instance of Marcus Brutus, one of the leaders in that war. When his party was vanquished, he was pardoned and purchased the position of a quaestor's clerk. Then contriving to win the favour, first of Maecenas and later of Augustus, he held a prominent place among the friends of both. How fond Maecenas was of him is evident enough from the well known epigram:

"If that I do not love you, my own Horace, more than life itself, behold your comrade leaner than Ninnius."[1]

But he expressed himself much more strongly in his last will and testament in this brief remark to Augustus: "Be as mindful of Horatius Flaccus as of myself." Augustus offered him the post of secretary, as appears in this letter of his to Maecenas: "Before this I was able to write my letters to my friends with my own hand; now overwhelmed with work and in poor health, I desire to take our friend Horace from you. He will come then from that parasitic table of yours to my imperial board, and help me write my letters."[2] Even when Horace declined, Augustus showed no resentment at all, and did not cease his efforts to gain his friendship. We have letters from which I append a few extracts by way of proof: "Enjoy any privilege at my house, as if you were making your home there; for it will be quite right and proper for you to do so, inasmuch as that was the relation which I wished to have with you, if your health had permitted." And again, "How mindful I am of you our friend Septimius can also tell you; for it chanced that I spoke of you in his presence. Even if you were so proud as to scorn my friendship, I do not therefore return your disdain." Besides this, among other pleasantries, he often calls him "a most immaculate libertine "[3] and "his charming little man," and he made him well to do by more than one act of generosity. As to his writings, Augustus rated them so high, and was so convinced that they would be immortal, that he not only appointed him to write the Secular Hymn, but also bade him celebrate the victory of his stepsons Tiberius and Drusus over the Vindelici, and so compelled him to add a fourth to his three books of lyrics after a long silence. Furthermore, after reading several of his "Talks,"[4] the Emperor thus expressed his pique that no mention was made of him: "You must know that I am not pleased with you, that in your numerous writings of this kind you do not talk with me, rather than with others. Are you afraid that your reputation with posterity will suffer because it appears that you were my friend?" In this way he forced from Horace the selection which begins with these words:

"Seeing that single-handed thou dost bear the burden of tasks so many and so great, protecting Italy's realm with arms, providing it with morals, reforming it by laws, I should sin against the public weal, Caesar, if I wasted thy time with long discourse."[5]

In person he was short and fat, as he is described with his own pen in his satires[6] and by Augustus in the following letter: "Onysius has brought me your little volume, and I accept it, small as it is, in good part, as an apology. But you seem to me to be afraid that your books may be bigger than you are yourself; but it is only stature that you lack, not girth. So you may write on a pint pot, that the circumference of your volume may be well rounded out, like that of your own belly."

It is said that he was immoderately lustful; for it is reported that in a room lined with mirrors he had harlots so arranged that whichever way he looked, he saw a reflection of venery. He lived for the most part in the country on his Sabine or Tiburtine estate, and his house is pointed out near the little grove of

Tiburnus. I possess some elegies attributed to his pen and a letter in prose, supposed to be a recommendation of himself to Maecenas, but I think that both are spurious; for the elegies are commonplace and the letter is besides obscure, which was by no means one of his faults.

He was born on the sixth day before the Ides of December in Dec. 8, 65 B.C. the consulate of Lucius Cotta and Lucius Torquatus, and died on the fifth day before the Kalends of the same month in the consulship of Gaius Marcius Censorinus and Gaius Asinius Gallus, fifty-Nov. 27, 8 B.C. nine days after the death of Maecenas, in his fifty-seventh year. He named Augustus as his heir by word of mouth, since he could not make and sign a will because of the sudden violence of his ailment. He was buried and laid to rest near the tomb of Maecenas on the farther part of the Esquiline Hill.

THE LIFE OF TIBULLUS

"Thee too, Tibullus, companion of Vergil, envious death sent in youth to the Elysian fields, that there might be no one to mourn tender loves in elegy, or sing the wars of kings in heroic verse."[1]

Albius Tibullus, a Roman knight, remarkable for his good looks and conspicuous for his personal elegance, was devoted above all others to Messala Corvinus. He was his tent companion[2] in the war in Aquitania[3] and was given military prizes.[4] In the judg-30-27 B.C. ment of many men he holds the first place among writers of elegy. His amatory letters, too, though short are very useful.[5] He died in youth, as is indicated by the epigram written above.

THE LIFE OF AULUS PERSIUS FLACCUS

Aulus Persius Flaccus was born the day before the Nones of Dec. 4, 34 A.D. December in the consulship of Fabius Persicus and Lucius Vitellius, and died on the eighth day before the Kalends of December, when Publius Marius and Afinius Gallus were consuls. He was born at Volaterrae in Etruria, was a Roman knight, but was connected by blood and by marriage with men of the senatorial order. He died on his estate near the eighth milestone of the Appian Way. Nov. 24, 62 A.D.

His father Flaccus died when his son was about six years old, leaving him to the care of a guardian. His mother, Fulvia Sisennia, afterwards married a Roman knight named Fusius, but buried him also within a few years.

Flaccus studied until the twelfth year of his age at Volaterrae, and then at Rome with the grammarian Remmius Palaemon[1] and the rhetorician Verginius Flavus. When he was sixteen years old he became so intimate a friend of Annaeus Cornutus that he never left his side; and from him he obtained some knowledge of philosophy.

From early youth he enjoyed the friendship of Caesius Bassus, the poet, and of Calpurnius Statura, who died in youth, while Persius still lived. Servilius Nonianus he revered as a father. Through Cornutus he came to know Annaeus Lucanus also, a pupil of Cornutus and of the same age as himself. Lucan so admired the writings of Flaccus, that when the author read them in the usual way,[2] he could hardly wait until he finished before saying that they were true poems, and his own mere child's play. Towards the end of his life he made the acquaintance also of Seneca, but was not impressed by his talents.

At the house of Cornutus he enjoyed the society of two learned and venerable men, who were then eagerly pursuing philosophical studies: Claudius Agathernus, a physician of Lacedaemon, and Petronius Aristocrates of Magnesia, whom he admired exceedingly and emulated, although they were of the same age as Cornutus, while he was a younger man. He was also for nearly ten years so great a favourite of Paetus Thrasea that he sometimes even travelled abroad with him; and Paetus's wife, Arria, was a relative of his.

He was very gentle in manner, of virginal modesty and very handsome; and he showed an exemplary devotion to his mother, sister, and aunt.

He was good and pure.

He left about two million sesterces to his mother and sister, and a letter addressed only to his mother. He requested her to give Cornutus a hundred thousand, as some say, or according to others, fifty thousand sesterces, and twenty pounds of silver plate, besides about seven hundred volumes of Chrysippus, or his entire library. But Cornutus, while accepting the books, turned over the money to the sisters[3] whom their brother had made his heirs.

He wrote rarely and slowly. This very volume[4] he left unfinished, and some verses were taken from the last book, that it might have the appearance of completion. Cornutus made some slight corrections, and on the request of Caesius Bassus that he might publish it, turned it over to him for that purpose.

In his boyhood Flaccus had written a *praetexta*,[5] one book describing his travels, and a few verses on the mother-in-law of Thrasea,[6] who had killed herself before her husband. All these Cornutus advised the poet's mother to destroy.

As soon as his book appeared, men began to admire it and to buy it up rapidly.

He died of a stomach trouble in the thirtieth year of his age. As soon as he left school and his teachers, he conceived a strong desire to write satires from reading the tenth book of Lucilius. The beginning of this he imitated with the intention at first of criticizing himself; but presently turning to general criticism,[7] he so assailed the poets and orators of his day, that he even attacked Nero, who was at that time emperor. His verse on Nero read as follows: "King Midas has ass's ears," but Cornutus by merely changing the name, and writing "Who has not an ass's ears?" so altered it that Nero might not think that it was said of him.

THE LIFE OF LUCAN

Marcus Annaeus Lucanus of Corduba made his first appearance as a poet with a "Eulogy of Nero" at the emperor's Quinquennial Contests,[1] and then gave a public reading of his poem on the "Civil War" waged between Pompey and Caesar. In a kind of introduction to the latter, comparing his time of life and his first essays with those of Vergil, he had the audacity to ask:

"How far, pray, do I fall short of the Culex[2]"?

In his early youth, learning that his father was living in the remote country districts because of an unhappy marriage . . . . He was recalled from Athens by Nero and made one of his intimate friends, besides being honoured with the quaestorship; but he could not keep the emperor's favour. For piqued because Nero had suddenly called a meeting of the senate and gone out when he was giving a reading, with no other motive than to throw cold water on the performance,[3] he afterwards did not refrain from words and acts of hostility to the prince, which are still notorious. Once for example in a public privy, when he relieved his bowels with an uncommonly loud noise, he shouted out this half line of the emperor's, while those who were there for the same purpose took to their heels:

"You might suppose it thundered 'neath the earth."

He also tongue-lashed not only the emperor but also his most powerful friends in a scurrilous poem. Finally he came out almost as the ringleader[4] in the conspiracy of Piso, publicly making great talk about the glory of tyrannicides, and full of threats, even going to the length of offering Caesar's head to all his friends. But when the conspiracy was detected, he showed by no means equal firmness of purpose; for he was easily forced to a confession, descended to the most abject entreaties, and even named his own mother among the guilty parties, although she was innocent, in hopes that this lack of filial devotion would win him favour with a parricidal prince. But when he was allowed free choice of the manner of his death, he wrote a letter to his father, containing corrections for some of his verses, and after eating heartily, offered his arms to a physician, to cut his veins. I recall that his poems were even read in public,[5] while they were published and offered for sale by editors lacking in taste, as well as by some who were painstaking and careful.

THE LIFE OF PLINY THE ELDER

Plinius Secundus of Novum Comum, after performing with energy the military service required of members of the equestrian order, administered several important stewardships in succession with the utmost justice. Yet he gave so much attention to liberal studies, that hardly anyone who had complete leisure wrote more than he. For instance, he gave an account in twenty volumes of all the wars which were ever carried on with Germany, besides completing the thirty-seven books of his "Natural History." He lost his
79 A.D. life in the disaster in Campania. He was commanding the fleet at Misenum, and setting out in a Liburnian galley[1] during the eruption of Vesuvius to investigate the causes of the phenomenon from nearer at hand, he was unable to return because of head winds. He was suffocated by the shower of dust and ashes, although some think that he was killed by a slave, whom he begged to hasten his end when he was overcome by the intense heat.

THE LIFE OF PASSIENUS CRISPUS

Passienus Crispus, a native of Visellium, began his first speech in the senate with these words: "Conscript fathers and you, Caesar," and was in consequence highly commended by Tiberius, though not sincerely. He voluntarily pleaded a number of cases in the court of the Hundred,[1] and therefore his statue was set up in the Basilica Julia.[2] He was twice consul. He married twice: first Domitia and then Agrippina, respectively the aunt and the mother of the emperor Nero. He possessed an estate of two hundred million sesterces. He tried to gain favour with all the emperors, but especially with Gaius Caesar, whom he attended on foot when the emperor made a journey. When he was asked by Nero[3] in a private conversation whether he had commerce with his own sister, as the emperor had with his, he replied "Not yet"; a very fitting and cautious answer, neither accusing the emperor by denying the allegation, nor dishonouring himself with a lie by admitting it. He was slain by the treachery of Agrippina, whom he had made his heir, and was honoured with a public funeral.

ENDNOTES

GENERAL CHARACTERISTICS

[1] *Die griechisch-römischen Biographie,* Leipzig, 1901.

[2] These were originally designed as introductions to works of literature, and their material was drawn in a great measure from those works themselves; but they were afterwards extended to men eminent in other fields. For fuller details on this and other points I may refer to my paper "Suetonius and his Biographies" in the *Proc. of the Amer. Philosophical Soc.*, lii. pp. 206 ff.

[3] *Calig.* xix. 3.

[4] *Nero,* lvii. 2; *Dom.* xii. 2.

[5] See Dennison, *Amer. Jour. of Arch.*, sec. series, ii. pp. 26 ff.

[6] See *Aug.* ix., lxi.; *Tib.* lxi. 2.; *Cal.* xxii. l.; *Nero,* xix. 3.

[7] See, however, *Tib.* xxi. 2; *Tit.* i.

[8] See H. T. Peck, *Julius and Augustus,* Introduction, pp. v ff.

MANUSCRIPTS

[1] Ω is used by Preud'homme to designate the manuscript mentioned on p. xiii.

[2] See especially C. L. Smith and A. A. Howard, *Harvard Studies in Class. Phil.*, xii. pp. 54 ff. and 261 ff.

[3] For different opinions as to the history of the manuscripts see Geer, *Class. Weekly,* xxiv. 4 ff. and Rand, *Harv. Stud. Class. Phil.* xxxvii. 1–48, especially 20–25 and 37–39.

BOOK I

[1] 85/84 B.C., according to the chronology of Suetonius, which makes the year of Caesar's birth 100 B.C. The arguments in favour of 102 are however very strong.

[2] By Marius and Cinna, consuls in 86; see Veil. 2. 43. 1.

[3] A chaplet of oak leaves, given for saving the life of a fellow-citizen, the Victoria Cross of antiquity.

[4] See chap. lxxiv. 1.

[5] The festival of Bona Dea, from which all men were excluded.

[6] The towns beyond the river Po, such as Verona, Comum, and Cremona, wished to obtain the rights of citizenship, which had been given to many of the Italian towns at the close of the Social War (89–88 B.C.).

[7] *Forum ornare* was the technical term for the display there by the aediles of the material to be used in their public shows.

[8] As *iudex quaestionis,* an office held by Caesar between the aedileship and the praetorship.

[9] As *iudex perduellionis,* or *duumvir perduellionis,* one of a commission of two men appointed to try cases of high treason. Of these one was selected by lot (*sorte ductus*) to conduct the trial, if a trial were necessary, and pass sentence. An appeal was allowed and the duumvir then brought the case before the *comitia centuriata* (in the regal period before the *comitia curiata*). See Livy 1. 26. 5 ff.; Cic. *Rab.* 4.

[10] As governor of Egypt; see chap. xi.

[11] Namely, Gnaeus Pompeius.

[12] When the consuls went to the Capitol to offer sacrifice at the commencement of their term of office (on January 1), their friends escorted them to the temple and back to their homes. Caesar took advantage of the absence of the aristocrats for his attack on Catulus.

[13] Novius seems to have been *quaesitor.* a special commissioner appointed to conduct the investigation (*quaestio*) of the Catilinarian conspiracy; perhaps we should read *quaesitorem.*

[14] That is, without waiting for the decrees of the senate which formally confirmed the appointments of the new governors, and provided them with funds and equipment.

[15] If *silvae callesque* should stand in the text, it is used in a different sense from *calles* in Tac. *Ann.* 4. 27. It seems to designate provinces where the duties of the governor would be confined to guarding the mountain-pastures and keeping the woods free from brigands. The senate would not run the risk of letting Caesar secure a province involving the command of an army. Cf. xxi. and see *Proc. Amer. Phil. Assoc.* xliv. xlvii.; *Amir. Jour. of Phil.* xxxvi. 323 ff.

[16] Business could be interrupted or postponed at Rome by the announcement of an augur or a magistrate that he had seen a flash of lightning or some other adverse sign; sometimes an opponent merely announced that he would "watch the skies" for such omens.

[17] Torrentius put *per iocum* after *signarent,* but such jesting would not be tolerated in actual legal documents.

[18] Through a special commission of twenty men.

[19] By making a speech of several hours' duration; Gell 4. 10. 8. The senate arose in a body and escorted Cato to prison, and Caesar was forced to release him.

[20] For his conduct during the war with Mithridates.

[21] That is, after the close of the business day, an indication of the haste with which the adoption was rushed through.

[22] Used in a double sense, the second unmentionable.

[23] A Celtic word meaning a crested lark (Plin. *N.H.* 11. 37) which was the device on the helmets of the legion.

[24] Roman measure; about 3106 English miles, taking the Roman foot (296 mm.) as 0·97 English.

[25] For this and similar sums see Index, s.v. *sestertius.*

[26] When ordinarily they would be put to death.

[27] That is, in correcting the bill after it had been passed and filed, as explained in the following sentence.

[28] When the senate passed a decree that Caesar should disband his army before a given date, the tribunes Mark Antony and Quintus Cassius exercised their privilege and vetoed it (Caesar, *B. C,* 1 .2. 6–7); not only did the senate disregard the veto, but the tribunes were obliged to seek safety in flight (*id.* 1 .5. 1–2).

[29] 3. 82; cf l. 26.

[30] *Phoenissae,* 524 f.

[31] Way.

[32] Knights (as well as senators) had the privilege of wearing a gold ring, and must possess an estate of 400,000 sesterces.

[33] *Per tumultum* is a strong expression for *contra legem* or *extra ordinem,* since the Lex Sempronia provided that the consuls be appointed to their provinces before election; cf xix. 2. See Greenidge, *ROM.* Pub. Life, 285 and 322.

[34] The *prandium* was the first substantial meal of the day, taken about noon; the translation “dinner” is used advisedly.

[35] In token of his restoration to the rank of knight, which he forfeited by appearing on the stage; see chap. xxxiii.

[36] The first fourteen rows above the orchestra, reserved for the knights by the law of L. Roscius Otho, tribune of the commons, 67 B.C.

[37] *Euripus,* the strait between Euboea and Boeotia, was used also as a common noun, meaning “a ditch” or “canal.”

[38] The year had previously consisted of 355 days, and the deficiency of about eleven days was made up by inserting an intercalary month of twenty-two or twenty-three days after February.

[39] Plebeians, who collected the *tributum* and paid the soldiers, apparently heads of the tribes; see Varro, *L.L.* v. 181; Momma. *Staatsr.* iii. 189 ff.

[40] The derivation of *parricida* is uncertain, but it cannot come from *pater* and *caedo.* In early times it meant wilful murder of a freeman; XII. Tab. ap. Fest. *s.v., si qui hominem liberum dolo sciens morti duit, paricidas esto;* later, it was associated by popular etymology with *pater* and *caedo,* and used also in the modern sense of the word.

[41] Epilepsy, called *morbus comitialis,* because an attack was regarded as sufficient cause for the postponement of elections, or other public business. Sometimes a seizure was feigned for political reasons.

[42] *Latus clavus,* the broad purple stripe, is also applied to a tunic with the broad stripe. All senators bad the right to wear this; the peculiarity in Caesar's case consisted in the long fringed sleeves.

[43] While a girdle was commonly worn with the ordinary tunic, it was not usual to wear one with the *latus clavus; Quint.* 2. 3. 138. The looseness of the girdle was an additional peculiarity.

[44] The word play on *tertia (pars)* and *Tertia,* daughter of Servilia, as well as on the two senses of *deducta,* is quite untranslatable. The first meaning is given in the translation, and the second is implied in the following sentence. *Cf.* Macrobius, *Saturnalia,* 2. 2. 5.

[45] M. Actorius Naso; see chap. ix. 3.

[46] The words *liberorum quaerendorum causa* are a legal formula indicating that the purpose of marriage is to beget legal heirs.

[47] Caesar was in reality *propraetor,* but *proconsul (pro consule)* is sometimes used of the governor of a province, regardless of his rank.

[48] Apparently about two-thirds the usual price: see Index, s.v. *sestertius* .

[49] Cic. *Brut.* 261. See *Trans. Amer. Phil. Assoc.* xlvi. 47.

[50] That is, a speech in which he competed with other advocates for the right to conduct a prosecution.

[51] Cic. *Brut.* 262.

[52] *De Bell. Gall.* viii, preface, 5–6.

[53] That is, Caesar reduced his reports to book form. If the book was a *roll,* the writing was arranged in columns, parallel with the edges (or long sides) of the roll. If it was a *codex,* several sheets were folded and fastened together and the writing was arranged on each page in one or two columns. His predecessors merely took a sheet, or sheets, and wrote from side to side and from top to bottom, without columns or margins.

[54] Through Gaius Volusenus (Caes. *B.G.* 4. 21. 1). Suetonius's words *per se* do not necessarily imply that Caesar went to Britain himself for this purpose.

[55] The significance of this name can only be conjectured. Salutio was an actor of mimes, mentioned by Pliny, *N.H.* 7. 54 and 35. 8.

[56] The standard of the legion was a silver eagle with outstretched wings, mounted on a pole which had a sharp point at the other end, so that it could be set firmly in the ground.

[57] *Rostratae naves,* ships of war provided with brazen beaks *(rostra)* or rams.

[58] Probably some woodcutter's hut; *deversorium* means ' inn, lodging.'

[59] Catull. 29 and 57.

[60] See chap. i. 2.

[61] At the theatre.

[62] For carrying his statue among those of the gods.

[63] Playing on the double meaning of *cor,* also regarded as the seat of intelligence.

[64] That is, "make me restore the republic."

[65] The white fillet was emblematic of royalty.

[66] With a pun on Rex as a Roman name; cf. Horace, *Serm.* 1. 7, etc.

[67] The college of fifteen priests (*quindecimviri sacris faciundis*) in charge of the Sybilline books.

[68] *Bonum factum* (*sit*) was a formula prefixed to edicts, here used in jest; cf. the similar formulas in proposals to the senate, *Aug.* lviii. 3, *Calig.* xv. 3.

[69] See note on xlv. 3.

[70] The *pons suffragiorum,* a temporary bridge of planks over which the voters passed one by one, to cast their ballots; Cic. *Ad Att.* i. 14; Ovid, *Fasti,* v. 634.

[71] Properly said of a temple; according to Florus, 4. 2. 91; one of the honours bestowed on Caesar was *fastigium in domo;* cf. Plutarch, *Caesar,* lxiii. 6, "a gable-ornament" (L.C.L.).

[72] Possibly "from behind," though it is hard to see how a wound *paulo infra iugulum* could have been dealt from that position. *Aversum* has better mss. authority than *adversum,* is *a priori* more probable, and is supported by Plutarch's version; but it may mean "turned away."

[73] A pointed instrument of bone or metal, for writing on waxen tablets.

[74] To inherit a share of his estate in the event of the death of the heirs in the first degree or their refusal to accept the inheritance; it was often a mere compliment.

[75] Cf. the apparition at the Rubicon; chap. xxxii.

[76] Caesar was beloved by the Jews, not only because he had overthrown Pompey, who had violated their Holy of Holies, but because of many acts of kindness besides.

[77] *Cyropedeia,* 8. 7.

[78] About an hour before sunset.

BOOK II

TIBERIUS

[1] Plebeian families in the senate enrolled in addition to the patricians. On ch. ii. see Geer, *A.J.P.* lv, 337 ff.

[2] In his Memoirs; see chap. lxxxv. 1.

[3] *Ad Quint. Frat.* 1. 1. 21.

[4] Q. Cicero was really *propraetor;* see note on *Jul.* liv. 1.

[5] *Imagines* were waxen masks of ancestors of noble (*i.e.,* senatorial) rank, kept in the hall (*atrium*) of their descendants.

[6] See *Jul.* xx. 3, note.

[7] According to the *Thes. Ling. Lat. s.v. collybus,* Suetonius misunderstood Cassius, who used *collybus* of a kind of cake. In general, see Scott, *Mem. Amer. Acad. in Rome,* xi 12f.

[8] *i.e.* Hadrian.

[9] *Annales,* 502, Vahlen.[2]

[10] Since the time of Sulla only senators were eligible for the position of tribune.

[11] Cic. *Epist.* 11. 20. 1; according to Vell. Paterc. 2. 62, Cicero punned on the double meaning of *tollo,* "raise" and "put out of the way."

[12] A game still common in Italy, in which the contestants thrust out their fingers (*micare digitis*), the one naming correctly the number thrust out by his opponent being the winner.

[13] The term applied to a victorious general by his soldiers.

[14] See note on *Jul.* xxxix. 2.

[15] The sacred precinct at Alexandria (*τὸ καλούμενον Σῆμα, περίβολος ἦν,* Strabo, 17. 1. 8) containing the tombs of Alexander and of the kings.

[16] The *nomenclator* (*nomenculator*) was a slave whose duty it was to remind his master, or mistress, of the names of persons.

[17] Applied to expeditions commanded by others, since as commander-in-chief he took the auspices before the army set out.

[18] Crassus lost his standards at the battle of Carrhae in 53, and Antony through the defeat of his lieutenants in 40 and 36 B.C.

[19] In the reign of Numa, and in 235 B.C., after the first Punic war.

[20] The ovation was a lesser triumph, in which the general entered the city on foot, instead of in a chariot drawn by four horses (whence the term *triumphus curulis*), and with other difference described by Gellius, 5. 6.

[21] That is, executed every tenth man, selected by lot.

[22] Instead of the usual rations of wheat.

[23] Carrying the pole to measure off the camp, or clods for building the rampart, was the work of common soldiers; hence degrading for officers.

[24] Cf. *Jul.* lxxvii. 2.

[25] That is, he kept them apart from the rest in the companies in which they were first enrolled.

[26] The *phalerae* were discs or plates of metal attached to a belt or to the harness of horses.

[27] *Se precipitaverit* means "hurled himself headlong," perhaps into the Tiber; more probably from some high place such as the Tarpeian Rock, or the roof of a building.

[28] See chap. ci.

[29] Suetonius is brief to the point of obscurity. The idea seems to be that the intentions of Augustus in establishing the principate, and the effect of the new régime on the public welfare, were equally good.

[30] *Latericiam* is strictly "of sun-dried brick."

[31] See *Jul.* lxxi.

[32] See Index under Salus, and Dio 37. 24; 51. 20.

[33] *Exigere* is the technical term tor making weights and measures correspond with the standards in charge of the aediles; see *C.I.L.* XIV. 4124. 1, 2; X. 8067. 2; etc.

[34] According to Richter, *Topographie von Rom*, p. 229, the *regia* was the main door, leading from the stage of the theatre to the colonnade.

[35] The *ergastula* were prisons for slaves, who were made to work in chains in the fields.

[36] *Collegia*, or guilds, of workmen were allowed and were numerous; not infrequently they were a pretext for some illegal secret organization.

[37] *Sordibus* refers especially to the mourning garb in which it was usual for the accused to appear in public.

[38] That is, if he failed to win his suit, he should suffer the penalty that would have been inflicted on the defendant, if he had been convicted.

[39] Men whose property amounted to 200,000 sesterces, or half of a knigt's estate.

[40] Parricides were sewn up in a sack with a dog, a cock, a snake, and a monkey, and thrown into the sea or a river. The word is here used in its modern sense; cf. *Jul.* xlii. 3.

[41] These consisted of various immunities, especially those connected with the *ius trium liberorum* (see Introd. p. x).

[42] Orcivi or Orcini, "freedmen by the grace of Orcus," were slaves set free by their master's will. The *Orcivi senatores* were those admitted by Mark Antony under pretence that they had been named in the papers left by Caesar.

[43] Cf. *Jul.* xx. 1.

[44] A very ancient tribunal, consisting at first of 105 members, three from each tribe, but later of 180. It sat in the Basilica Julia, with a spear (*hasta*), the ancient symbol of Quiritary ownership, planted before it. It was divided into four chambers, which usually sat separately, but sometimes altogether, or in two divisions.

[45] The *decemviri stlitibus iudicandis.*

[46] See note on cap. xxii.

[47] That is, were so old or infirm that they could not ride, or would cut a sorry figure if they did.

[48] See note on chap. x. 2.

[49] See note on *Jul.* xxxix. 2, and cf. chap. xiv,

[50] Cf. *Jul.* xli.

[51] Augustus was a member of the latter because of his connection with the Octavian family; of the former, through his adoption into the Julian *gens.*

[52] That is, even by *iusta libertas*, which conferred citizenship. Slaves who had been punished for crimes (*facinora*) or disgraceful acts (*flagitia*) became on manumisson *dediticii, "prisoners of war."*

[53] Verg. *Aen.* 1. 282.

[54] *Congiarium*, strictly a distribution of oil (from *congius*, a liquid measure) came to be used of any largess.

[55] The *tesserae nummulariae* wore small tablets or round hollow balls of wood, marked with numbers. They were distributed to the people instead of money and entitled the holder to receive the sum inscribed upon them. Grain, oil, and various commodities were distributed by similar; tesserae cf. chap. xl. 2; *Nero*, xi; *Dom.* iv.

[56] Cf. *Jul.* xxxii. 1.

[57] Cf. *Jul.* xxxix. 2.

[58] The auditorium was divided horizontally into three parts: *ima* (*prima*), *media*, and *summa (ultima) cavea*.

[59] This puzzling statement is thus explained by Baum. Crusius: "*i.e.* ex aedibus proxime adjacentibus, unde prospectus erat in Circuin. Coenacula autem in sunimis aedibus esse solebant. Idem narrat Dio 57. 11 de Tiberio: *τοὺς τῶν ζππων ἀγῶνας ἐξ οἰκίας καὶ αὐτὸς τῶν ἀπελευθέρων τινὸς πολ λάκις ἑώρα τινὸς πολ λάκις ἑώραϊὸ*

[60] *Pulvinar* was originally a sacred couch for a god. The honour was given to Julius Caesar (see *Jul.* lxxvi. 1) and the term was later applied, as here, to the place reserved for the emperor and his family; cf. *Claud*, iv. 3.

[61] That is, given at Rome in the Greek language and dress, sometimes by Greek actors.

[62] Those of Pompey, Balbus, and Marcellus.

[63] That is, his middle finger, *infamis digitus;* it implied a charge of obscenity; cf. *Calig.* lvi. 2.

[64] That is, appointed them to the offices of *tribunus cohortis*, *praefectus alae*, and *tribunus legionis*, usually open only to knights.

[65] A limited citizenship, taking its name from the old Latin cities and varying in different cases and at different times.

[66] *Diploma*, strictly any document written on a two-leaved tablet, is used especially of those which secured to travellers the use of the public post (see chap. xlix. 3) and other privileges; cf. Cic. *Ad fam.* 6. 12.

[67] *Dominus*, "master," in the time of the Republic indicated the relation between master and slaves. Tiberius also shrank from it (*Tib.* xxvii.), and it was first adopted by Caligula and Domitian. From the time of Trajan it was usual in the sense of "Lord" or "Sire."

[68] That is, they did not make a morning call on him, as in other days.

[69] See chap. xxxv. 1.

[70] The Romans in their wills often express their opinion freely about public men and affairs; cf. chap. lxvi., and Cassius Dio, 58. 25, where it is said that Fulcinius Trio, who died in prison, bitterly assailed Tiberius in his will.

[71] The movable seats provided for the advocates, witnesses, etc.

[72] The custom of defending an accused person by a general eulogy of his character was forbidden by Pompey in his third consulship (Dio, 40. 52), but was nevertheless resorted to, even by Pompey himself (Dio, 40. 55).

[73] September 22 and 23.

[74] Probably of the scribes and other minor officials.

[75] One's tutelary divinity, or familiar spirit, closely identified with the person himself.

[76] The form of purchase consisted in thrice touching a balance (*libra*) with a penny (*as*), in the presence of the praetor.

[77] A record of the events of the imperial household. The custom of keeping such a day-book apparently dated from the time of Augustus. See Friedländer, *Roman Life and Manners* (Eng. Trans.), IV. p. 56.

[78] The host usually occupied the *summus locus* on the *imus lectus.*

[79] Ancient divisions of the citizens for political purposes. In cases of adoption the *curiae* were represented by thirty lictors, presided over by the pontifex maximus. This form of adoption was usual with adults; cf. cap. lxiv. 1.

[80] Pandataria.

[81] Planasia.

[82] *Iliad* 3. 40, where the line is addressed by Hector to Paris, with the verbs in the second person.

[83] See chap. xlvii., at the beginning.

[84] As well as Salvidienus.

[85] That is, while a private citizen could quarrel and make up with his friends, the emperor's position made his anger fatal.

[86] That is to say, holding the highest place in the *ordo* (*senatorius, equestris, plebeius*) of which he was a member.

[87] Cf. chap. lvi. 1 and the note.

[88] A double word-play on *orbem,* "round drum" and "world," and *temperat,* "beats" and "sways."

[89] Probably referring to Livia.

[90] The *choragus* at Athena had charge of the costuming and stage setting of plays. On the passage in general, see Scott, *Mem. Amer. Acad. in Rome,* xi. 30 ff.

[91] According to some, the choragus; others regard it as the name of a place.

[92] *Corinthiarius*: coined in jest on the analogy of *argentarius*; used in inscr. of slaves in charge of the *vasa Corinthia.*

[93] Cf. chap. xli. 1.

[94] When the freedom of the Saturnalia justified it.

[95] When only aces appeared, the throw was called *canis*; when all the dice turned up different numbers, *Venus.*

[96] The "five-day" festival of Minerva, March 20–25; see Index.

[97] Commonly called *peperino,* a hard grey volcanic stone with black nodules resembling peppercorns.

[98] Cf. chap. lxxxii. 1.

[99] With reference to the study of Archimedes, or perhaps to the general use of such elevated rooms in Syracuse.

[100] "Little workshop"; a diminutive from τέχνη.

[101] Opposed to *vestis forensis* or *forensia (vestimenta);* cf. *Vit.* viii. 1.

[102] The *cena recta* was a regular dinner, at which the guests reclined on couches at a table, contrasted with *sportula,* an informal meal (*Claud.* xxi. 4) or a distribution of food. See Friedlander, *Roman Life and Manners* (Eng. trans.), IV. pp. 77 ff.

[103] See chap. lxxii. 2.

[104] Tellers of marvellous tales; cf. Juv. 15. 16, and Mayor *ad loc.* Doubtless the same as the *fabulatores,* lxxviii. 2, below.

[105] Not the same as *regia* in xxxi. 5; see *Trans. Amer. Phil. Assoc.* xlvi. 35 ff.

[106] That is, grapes suited for eating and not for making wine; cf. Mart. 13. 22; Colum. 3. 2.

[107] Like an acid wine.

[108] That is, without a blanket over his feet, because he had his shoes on.

[109] *Lucubratoriam,* "for working by lamp-light."

[110] The so-called "Roman nose."

[111] Roman measure; a little less than five feet seven inches (5·58) English.

[112] Ursa major, Charles's Wain, the Great Dipper.

[113] Apparently a form of poultice; some read *habenarum* and explain as a kind of truss.

[114] Cf. Hor. *Epist.* 1. 15. 2–3.

[115] Cf chap. lxxii. 1, note *b.*

[116] *Albulae aquae* were the sulphur springs which flow into the Anio between Rome and Tivoli (Tibur).

[117] The *pila* was a small hard ball. Three players stood at the three points of a triangle (whence the game was called *trigon*) and passed the ball from one to the other. A skilful player used his left hand as well as his right.

[118] The *folliculus* was a large light ball. The players wore a guard on the right arm, with which they struck the ball, as in the Italian *gioco del pallone.*

[119] Many games were played with nuts; cf. Hor. *Serm.* 2. 3. 171, Mart. 5. 84, etc.

[120] See chap. lxxxi. at the end.

[121] Brutus published a eulogy of Cato in 46 B.C.; cf. Cic. *ad Att.* 12. 21.

[122] Evidently two archaizing grammarians of the day.

[123] See *De. Grammaticis,* x, at the end.

[124] Thus characterized in contrast with the studied simplicity of the Attic school of orators.

[125] *See* Index.

[126] Cf. Catull. 67. 21, *languidior tenera beta.* All these words, which Augustus is said to have used, are colloquialisms or slang, and the exact form and derivation of many of them are uncertain.

[127] Since *sumus* was originally enclitic, the forms *simus, sumus* may have represented the sound between *u* and *i* in *maximus, maxumus*, etc. Or *simus* may have been formed on the analogy of *agimus* and similar forms.

[128] *Domuos* is the earlier form of the genitive, with the suffix *-os, domus* the later, with the suffix *-s*. There was no form *domos*, and if Augustus used it, he probably did so on the analogy of *domos, domus* in the acc. plur.

[129] Cf. *Jul.* lvi. 6–7, and Aul. Gell. 17. 9. 1–5.

[130] *Religiones* includes both religious belief and regard for omens and portents.

[131] Pliny, *N. H.* 2. 55, says that the laurel tree (cf. *Tib.* lxix.) and the seal are never struck by lightning; and also that lightning never goes more than five feet below the ground.

[132] Chap. xxix. 3.

[133] This is not in accordance with the emperor's character (cf. chap. lvii), and Suetonius may have confused him with Caligula; see *Calig.* xlii. Yet there are records of many such acts of humility to propitiate Nemesis; see Casaubon *ad loc.*

[134] The Roman month was divided into periods of eight days, lettered in the Calendar from A to H. The last of these, every ninth day (*nundinae*) according to the Roman reckoning, was a market day.

[135] Because of its resemblance to *non is* (from *eo*); cf. Cic. *de Div.* 2. 84; or perhaps merely because it contained *non.*

[136] Into the Eleusinian mysteries of Ceres.

[137] The decree was not complete until this was done; cf. *Jul.* xxviii. 3.

[138] *i.e.* "Discourses about the Gods." Aristotle wrote a work with the same title.

[139] The *genius*, or familiar spirit (see note on chap. lx.), was often represented by a serpent, and those of husband and wife by two serpents; *e.g.* in Pompeian frescoes.

[140] To avoid profanation of the sacred rites.

[141] Otherwise unknown; Müller would read *Caesarem Drusum.* Stahr believes that the reference is to the Eulogy in chap. c. 3.

[142] Apparently another name for the via Appia; see *C.I.L.* i. 129).

[143] Instead of kissing him directly.

[144] *See* note on *Jul.* xv.

[145] Marked by the broad purple stripe (*latus clavus*). Augustus was not yet a senator, but the privilege of wearing the laticlave was doubtless one of the honours conferred on him by Caesar.

[146] Prosper (εὐτυχής "fortunate").

[147] Victor (νικῶν).

[148] The *lustrum* was a sacrifice of purification, made every five years by one of the censors, after the completion of the census, or enumeration of the Roman people. The sacrifice consisted of the *suovetaurilia*, the offering of a pig, a sheep, and a bull. *Lustrum* was also applied to the five-year period.

[149] The *pallium* was the distinctive dress of the Greeks, as the *toga* was of the Romans.

[150] Greek youths between the ages of eighteen and that of full citizenship, who had regular gymnastic training as a part of their education. The Greek training survived in Capreae, which until recently (see chap. xcii. 2) had belonged to Naples.

[151] The Land of Do-nothings. As there is no island "near Capreae," I take *Capreis* as locative, and *vicinam* as partitive. But see McDaniel, *T.A.P.A.*, xlv. 17 ff. and Della Corte, *Apragopoli, etc.* and *Augustiana* (Naples, 1933, 1934). The latter reads *Capreas* and takes *insula*, as "aggregato civico" (*pagus* or *vicus*).

[152] *Κτίστς*, the Greek name for the founder of a city or colony.

[153] Beneventum; chap. xcvii. 3.

[154] *i.e.* open through weakness.

[155] Or closed.

[156] See *Claud.* vi. 1.

[157] Augustus and Augusta, but Tiberius did not assume the title until it was conferred on him by the senate; Dio 57. 2–3.

[158] See note on *Jul.* lxxxiii. 2.

[159] See chap lxiv. 1.

[160] Probably those with which he was connected (see chap. xl. 2); Lipsius suggested *tribulibus.*

[161] That is, on their death; a common euphemism.

[162] The original of this inscription is lost, but the greater part of a copy inscribed in Greek and Latin on marble is preserved at Ancyra in Asia Minor and is known as the *Monumentum Ancyranum.*

BOOK III

[1] 504 B.C. in the traditional chronology.

[2] See note on *Aug.* xxii.

[3] 449 B.C. in the traditional chronology.

[4] Cybele, a Phrygian goddess worshipped near Mount Ida. In the year 204 B.C. her cult was introduced into Rome, where she was worshipped as the Magna Mater.

[5] Cf. *Jul.* xx. 4.

[6] That is, affixed the mark of ignominy (*nota*) to their names on the census roll.

[7] *Ad pilleum*: the *pilleus*, a close-fitting felt cap, was given to slaves on manumission, as a token of freedom.

[8] See *Aug.* lxii. 2.

[9] See *Aug.* xxii.

[10] Cf. *Jul.* xxxix. 2.

[11] The one built by Statilius Taurus; see *Aug.* xxix. 5.

[12] *Rudiarius*: presented with the *rudis*, or wooden sword, a symbol of honourable discharge; cf. Hor. *Epist.* 1. 1 .2.

[13] A child at birth was laid at his father's feet. He then acknowledged him by taking him in his arms (*tollere*), or the child was disowned and cast out (*expositus*).

[14] Cf. *Aug.* lxiii. 2.

[15] See note on *Aug.* xxxii. 1.

[16] Cf. *Aug.* xxi. 3.

[17] Transalpine Gaul was called *Comata*, "long-haired." The southern part was called *Braccata*, "breeches-wearing," and Cisalpine Gaul, *Togata.*

[18] *i.e.* celebrating a *iustum triumphum*; see note on *Aug.* xxii., and cf. Veil. 2. 121. For a different version see Dio, 54. 31.

[19] Since he was quaestor in 23 B.C. and consul for the first time in 13 B.C., *paene iunctim* is used loosely, to indicate a general disregard of the ages required for the various offices and the prescribed intervals.

[20] Cf. *Aug.* lxvi. 3.

[21] The title of *legatus* gave him an official position and concealed the fact that his absence was a forced one.

[22] The Greek dress; see note on *Aug.* xcviii. 3.

[23] In Gallia Comata, where Tiberius had been governor see chap. ix. 1.

[24] Gaius Caesar.

[25] Cf. *Aug.* xxvi. 2.

[26] "The Keels," the western end of the southern slope of the Esquiline, near S. Pietro in Vincoli; it was so named from certain buildings upon it; see Serv. *ad Aen*, viii. 361.

[27] *Peculium* was the term applied to the savings of a slave or of a son under his father's control, which they were allowed to hold as their own property, though technically belonging to the master or father.

[28] At tha Porta Triumphalis, at the head of the senate, who met the triumphing general there, and joined in the procession.

[29] Ordinarily the leaders of the enemy were strangled in the *carcer*, or dungeon, at the foot of the Capitoline Hill.

[30] See *Aug.* xcvii. 1.

[31] If the text is correct, the reference is to Tiberius' literary tastes; cf. Horace, *Odes*, 3. 4. 37 ff.; *Epist.* 1. 3.

[32] Cf. Enn. *Ann.* 370 V^2; where *cunctando* takes the place of *vigilando.*

[33] Literally, "by the god of Truth"; Fidius was one of the surnames of Jupiter.

[34] *Iliad*, 10. 246 f.

[35] A Greek proverb; cf. Ter. *Phorm.* 506 and Donatus, *ad loc.*

[36] The *secespita*, or sacrificial knife, had a long, sharp point and a double edge, with an ivory handle ornamented with gold and silver.

[37] *Civilis* means "suited to a citizen" (of the days of the Republic). His conduct was that of a magistrate of the olden time, who had regard to the laws and the rights of his fellow-citizens.

[38] The reference is to an oath taken by all the citizens to support what the emperor had done in the past and might do in the future; see Dio, 57. 8.

[39] Cf. *Jul.* lxxvi. 1.

[40] See note on *Jul.* ii. This had been conferred on Augustus *honoris causa,* as the saviour of all the citizens.

[41] See *Aug.* ci. 2. On xxiv-xl. see the commentary of A. J, Rietra, The Hague, 1927.

[42] See *Aug.* liii. 1.

[43] See note on chap. xxvi. 1.

[44] The flattery of the term *dominos* is the more marked because Tiberius himself shrank from it; cf. xxvii.

[45] That is, the granting to an individual or a company of the exclusive right to sell certain commodities. Forbidden in *Cod. Just.* 4. 59. 1.

[46] That is, to make use of the public post; see *Aug.* xlix. 3, and Cic. *de Leg.* 3. 18.

[47] See *Aug.* xxv. 3.

[48] Consisting of prayers for the emperor' welfare; see Dio, 57. 11, and cf. Plin. *Epist.* 10. 1, *Fortem te et hilarem, Imperator optime, et privatim et publice opto.*

[49] The designation of the seventh day of the week (Saturday) by the Jewish term "Sabbath" seems to have been common; cf. *Aug.* lxxvi. 2.

[50] That is, at one end of the curved platform, to leave room for the praetor in the middle; cf. Tac. *Ann.* 1. 75, *iudiciis adsidebat* in cornu tribunalis, *ne praetorem curuli depelleret.*

[51] See note on *Jul.* xvii. 1.

[52] Cf. *Aug.* Ixx. 2.

[53] Both an hygienic and a moral measure, see Plin. *N.H.* 26. 1 ff., and Mart. xi. 98.

[54] *Strena,* Fr. étrenne, literally "an omen," meant strictly gifts given for good luck.

[55] That is, of four times the value of the one which he received.

[56] The punishments for adultery had been made very severe by Augustus (cf. *Aug.* xxxiv.). To escape these some matrons registered with the aediles as prostitutes, thereby sacrificing their rights as matrons, as well as their responsibilities; cf. Tac. *Ann.* 2. 85.

[57] The first of July was the date for renting and hiring houses and rooms; hence it was "moving-day." See Mart. 12. 32.

[58] To determine his province or the sphere of his duty. The reason for his divorcing his wife is problematical. Evidently his marriage brought him some advantage which no longer existed after his province was determined.

[59] That is, the supporters and partisans of the rival actors; see Tac. *Ann.* 1. 77.

[60] The members of the local senate.

[61] Taking refuge in temples and holy places, to avoid punishment for crimes; for its abuse see Tac. *Ann.* 3. 60.

[62] The same proverb is mentioned by Cic. *ad Att.* 13. 12. The reference is to an Athenian actor of mimes, who imitated the movements of running but remained in the same spot; cf. Xen. *Symp.* 3. 11; Plut. *Agis,* 21.

63 That is, to make some amends for his conduct.

64 See Mommsen, Staatsr. 3, 489, n. 4.

65 See Index *s.v.* Biberius.

66 Probably the emperor took a sip from the huge vessel and passed it to the man, who drained it to the dregs; cf. Verg. *Aen.* 1. 738. Since the amphora as a measure contained about seven gallons, the word is here probably used of a large tankard of that shape.

67 See chap. lvi.

68 Cf. *Aug.* xli. 1; Tac. *Ann.* 2. 37.

69 This occurred twice, in 27 and 36; see Tac. *Ann.* 4. 64 and 6. 45. The second fire was on and near the Aventine.

70 The decree is quoted by Tac. *Ann.* 6. 17. The purpose was to put the money into circulation and at the same time to allow the debtors to pay in land.

71 According to Tacitus (*Ann.* 4. 64) this was done by the senate, because the statue of Tiberius remained uninjured in the midst of the burned district.

72 The standards had a sacred character; see, for example, Tac. *Ann.* 1. 39. 7; and the head of the reigning emperor was often placed under the eagle or other emblem.

73 Since he would save the rewards to be paid on the completion of their term of service.

74 Under pretence that they were hoarding money for revolutionary purposes. Caesar had limited the amount to be held by any one person in Italy to 60,000 sesterces; cf. Tac. *Ann.* 6. 16; Dio, 41. 38.

75 But cf. chap. xi. 4, above.

76 See note on chap. xv. 2.

77 *Sacrarium* is really a shrine (perhaps to Augustus) in which the letters had been deposited.

78 A sign that he was condemned to death; the noose was for strangling him and the hooks for dragging his body to the Tiber.

79 With A play on the double meaning of *debitum.*

80 A knight must possess four hundred thousand sesterces; Tiberius, as the adopted son of Augustus, had no property. See chap. xv. 2.

81 That is, not even a Roman citizen, since an exile lost his citizenship; still less a knight.

82 Sulla adopted the surname Felix.

83 Cf. *Calig.* xxx. 1.

84 If the text is correct, *primae cohortes* would seem to refer to the praetorians.

85 Of Fortuna Primigenia.

86 Cf. chap. xxvi. 2.

87 Since Tiberius and Sejanus were consuls for the year, the reference is to *consules suffecti*, appointed to succeed to the honour for a part of the year, probably from July 1st.

88 A somewhat similar method of telegraphy is mentioned at the beginning of the *Agamemnon* of Aeschylus as the means of sending the news of the fall of Troy to Mycenae.

[89] Where the senators sat at the theatre; cf. *Aug.* lv.

[90] For this meaning of *parricidium* see note on *Jul.* xlii. 3.

[91] Quoted also by Tac. *Ann.* 6. 6.

[92] That is, the change in his character and its consequences.

[93] One of the strongest arguments against the truth of the tales of his debauchery.

[94] See note on *Aug.* xc.

[95] The *grammaticus* was a critic and teacher of literature, but "grammarian" has become conventional in this sense, as well as in its more restricted meaning.

[96] "Monopoly," a Greek word transliterated into Latin; see note on chap. xxx.

[97] The Greek word for inlaid figures of metal riveted or soldered to cups. There is no exact equivalent in Latin, but Cicero twice uses the transliterated form *emblema* (*In Verr.* 4. 49). See E. E. Strong, *Rom. Art,* ii. 39, with illustration.

[98] See *Jul.* xxxix. 4.

[99] This statue, which took its name from Temenos, a suburb of Syracuse, was a celebrated one; cf. Cic. *In Verr.* 2. 4. 119.

[100] Of Augustus, on the western slope of the Palatine Hill.

[101] *Pharos,* the lighthouse at Alexandria, became a general term. Cf. *euripus, Jul,* xxxix. 2.

[102] The exact point is not clear. Perhaps an amphitheatre was chosen for the sake of ignominy, as well as to furnish accommodation for spectators, and that of Atella was near Misenum. Or it may have been because of Tiberius's failure to entertain the people with shows (see chap. xlvii.) that it was proposed to make a farce of his funeral in Atella, the home of the popular Atellan farces. Criminals were often punished in the amphitheatres; see *Calig.* xxvii. and Friedländer, *Rom. Life and Manners,* iv, p. 190.

BOOK IV

[1] That is, without holding the intermediate offices; the interval between his quaestorship and consulship was five years.

[2] Cf. *Tib.* xxv. 2.

[3] Cf. *Tib.* lii. 3.

[4] *See note on Tib.* xxvi. 1.

[5] Fuller details are given by Tac. *Ann.* 2. 69. 5. Such spells were often inscribed on leaden tablets (*defixiones; plumbeis tabulis,* Tac.), specimens of which have come down to us.

[6] See note on *Aug.* ci. 3.

[7] See note on *Tib.* vii. 2.

[8] A title originally applied to the king of Persia and transferred to the king of the Parthians.

[9] The Saturnalia, see Index and cf. note on *Aug.* lxxi. 1.

[10] See *Tib.* liv.

[11] The *acta publica* or *acta diurna*, an official publication of important events.

[12] Chap. vii.

[13] "Little Boots" (though really singular number). The *caliga*, or half-boot, was regularly worn by the soldiers.

[14] See *Tib.* lxxvi.

[15] They were compelled to fulfil their vows; see chap. xxvii. 2.

[16] Cf. *Vit.* ii. 4.

[17] Of Augustus; see *Aug.* c. 4.

[18] Originally the title of the commander of the knights who were under forty-five and in active service. Conferred on C. and L. Caesar by Augustus, it became the designation of the heir to the throne, and was later assumed by the emperors themselves.

[19] The consuls in making propositions to the senate began with a set formula (cf. *Aug.* lviii. 2, *Jul.* lxxx. 2), wishing success to the emperor, or in earlier days to the State.

[20] See *Tib.* xliii. 1.

[21] Cf. *Aug.* xxxv. 2.

[22] See *Aug.* xxviii. 1 and ci. 4.

[23] *Ducentesimam* (*sc. partem*), one half of one per cent.

[24] An error, since he was consul in 39, 40, and 41.

[25] See *Aug.* xxix. 5.

[26] To be scrambled for by the spectators.

[27] *Africanae*, supply *bestiae* and see Index.

[28] On the houses adjoining the Circus; called *Maeniana* after a certain Maenius, who was supposed to have been the first to build such balconies.

[29] Over three and a half Roman miles.

[30] See *Tib.* lv.

[31] See note on *Tib.* vi. 4.

[32] Obviously not a choice, but determined by the degree of success of the contestants.

[33] See *Claud.* xx. 1.

[34] Cf. *Jul.* xliv. 3.

[35] *Iliad* 2. 204.

[36] Under Caligula the so-called "principate" had become an absolute monarchy. Caligula proposed to assume the pomp of a king.

[37] The chryselephantine statue of Zeus by Pheidias; see chap. lvii. 1.

[38] *Iliad*, 23. 724, where after a long and indecisive wrestling bout Ajax thus challenges Odysseus to settle the contest. *Ανάειρε* is doubtless used in a double sense, perhaps with aposiopesis, "Raise me up (to heaven), or thee I'll—."

[39] See *Aug.* xvi. 1.

[40] The *stola* was the characteristic dress of the Roman matron, as the *toga* was that of the man.

41 See note on *Tib.* xxxvii. 3.

42 By adoption; see chap. xv. 2.

43 Or perhaps, in short linen tunics.

44 This remark shows the regard in which the empty title of "consul" was still held.

45 The reason for the term *decimas*, if the reading be correct, is uncertain; cf. note on *Aug.* xli. 2. Obviously his purpose was to lead the rabble to occupy the knights' seats before the plays began, and thus to start a fight.

46 The meaning of *paegniarii* is uncertain; they may have carried *arma lusoria* or arms incapable of causing death. See Friedländer, *Roman Life and Manners*, Eng. trans. iv. p. 179.

47 The *elogium* was the tablet on which the charge against the prisoner was recorded.

48 It seems probable that there happened to be a bald-headed man at each end of the line; the expression became proverbial.

49 See chap. xiv. 2.

50 See *Aug.* lx.

51 "Immobility," a Stoic virtue. Since in Gaius this took the form of callous indifference to suffering and to public opinion, it became *inverecundia*.

52 Accius, *Trag.*, 203.

53 See chap. xv. 4.

54 For punishment, or to fight in the arena.

55 See Index and Friedländer, *op. cit.* (p. 446, ftn. *b*) iv, 171 ff.

56 See *Aug.* xxiii. 1.

57 See *Tib.* xl.

58 See chap. xix.

59 See note on chap. xxx. 3.

60 The *popa* knocked down the victim with a mallet or with the back of an axe-head, and the *cultrarius* then cut the animal's throat.

61 Literally, "the cords," as an instrument of torture; cf. *Tib.* lxii. 2. On the whole passage cf. *Calig.* xxv. 3 and l. 2.

62 See chap. xxvi. 1.

63 He himself was bald; see chap. l. 1.

64 The "Giant Cupid" from κολοσσός and ἔρως.

65 The priest of Diana at Nemi, who must be a fugitive slave and obtain his office by slaying his predecessor.

66 A gladiator who fought from a British chariot; see note on chap. xxx. 3.

67 The Liburnian galleys, so-called from a people of Illyricum, were famous for their speed. They commonly had but one or two banks of oars.

68 That is, if anyone chanced to have received an addition to his income since the last census, he charged him with having made a false report to the censors, and of course confiscated his estate.

[69] The part occupied by Augustus and Tiberius, to which Caligula had made some additions.

[70] See note on *Aug.* xix. 1.

[71] See *Aug.* lvii. 1.

[72] *Sinus* means the bosom of the toga, which was often used as a pocket.

[73] Celebrated for its beautiful scenery, described by Pliny, *Epist.* 8. 8.

[74] Half the amount established by Augustus; see Dio, 55 .23.

[75] Ordinarily such vehicles were allowed to pass through the city streets only before sunrise or during the last two hours of the day. See Friedländer, *Roman Life and Manners,* Eng. trans. iv. p. 28.

[76] See *Aug.* xxix. 2.

[77] From *exploratores,* scouts or rangers.

[78] *Aen.* 1. 207.

[79] One of the various kinds of "torsion-engines" (*tormenta*) used by the Romans. The *ballista* cast stones, the *catapulta* large arrows or darts.

[80] The lighthouse at Alexandria.

[81] To the privy-purse, of course.

[82] See chap. ix.

[83] See *Aug.* xxiv. 2.

[84] See note on *Aug.* xxii.

[85] Cf. chap. iii. 1.

[86] See *Jul.* xlv. 1.

[87] After his murder; probably referring to the praetorians.

[88] Men were forbidden to wear silk garments; see Tac. *Ann.* 2. 33, *ne vestis serica viros* foedaret.

[89] The *cyclas* was a kind of robe worn by women and embroidered with gold and purple.

[90] Cf. *Aug.* xviii. 1.

[91] That is, if he succeeded better in his accusation, he took sides against the defendant, and *vice versa,* regardless of justice.

[92] Cf. chap. xxxii. 2.

[93] A festival in honour of gome god or goddess, celebrated with feasting, dancing, and plays of all kinds.

[94] About midnight, since the night was divided into four *vigiliae.*

[95] The *scabellum* was attached to the feet of dancers and sounded an accompaniment to their movements.

[96] See note on chap. xxx. 3. He disliked the *murmillones,* as the opponents of his favourites, the Thracians.

[97] The charioteers in the Circus were divided into four parties, distinguished by their colours, which were red, white, blue, and green. Domitian added two more; see Dom. vii. 1.

[98] The "stable" was in reality a kind of club, containing the quarters of the drivers as well as the stalls of the horses.

[99] The host at a dinner party often gave gifts to his guests to take away with them (hence called by the Greek name *apophoreta*); cf. *Aug.* lxxv.

[100] Swift, "Flyer."

[101] Cf. *Aug.* xlv. 4.

[102] Referring of course to the assassination of Julius Caesar.

[103] See chap. xxii. 3.

[104] It was called Cinyras, and its story is told by Ovid, *Metam.* 10. 298 ff.

[105] Its name was derived from a famous highwayman; cf. Juv. 8. 186.

[106] The actors *secundarum partium* entertained the spectators after a play by imitating the actions of the star.

[107] Hoc age means "pay attention" or "mind this" (Plutarch, *Numa,* xiv. 2, Perrin in L.C.L), its usual, if not its only sense from the time of Plautus. See *Class. Phil.* xxviii. 47 ff. Its use in sacrifices is doubtful, in spite of Varro, *L.L.* vi. 12.

[108] Another formula "Receive the fulfilment of your omen" *i.e.,* in naming Jupiter, the god of the thunderbolt and sudden death.

[109] With which they carried his litter.

[110] Gaius Julius Caesar Strabo, slain in 87 B.C. But the Dictator's father died a natural death, as did also Gaius Caesar, grandson of Augustus; see *Aug.* lxv. 1.

BOOK V

[1] See *Aug.* lxii. 2.

[2] Literally, "the blest," those on whom fortune smiles.

[3] The *fossae Drusinae,* two miles long, connecting the Rhine with the Yssel, to furnish a passage to the North Sea.

[4] See *Aug.* xxii.

[5] Cf. *Tib.* vii. 3.

[6] The reference is probably to the *scribae quaestorii,* the quaestor's clerks, who were the most important of the attendants upon the magistrates. They formed a guild composed of six *decuriae,* or divisions of ten, presided over by six officers called *sex primi curatorum.*

[7] *A decursus,* or *decursio.* Dio, 56. 42, describes the one about the funeral pyre of Augustus. After running around it in full armour, the soldiers cast into the fire the military prizes which they had received from the emperor; cf. *Jul.* lxxxiv. 4.

[8] See note on *Tib.* xxvi. l.

[9] The *spolia opima* were the armour of the leader of the enemy, taken from him in hand-to-hand combat by a Roman general.

[10] C. and L. Caesar; see *Tib.* xxiii. and Index.

[11] That is, on the anniversary of the dedication, which was in 13 B.C.

[12] That is, the age at which one was ordinarily freed from tutelage. The usual formula is *in suam tutelam venire,* Cic. *De. Orat.* i. 39. 180.

[13] Of relatives and friends.

[14] The future emperor.

[15] Claudius.

[16] Celebrated by Augustus in 12 A.D. in honour of Mars Ultor; cf. *Aug.* xxix. 1 and 2.

[17] The two Greek words, ἄρτιος and ὁλόκληρος, mean "complete," "perfect of one's kind;" the meaning therefore is "if he have his five senses."

[18] See note on *Aug.* xlv. l.

[19] See note on *Jul.* lxxxiii. 2; the heirs in the third degree had little or no prospect of receiving their inheritance.

[20] December 21 and 22, an extension of the Saturnalia, when it was customary to make presents of little images of various kinds (*sigilla*); also the name of a quarter or street in Rome, see chap. xvi. 4; *Nero,* xxviii. 2.

[21] Founded by Tiberius for the worship of the Deified Augustus.

[22] Of his house.

[23] Gauis appointed a number of consuls at once, who drew lots for the year when they were to hold the office.

[24] See *Calig.* viii. 1 and xxiv. 3.

[25] The Rhine.

[26] See *Calig.* xxii. 3.

[27] He had borrowed money from the public treasury for his entrance fee into the new priesthood, and pledged his estates as security.

[28] That is, the prefects of the treasury, chosen from the praetors and ex-praetors (see *Aug.* xxxvi). Claudius later restored the charge of the treasury to the quaestors (see chap. xxiv. 2).

[29] *in vacuum*; the meaning is uncertain. It perhaps means that the advertisement was merely a matter of form, though none the less humiliating.

[30] "Hope" of becoming emperor; "confidence" that he had escaped death.

[31] By restoring the republic.

[32] For carrying her image; see *Calig.* xv. 1, and cf. *Tib.* li. 2.

[33] Germanicus.

[34] See *Aug.* xcviii. 5. The comedy was doubtless written by Germanicns; see *Calig.* iii. 2.

[35] See *Jul.* lxxvi. 1.

[36] With garlands and perfumes; cf. note on *Tib.* xlviii. 2.

[37] See note on *Jul.* lxii. It was considered a bad omen if it was difficult to pull the standards from the ground.

[38] Before his own tribunal.

[39] More literally "the decuries for court duty," to distinguish them from the decuries of knights, scribes, etc.

[40] That is, he enjoyed the privileges of the *ius trium liberorum,* one of which was freedom from jury duty.

41 Cf. Dio, 60. 28.

42 Only a Roman citizen had the right to wear the toga.

43 On these see *Aug.* xxxix.

44 By affixing the *nota,* or mark of disgrace, to their names on the census-list.

45 Referring to the street or quarter; see note on chap. v.

46 Suetonius is vague. Dio, 60. 19, says that one Bericus, who had been expelled from the island during a revolution, persuaded Claudius to send troops there. Possibly the reference is to the deserters mentioned in *Calig.* xliv.

47 A suburb of Rome, lying north of the city, outside of the Servian wall.

48 A large building in the campus Martius, where the votes cast in the elections were sorted and counted; according to Dio, 55. 8, the largest building ever covered by a single roof.

49 Passed in 9 A.D., after the failure of Augustus' law *de maritandis ordinibus*; see *Aug.* xxxiv.

50 See note on *Aug.* xlvii.

51 These were numerous and varied; cf. Dio, 55. 2.

52 This had been brought by Gaius from Heliopolis and set up in the *spina* of his circus, near the Vatican hill. It now stands before the cathedral of St. Peter. The great ship in which it was transported to Rome from Alexandria is described by Pliny, *N.H.* 16. 201.

53 Pompey placed the double temple of Venus and Victory at the top of his theatre, so that the seats of the auditorium formed an approach to it.

54 See *Aug.* xxxi. 4.

55 Built by Gaius; see note on chap. xx. 3 and Index *s.v. Vaticanum.*

56 The *carceres* were compartments closed by barriers, one for each chariot. They were probably twelve in number and were so arranged as to be at an equal distance from the starting point of the race. When the race began, the barriers were removed. The *metae,* or "goals," were three conical pillars at each end of the *spina,* or low wall which ran down the middle of the arena, about which the chariots had to run a given number of times, usually seven; see *Dom.* iv. 3.

57 See note on *Aug.* lxxiv.

58 Instead of keeping it covered with his toga, an undignified performance for an emperor.

59 "The Dove," nickname of a gladiator.

60 The symbol of discharge; cf. Hor. *Epist.* 1. 1. 2.

61 See note on *Calig.* xxxv. 3.

62 About to die; one of Claudius's feeble jokes, which the combatants pretended to understand as meaning that they need not risk their lives in battle.

63 See chap. xxx. below.

64 That those whom he had selected were worthy of the honour.

[65] See *Galba* xiv. 3, from which it appears that Claudius made the summer and autumn seasons continuous, and did away with the winter term.

[66] The *relegatio* was a milder form of exile, without loss of citizenship or confiscation of property, but in this case the offenders were not banished, but confined to the city and its immediate vicinity.

[67] The *procuratores* were the emperor's agents, who performed various administrative duties throughout the empire. They were members of the equestrian order and were ranked on the basis of their annual stipend as *trecenarii, ducenarii, centenarii,* and *sexagenarii,* receiving respectively 300,000, 200,000, 100,000, and 60,000 sesterces.

[68] A common reason for this was the desire to engage in business, which senators were not allowed to do.

[69] The state treasury, located in the temple of Saturn in the Forum; cf. *Aug.* xxxvi.

[70] According to Tac., *Ann.* 11. 20, this was done by the legions in Germany.

[71] That is, if their own freedmen proved ungrateful and they wished to bring suit against them.

[72] In the Tiber at Rome, so-called from its temple of Aesculapius.

[73] That is, the gentile names such as Claudius, Cornelius, etc.; apparently forenames (Gaius, Lucius, and the like) and surnames (Lentulus, Nasica) might be assumed, although a foreigner often retained his native name as a surname.

[74] The part of the Esquiline hill on both sides of the Servian wall; occupied in part by the Gardens of Maecenas; see Hor. *Serm.* 1. 8. The place of execution seems to have been outside of the Porta Esquilina.

[75] Another form of Christus; see Tert. *Apol.* 3 (at the end). It is uncertain whether Suetonius is guilty of an error in chronology or is referring to some Jew of that name. The former seems probable because of the absence of *quodam.* Tacitus, *Ann.* 15. 44, uses the correct form, Christus, and states that He was executed in the reign of Tiberius.

[76] The gender is not significant; cf. Livy 1. 24; Varr. *R. R.* 2. 49.

[77] See Livy 1. 24.

[78] Of Claudius from Urgulanilla.

[79] Either Suetonius is in error here, or the text is corrupt, since Claudius' second consulship did not begin until 42, and he began to reign Jan. 25, 41.

[80] A common military prize.

[81] Only two of these are known, both named Drusilla. One was the daughter of Juba II., king of Mauretania, and the other of Herod Agrippa I., of Judaea; the latter was previously married to Azizus, king of Emesa.

[82] Otherwise restricted to knights.

[83] Chap. xxv.

[84] The *fulcra* were the ends of the couches on which the pillows were placed; see *Class. Rev.* 3, pp. 322 ff.

[85] Cf. *Aug.* lxiv. 3.

[86] Their feasts were proverbial for luxury; see Hor. *Odes,* i. 37. 2.

[87] See *Aug.* xxxiii. 1.

[88] See Livy, i. 26. 6; *Nero,* xlix. 2; *Dom.* xi. 2–3.

[89] Their faces were not covered by helmets; see Index, s.v. *retiarius.*

[90] According to Pliny, *N.H.* 28. 34, game killed with a knife with which a man had been slain was a specific for epilepsy.

[91] Those who fought during the midday interval, perhaps the *paegniarii*; see note on *Calig.* xxvi. 5, with the reference to Friedländer there given.

[92] A structure with several movable stories, for show pieces and other stage effects; see Juv. 4. 122, and Mayor's note.

[93] See note on *Aug.* xix. 1.

[94] Chap. xii.

[95] Chap. xiii.

[96] Of the prætorian guard, in the north-eastern part of the city.

[97] Narcissus.

[98] See note on chap. xxiii. 2.

[99] See *Tib.* xxxiv. 1. Claudius apparently allowed greater freedom. The restrictions were renewed by Nero (see *Nero,* xvi. 2), and according to Dio, 60. 6, Claudius himself (later?) issued an edict forbidding the sale of dressed meats and hot water, as well as abolishing the drinking-booths.

[100] Obviously some man proverbial for his folly; but nothing is known about him.

[101] The famous historian.

[102] Because he stammered; see chap. xxx.

[103] His grandmother Octavia was the widow, and his mother Antonia the daughter, of Mark Antony.

[104] These were Ⱶ, to represent the sound between *u* and *i* in *maxumus, maximus,* etc.; Ↄ, for the sound of *bs* as *ps;* Ⅎ for consonant *u.*

[105] See *Jul.* xx. 1, at the beginning.

[106] *i.e.* in Greek; cf. *Tib.* lxxi.

[107] Referring to the cohort on guard at the Palace; cf. chap. x.

[108] *Iliad,* 24. 369; *Odyss.* 21. 133.

[109] A proverbial expression, derived from the story of Telephus, who when wounded by Achilles was told by the oracle that he could be cured only by the one who dealt the blow. Achilles cured him by applying rust from his spear to the wound.

[110] That is, a legitimate heir to the throne.

[111] The northern spur of the Capitoline Hill.

[112] The formula was "*Di meliora* (*duint*)!" "May the Gods grant better things," *i.e.* "the Gods forbid!"

BOOK VI

[1] The youths were Castor and Pollux, and the victory that at Lake Regillus, in 498 B.C., according to the traditional chronology.

[2] Suetonius is in error here; it was the father of the tribune who defeated the Allobroges.

[3] *Os* has about the force of "cheek" in colloquial English.

[4] See *Jul.* xxxiv. 1.

[5] Proposed by Q. Pedius, Caesar's colleague in the consulship.

[6] The Pedian law.

[7] That is, as his executor. The maker of a will choae a man to whom he made a symbolic sale *(per aes et librum; see Aug.* lxiv. 1) of all his goods in the presence of witnesses. The purchaser then made the designated payments to the heirs and legatees.

[8] *Aug.* lxiv. and lxv.

[9] Gouging out the eyes seems to have been a favourite mode of attack among the Italians, cf. *Aug.* xxvii. 4, *Nero* xxvi. 2, and the frequent allusions in comedy.

[10] And paid for through the bankers; cf. *perscriptum fuisset, Jul. xlii.* 2.

[11] In his capacity as praetor; this was adding insult to injury, since the edict did not affect the present case.

[12] See note on *Tib.* vii. 2.

[13] See note on *Tib.* vii. 2 and cf. *Aug.* v.

[14] Boys on the ninth day after birth, and girls on the eight, were purified by a sacrifice and given a name; the ceremony was called *lustratio.*

[15] That is, *as* if the story had a better foundation, and the serpent had really saved his life through divine agency.

[16] So the mss., but it should be the twelfth *(Lipsius) or* thirteenth *(Oudendorp).*

[17] That is, his adoptive father Claudius.

[18] *See* note *d* on *Claud.* i. *3.*

[19] See note *e* on *Claud.* xlii. l.

[20] Cf. Tac. *Ann.* 12. 68.

[21] See *Claud.* xix.

[22] *Cf. Vesp.* xvii.

[23] Cf. *Aug.* liii. 3, *nullo submonente.*

[24] An honour previously conferred only on generals after a great victory; cf. *Jul.* xxiv. 3, at the end.

[25] That is, the part which he had read.

[26] In commemoration of the first shaving of his beard; see chap. xii. 4, below.

[27] This had previously been done only at the theatre (see note on *Jul.* xxxix. 2); senators were first given special seats at the Circus by Claudius; see *Claud.* xxi. 3.

[28] A tight-rope, sloping downwards across the arena; cf. *Galba,* vi.

[29] The musicians, machinists, etc.; cf. *Claud.* xxxiv. 2.

[30] Cf. *Jul.* xxxix. l. Originally war dances, their scope was extended to pantomime of all kinds, as appears from what follows.

[31] See note on *Aug.* xcviii. 3.

[32] The *podium* in the amphitheatre was a raised platform, close to the arena, on which the imperial family, the curule magistrates, and the Vestal virgins sat on curule chairs. Nero reclined there on a couch.

[33] In the broad sense, including poetry and oratory.

[34] The baths, the *Thermae Neronianae,* were in the Campus Martius, near the Pantheon. The gymnasium, the first permanent building of the kind at Rome, was attached to the baths.

[35] And to act as judges.

[36] Cf. *Aug.* xliv. 3.

[37] Of Pompey.

[38] See note on *Aug.* xiii. 2.

[39] This was usual only when a triumph was celebrated.

[40] See note on *Aug.* xxii.

[41] He assumed a fifth consulship in 68; see chap. xliii. below.

[42] See *Jul.* lxxvi. 2, where, however, the man's name is not mentioned.

[43] *See Aug.* lxv. 2.

[44] This was undoubtedly after the great fire; see chap. xxxviii.

[45] Various attempts had however been made to check this form of luxury; see note on *Claud.* xl. l.

[46] Because of their disorderly conduct; see chap xxvi. 2, and Tac. *Ann.* 13. 25.

[47] The tablets consisted of three leaves, two of which were bound together and sealed. The contract was written twice, on the open leaf and on the closed ones. In cases of dispute the seals were broken in the presence of the signers and the two versions compared.

[48] As witnesses. The testator afterwards wrote the names of the heirs on these leaves.

[49] The Cincian law of 204 B.C. forbade fees. Augustus renewed the law in 17 B.C. (Dio, 54. 18). Claudius limited fees to 10,000 sesterces (Tac. *Ann.* 11. 5-6). The senate again abolished fees at the beginning of Nero's reign (Tac. *Ann.* 13. 5), but Nero apparently revived the law of Claudius, with a provision against the addition of "costs."

[50] Instead of coming before the prefects of the treasury; cf. *Claud.* ix. 2.

[51] That is, his adoptive father Claudius.

[52] Of Corinth; cf. *Jul.* xliv. 3.

[53] Roman measure; a little over 5ft. 8in. English.

[54] *Cf. Gell.* 13. 31. 3.

[55] It collapsed in consequence, but not until the audience had dispersed; see Tac. *Ann.* 15. 34.

[56] Literally, "full-packed," *i.e.* full of sound, sonorous.

[57] The first seems to have derived its name from the sound, which was like the humming of bees, the second and third from clapping with the hands rounded or hollowed, like roof-tiles, or flat, like bricks or flat tiles.

[58] See chap. xii. 3.

[59] Probably asking for the favourable attention of the audience; cf. Dio, 61. 20 and chap. xxiii. 3.

[60] That is, those given by the magistrates; under the Empire all but the emperor were *privati,* regardless of their official positions.

[61] By his guardian and teachers.

[62] See note on *Calig.* lv. 2.

[63] The signal for the start.

[64] Chap. xix. l.

[65] Cf. Juv. viii. 224 ff.

[66] Of the theatre; for a similar use of *murus* see chap. xxxviii. l.

[67] *Oppida,* the term applied to the towers and other structures at the entrance to the Circus, seems to be used here of the corresponding part of the theatre.

[68] The use of a handkerchief was not allowed; see also Tac. *Ann.* 16. 4.

[69] The *hypocrites (hypocrita)* made the gestures and accompanied the tragic actor on the flute, as he spoke his lines.

[70] The heralds for the great festivals were selected by competition among the rival candidates.

[71] The Greek term *hieronices,* "victor in the sacred games," indicates the religious nature of the festivals.

[72] That is, with local self-government, not with actual independence.

[73] See note *d* on chap. xxiv.

[74] See chap. xx. 3.

[75] To make more room for the procession, which passed through the Circus (Dio, 63. 20). The reference is probably to the gateway at the eastern end, through which the procession entered and passed out again, after marching around the *spina* (see note on *Claud.* xxi. 3). Suetonius mentions only the exit from the Circus. In his time the gateway was formed by the Arch of Vespasian and Titus, erected by Domitian in 81 A.D.

[76] That is, song-birds, as a compliment to Nero's voice; the other offerings were also typical of his art and his triumph.

[77] Cf. *Aug.* lxxxiv. 2.

[78] *Quintana* is really the market of a camp, named from the *Quintana via,* one of the streets of a Roman camp, on which the market was regularly placed

[79] See note on chap. v. 1.

[80] Julius Montanus; *see* Tac. *Ann.* 13. 25.

[81] And their bands of partisans; see chap. xvi. 2.

[82] Made for sea-fights; see *Aug.* xliii. l; *Tib.* lxxii. l.

[83] With *mitellita* and *rosaria* we may supply cena; the former means a banquet at which silken turbans were a distinguishing feature.

[84] Cf. *Claud.* xvi. 4.

[85] Used in a double sense.

[86] That is, could balance the account of their expenditures.

[87] See chap. xii.

[88] That is, for each pip of the winning throw.

[89] Celebrated horseman of Mauretania.

[90] See note on *Aug.* xxv. 3

[91] That is, with three parallel rows of columns.

[92] One may compare Hadrian's villa at Tibur (Tivoli) with its Canopus, its Vale of Tempe, and the like.

[93] Suetonius' brevity is here inexact; it was evidently the spherical ceiling which revolved.

[94] That is, had left him nothing in their wills, or an insufficient amount.

[95] See chap. xxiv. 2.

[96] Of course confiscating their property.

[97] According to Dio, 60. 35 (at the end) the saying was original with Nero; but as Dio calls it "a remark not unworthy of record," it perhaps became proverbial among the Greeks.

[98] But cf. chap. ix.

[99] The pun on *morari,* "to linger, remain" and *mōrari,* "to play the fool," seems untranslatable.

[100] Against assassination *(De sicariis),* including poisoning, passed by Sulla and renewed by Julius Caesar.

[101] For her past offences; see Tac. *Ann.* 12. 66.

[102] See Juv. i. 71 f.

[103] The inventor was his freedman Anicetus; Tac. *Ann.* 14. 3.

[104] See *Aug.* lxxi. 3.

[105] Given by the future emperor Otho; see *Otho,* iii.

[106] Tacitus tells us that some denied this; *Ann.* 14. 9.

[107] That is, "when I see you arrived at man's estate." The first shaving of the beard by a young Roman was a symbolic act, usually performed at the age of twenty-one with due ceremony; see chap. xii. 3, above. According to Tac. *Ann.* 14. 15, and Dio, 61. 19, Nero first shaved his beard in 59 A.D. at the age of twenty-one and commemorated the event by establishing the *Juvenales ludi* or Juvenalia (chap. xi. 1).

[108] A brutal pun. Just as the consular *insignia* or *ornamenta* were given in place of the regular office (see *Claud,* v.), and the triumphal *insignia* in place of a triumph, so Octavia ought to be content with being the emperor's wife in name only.

[109] Anicetus was at the time prefect of the praetorian fleet at Misenum; see Tac. *Ann.* 14. 62.

[110] See *Claud,* xxvii. l.

[111] Seneca's speech and Nero's reply are preserved by Tacitus *(Ann.* 14. 53-56).

[112] Pallas and Doryphorus; see Tac. *Ann.* 14. 65.

[113] Tacitus mentions two comets, one in 60 and the other in 64; see *Ann.* 14. 22; 15. 47.

[114] As Dio says (62. 24) "they desired at the same time to be rid of these evils *and to give Nero his release from them."* Death was the only remedy for one as far gone in wickedness; hence in attempting to apply this remedy, they were doing him a favour. Cf. also Tac. *Ann.* 15. 68.

[115] The *capsarii* carried the children's books and writing materials in a box *(capsa).*

[116] The Greek word means "a glutton," or something Stronger,

[117] Such a salutation was usual; see Plin. *Paneg.* xxiii.

[118] A line put by Dio, 58. 23, into the mouth of Tiberius. It is believed to be from the *Bellerophon,* a lost play of Euripides.

[119] But cf. Tac. *Ann.* 15. 38.

[120] *Insulae* here refers to blocks of houses, or tenements, in which rooms were rented to the poorer classes; *domus* to detached houses or mansions.

[121] A tower connected with the house and gardens of Maecenas on the Esquiline; see Hor. *Odes, 3.* 29. 10, *molem propinquam nubibus arduis.* It was probably connected with the Palatine by the *domus transitoria; see* chap. xxi. 2 and Tac. *Ann.* 15. 39, whose account, as well as that of Dio, 62. 18, differs from that of Suetonius.

[122] Probably a composition of his own; cf. Juv. 8. 221 and *Vitell.* xi. 2.

[123] Venus Libitina, in whose temple funeral outfits and a register of deaths were kept; cf. Hor. *Serm,* ii. 6, 19.

[124] Coamuldunum (Meldon) and Verulanium (St. Albans); according to Xiphilinus (61. 1) 80,000 perished.

[125] See the reference to the *Rh. Mus.* in the textual note. The numerical value of the Greek letters in Nero's name (1005) is the same as that of the rest of the sentence; hence we have an equation, Nero = the slayer of one's own mother.

[126] Referring to Nero's design mentioned in chap. xxxvii. 3.

[127] If the text is right, the remark must be of a general nature ("us" = mankind). Dio, 63. 27, who reads *διαθρεψει,* says that Nero when planning to kill the senators, burn Rome, and sail to Alexandria, said: "Even though we be driven from our empire, yet this little artistic gift of ours shall support us there"; *i.e.* at Alexandria.

[128] Cf. chap. vii. 1.

[129] This and the following sentences show Nero's utter failure to realize the real gravity of the situation and his fluctuation between panic fear and fatuous confidence.

[130] Implying that Nero would have been the centre of attraction, if he were not otherwise engaged.

[131] Since Nero commanded the army, the consul in question must be himself; hence the *se* of ζ is unnecessary.

[132] Instead of to their landlords. These people had no rating on the census list and their contribution took this form.

[133] That is, tested by fire; see Pliny, *N.H.* 33. 59.

[134] By using, for his own purposes, ships which would otherwise have been loaded with grain; but the text and the meaning are uncertain.

[135] Doubtless an allusion to the long hair which he wore during his Greek trip; see chap. li.

[136] In contrast with those of the stage.

[137] The one in which parricides were put; see *Aug.* xxxiii. 1. But the text and the meaning are uncertain.

[138] There is obviously a pun on *Galli,* "Gauls," and *galli,* "cocks," and on *cantare* in the sense of "sing" and of "crow."

[139] Punning of course on Vindex, the leader of the revolt.

[140] On the first of January, for the prosperity of the emperor and the State.

[141] Of course used in a double sense.

[142] Pliny, *N.H.* 37. 29, tells us that the cups were of crystal.

[143] Verg. *Aen.* 12. 646.

[144] In the Palace.

[145] See chap. xxx. 2.

[146] The word *percussor* implies experience in dealing death. Nero wished to be killed swiftly and painlessly.

[147] Referring to a drink of his own contrivance, distilled water cooled in snow; cf. Pliny, *N.H.* 31. 40.

[148] *Cella* implies a small room, for the use of slaves.

[149] The water was for washing the corpse and the fire for burning it.

[150] Cf. *Claud.* xxxiv. 1.

[151] Two pieces of wood, fastened together in the form of a V.

[152] *Iliad.* 10. 535.

[153] See *Domit.* xiv. 4.

[154] See *Galba,* xiv. 2.

[155] The modern Pincio.

[156] The *synthesina* (sc. *vestis*), was a loose robe of bright-coloured silk, worn at dinner, during the Saturnalia, and by women at other times. Nero's is described by Dio, 63, 13, as "a short, flowered runic with a muslin collar."

[157] Probably meaning "in slippers."

[158] See note on *Aug.* xcvii. 1. Here *lustrum* is applied to the five-year period of the Olympic games.

[159] Atargatis, the principal deity of Northern Syria, identified with Magna Mater and Caelestis; often mentioned in inscriptions and called by Apul. *Metam.* 8. 25, *omnipotens et omniparens.*

[160] See note on *Tib.* iv. 2.

[161] In 88, Terentius Maximus by name; another pseudo-Nero had appeared in 70; see Tac. *Hist.* 2. 8.

BOOK VII

[1] Nero was the last who bore the name because of connection with the family of Augustus; after him it became a designation of rank.

[2] "The Hen Roost."

[3] Those which they carried in their triumph, according to Pliny, *N.H.* 15. 136 f.

[4] No such temple is known.

[5] No existing inscription confirms this statement.

[6] That is, of those of the Sulpicii who bore the surname Galba.

[7] The gum of a Syrian plant; see Pliny, *N.H.* 12. 126.

[8] See *Nero,* iii, 1.

[9] That is, after his consulship. Tiberius doubtless suspected him of a desire to enrich himself at the expense of the provincials; cf. *Tib.* xxxii. 2, at the end.

[10] The usual procedure, to avert the evil omen.

[11] Proverbial for "never," like the Greek Kalends (*Aug.* lxxxvii. 1).

[12] To marry and rear a family was regarded as one of the duties of a good citizen.

[13] Cf. *Nero,* xi. 2.

[14] That is to say, entering office on January 1, and with his colleague, L. Cornelius Sulla, giving his name to the year.

[15] Either Suetonius is in error or the manuscripts; the name should be Gnaeus.

[16] See *Calig.* xliii. and xliv.

[17] Cf *Calig.* xxvi. 2.

[18] Except in special cases, the governors were appointed by lot from among those who were eligible.

[19] The *modius* was 8 .75 litres.

[20] See note on *Jul.* lxxix. 3.

[21] The *sodales Titii* were an ancient priesthood of uncertain origin. The tradition arose that they were established to keep up the ancient Sabine worship, and named from Titus Tatius.

[22] See note on *Claud.* vi. 2.

[23] So as to be able to leave the country on short notice.

[24] See note on Claud. xxiv. 1.

[25] Such predictions, like the responses of oracles, were in verse.

[26] Instead of the emperor, as heretofore.

[27] *Evocati* were soldiers who, after serving their time, were invited to continue their service. It is here an honorary title.

[28] See note on *Jul.* xxxiii.

[29] See chap. x. 1.

[30] See note on chap. i.

[31] See note on *Claud.* xxiv. 1.

[32] Cf. *Aug.* xxiv. 2; *Calig.* xlviii. 1.

[33] See *Aug.* xlix. 1; *Calig.* lviii. 3.

[34] Doubtless many of them were false or exaggerated. Galba's frugality was naturally regarded as stinginess by a people accustomed to a prince like Nero; see *Nero,* xxxi. 1.

[35] Plutarch, *Galba,* xvi., gives the story quite a different aspect, saying that the gift was of gold pieces, and that Galba said that it came from his own pocket, and not from the public funds.

[36] The text is uncertain, but obviously the song ridiculed a stingy old countryman.

[37] Cf. the inimitable sentence of Tac. (*Hist.* l. 49) *maior privatus visus, dum privatus, et omnium consensu capax imperii, nisi imperasset.*

[38] *See* note on *Jul.* xxxiii.

[39] Prefect of the praetorian guard.

[40] See note on *Claud.* xv. 1.

[41] See *Claud.* xxiii. 1, and the note.

[42] These offices were numerous and varied. Since his apparent purpose was to check ambition and avarice, the senatorial offices referred to were probably military commands and governorships, and the equestrian, procuratorships; see note on *Claud.* xxxiv. 1.

[43] According to Plutarch (*Galba,* 2) it was Nymphidius Sabinus, prefect of the praetorian guard, who made this promise. *Praepositi* would include those who followed his example.

[44] See chap. xi.

[45] As he was on his way to Rome.

[46] See chap. iv. 3.

[47] The fire should have been blazing brightly and a youth clad in white should have carried the incense in a proper box (*acerra,* see chap. viii.), and the wine in a more costly and appropriate vessel.

[48] Of Piso.

[49] Of the praetorian guard.

[50] Which he had hitherto refused; see chap. xvi. 1.

[51] See note on *Calig.* lviii. 2.

[52] In the Forum; see *Aug.* lvii. 1, and Index.

[53] *Iliad,* 5. 254; *Odyss.* 21. 426.

[54] The meaning of this passage is uncertain and the interpretations various; see the long note in the ed. of Baumgarten-Crusius. The meaning of *super manus is* particularly dark; the most plausible suggestion is that it is equivalent to *ante se.*

[55] Like Maecenas, Otho was *Tyrrhena regum progenies*; Hor. *Odes,* 3. 29. 1.

[56] See *Claud.* xiii. and xxxv. 2.

57 Suetonius does not mention this among the conspiracies against Claudius; see *Claud.* xiii.

58 Instead of the modern blanket a *sagum,* or military cloak, was used, whence the operation was called *sagatio.*

59 The penalty for extortion was expulsion from the senate; see *Jul.* xliii. 1.

60 See note on *Nero,* xxxiv. 2.

61 According to Tac. *Ann.* 13. 45, the marriage was a real one, as is also implied below; see note *d.*

62 See note[c] above.

63 Tacitus and Plutarch give Ptolemaeus as the name of the astrologer.

64 Between the adoption and the death of Galba, a space of five days.

65 A pillar covered with gilded bronze, erected by Augustus, in 20 B.C., on which were engraved the names of the principal cities of the empire and their distance from Rome. The Roman roads were supposed to converge at that point, but the distances on them were reckoned from the gates.

66 Proverbial of undertaking something beyond one's powers; cf. Cic. *ad Att.* ii. 16.

67 To Ostia.

68 Of the armoury.

69 This difficult passage is obscure because of its brevity and perhaps through corruption of the text The same story is told by Tacitus (*Hist.* 1. 80) and Plutarch (*Otho,* 3.), but the three accounts seem to vary. According to Suetonius the arms were sent from the praetorian camp to Ostia, to fit out the (eighteenth) cohort, and that the riot started in the praetorian camp; the account of Tacitus seems to imply that it was the soldiers from Ostia (joined by the praetorians) that burst into Otho's dining room: *insidentes equis* urbem ac Palatium *petunt.* The arms in question would seem to be a part of those belonging to the cohort; hence *remitti.* See however Hofstee, *ad loc.*

70 From the temple of Mars, to be carried through the streets in the sacred procession. To begin any enterprise during that time was considered unlucky, and weddings were avoided; see Ovid, *Fasti,* iii. 393.

71 Cybele, whose festival was from March 24 to 30.

72 Tacitus, *Hist.* 2. 24, says *locus Castorum* (= *Castoris et Pollucis*) *vocatur,* and that it was twelve miles from Cremona. There was probably a temple there to the Twin Brethren.

73 See Tac. *Ann.* 2. 48.

74 See *Calig.* xiv. 3.

75 See *Claud.* xxix. 1.

76 See *Claud.* xxi. 2.

77 See *Tib.* xliii. 1.

78 See *Nero,* xii. 3 and xxi.

79 A faction in the Circus; see note on *Calig.* lv. 2.

80 *Supinis manibus,* "with hands uplifted," to the gods in gratitude.

81 See *Aug.* xxxii. 2.

82 Cf. *Aug.* lxxiii. and the note. See also Seneca, *De Tranq. An.* l. 5, *placet . . . non ex arcula prolata vestis . . . sed domestica et vilis, nec servata nec sumenda sollicite.*

83 Vienne, on the Rhone.

84 See chap. xviii. below.

85 In deserting Galba for Otho.

86 Modern Cologne.

87 See note *c* on *Calig.* liv. 2. The connection suggests an orgy in celebration of his victory.

88 A day of special ill omen because of the defeat by the Gauls in 390 B.C.

89 *Dominicus* (*liber*) was the name applied to a collection of Nero's compositions.

90 A drink made of sour wine or vinegar mixed with water.

91 The *ientaculum* was ordinarily a very light breakfast; Vitellius made a banquet of it.

92 Probably referring to the colossal statue of Athena Promachos on the Acropolis at Athens. Pliny, *N.H.* 35. 163 ff., says that the platter cost a million sesterces, and that to make it a special furnace was built in the open fields.

93 That is, from the eastern to the western limits of the Roman world.

94 See *Calig.* liv. 2.

95 *Vernaculus* and *verna* are used by Martial 10. 3. 1 and 1. 41. 2 in the sense of "buffoons," a meaning derived from the proverbial insolence of the *vernae,* or home-born slaves. The connection of the word here with *mathematicis,* and the fact that only the astrologers are mentioned in what follows, would seem to imply that the lampoons of these jesters contained predictions about Vitellius.

96 That is, the astrologers, for whom *Chaldaei* became a general term.

97 See note on *Jul.* lxxx. 2.

98 As a sign that he was willing to renounce the power of life and death over the people; Tac. *Hist.* 3. 68.

99 Chap. ix., above.

100 *Gallus* means "a cock," as well as "a Gaul."

BOOK VIII

1 See note on *Galba,* x. 3.

2 A tax of five per cent. on the value of every slave who was set free, paid by the slave himself or by his master.

3 A position held by tried and skilful officers, especially centurions of the first grade (*primipili; C. I. L.* iii. 6809, etc.). Cf. Vegetius, *Epit. Rei Milit.* 2. 10, *is post longam probatamque militiam peritissimus omnium legebatur, ut recte doceret alios quod ipse cum laude fecisset.*

[4] The *anteambulo* was the client who walked before his patron on the street and compelled people to make way for him; cf. Mart. 2. 18. 5, *tumidique anteambulo regis,* where *regis* means "patron," as in Hor. *Epist.* 1. 17. 43 and elsewhere.

[5] See *Calig,* xlviii. and xlix.

[6] Lepidus and Gaetulicus; see *Claud.* ix. 1.

[7] The senate.

[8] See note on *Aug.* xlvii.

[9] See *Claud.* xvii.

[10] The Isle of Wight.

[11] *Mango* (cf. Gk. *μάγγανον*, "charm") was the term applied to a dealer in slaves, cattle, or wares, to which he tried to give an appearance of greater value than they actually possessed. The nickname applied to Vespasian implies that his trade was in mules.

[12] See *Nero,* xxii. ff.

[13] Probably of auxiliaries.

[14] The hand was typical of power, and *manus* is often used in the sense of *potestas.*

[15] Of Nero's lodging.

[16] July 11; according to Tac. *Hist.* 2. 79, it was the fifth day before the Nones, July 3.

[17] Governor of the neighbouring province of Syria.

[18] The strategic importance of Egypt is shown by Tac. *Ann.* 2. 59; cf. *Jul.* xxxv. 1 (at the end); *Aug.* xviii. 2.

[19] The freedman's name, connected with Greek Βασιλεύς, "king," was an additional omen.

[20] They were stationed at Ostia and Puteoli as a fire brigade (see *Claud.* xxv. 2), and the various divisions were on duty now in one town, now in the other, and again in Rome.

[21] Literally, "on his own neck"; in a basket.

[22] The Colosseum, known as the Flavian amphitheatre until the Middle Ages.

[23] That is, a citizen could return the abuse of another citizen, regardless of their respective ranks.

[24] During the civil wars.

[25] See note on *Aug.* xxxvi.

[26] In the legal sense; *filii familiarum* were sons who were still under the control of their fathers, regardless of their age; cf. *Tib.* xv. 2.

[27] His tribunician power was reckoned from July 1, 69, the day when he was proclaimed emperor by the army. The meaning of the sentence is not clear.

[28] See *Claud.* xxxv.

[29] See chap. vi. 4. He boasted that the rule had been at his disposal and that he had given it to Vespasian; see Tac. *Hist.* 4. 4.

[30] Implying that Mucianus was effeminate and unchaste.

[31] A made-up name from *morbus,* "illness"; the expression is equivalent to "go to the devil."

[32] That is, in their superscriptions; see note on *Tib.* xxxii. 2.

[33] *Cogere (redigere) in ordinem* is used of one who resists or does not show proper respect to a magistrate; that is, attempts to reduce him to the level of an ordinary citizen. It seems to have been originally a military expression. Cf. *Claud.* xxxviii. 1; Pliny, *Epist.* 1. 23. 1; Livy, 3. 51. 13.

[34] This had been increased to 1,200,000 sesterces by Augustus.

[35] See note on *Aug.* xli. 2.

[36] Doubtless referring to the statue of Venus consecrated by Vespasian in his temple of Peace, the sculptor of which, according to Pliny, was unknown. The Venus of Cos was the work of Praxiteles.

[37] The colossal statue of Nero; see *Nero,* xxxi. 1.

[38] See *Aug.* lxxiv. and the note.

[39] See note [d] on *Calig.* lv. 2.

[40] The Matronalia or feast of married women; see Hor. *Odes,* 3. 8, 1.

[41] A transliterated Greek word, *κυβιοσάκτης*, meaning "dealer in square pieces (*κύβυι*) of salt fish,"

[42] According to Celsus, 2. 1, *quadratum* is applied to a well-proportioned body, neither slender nor fat.

[43] Cf. Macrobius, *Saturn.* 2. 1. 9, *impudica et praetextata verba;* Gell. *N.A.* 9. 10. 4, *non praetextatis sed puris honestisque verbis.* Various explanations of the term are given. It perhaps means words such as boys use; but see Festus, s. v. *praetextum sermonem.*

[44] *Plaustra* was the original form of the word for "wagons," but there was also a plebeian form *plostra*; see Hor. *Serm.* 1. 6. 42 and cf. *Claudius, Clodius.*

[45] *Iliad* 7. 213.

[46] Menander, Fr. 223. 2, Koch.

[47] Of Augustus; see *Aug.* c. 4.

[48] The connection between the *stella crinita* and the long hair of the Parthian king is obvious; it does not seem accidental that Calvina is connected with *calvus,* "bald," though this word-play seems to have been overlooked.

[49] Claudius and Nero reigned thirteen and fourteen years respectively; Vespasian, ten; Titus, two; and Domitian, fifteen.

[50] Some building of seven stories; the famous Septizonium on the Palatine was the work of Septimius Severus.

[51] Cf. *Nero,* xxxiii. 2 and 3.

[52] See *Galba* xiv. 2, and note [e].

[53] By the accession of his father Vespasian.

[54] See *Aug.* xiii. 2.

[55] See *Nero.* xv. 2, and note [a].

[56] See note on *Vesp.* ix.

[57] See *Aug.* xliii. 1.

[58] When the water had been let out; cf. *Nero,* xxvii. 2.

59 By humorously pretending to wrangle with those who favoured other gladiators than the Thracians; see Index, s.v. *gladiator.*

60 Implying that it was his personal loss, which he would make good.

61 To propitiate the gods, who were supposed to inflict such evils upon mankind by way of punishment.

62 The office was seldom taken so seriously. Julius Caesar, for instance, held it during his campaigns in Gaul.

63 The weapons of gladiators were regularly examined by the *editor,* or giver of the games, to see if they were sharp enough; cf. Dio, 68. 3, who tells a similar story of the emperor Nerva.

64 Possibly Domitian's charge was true; cf. *Dom.* ii. 3.

65 The old homestead at Cutilae, near Reate; see *Vesp.* xxiv. That this continued to be a *villa rustica* is implied in *Vesp.* ii. 1.

66 Various quarters and streets of the city were designated in this way; cf. *ad Capita Bubula, Aug.* v.; *ad Pirum,* Mart. 1. 117. 6. *Ad Malum Punicum* was a street on the Quirinal hill, probably corresponding with the modern Via delle Quatro Fontane; see Platner, *Topography of Rome,* p. 485.

67 Cf. *Otho,* xii. 1, at the end.

68 See note on *Galba,* i.

69 As son of the emperor.

70 That is, in the provinces.

71 He was but eighteen years old at the time.

72 The usual procedure for a youthful prince; cf. *Tib.* vi. 4.

73 See note on *Galba,* vi. 1. The reference is to his consulships before he became emperor; see chap. xiii. 3.

74 That is, twice as large as his brother's.

75 Titus had the ability to do this; cf. *Tit.* iii. 2, at the end.

76 See chaps. ix. and xi. 1.

77 See note on *Vesp.* ix. 1.

78 See note on *Claud.* xxi. 2.

79 See note on *Claud.* xxi. 3.

80 As well as in poetry.

81 Established for the worship of the deified Flavian emperors, after the manner of the Augustales; see note on *Claud.* vi. 2.

82 See *Aug.* lxxi. 3.

83 While the spectators remained in their seats; cf. Dio, 67. 4.

84 Represented in many cases by *tesserae,* or tickets; see note [b] on *Aug.* xli. 2.

85 In 80; it had previously been destroyed by fire in 69; see *Vit.* xv. 3.

86 Who finished and dedicated it; it was also called the *Forum Transitorium* because it connected the Forum of Augustus with the Forum Pacis, as well as the Subura with the Forum Romanum. It occupied a part of the Argiletum.

[87] Or Music Hall.

[88] See chap. iv. 2.

[89] Tac *Agr.* 39 says that his unjustified triumph over the Germans (and the Dacians) was a laughing-stock.

[90] See *Nero,* xvi. 2.

[91] See *Aug.* lxxiv.

[92] See *Calig.* lv. 2.

[93] See chap. xiv. 2.

[94] That is, those which had formerly been restricted to the senatorial order.

[95] Where the soldiers deposited their surplus money with the general for safe keeping, until the end of their term of service; see Veget. 2. 20 and for fuller details Grenfell, Hunt, and Hogarth, "Fayoum Towns and their Papyri," pp. 252 ff., where the accounts of two soldiers of about the year 180 are published.

[96] That is, raised the amount from nine to twelve *aurei.* The *aureus* contained 100 sesterces and was equal to a little over a pound sterling, or five dollars.

[97] That is, to gain favour with influential men or their advocates; cf. *Tib.* xxxiii.

[98] Cf. *Nero,* xvii.

[99] That is, all who sat in judgment on the same case.

[100] As censor.

[101] *De nefanda Venere.*

[102] *Georg.* 2. 537.

[103] Probably referring to new senators, entering the House for the first time.

[104] Nothing is known of this law. Livy, 21. 63. 3–4 mentions a law of Q. Claudius, which forbade senators to engage in business, and that law may have had a chapter referring to the *scribae quaestorii* and other "civil servants"; or, as some suppose, Publius Clodius may have passed such a law.

[105] That is, charges which resulted in the confiscation of the goods of the accused to the privy purse.

[106] See chap. iii. 1.

[107] Implying unfairness on the part of Domitian, who favoured the Thracians; cf. Pliny, *Paneg.* xi. and xxxiii.

[108] There is an added insult in *parmularius,* "one armed with the buckler," "a Thracian," as applied to a Roman citizen (*pater familias*).

[109] See chap. i. 3.

[110] Part of a course of training; cf. *Nero,* xx. 1.

[111] See *Nero,* xlix. 2.

[112] A tax of two drachmas a head, imposed by Titus in return for free permission to practise their religion; see Josephus, *Bell. Jud.* 7. 6. 6.

[113] These were doubtless Christians, whom the Romans commonly confounded with the Jews.

[114] See *Vesp.* iii.

[115] *Iliad.* 2. 204.

[116] *Pulvinar* here means the couch for the images of the gods; cf. *Aug.* xlv. 1.

[117] See chap. iv. 5.

[118] See note on *Aug.* liii. 1.

[119] See chap. iv. 4.

[120] *Arci* is a transliteration of the Greek word ἀρκεῖ with a pun on its resemblance in sound to *arcus,* "arch."

[121] See chap. vii. 2.

[122] Cf. Ovid, *Fasti,* 1. 357.

[123] A toga ornamented with horizontal stripes of purple, worn by the knights on public occasions, as well as by the early kings and the consuls; Tac. *Ann.* 3. 2; Val. Max. 3 .2 .9.

[124] According to Pliny, *N.H.* 36. 163, a hard, white, translucent stone discovered in Cappodocia in the reign of Nero. According to Tzetzes, *Lyc.* 98, φεγγίτης = σεληνίτης, "moon-stone." Pliny also mentions similar mirrors of black obsidian; *N.H.* 36. 196.

[125] Cf. *Nero,* xl. 2.

[126] See *Nero,* xlix. 4.

[127] It was evidently on a metal plate, attached to the marble base.

[128] See *Vesp.* v. 4.

[129] Fortuna Primigenia; cf. *Tib.* lxiii. 1.

[130] Including the burning of the body, to prevent the fulfilment of the prophecy.

[131] Niece of Domitian.

[132] See *Aug.* vii. 1.

[133] This in its connection suggests the blush of modesty, but cf. Tac. *Agr.* 45, *ille vultus et rubor quo se contra pudorem muniebat;* and in general, Sen. *Epist.* 11. 3. Doubtless Domitian's ruddy complexion was a recommendation in his youth.

[134] *Iliad,* 21. 108.

[135] Cf. *Tit.* v. 2. The bow and arrow were not included by the Romans in the term *arma.*

[136] Cf. chap. ii. 2.

[137] The great library of Ptolemy Philadelphus at Alexandria was destroyed during Caesar's Alexandrine war. The Pergamene library was given by Antony to Cleopatra and transferred to Alexandria, where it was kept in the temple of Serapis. It was frequently damaged during civil disturbances. Burmann thinks that the reference is to the latter; but the plural suggests both.

[138] Named after C. Matius, a friend of Augustus and a writer on cookery and gardening.

[139] Cf. *Juv.* ii. 32 f.

[140] Votice shields, adorned with the emperor's image; see *Calig.* xvi. 4.

[141] Cf. Plin. *Paneg.* lii.

[142] The Capitoline hill was sometimes called mons Tapeius, from the Tarpeian Rock at its south-west corner. It was not, however, the original name of the hill, as some Roman antiquarians supposed.

PART II

PREFATORY NOTE

[1] The date is variously given: 1455, Teuffel, *Gesch. d. röm. Lit.6*; 1457–8, Gudeman, *Grund. z. Gesch. d. kl. Phil.;* etc.

[2] Enoc's discovery of this manuscript has been doubted by some, but is now accepted by most scholars.

[3] Except for one *quaternio,* now at Esinus (Jesi).

[4] *Rhein. Museum,* 61 (1906), p. 543.

[5] See Volume I, p. xi.

[6] Hieronymus used the *De Viris Illustribus* of Suetonius as his model in the composition of a work of the same title, devoted to the worthies of the Church, as well as in his translation and enlargement of the "Chronicle" of Eusebius. From the latter numerous fragments of the *De Viris Illustribus* of Suetonius have been recovered, and the general plan of his work made out.

[7] See Volume I, p. x, footnote 1.

[8] For the manuscripts and their sigla see pp. 450 and 451.

[9] This is given on p. 450.

[10] See for example Porphyrio on *Epist.* 2. 1. 1.

[11] See especially G. Körtge, *In Suet. de Viris Ill. libros Inquisitionum Caput Primum, Halis Saxonum,* 1899, pp. 41 ff.

[12] *Gesch. d. röm. Litt.,* in Müller's *Handbuch,* viii. 3, p. 53.

DE GRAMMATICIS ET RHETORIBUS

[1] The names in brackets are omitted by Reifferscheid; those in parenthesis are added by him.

[2] Iulius Tiro, *mss.*

ON GRAMARIANS

[1] *See* note on *Tib.* lxx. 3.

[2] Livius Andronicus came from Tarentum, and Ennius was a native of Rudiae in Calabria.

[3] *praeco.*

[4] From *stylus,* an instrument for writing; see note on *Jul,*. lxxxii. 2.

[5] The pun consists in likening him to the Sicilian Daphnis, the "ideal shepherd," whom Pan taught to play the shepherd's pipe. If we read ἄγασμα, the meaning is "the prodigy (or 'wonder-child') of Pan." The early commentators saw a reference to Pan's love for the flocks and shepherds (cf. Verg. *Buc.* ii. 33.) and an implication that Lutatius was *rusticus or pecus.*

[6] The text is certainly corrupt and the meaning is uncertain; see Ihm, *Rh. Mus.* 61, p. 550.

[7] "Men of letters," from *littera,* while *grammaticus* is from the corresponding Greek word γράμμα.

[8] "Man of learning, scholar."

[9] *Sicci* and *aridi* both mean "dry, juiceless."

[10] The text and the meaning are uncertain, but it is obvious from the preceding sentence that we must have two *cognomina.* The man's name appears to have been M. Saevius Postumius Nicanor. Thus he was Saevius Nicanor, Saevius Postumius, and Marcus. The meaning of the verbs and of the lines as a whole is obscured by the lack of a context. The textual variants show that the mss. had the spelling Posthumius.

[11] The Tablet.

[12] See note on *Tib.* vii. 2.

[13] That is, the man who found and reared him.

[14] Literally, "on market days"; see note on *Aug.* xcii. 2.

[15] *Elenchus* is a transliteration of the Greek ἔλεγχος, "refutation," "cross-examination." The work was apparently an attack on *the Annals,* like those on the writings of Vergil; cf. the *Life of Vergil,* 44 and 45.

[16] That is, in a garret.

[17] The word is evidently corrupt; perhaps we should read Perialges (περιαλγής), "The Sorrowful Man." Turnebus suggested περὶ ἀλογίας, a treatise on the folly of teachers in submitting to such unjust treatment.

[18] Cf. *Tib.* xi. 3.

[19] *Epist.* 2. 1. 70.

[20] Varro Murena. Macrobius, *Saturn.* 2. 6, tells the same story of Galba, father of the emperor (cf. *Galba,* iii), but gives the reply of Orbilius as: *in sole gibbos soleo fricare,* "I rub humps in the sun." Neither remark seems to have any point except the allusion to Murena's deformity, unless Suetonius's version means "I put them into the background," or "consign them to obscurity." The commentators confine themselves to quoting Macrobius.

[21] The text is corrupt and no satisfactory emendation has as yet been proposed; see Ihm, *Rh. Mus.* 61, p. 551. Vahlen, *Index Lectionum,* Berlin, 1877, suggested *theoremata,* which would give the meaning "and afterwards taught his (Gnipho's) theories."

[22] A Greek word, equivalent to *Silva,* meaning literally "timber" for building, and used metaphorically of material in a rough form; here of material for oratory.

Silva is also applied technically to hasty and more or less extempore productions; cf. *Quint.* 10. 3. 17, *diversum est huic eorum vitium, qui primo decurrere per materiam stilo quam velocissimo volunt et sequentes calorem atque impetum ex tempore scribunt; hanc silvam vacant.*

23 That is, his own, without borrowing or imitation.

24 Dictynna is a name of Diana as goddess of the chase, from *δίκτυον*, "hunting-net."

25 *Unum expedire nomen,* "make shift to find one name," as surety for his debts.

26 That is, "what a fate for a man with such a mind and heart." *Cor* here, as often, ="intelligence," and *iecur* may have the same meaning, although it is commonly spoken of as the seat of the emotions, especially anger and the like.

27 The *calatores,* literally "summoners," were attendants on the augurs and other religious officials.

28 *Catasta was* the scaffolding or platform on which slaves were exposed to view at public sales.

29 *Ad Fam.* 9. 10.

30 The critical mark used to indicate spurious or interpolated lines; that is, Vidius denies the debt.

31 *Ad Att.* 12. 26.

32 See note on *Tib.* xv. 1.

33 Cf. *Aug.* lxvi. 1–2.

34 Q. Lutatius Catulus; see chap. iii. and Index.

35 A semi-circular place for sitting; applied also by Vitruvius, 9. 9. 1, to a kind of sundial.

36 The *Fasti Praenestini,* of which fragments have come down to us.

37 A *pergula* was an upper floor or balcony on the front of a house; such balconies were used as shops, studios, schools, and the like; cf. *Aug.* xciv. 12.

38 *Aug.* lxii. 2.

39 *Aug.* xxix. 3.

40 See note on *Tib.* vii. 2.

41 *See Aug.* xxix. 4.

42 The *fabulae togatae* presented scenes from Roman life, in contrast with the *fabulae palliatae,* or comedies adapted from the Greek.

43 See note on *trabea,* Dom. xiv. 3. In the *trabeatae* the characters were knights or other wearers of the *trabea.*

44 To dodge a blow delivered with the right hand; cf. Verg. *Aen.* v. 428, *abduxere retro longe capita ardua ab ictu;* part of the instruction to a boxer.

45 *Os* is of course used in a double sense, figuratively as above, and literally, of a pugilist's battered visage.

46 As *paedagogus,* cf. *Nero,* xxxvi. 2, etc.

47 3. 50 ff.

48 Naturally, on literary and grammatical topics

49 See note on *Hyle,* chap. x.

ON RHETORICIANS

[1] This word, like *grammaticus,* had a different force from that of the corresponding English word; it meant a teacher of declamation and oratory.

[2] Cf. Seneca, *Controv.* 1. praef. 11 ff.

[3] Cf. *Aug.* lxxxiv. 1.

[4] That is, stories and fables (Gk. ἀπόλογοι) introduced by way of illustration. Cf. Quint. 5. 11. 19 ff.

[5] They corresponded in general with the Roman *suasoriae,* which with the *controversiae* formed the stock exercises of the schools of rhetoric.

[6] The dress of a freeborn youth of good family; cf. *Jul.* lxxxiv. 4. The *bulla* was also a badge of free birth.

[7] Συθέσεις, "Compositions."

[8] The letter has not been preserved.

[9] That is, his speech in support of the charge against Caelius.

[10] Used in a double sense, implying that he had ruined his eyes by dissipation and late hours in Antony's company.

[11] Used in a double sense; she tempts me (1) to write a sharp epigram on her; (2) to lance her cheek.

[12] See note on *Aug.* xli. 2.

[13] 2. 17. 42–43.

[14] The *iugerum* is literally about two-thirds of an acre.

[15] See note on *Aug.* xxxvi.

[16] The story is told in more detail in Seneca, *Controv.* 7, Praef. 7. The defendant wished to settle the case by taking oath to the truth of his contention, which was permitted, provided the opposing counsel gave his consent. Albucius said, "I consent, provided I may dictate the oath." But when he challenged his opponent to swear by the ashes of his father and mother who lay unburied, and the latter accepted the condition, Albucius declared that he was speaking figuratively, and had not intended to give his consent.

[17] Pliny complains of this nuisance in *Epist.* 2. 14. 10 ff.

ON POETS

[1] Cf. Hor. *Epist.* 1. 10. 26 ff.: *Non qui Sidonio contendere. callidus ostro Nescit Aquinatem potantia vellera fucum, Certius accipiet damnum propiusve medullis, Quam qui non poterit vero distinguere falsum.*

[2] *facillime agitare* means "to live most comfortably," or, "most free from care"; cf. Ter. *Adelph.* 501, and the Greek ῥεῖα ζῶντες. In an opposite sense we have *difficultate nummaria, Tib.* xlviii. 1.

[3] Text and meaning are uncertain. Dziatzko suggested *submaeret (poeta) Hecyra sexta exclusa fabula.*

4 The *didascalia.*

5 That is, presumably, the beginning of the play of Menader on which the *Adelphoe* is based,

6 See note *c* on *Vesp.* xix. 1.

7 See note on *Rh. v.*

8 In his celebrated "canon," Gell. 15. 24.

9 "Meadow," a fanciful title for a book of miscellaneous contents, like the "Sylvae" of Statius, the "Pratum" of Suetonius, and the like.

10 Perhaps, "amid a hush of silence" in the audience. Because of the awkwardness of *voce . . . vocibus* Ritschl preferred *motibus* (*animi*).

11 Referring to Julius Caesar.

VERGIL

1 "The Maiden."

2 *Ecl.* 5. 20.

3 *Culex,* 413 f.

4 2. 34. 65 f.

5 *Aen.* 6. 884 f.

6 *Aen.* 6. 164

7 *Aen.* 6. 165.

8 Cf. *Aug.* ci, 3.

9 *Aen.* 3. 340. This is no real exception, for we probably have the line as Vergil intended to leave it. Andromache purposely avoids naming the *amissae parentis* (341).

10 "Plough naked, naked sow."

11 "A chill will give you the fever."

12 The scourge of Aeneas.

13 See *Aug.* lxxxvi. 2.

THE LIFE OF HORACE

1 Ninnius is unknown, but if the reading be correct, he was notorious for his leanness; cf. Telegenius, *Claud.* xl. 3.

2 It seems probable that there is a word-play on the double sense of *rex,* "king" and "wealthy patron," since Augustus would hardly use *regiam* literally of his table. The meaning would then be "let the parasite change tables (and patrons)."

3 See Th. Birt, Müller's *Handbuch,* 1^3. 3. 166

4 *Sermones* was apparently the title which Horace gave his "Satires"; the term *saturae* is broader and covers the Epistles as well; see p. 488 and note *b.*

5 *Epist.* 2. 1. 1 ff.

6 *Epist.* 1. 4. 15; 1. 20. 24; see note on p. 487.

THE LIFE OF TIBULUS

[1] Written by Domitius Marsus.

[2] Cf. *Jul.* ii.

[3] Messala was sent to Aquitania soon after the battle of Actium (App. B.C. 4. 38); he celebrated his triumph in 27.

[4] See *Aug.* xxv. 3.

[5] This is quite meaningless, so far as anything we know of Tibullus is concerned.

THE LIFE OF AULUS PERSIUS FLACCUS

[1] See *Gr.* xxiii.

[2] That is, gave a public reading.

[3] There is clearly something wrong here; elsewhere but one sister is mentioned.

[4] The collection of six satires, for which this Life was used as an introduction.

[5] A Roman tragedy.

[6] The elder Arria.

[7] Text and meaning are uncertain; see Marx, *Lucilius,* 2, p. 145.

THE LIFE OF LUCAN

[1] See *Gr.* xxiii.

[2] That is, gave a public reading.

[3] There is clearly something wrong here; elsewhere but one sister is mentioned.

[4] The collection of six satires, for which this Life was used as an introduction.

[5] A Roman tragedy.

[6] The elder Arria.

[7] Text and meaning are uncertain; see Marx, *Lucilius,* 2, p. 145.

THE LIFE OF PLINY THE ELDER

[1] See *Calig.* xxxvii. 2.

THE LIFE OF PASSIENUS CRISPUS

[1] See note on *Aug.* xxxvi.

[2] In the Roman Forum.

[3] Gaius is obviously intended, instead of Nero.

INDEX

Beside proper names, the Index includes the Latin words which are taken over into the translation, and a few others which seem to require explanation. The references are to chapter and section. The following abbreviations are used: A., *Augustus;* Cal., *Caligula; Cl., Claudius:* D., *Domitian; G., Galba; J., Julius (Caesar); N., Nero; O., Otho;* T., *Tiberius;* Tit., Titus; V., *Vespasian;* Vit., *Vitellius; Gr., De Grammaticis;* Rh., *De Rhetoribus;* Ter., *Life of Terence;* Verg., *Life of Vergil;* Hor., *Life of Horace;* Tibull., *Life of Tibullus;* Luc., *Life of Lucan;* Pers., *Life of Persius;* Plin., *Life of Pliny.;* Pass., *Life of Passienus Crispus.*

ABORIGINES, Vit. I. 2. A name applied to the primitive inhabitants of Latium.

Accius, Cal. XXX. 1 (quoted); cf. T. LIX. 2. An early Roman poet (170–86 B.C.), especially famous for his tragedies.

Acerronius Proculus, Cn., Tib. LXXIII. 1. Consul in 37 A.D.

Achaia, Tib. IV. 3, VI. 2; Cal. XXI.; Cl. XXV. 3, XLII. 1; N. XIX. 2, XXII. 3; V. V. 5, VIII. 4. The Roman province, comprising all of Greece south of Macedonia.

Achaica, *see* Mummia.

Achaicus, -a, -um, *adj.* from Achaia: *peregrinatio,* N. XIX. 1, LI.; V. IV. 4.

Achilles, T. LXX. 3.

Acilius, *see* Atilius.

Acilius (C.), J. LXVIII. 4 (*bis*).

Acilius Aviola (M'.), Cl. XLV. Consul in 54 A.D.

Acilius Glabrio, D. X. 2. Consul in 91 A.D.

Acte, N. XXVIII. 1, L. A freed-woman beloved by Nero.

Actiacus, -a, -um, *adj.* from Actium: *bellum,* A. IX.; *triumphus,* A. XXII.; T. VI. 4; *victoria,* A. XVIII. 2; Cal. XXIII. 1 (*plural*); Verg. 27.

Actium, A. XVII. 2, 3, XVIII. 2, XCVI. 2. A promontory in north-western Acarnania at the entrance to the Ambracian Gulf, off which

Aethiopes, Cal. LVII. 4. The people of Aethiopia.
Aethiopia, J. LII. 1. A country in the interior of Africa.
Aetna, Verg. 19. The name of a poem.
Aetnaeus, -a, -um, *adj.* from Aetna, the volcano in western Sicily: *vertex,* Cal. LI. 1.
Aetolla, A. XVII. 3. A district in the western part of central Greece.
Afer, *see* Tedius *and* Terentius.
Afer, -ra, -rum, *adj.* meaning African: *generis,* A. IV. 2; *pugiles,* Cal. XVIII. 1. *See* Afri.
Aflnius Gallus, Pers.
Afranius (L.), N. XI. 2; Ter. V. A Roman writer of *fabulae togatae,* or plays based upon Italic life. He lived in the latter part of the second century B.C.
Afranius, L., J. XXXIV. 2, LXXV. 2, 3. One of Pompey's generals.
Afri. Ter. I.
Africa, J. xxxv. 2, XXXVI., LIX., LXX. (*bis*); A XVI. 4, XLVII.; T. XXXI. 2; N. XXXI. 4; G. VII. 1, VIII. 1, XI; O. 1. 2; Vit. V.; V. III., IV. 3. Usually applied to the Roman province.
Africanus, -a, -um, *adj.* from Africa: *triumphus, J. XXXVII.* 1, A. VIII. 1; as subst., *Africanae (sc. bestiae),* Cal. xvm. 3; Cl. XXI. 3. Panthers or leopards.
Africanus, *see* Fabius *and* Scipio.
Africus, -a, -um, *adj. to* Africa: *bellum,* J. LVI. 1.
Agamemnon, T. LXI. 3.
Agathernus, *see* Claudius.
Agermus, L., N. XXXIV. 3.
Agrippa, M., A. XVI. 2, XXV. 3, XXIX. 5, XXXV. 1, XLII. 1, LXIII. 1 (*bis*), *LXIV.* 1 (*bis*), LXVI. 3, XCIV. 12, XCVII. 1; T. VII. 2, x. 1; Cal. VII., XXIII. 1; Gr. XVI.
Agrippa Postumus, M., A. XIX. 2, LI. 1, LXIV. 1, LXV. 1, 4; T. xv. 2 (*bis*), XXII., XXV. 1. Son of the preceding and grandson of Augustus.
Agrippina, T. VII. 2, 3 (*bis*). Granddaughter of Atticus.
Agrippina, A. LXIV. 1 (*bis*), *LXXXVI.* 3; T. LIII. 1; Cal. VII., VIII. 1, 3, 4 (*bis*). Granddaughter of Augustus and wife of Germanicus, known as "the elder Agrippina."
Agrippina, Cal. VII.; Cl. XXVI. 3 (*bis*), XXIX. 2, XXXIX. 2, XLIII., XLIV. 1, 2; N. V. 2, VI. 1, 2, XXVIII. 2, XXXIX. 3; G., V. 1; V., IV. 2, IX. 1; Pass. (*bis*). Mother of Nero, known as "the younger Agrippina."
Agrippinensis, -e, *adj.* from Agrippina: *Colonia,* Vit. X. 3. Modern Cologne.
Ahenobarbi, N., I. 1, 2.
Ahenobarbus, *see* Domitius and Nero (the emperor).
Aiax, A. LXXXV. 2. The name of a tragedy begun by Augustus.
Alani, D. II. 2. A warlike people of Scythia.
Alauda, J. XXIV. 2. The name of a legion; *see* note.
Albanum, N. XXV. 1; D. IV. 4; Ter. I., V. A uame applied to various villas in the Alban region; later a town, modern Albano.
Albanus, -a, -um, *adj.* from Alba: *columnae, A. LXXII.* 1 (*see* note); *mons,* CJ IV. 3 (modern Monte Cavo); *secessus,* D. XIX., the villa of Domitian at Albanum.

Albia Terentia, O. I. 3. Mother of the emperor Otho.
Albis, A. XXI. 1. A river of Germany, the modern Elbe.
Albuctus Silus, C., Rh. VI.
Albudignus, Cl. XX. 1; *see* note on text. A spring in the Sabine country, one of the sources of the Aqua Claudia and Aqua Marcia.
Albulae (aquae), A. LXXXII. 2 (*see* note); N. XXXI. 2.
Alcmaeon, N. XXXIX. 2. Son of Amphiaraus. He slew his mother and was pursued by the Furies. Alexander, Verg. 9. *See also* Cornelius and Tiberius.
Alexander, Magnus, J. VII. 1 (*bis*); A. XVIII. 1, L., XCIV. 5; Cal. LII.; N. XIX. 2.
Alexandria (also -ea), J. XXXV. 1, 2, LXIV., LXXVI. 3, LXXIX. 3; A. XVII. 3, LXXI. 1; T. LII. 2; Cal. XLIX. 2; Cl. XVI. 2, XLII. 2; N. XX. 3; V. VII. 1; Tit. v. 3; D. XX.; Gr. VII., xx. The city in Egypt, at the mouth of the Nile.
Alexandria, N. L. Nurse of Nero.
Alexandrini, J. XI.; N. XX. 3; V. XIX. 2.
Alexandrinus, -a, -um, *adj.* from Alexandria: Gr. xx.; *bellum, J. LVI.* 1; T. IV. 1; *merces,* A. XCVIII. 2; *navis,* A. XCVIII. 2; N. XLV. 1; G. X. 4; *peregrinatio,* N. XIX. 1 (bis); *pharus,* Cl. XX. 3. The lighthouse; *triumphus,* J. XXXVII. 1; A. XXII., XLI. 1.
Alexis, Verg. 9.
Alfenus Varus, Verg. 19.
Alliensis, -e, *adj.* from Allia, a small river eleven miles north of Kome, the scene of the defeat by the Gauls in 390 B.C.: *dies,* Vit. XI. 2; the anniversary of the defeat, regarded as a day of ill-omen.
Allobroges, N. II. 1. A people of Gallia Narbonensis. whose territories extended from Lake Geneva southwest to the Rhone.
Alpes, J. xxv. 1, LVI. 5; A. LXXIX. 1; Cal. XXI., LI. 3; N. XVIII.; O. IX. 2.
Alpinus, -a, -um, *adj.* from Alpes: *gentes,* T. IX. 2.
Amazones, J. *XXII.* 3. A mythical race of female warriors, whose home was near the river Thermodon in Pontus.
Amazonicus, -a, -um, *adj.* from Amazones: *secures peltaeque,* N. XLIV. 1.
Ambitarvius, Cal. VIII. 1. A village near Confluentes (modern Coblenz).
Ambrani (?), J. IX. 3. *See* note on text.
Ampius, T., J. LXXVII.
Ancharia, A. IV. 1. First wife of C. Octavius, father of Augustus.
Ancus Marclus, J. VI. 1. Fourth king of Rome.
Andes, Verg. 2. A small place near Mantua.
Andria, Ter. II. The "Maid of Andros"; the name of Terence's first comedy.
Andronicus, *see* Pompilius.
Anicetus, N. XXXV. 2 (*see* note).
Anio (gen. Anienis), T. I. 1. A river flowing into the Tiber just north ot Rome.
Anio novus, Cl. XX. 1. An aqueduct built by Claudius, which brought water from the upper course of the Anio to Borne.
Annaeus, *see* Cornutus, Lucanus *and* Seneca.

dagger to her husband, saying: "Paetus, it does not pain me,"
Arria, Pers. Daughter of the preceding and wife of Thrasea.
Arruntius, *see* Furius.
Artabanus, T. LXVI; Cal. XIV. 3; Vit. II. 4. A king of the Parthians.
Arverni, N. II. 1. A tribe of south-eastern Gaul.
Asclepiades, A. XCIV. 4. A philosopher of Mendes, a town of Egypt.
Ascletario, D. XV. 3. An astrologer.
Asconius Pedianus, Verg. 10, 46.
Asellius Sabinus, T. XLII. 2.
Asia, J. II., IV. 2, XXII. 2, XXVIII. 1. XXXIX. 1, LXIII.; A. III. 2, XVII. 3, XXVI. 3; T. XLVIII. 2; Cal. LVII. 3, LVIII. 1; V. I. 2; D. X. 2; Gr. VI.; Ter. IV.; Verg. 35.
Asiaticus, -a, -um, *adj.* from Asia: *oratores, A. LXXXVI.* 3.
Asiaticus, Vit. XII
Asilllus, Cal. VIII. 4.
Asinius Epicadius, Cl. XIX. 1, 2.
Asinius Gallus, C., Cl. XLI. 3; Gr. XXII., Hor. Son of Asinius Pollio and consul in 9 B.C.
Asinius Gallus, C., Cl. XIII. 2. Grandson of Asinius Pollio.
Asinius Marcellus, Cl. XLV. Consul In 54 A.D.
Asinius Pollio, J. xxx. 4, LV. 4, LVI. 4; A. XXIX. 6, XLIII. 2; Cl. XIII. 2; Gr. X. (*ter*); Verg. 9,19. A celebrated orator, soldier, statesman and patron of literature. Author of a history of the war between Pompey and Caesar, and of tragedies mentioned by Hor. *Odes,* 2, 1.
Asprenas, *see* Nonius.
Astici ludi, T. VI. 4 (*see* note); Cal. XX.
Astura, A. XCVII. 3, T. LXXII. 2; A small Island on the coast of Latium near Antium, where many distinguished Romans had villas; later joined to the mainland by a causeway; modern Astura (Torre d'Astura). asturco, N. XLVI. 1. A horse from Asturia in Hispania Tarraconensis.
Atalanta, T. XLIV. 2. Daughter of Iasius of Arcadia, beloved by Meleager.
Ateius Capita, Gr. X., XXII. (*bis*).
Ateius Praetextatus Philologus, L., Gr. VII., X. (*bis*).
Atella, T. LXXV. 3, Verg. 27. An Oscan town in Campania, north of Naples; *see* Atellana.
Atellana (fabula), Cl. XXVII. 4; N. XXXIX. 3. A farce of Oscan origin named from Atella, and representing scenes from everyday life by stock characters. In later times such farces were sometimes given after a tragedy and called *Atellanica exodia.*
Atellanicus, -a, -ura, *adj.* from Atella: *exhodio,* T. XLV.
Atellanus, -a, -um, *adj.* from Atella: *actor,* G. XIII
Athenae, A. LX., XCIII.; Gr. X., XV.; Verg. 35; Luc.
Athenodorus, Cl. IV. 5.
Atilius (C), J. LXXXIV. 2 (*see* note on text), Ter. V. An early Roman writer of comedies and tragedies.
Atia, A. IV. 1 (*bis*), XCIV. 4 (*ter*). Mother of Augustus.
Atius Balbus, M., A. IV. 1 (*bis*). Husband of Julia, sister of Julius Caesar.
Atratinus (Sempronius), Rh. II.
Atta, *see* Claudius.
Attalus, Gr. II. Attalus II, king of Pergamum from 159–138 B.C.

Aviola, *see* Acilius.

Avitus, *see* Octavius.

Axius, J. IX. 2.

Baiae, A. XVI. 1, LXIV. 2; T. VI. 3; Cal. XIX. 1; N. XXXI. 3; XXXIV. 2. A town at the northern end of the Bay of Naples, a favourite watering-place of the Romans.

Baianus sinus, Cal. XIX. 3; N. XXVII. 3.

Balbillus, N. XXXVI. 1.

Balbus, *see* Atius *and* Cornelius.

Baliaris insula, G. X. 1. One of two islands la the Mediterranean near the eastern coast of Spain; modern Majorca and Minorca.

Ballista, Verg. 17 (*bis*). A schoolmaster.

Barbatus, *see* Valerius.

Basilides, V. VII. 1 (*see* note).

Bassus, *see* Caesius.

Batavi, Cal. XLIII.

Bato, T. XX. A leader of the Pannonians.

Bauli, N. XXXIV. 2; *cf.* Cal. XIX. 1. A small town of Campania between Misenum and Baiae.

Beccus (-o), Vit. XVIII.

Beneventanus, -a, -um, *adj.* from Beneventum: Gr. IX.

Beneventum, A. XCVII. 3; N. XXXVI. 1, Gr. IX. A town in Samnium, modern Benevento.

Berenice, Tit. VII. 1, 2, Daughter of Agrippa I, king of Judaea.

Berytius, -a, -um, *adj.* from Berytus, a city of Phoenicia: Gr. XXIV.

Bessi, A. III. 2. A mountain tribe of the Thracians.

Betriacensis, -e, *adj.* from Betriacum; *victoria*, Vit. X. 1; *copias*, Vit. XV. 2; *acie*, V. V. 7.

Betriacum (also Bedriacum and Bebriacum), O. IX. 2. A village of orthern Italy between Verona and Cremona.

Bibaculus, *see* Furius.

Biberius Caldius Mero, T. XLII. 1. A name coined in jest after Tiberius Claudius Nero, from *bibo*, drink, *cal(i)dus*, hot, and *merum*, unmixed wine.

Bibulus, M., J. IX. 2, X. 1, XIX. 1 (*bis*), 2, XX. 2 (*ter*), XXI., XLIX. 2.

Bithynia, J. II. (*bis*), XXXIX. 1, XLIX. 1, 3. A district of northern Asia Minor on the Propontis (Sea of Marmora) and the Euxine (Black Sea).

Bithynicus, -a, -um, *adj.* from Bithynia: *fornicem*, J. XLIX. 1; *reginam*, J. XLIX. 2.

Bogudes (?), gen. Bogudis, J. LII. 1.

Bononia, A. XCVI. 1. Modern Bologna.

Bononiensea, A. XVII. 2; N. VII. 2. The people of Bononia.

Boter, Cl. XXVII. 2. A freedman of Claudius.

Bovillae, A. C, 2 (*bis*). An ancient town of Latium on the Appian Way, about twelve miles from Rome.

Breuci, T. IX. 2. A people of Pannonia.

Britanni, J. XXV. 2; Cal. XLIV. 2.

Britannia, J. XXV. 2, XLVII., LVIII. 1; Cal. XIX. 3; Cl. XVII. 1, XXI. 6; N. XVIII., XL. 2; V. IV. 1 (*bis*); Tit. IV. 1; D. X. 3.

Britannicus, -a, -um, *adj.* from Britannia: *clades*, N. XXXIX. 1; *expeditio*, G. VII. 1; Vit. II. 4; *triumphus*, Cl. XXVII.

Britannicus, Cl. XXVII. 1 (Germanicus), XXVII. 2, XLIII.; N. VI. 4, VII. 1, XXXIII 2 (*bis*), 3; Tit. II. 1 (*ter*). Son of the emperor Claudius.

Brixellum, O. IX. 1. A town of northern Italy on the Po between Parma and Mantua; modern Brescello.

Bructerus, T. XIX. One of the Breucteri, a Germanic people, occupying the territory of modern Westphalia.

Brundisium, J. XXXIV. 1, LVIII. 2; A. XVII. 3 (*bis*); Rh. I.; Verg. 35. A seaport of south-eastern Italy, the regular point of departure for Greece and the Orient; modern Brindisi.

Brutus, D., T. LXXX. 4, LXXXI. 4, LXXXIII. 2; A. X. 2, 3. One of the conspirators against Caesar's life.

Brutus, L., J. LXXX. 3 (*bis*). The first Roman consul.

Brutus, M., J. XLIX. 2, L. 2, LV. 1, LVI. 1, LXXX. 4, LXXXII. 2, LXXXV.; A IX., X. 1, XIII. 1, LXXXV. 1; T. LXI. 3; N. III. 1; G. III. 2; O. X. 1; Gr. XIII.; Rh. VI.; Hor. Leader with Cassius of the conspiracy against Caesar's life.

Bubula, ad capita, A. V. Probably the name of a street or quarter at the north-east corner of the Palatine Hill.

Bucolica, Gr. XXIII.; Verg. 9, 19, 25, 26, 43. The Bucolics of Vergil.

Burrus (Afranius), N. XXXV. 5. Prefect of the praetorian guard under Claudius and Nero.

Bursenus, Gr. XI.

Byzantium, V. VIII. 4. A city of Thrace on the Bosphorus, modern Constantinople.

Caecilius Atticus, Q., T. VII. 2; Gr. XIV., XVI. T. Pomponius Atticus, the friend of Cicero, after his adoption by Q. Caecilius, called Q. Caecilius Pomponianus Atticus.

Caecilius Epirota, Q., Gr. XVI. (*bis*).

Caeciliua Metellus, Q., J. XVI. 1, LV. 3. A tribune of the commons.

(Caecilius) Metellus, Q., A. LXXXIX. 2. Cons. in 143 B.C., and famous as an orator.

(Caecilius) Metellus Numidicus, Q., Gr. III.

Caecilius (Statius), Ter. II. (*bis*), V. The famous comic poet (219–166 B.C.).

Caecina, A., J. LXXV. 5.

Caecina, A., Tit. VI. 2. Consul in 69 A.D.

Caecus, *see* Claudius.

Caelius mons, T. XLVIII. 1 (*bis*); V. IX. 1. One of the hills of Rome, between the Aventine and the Esquiline.

Caelius, M., Rh. II.

Caenis, V. III. XXI.; D. XII. 3.

Caepio, *see* Fannius, Rustius, Servilius.

Caeruleus fons, Cl. XX. 1. A spring in the Sabine territory, one of the sources of the aqua Claudia.

Caesar, *see* Augustus, Claudius, Domitianus, Gaius, Iulius, Nero, Sulpicius Galba, Tiberius, Vespasianus, Vitellius. Caesares, Cal. LX.; Cl. I. 5, X. 4; G. I., XII. 2; Tit. VIII. 1; Caesarum *aedes*, G. I.; *domus*, G. 2; *imagines*, Cal. XIV. 3, XXIII. 1; *memoria ac templa*, Cal. LX.; *nemus*, A. XLIII. 1; *potestas*. T. XIV. 2; *progenies*, G. I.

Caesar Strabo (C. Iulius), J. LV. 2. Aedile in 90 B.C., an orator and writer of tragedies.

Caesar, C., A. XXVI. 2, XXIX. 4, LXIV. 1 (*bis*), LXV. 1 (*bis*), 2, LXVII. 2, XCIII.; T. XI. 5, XII. 2, XIII. 1, 2, XV. 2, XXIII.; N. V. 1. Grandson and adopted son of Augustus.

Capito, *see* Ateius *and* Fonteius.

Capitolinus, -a, -um, *adj.* from Capitolium: *area,* Cal. XXII. 4, XXXIV. 1; *certamen,* D. XIII. 1. *See also* Catulus, Iuppiter, Venus.

Capitolium, J. X. 1, XV., XXXVII. 2, LIV. 3, LXXIX. 2; A. XXIX. 1, LVII. 1, LIX., XCI. 2, XCIV. 8, 9 (*bis*); T. I. 2, II. 4, III. 2, XX.; Cal. VI. 1, XVI. 4, XXII. 4, XLVI., LX.; Cl. II. 2, X. 3, XXII., XXIV. 3; N. XII. 4, XIII. 2, XLVI. 2; Vit. XV. 3; V. VIII. 5, XVIII.; D. I. 2, V. (*bis*), XIII. 2, XV. 2, XXIII. 2. The temple of Jupiter Optimus Maximus, with Juno and Minerva, on the Capitoline hill. Also applied to the whole of that summit of the hill and to temples to the same triad of gods in other cities of Italy: Beneventi, Gr. IX.; Capuae, T. XL.; Cal. LVII. 2.

Cappadocia, Cal. I. 2; V. VIII. 4. A country in the eastern part of Asia Minor.

Cappadox, *adj.* to Cappadocia: T. XXXVII.4.

Capreae, A. LXXII. 3, XCII. 2, XCVIII. 1, 3, 4; T. XL., LX., LXII. 2, LXXIII. 1, LXXIV; Cal. X. 1, Vit. III. 2; cf. T. XLV. An island near Naples, modern Capri.

Caprensis, -e, *adj.* from Capreae: *secessus,* T. XLIII. 1.

Capricornus, A. XCIV. 12. One of the signs of the Zodiac.

Caprineus, T. XLIII. 2.

Capua, J. LXXXI. 1 (*bis*); T. XL.; Cal. LVII. 2. An ancient city of Campania.

Capys, J. LXXXI. 1 (*bis*). Founder and king of Capua.

Carchedoniaca, Cl. XLII. 2 (*bis*). A History of Carthage, by the emperor Claudius, from Καρχηδών, the Greek name of the city.

Carinae, T. XV. 1 (*see* note); Gr. XV.

Carmelus, V. V. 6. The god of Mount Carmel in Phoenicia.

Carnulus, T. LXI. 5 (*bis*).

Carthago, Ter. I. (*bis*).

Carthago Nova, G. IX. 2. A seaport of south-eastern Spain; modern Carthagena.

Carthaginiensis, -e, *adj.* fcom Carthago: *see* Sulpicius.

Carvilius Pictor, Verg. 44.

Cascae, J. LXXXII. 1, 2. Two brothers, members of the conspiracy against Julius Caesar.

Caspiae Portae, N. XIX. 2. A pass through the range of mountains south-east of the Caspian Sea.

Cassiope, N. XXII. 3. A town of Corcyra (modern Corfu).

Cassius, N. XXII. 3. An epithet applied to Jupiter as the tutelary divinity of Cassiope.

Cassius, Cal. LVII. 1.

Cassius, C., J. LXXX. 4, LXXXV.; A. IX., x. 1; T. LXI. 3; N. III. 1, XXXVII. 1; G. III. 2; O. X. 1; Gr. XIII. Leader with M. Brutus of the conspiracy against Julius Caesar.

Cassius, L., J. LXIII.; Gr. XIII.

Cassius Chaerea, Cal. LVI. 2, LVII. 3, LVIII. 2 (*bis*).

Cassius Longinus, L., Cal. XXIV. 1, LVII. 3. Consul in 30 A.D.

Cassius Longinus, N. XXXVII. 1.

Cassius Parmensis, A. IV. 2. A poet, who was one of the murderers of Julius Caesar; cf. Hor. *Epist.* 1. 4. 3.

Cassius Patavinus, A. LI. 1.

Cassius Scaeva, J. LXVIII. 4 (*bis*). One of Caesar's centurions.

Cassius Severus, A. LVI. 3; Cal. XVI. 1; Vit. II. 1; Gr. XXII. A distinguished orator, noted for the bitterness of his style; *cf.* Plin. *N.H.* 7. 55.

Castor, J. X. 1; T. XX; Cal. XXII. 2; O. IX. 2 (ad Castoris).

Castricius, A. LVI. 4.

Catalepton, Verg. 17.

Catilina (L. Sergius), J. XIV. 1, XVII. 1 (*ter*); A. III. 1, XCIV. 5.

Cato (M. Porcius Censorinus), A. LXXXVI. 3; Gr. XV. The celebrated orator, historian and statesman (234–149 B.C.).

Cato, M. (Porcius Uticensis), J. XIV. 2, XIX. 1, XX. 4, XXX. 3, LIII. 1; A. XIII. 2, LXXXV. 1, LXXXVII. 1. The grandson of Cato the Censor (95–46 B.C.). A type of austere virtue.

Cato, *see* Valerius.

Catulinus, -a, -um, *adj.* from Catulus, referring to Q. (Lutatius) Catulus Capitolinus; Gr. XVII.

Catullus, *see* Valerius.

Catulus Capitolinus, Q., J. XV.; A. XCIV. 8 (*bis*); G. II., III. 4; Gr. III. A prominent leader of the aristocratic party, who restored the Capitol after its destruction in 83 B.C.

Cauchi (also Chauci), Cl. XXIV. 3. A people of north-eastern Germany near the mouth of the Visurgis (Weser).

Cauchius, *see* Gabinius Secundus.

Caudex, *see* Claudius.

Cebenna mons, J. XXV. 1. A mountain range in southern Gaul, the modern Cervennes.

Cebes, Verg. 9 (*bis*).

Celadus, A. LXVII. 1.

Censorinus, *see* Marcius.

centumviralis, -e, *adj.* from centumviri: *hasta,* A. XXXVI. (*see* note); *lis,* Rh. VI.

centumviri, D. VIII. 1. Members of the Court of the Hundred Judges; *see* note on A. XXXVI.

Ceraunii montes, A. XVII. 3. A mountain range in north-eastern Epirus, also called Acroceraunia, ending in a promontory of the same name, the "Thunder Cape."

Cercei, A. XVI. 4; T. LXXII. 2. A promontory and town on the coast of Latium.

Cerealis, *see* Civica.

Ceres, A. XCIII; N. XII. 4. The Italian goddess identified with the Greek Demeter, goddess of agriculture; in the two cases cited used of Demeter herself.

Cerrinius Gallus, A. LIII. 3.

Cerylus, V. XXIII. 1.

Cestius Gallus, T. XLII. 2.

Chaerea, *see* Cassius.

Chaldaei, V. XIV. 4; D. XIV. 1. An Assyrian people, noted tor their knowledge of astronomy and astrology; hence a designation of astrologers in general.

Chares, *see* Oppius.

Charicles, T. LXXII. 3. A physician.

Chatti, D. VI. 1 (*bis*). A people of western Germany, near the Rhine.

Chattus, -a, -um, *adj.* to Chatti: *mulier.* Vit. XIV. 5.

Chii, T. VIII. The people of Chios, an island in the Aegean Sea, on the coast of Ionia.

Chrestus, Cl. XXV. 4; *see* note.

Christiani, N. XVI. 2.

Chrysippus, Pers. A celebrated Stoic philosopher, born at Soli in Cilicia in 280 B.C.

Clitumnus, Cal. XLIII. A river of southern Umbria, celebrated for the clearness of its water, and described by Pliny, *Epist.* 8. 8. Also a grove at its source, sacred to Juppiter Clitumnus.
Clodianus, D. XVII. 2.
Clodius (Pulcher), P., J. VI. 2, XX. 4, XXVI. 1, LXXIV. 2; A. LXII. 1; T. II. 4. The notorious tribune and opponent of Cicero.
Clodius, Sex., Rh. V. (*bis*).
Clodius Licinus, Gr. XX.
Clodius Macer, G. XI.
Clodius Pollio, D. I. 1.
Clodius, Servius, Gr. III. (*bis*). Clodius, -a, -um, *adj.* to Clodius: *lex*, D. IX. 3.
Clunia, G. IX. 2. A city of northern Spain, in the country of the Arevaci.
Cluvius Rufus, N. XXI. 2.
Cocceianus, *see* Salvius.
Codeta minor, J. XXXIX. 4. A marshy place on the right bank of the Tiber, opposite the Campus Martius.
Colosseros (from Κολοσσος and ὠΕρως), Cal. XXXV. 2.
Colossus, N. XXXI. 1; a colossal statue of Nero in the vestibule of the Golden House. *Cf.* V. XVIII.
Columbinus, -a, -um, *adj.* from Columbus, a gladiator: *venenum*, Cal. LV. 2.
Columbus, Cal. LV. 2.
Comata, *see* Gallia.
Commagene, V. VIII. 4. A district in the northern part of Syria, bordering on the Euphrates.
Commagenus, -a, -um, *adj.* from Commagene: Cal. XVI. 3.
Compitales Lares, Aug. XXXI. 4. Tutelary gods, having shrines at the cross-roads (*compita*).
Compitalia, Ter. V. A play of Afranius.
Compitalicii ludi, Aug. XXXI. 4. Games celebrated at the Compitalia, the festival of the Compitales Lares, in the early part of January.
Comum, *see* Novum Comum.
Concordia, T. XX.; Vit. XV. 4. A Roman goddess with a temple at the western end of the Forum, at the foot of the Capitoline hill. A title given to Vitellius, Vit. XV. 4 (*bis*).
Confluentes, Cal. VIII. 1. A town at the confluence of the Moselle and the Rhine, modern Coblentz.
Cordubensis, -e, *adj.* from Corduba, a city of southern Spain, modern Cordova: A. LI. 2; Luc.
Cordus, *see* Cremutius.
Corfinium, J. XXXIV. 1; N. II. 2. A city of the Paeligni in central Italy, modern Pelino.
Corinthiarius, A. LXX. 2; *see* note.
Corinthius, -a, -um, *adj.* from Corinthus: *vasa*, A. LXX. 2 (*bis*); T. XXXIV. 1. Vessels made of Corinthian bronze and highly prized.
Corinthus, G., III. 4.
Cornelia, J. I. 1, VI. 1, 2. First wife of Julius Caesar.
Cornelia, D. VIII. 4. A chief Vestal.
Cornelii, J. LIX.
Cornelius, A. XXVI. 1; *see also* Scipio *and* Sulla.
Cornelius, -a, -um, *adj.* to Cornelius: *legibus*, J. XI.; *lege*, A. XXXIII. 2.
Cornelius Alexander, surnamed Polyhistor and Historia, Gr. XX.
Cornelius Balbus, J. LXXVIII. 1, LXXXI. 2; A. XXIX. 5.
(Cornelius) Cinna (L.), J. I. 1. Consul with Marius.
(Cornelius) Cinna, L., J. V. Son of the preceding.

Cynicus, *see* Demetrius *and* Isidorus.
Cynobellinus, Cal. XLIV. 2. A king of the Britons.
Cyrenae, V. II. 3. A Greek city on the northern coast of Africa, between Carthage and Alexandria.
Cyrus, J. LXXXVII. Cyrus the Great, founder of the Persian Empire; the subject of Xenophon's *Cyropaedeia.*
Cyziceni, Tib. XXXVII. 3. The people of Cyzicus, a city of north-western Asia Minor.

Daci, J. XLIV. 3; A. VIII. 2, XXI. 1; T. XII.; D. VI. 1 (*bis*). The people of Dacia, on the northern bank of the Danube.
Dalmatae (also Delmatae), T. IX. 2. The people of Dalmatia.
Dalmatia (also Delmatia), A. XXI. 1; Cl. XIII. 2; O. IX. 3. A country on the eastern shore of the Adriatic.
Damoetas, Verg. 43.
Danuvius, T. XVI. 2. The Danube.
Daphnis, Verg. 14; *see also* Lutatius.
Dareus,Cal. XIX. 2. A Parthian boy.
Datus, N. XXXIX. 3. An actor.
December mensis, J. XL. 2, A. XXXII. 3, LXXI. 1; Cal. VI. 2; Hor. (*bis*); Pers. (*bis*).
Delmatia, *see* Dalmatia.
Delmaticus, -a, -um, *adj.* from Delmatia (Dalmatia): *bellum,* A. XX.; *triumphus,* A. XXII.
Delphi, N. XL. 3. The chief city of Phocis in Greece, famous for its oracle.
Demetrius Cynicus, V. XIII.
Demochares, A. XVI. 3.
denarius, A. LVII. 2, LXI. 4, LXVII. 2; T. XLVIII. 2; Cal. XLVI. A Roman coin containing ten, and afterwards eighteen, asses; equal to about 8*d.* or 16 cents.
Dertosa, G. X. 4. A town of Spain, near the mouth of the Iberus (Ebro).
Dialis, -e, *adj.* to Juppiter (cf. Diespiter): *flamen,* J. I. 1, the special priest of Jupiter; *flamonium,* A. XXXI. 4; *sacerdote,* D. IV. 4.
Diana, A. XXIX. 5. The Roman goddess identified with the Greek Artemis.
Diana, Gr. XI. (*bis*). A poem of Valerius Cato.
Dictynna, Gr. XI; SEE note.
Dido, N. XXXI. The well-known queen of Carthage.
Didymeum, Cal. XXI. A sanctuary of Apollo Didymaeus at Didyma, a city of Ionia near Miletus.
Diodorus, V. XIX. 1. A lyre-player.
Diogenes, T. XXXII. 2. A grammarian.
Diomedes, A. LXVII. 1. A steward of Augustus.
Dionysius, A. LXXXIX. 1. Son of Areus, a philosopher.
Dionysius Scytobrachion, Gr. VII. "Dionysius of the leathern arm," an hiatorian of Mytilene.
Dioscurides, A. L.
Dirae, Verg. 17.
Diribitorium, Cl. XVIII. 1 (*see* note).
Dis, O. VIII. 3. God of the Under World, another name for Pluto.
Dius Fidius, T. XXI. 6. God of Faith, at first identified with Juppiter and later with the Sabine deity Semo Sancus.
Dolabella, *see* Cornelius.
Domitia Lepida: *Lepida,* N. V. 2, VI. 3, VII. 1; *Domitia,* Pass. Aunt of the emperor Nero.

Domitia Longina, T. X. 2; D. I. 3, III. 1 (*Augusta*); XXII. Wife of the emperor Domitian.
Domitianus, the emperor: *Domitianus*, V. I. 1, III.; D. I. 1 (*bis*), XIII. 2, XXIII. 2; *Caesar*, D. I. 3, III. 1, XII. 2; *Germanicus*, D. XIII. 3; *Divus*, D. XXIII. 1.
Domitianus, D. XV. 1. Son of Flavius Clemens.
Domitianus mensis, D. XIII. 3.
Domitii, N. I. 2, L.
Domitilla, *see* Flavia.
Domitius (Cn.), N. II. 1. Grandfather of Nero's grandfather.
Domitius (Cn., *mss.* T.), A. XVII. 2; cf. N. III. Great-grandfather of the emperor Nero.
Domitius (L.), J. XXIII. 1, XXIV. 1 (*bis*); cf. N. II. 2. Father of Nero's great-grandfather.
Domitius, N. IV. Grandfather of the emperor Nero.
Domitius Ahenobarbus, L., N. I. 1. The first to bear the surname.
Domitius Ahenobarbus (Cn.), N. VI. 1, IX., XXVIII.; G. V. 1, VI. 1 (*mss.* L.); O. II. 1; Vit. II. 2; cf. N. V. Father of the emperor Nero.
Domitius Ahenobarbus, Cn., Rh. I.; cf. N. II. 1.
Domitius Marsus, Gr. IX., XVI; cf. Tibull. A poet of the Augustan Age.
Domitius, -a, -um, *adj.* to Domitius: *gens*, N. I .1.
Domus publica, J. XLVI. The official residence of the pontifex maximus, near the temple of Vesta in the Forum.
Dorice, *adv.* from Doricus, "Doric," T. LVI.
Doris, -idis, *adj. sc. dialectus*, T. LVI. The Doric dialect.
Doryphoros, N. XXIX. A freedman.
Drausus, T. III. 2.
Druidae, Cl. XXV. 5. The Druids, a Gallic priesthood, with cruel and barbarous rites, abolished by Claudius.
Drusi, *see* Livii.
Drusilla, *see* Julia, Livia.
Drusinus, -a, -um, *adj.* from Drusus *fossae*, Cl. I. 2 (*see* note).
Drusus, *see* Claudius.
Drusus, T. III. 2. The first of the name.
DrusuS, T. VII. 1. Grandfather of Tiberius.
Drusus, T. LIV. 1, 2, LXV. 2; Cal. VII., XII. 1; Cl. IX. 1; O. I. 3. Son of Germanicus Caesar.
Drusus, Cl. XXVII. 1 (*bis*). Son of the emperor Claudius.
Drusus (Decimus and Nero; *see* Cl. I. 1): *Drusus*, A. XCIX. 1; T. VII. 3, L. 1, LXXVI.; Cal. I. 1; Cl. I. 1, 2, XI. 3, XLVI.; Hor.; *Nero*, T. IV. 3; *Germanicus*, Cl. I. 3. Brother of Tiberius.
Drusus, C., A. XCIV. 6.
Drusus Caesar, A. C. 3, CI. 2; T. VII. 2, XV. 1, XXIII., XXV. 3, XXXIX., LII. 1 (*bis*), LIV. 1, LV., LXII. 1; Vit. III. 2. Son of the emperor Tiberius.
Dyrrachium, J. XXXVI., LVIII. 2, LXVIII. 3. A town in the southern part of Illyricum, nearly opposite Brundisium.
Dyrrhacinus, -a, -um, *adj.* from Dyrrachium: *munitione*, J, LXVIII. 2.

Eficius Calvinus, Gr. III.
Egloge, N. L. A nurse of Nero.
Eglogus, Q. (?), Vit. I. 2.
Egnatius, M., A. XIX. 1.

Electra, J. LXXXIV. 2 (*see* note on text). A tragedy of Sophocles, rendered into Latin by Atilius.
Elenchi, Gr. VIII.; *see* note.
Elephantis T. XLIII. 2. A Greek writer on amatory subjects, of uncertain date; cf. Mart. 12 .43 .4.
Eleusinius, -a, -um, *adj.* from Eleusis, the city of Attica, famous for the Eleusinian mysteries: *sacra,* Cl. XXV. 5; N. XXXIV. 4; cf. A. XCIII.
Elogus, Q., *see* Eglogus.
Elysius, -a, -um, *adj.* from Elysium: *compos,* Tibull.
Ennia Naevia, Cal. XII. 2, XXVI. 1.
Ennius, Q., A. VII. 2; cf. T. XXI. 5; Gr. I. (*bis*), II. (*bis*), VIII. The "Father of Roman poetry," who lived from 239 to 169 B.C.
Ennius, Gr. I. The "younger Ennius," a grammarian who flourished from 140 to 100 B.C.
Epaphroditus, N. XLIX. 3; D. XIV. 4.
Epicadius, *see* Asinius *and* Cornelius.
Epicureus, -a, -um, *adj.* from Epicurus, the famous philosopher: *cuiusdam,* Gr. VI.; *sectae,* Gr. VIII.
Epidius, M., Rh. IV. (*ter*).
Epidius Marullus, J. LXXIX. 1, LXXX. 3. A tribune of the commons.
Epidius, of Nuceria, Rh. IV.
Epigrammata, Verg. 17.
Epirota, Gr. XVI. (*bis*). Of Epirus, a surname of Q. Caecilius.
Eratosthenes, Gr. X. A famous scholar and writer, born at Cyrene in 276 B.C. A librarian of the great Library at Alexandria.
Eros, Verg. 34; *see also* Staberius.
Erycina, Cl. XXV. 5. A surname of Venus, from her shrine at Mt. Eryx in the western part of Sicily.
Esius, *see* Aesius.
Esquiliae, T. XV. 1; N. XXXI. 1; Hor.; Verg. 13. The largest of the hills of Rome, the Esquiline, in the western part of the city. Plural because it consisted of several different parts.
Esquilinus campus, Cl. XXV. 3; *see* note.
essedarius, *see* gladiator.
Etruria, J. XXXIV. 1; O. I. 1; Pers.
Etruscus, -a, -um, *adj.* to Etruria: *lingua,* A. XCVII. 2.
Eulogius, Q., *see* Eglogus.
Eunoe, J. LII. 1. A Moorish queen.
Eunuchus, Ter. II. "The Eunuch," one of the plays of Terence.
Euphorion, T. LXX. 2. A Greek elegiac poet of the Alexandrine school, noted for his ornate and obscure style. He was born at Chalcis in 276 B.C.
Euphrates, Cal. XIV. 3. The well-known river of Syria.
Euripides, J. XXX. 5; cf. A. XXV. 4. The Athenian tragic poet.
Eutychus, Cal. LV. 2. A charioteer.
Eutychus, A. XCVI. 2. A donkey-driver (*see* note).

FABIANUS, -a, -um, *adj.* from Fabia (tribus): *tribules,* A. XL. 2.
Fabius Africanus, Cl. II. 1. Consul in 10 A.D.
Fabius Labeo, Q., Ter. IV.
(Fabius) Maximus, Q., J. LXXX. 2.
Fabius Persicus, Pers.
Falacrina, V. II. 1. A village in the Sabine country north-east of Rome, near Reate.
Fannius Caepio, A. XIX. 1; T. VIII.
Fannius Strabo, C., Rh. I. Consul in 161 B.C.

Fucinus lacus, J. XLIV. 3; Cl. xx. 1, 2, XXI. 6, XXXII. A lake in the country of the Marsi, east of Rome, drained by Claudius.

Fulvia, A. XVII. 5, LXII. 1 (*bis*); Rh. V. Wife of Mark Antony.

Fulvia Sisennia, Pers.

Fulvius Nobilior, M., Ter. V. Consul in 159 B.C.

Fundanus, -a, -um, *adj.* from Fundi, T. V.; *decurione,* Cal. XXIII. 2; *see also* Galeria.

Fundi, T. V.; G. IV. 1, VIII. 1. A town of Latium on the Appian Way.

Furiae, N. XXXIV. 4. The Furies, the Greek Eumenides.

Furius, Ter., I. V.

Furius Bibaculus, Gr. IV., IX., XI. A Roman poet born 103 B.C., parodied by Horace, *Serm.* 2. 5. 39 ff.

(Furius) Camillus, T. III. 2, Cl. XXVI. 1. Dictator in 396 B.C.

(Furius) Camillus Arruntius, O. II. 1. Consul in 32 A.D.

Furius Camillus Scribonianus, Cl. XIII. 2, XXXV. 2, O. I. 2.

Furius Leptinus, J. XXXIX. 1.

Furnilla, *see* Marcia.

Fuscus, *see* Cornelius.

Fusius, Pers.

Gabinius, A., J. L. 1.

Gabinius Secundus Cauchius (P.), Cl. XXIV. 3.

Gadareus, -a, -um, *adj.* from Gadara, a town of Palestine, T. LVII. 1.

Gades, J. VII. 1. A city of southwestern Spain, modern Cadiz.

Gaetuli, Ter. I. A people of north-eastern Africa.

Gaetulicus, *see* Lentulus.

Gaianus, -a, -um, *adj.* from Gaius, referring to the emperor: *nex,* Tit. I.

Gaius (Caligula), the emperor: *Caligula,* Cal. IX.; (*Gaius,* T. LIV. 1, LXII. 3, LXXIII. 2, LXXV. 2, LXXVI; Cal. VIII. 3, 4, 5, XV. 3, XIX. 3, XXXVIII. 4, LVI. 2, LVIII. 2, LX.; Cl. VII., IX. 1, X. 1, XI. 1, 3, XX. 1, XXXVIII. 3; N. VI. 3, XXX. 1; G. VI. 3, VII. 1; O. VI. 1; Vit. IV., XVII. 2; V. II. 3; *C. Caesar,* Cal. I. 1, VII., VIII. 1, 2, XV. 3; Cl. XXVI. 3; N. VI. 2, VII. 1; G. VI. 2; Vit. II. 5; V. V. 3; Pass; *Caesar,* Cal. XXIX. 1, XXXIX. 2, XLI. 1, XLV. 3; Cl. IX. 1; *optimus maximus Caesar,* Cal. XXII. 1; *Jupiter Latiaris,* Cal. XXII. 2.

Galba, *see* Sulpicius.

Galeria Fundana, Vit. VI.

Galli, J. LXXVI. 3, LXXX. 2 (*bis*); Cal. XXIX. 2; Cl. XXV. 5; N. XL. 1, XLV. 2; G. III. 1, XVI. 2; sing. (*tributario*), A. XL. 3.

Gallia, J. XXV. 1, 2, LI., LIV.; A. XXI. 1; T. III. 2, IV. 1, IX. 2; Cal. VIII. 3, XX., XXXIX. 1; G. III. 2, VI. 3; Vit. X. 1; D. II. 1; Gr. VII., X.; *Cisalpina,* J. XXII. 1, XXIX. 2; *Citerior,* J. XXX. 1, LVI. 5; *Comata,* Transalpine Gaul, where the natives wore their hair long. J. XXII. 1; T. IX. 1; *Togata,* Gr. III., the Roman Province, where the toga was worn; *Transalpina,* J. XXIX. 2.

Galliae, J. XXII. 1, XXIV. 3, XXVIII. 1, XLIX. 4; A. LXXIX. 1; T. XLI., XLIX. 2; Cal. XLVII.; Cl. I. 3; N. XL. 4, XLIII. 1, 2; G. IX. 2, XII. 1.

Gallicanus, -a, -um, *adj.* from Gallia: *hominis,* Vit. XVIII.; *homines,* N. XLIII. 1.

Gallicus, -a, -um, *adj.* from Gallia: *belium,* J. LVI. 1 (*bis*); *bella,* J. LXIX.; N. XXXVIII. 2; *exercitus,* N. II. 2; *habitus,* J. LVIII. 1; *provincia,* Cl. XXIV. 2; *triumphus* J. XXXVII. 1, 2, XLIX. 4, LI.; *vocabulum,* J. XXIV. 2.

Gallinas, ad., G. I. (*see* note).

Gallius, M., T. VI. 3 (*bis*).

Gallius, Q., A. XXVII. 4.

Gallograecia, Cal. XXIX. 2.

Gallus, -a, -um, *adj.* to Galli: *miles,* N. XLI. 2.

Gallus, Gr. XI.; *see* also Afinius, Asinius, Cerrinius, Cestius, Cornelius, Plotius, Roscius, Sulpiciua.

Gallus, A. LXVIII. A priest of the Magna Mater (Cybele).

Gamala, Tit. IV. 3. A city of Judaea.

Gebenna, *see* Cebenna.

Gelotiana domus, Cal. XVIII. 3. A house on the south-western slope of the Palatine Hill, opposite the Circus Maximus.

Geminus, *see* Tanusius.

Gemoniae scalae, T. LIII. 2, LXI. 4, LXXV. 1, 2; Vit. XVII. 2. A flight of steps leading from the Forum to the Capitoline Hill, probably between the temple of Concord and the Carcer.

Genetrix, *see* Venus.

Genius: *Augusti,* A. LX. (*see* note); *Gai,* Cal. XXVII. 3.

Georgica, Verg. 20, 22, 25, 27, 43. The Georgics of Vergil.

Gergovia, J. XXV. 2. The principal town of the Arverni, in the eastern part ot Aquitania.

Germani, J. XXV. 2 (*bis*); A. XXI. 1, XLIX. 1; T. XVII. 1, XLI.; Cal. XLV. 1, LV. 2, LVIII. 3; Cl. I. 4, XXV. 4; N. XXXIV. 1; G. XII. 2; Plin.; *sing.* T. XXXVII, 4.

Germania, J. LVIII. 1; A. XXIII. 1; T. VII. 3, XVI. 1, XVII. 1, XVIII. 1, XX., XXV. 1; Cal. I. 1, IV., XIX. 3, LI. 3; Cl. IX. 1; G. VIII. 1, XI.; V. IV. 1; Tit. IV. 1; D. XVI. 1; *Inferior,* Vit. VIII. 1; *Superior,* G. XVI. 2; D. VI. 2 (cf. G. VI. 2; Vit. VIII. 2).

Germaniae, D. II. 1.

Germaniciani, T. XXV. 2; G. XX. 1. The soldiers of the army in Germany.

Germanicianus, -a, -um, *adj.* from Germania: *exercitus,* O. VIII. 1; V. VI. 2.

Germanicus, -a, -um, *adj.* from Germania: *belium,* T. IX. 1, 2; Cl. I. 2; N. 4, 1; *bella,* A. XX.; *expeditio,* Cal. XLIII.; gens, Cl. XXIV. 3; *legiones,* V. VI. 4; *res,* Vit. IX.; *sermo,* Cal. XLVII.; VICTORIA, V. II. 3.

Germanicus Caesar, A. XXXIV. 2, LXIV. 1, CI. 2; T. XV. 2, XXV. 2, 3, XXXIX., LII. 1, 2, 3, LIV. I, LV. LXI. 1, LXXVI.; Cal. I. 1, II., III. 1, VI., 1, VIII. 2, 3, 4 (*bis*), XIII., XLVIII.; Cl. I. 6, VII., XXVI. 3, XXIX. 1; N. V. 2; O. I. 3; Vit. II. 3. Son of Drusus and brother of Claudius.

Germanicus, *see* Britannicus, Claudius, Domitianus, Drusus, Vitellius.

Germanicus mensis, Cal. XV. 2; D. XIII. 3.

Germanus, *see* Germani.

Geryonis oraculum, T. XIV. 3.

Gesoriacum, Cl. XVII. 2. A town of Belgic Gaul on the Fretum Gallicum (English Channel), also called Bononia; modern Boulogne-sur-mer.

Getae, A. LXIII. 2. A Thracian people on the southern bank of the Danube, which separated them from the Dacians.

gigantum ossa, A. LXXII. 3. Bones of huge sea-monsters, collected by Augustus.

Glabrio, *see* Acilius.

gladiator, a professional fighter, trained for contests in the amphitheatre and elsewhere. The gladiatores had special names according to their armour and equipment; for full details see Friedlander, *Roman Life and Manners*, Eng. trans., iv. pp. 171 ff. The following are mentioned by Suetonius:

essedarii, who fought from Gallic chariots (*essedae*): Cal. XXXV. 3; Cl. XXI. 5.

meridiani, see note on Claud. XXXIV. 2.

murmillones, who fought with the *Thraeces* and with the *retiarii.* They derived their name from a kind of fish (μορμύρος or μορμύλος), an image of which they wore as a device on their helmets. Little or nothing is known about their armour: Cal. XXXII. 2, LV. 2; N. XXX. 2; D. X. 1.

oplomachi, heavy armed gladiators; according to Lipsius, a later name for the Samnites, derived from their large shield (ὅπλον): Cal. XXXV. 2.

paegniarii, Cal. XXVI. 5 (*see* note)

retiarii, "net-fighters," who were lightly armed and fought with uncovered heads. They carried a net, in which they tried to entangle their opponents, and a trident and dagger, with which they slew them, if successful: Cal. XXX. 3; Cl. XXXIV. 1.

secutores, the usual opponents of. the *retiarii.* They were armed with a sword, a shield, one greave, and a visored helmet: Cal. XXX. 3.

Thraeces, heavily armed gladiators, but distinguished from the *oplomachi* by the small Thracian buckler (*parma*) in place of the large shield. They wore greaves on both legs, a visored helmet, and a sleeve on the right arm, and carried a short curved or bent sword (*sica*). They fought with one another, with the *oplomachi,* and with the *murmillones:* Cal. XXXV. 2, LIV. 1, LV. 2; Tit. VIII. 2; D. X. 1.

Glycias, T. II. 2.

Glyco, A. XI. A physician.

Gnipho, *see* Antonius.

Gracchi, T. III. 2. The celebrated tribunes, Tiberius and Gaius Gracchus.

Graecanicus, -a, -um, *adj.* from Graecia: *toga,* D. IV. 4.

Graece, *adv.* from Graecus: T. LXXI.; Cal. XXXIX. 1, XLII. 1; N. VII. 2, XXXIX. 2; Tit. III. 2; D. IV. 4, XIII. 2; Gr. VII.; Rh. I.

Graecia, J. XXVIII. 1; T. XLIX. 2; Cal. XXII. 2; Cl. XVI. 2 (*provincia*); N. XXX. 1, XXVIII. 2, XXXIV. 4, LIII.; Ter. I., III., V.; Verg. 35.

Graeci, J. LII. 2, LXVIII. 4; A. XCVIII. 3; T. XLVI.; Cal. XXIX. 2; N. XXII. 3; Gr. I., IV. (*bis*); Rh. I. (*bis*); Ter. IV., V.; *semigraeci,* Gr. IV.

Graeculi, T. XI. 1, LVI.; *sing.,* Cl. XV. 4. Diminutive of Graecus, with a contemptuous or patronizing force.

Graecus, -a, -um, *adj.* to Graecia: *appellatione,* Rh. I.; *bibliotheca,* J. XLIV. 2; A. XXIX. 3, *certamen,* A. XLV. 2 (*see*

Hispaniae, J. XXVIII. 1; A VIII. 1, 2; T. XLIX. 2; N. XLII. 1; G. XII. 1. The Spanish provinces.

Hispanicus, -a, -um, *adj.* from Hispania: *verbo,* A. LXXXII. 2; *freto,* Vit. XIII. 2.

Hispaniensis, -e, *adj.* from Hispania: *triumphum,* J. XXXVII. 1; *victoriam,* J. XXXVIII. 2; *belli,* J. LVI. 1; *exercitu,* V. VI. 2.

Hispanus, -a, -um, *adj.* to Hispania, Gr. XX.

Historia, *see* Cornelius Alexander.

Histria, D. XII. 2. A country at the north-eastern end of the Adriatic Sea, south of Tergeste (Trieste).

Homericus, -a, -um, *adj.* from Homerus: *versus,* T. XXI. 6; Cl. XLII. 1; cf. A. LXV. 4; Cal. XXII. 1, 4; Cl. XLII. 1; N. XLIX. 3; G. XX. 2; V. XXIII. 1; D. XII. 3, XVIII. 2.

Homerius, -a, -um, *adj.* from Homerus: *scyphi,* N. XLVII. 1.

Homerus, Cal. XXXIV. 2; N. XLVII. 1; Verg. 21, 43, 46 (*bis*).

Horatius Flaccus, Q., Gr. IX.; Hor. (*quater*).

Hortalus, T. XLII. Grandson of Q. Hortensius.

Hortensianus, -a, -um, *adj.* from Hortensius: *aedes,* A. LXXII. 1.

Hortensius, Q., T. XLVII. The celebrated orator of the time of Cicero.

Hortulorum (collis), N. L. (*see* note).

Hyginus, *see* Julius.

Hylas, A. XLV. 4. An actor of pantomimes.

Hyle, Gr. X. (*see* note).

Iaccus, *see* Pescennius.

Ianiculum, Vit. I. 3. A long hill east of Rome across the Tiber; included in the modern city, but outside the Aurelian Wall.

Ianuariae Kalendae, J. XL. 2.

Ianus: *geminus,* N. XIII. 2; *Quirinus,* A. XXII.; *marmoreus,* A. XXXI. 5; *plur.* D. XIII. 2. An old Italic deity, represented with two faces fronting in opposite directions, also used for his temple, which was open in time of war and closed in time of peace; and in general for an arch.

Icarus, N. XII. 2. Son of Daedalus, with whom he attempted to fly from Crete across the Aegean Sea. Since he flew too high, the sun melted the wax with which his wings were held together. He fell into that part of the Aegean which was called from him the Icarian Sea, and was drowned.

Icelus Marcianus, N. XLIX. 4; G. XIV. 2, XXII. A freedman of the emperor Galba.

Idaeus, -a, -um, *adj.* from Ida, a mountain near Troy; *Mater deum,* T. II. 3.

Idus, the fifteenth of March, May, July, and October, and the thirteenth of the other months; J. LXXX. 4, LXXXI. 2, LXXXIII.; A. XV., XXXV. 3; Cal. LVII. 2; V. VI. 3; Verg. 2; Hor.

Ilerda, J. LXXV. 2, a town of northeastern Spain.

Ilias, Verg. 30.

Ilienses, T. LII. 2; Cl. XXV. 3 (*bis*); N. VII. 2. The people of Ilium.

Ilium, J. LXXIX. 3; N. XXXVIII. 2. Another name for Troy.

Illyricum, J. XXII. 1, XXIX. 2, XXXVI. (*bis*); A. XXI. 1, XXV. 2, XCVII. 3; T. XIV. 3, XVI. 1, 2, XVII. 1, XXI. 1, XXV. 1; O. 1, 2. A country on

the eastern shore of the Adriatic Sea, opposite Italy.
Illyricus, -a, -um, *adj.* to Illyricum: *exercitus,* A. XIX. 2.
Imperator, as a praenomen, J. LXXVI. 1; T. XXVI. 2, Cl. XII. 1.
Inalpinus, -a, -um, *adj.* from *in, Alpes: gentes,* A. XXI. 1.
Incendium, N. XI. 2. "The Fire," a *fabula togata,* or Roman play, of Afranius.
Incitatus, Cal. LV. 3. The name of a horse; *see* note.
Indi, A. XXI. 3. The people of India.
Indignatio, Gr. XI. A work of Valerius Cato.
Ineptiae, Gr. XXI. Title of a book of Gaius Melissus.
Inferum mare, A. XLIX. 1. "The Lower Sea," a term applied to the Tyrrhenian (Tuscan) Sea; *cf.* Superum mare.
Invictus, T. XVII. 2. A surname which the senate proposed to confer on Tiberius.
Ioci, Gr. XXI. The title of a book of Gaius Melissus.
Ionis villa, T. LXV. 2. The name of a villa at Capreae (Capri).
Iosephus, V. V. 6.
Isauricus, *see* Servilius.
Isiacus, D. I. 2. A priest of Isis.
Isidorus, N. XXXIX. 3. A cynic philosopher.
Isis, O. XII. 1. An Egyptian deity, whose worship was popular at Rome in the days of the Empire.
Isthmia (*sc. certamina*), N. XXIV. 2. The Isthmian games, celebrated every five years at Corinth.
Isthmus, J. XLIV. 3; Cat. XXI.; N. XIX. 2, XXXVII. 3. The Isthmus of Corinth.
Italia, J. XXVIII. 1, XXXVIII. 2, XLII. 1, LIV. 2, LXXV. 4, LXXIX. 3, LXXXI. 1; A. XIII. 3, XVII. 2, 3, XLV. 4, XLVI., LIX.; T. II. 2, VIII., XVI. 2, XXXVII. 1; Cal. XVI. 3; Cl. XVI. 2, XXIII. 2, XXV. 2; N. XXXI. 3, XXXIX. 3; Vit. XIV. 4; V. VII. 1; Tit. V. 3; D. VII. 2, X. 3; Rh. VI.; Hor.; Verg. 39.
Italici, V. IX. 2; Ter. I.
Italicus, -a, -um, *adj.* from Italia: *tirones,* N. XIX. 2.
Italus, -a, -um, *adj.* to Italia: *res,* Hor.
Iuba, J. XXXV. 2, LIX., LXVI., LXXI. Juba I, king of Numidia and a part of Mauretania. He sided with Pompey against Julius Caesar.
Iuba, Cal. XXVI. 1. Juba II, son of the above, brought by Julius Caesar to Rome, where he gained fame as a writer; afterwards restored to his kingdom.
Iudaea, A. XCIII.; Cl. XXIII.; G. XXIII.; Vit. IV. 5, V. 6; Tit. IV. 3, V. 2.
Iudaei, J. LXXXIV. 5; T. XXXVI.; Cl. XXV. 4; V. IV. 5, VIII. 1; *sing.* A LXXVI. 2.
Iudaicus, -a, -um, *adj.* from Iudaea *exercitus,* Vit. XV. 1, V. VI. 3; *fiscus,* D. XII. 2; *ritus,* T. XXXVI.; *triumphus,* D. II. 1; *vita,* D. XII. 2.
Iugurtha, J. XI. King of Numidia. He waged war with the Romans from 112 to 106 B.C., when he was conquered by Marius.
Iulia, J. VI. 1 (*bis*). Aunt of Julius Caesar and wife of Marius.
Iulia, J. LXXIV. 2; A. IV. 1, VIII. 1. Sister of Julius Caesar.
Iulia, J. I. 1, XXI., LXXXIV. 1; A. XCV. Daughter of Julius Caesar.
Iulia, A. XIX. 2, LXIII. 1 (*bis*) 2, LXIV. 1, LXV. 1, CI. 3, T. VII. 2 (*bis*), 3,

XI. 4, L. 1; Cal. VII. 1, XXIII. 1. Daughter of Augustus.
Iulia, A. LXIV. 1 (*bis*), LXV. 1, 4, LXXII. 3, CI. 3. Granddaughter of Augustus.
Iulia, Cl. XXIX. 1. Granddaughter of Tiberius.
Iulia, D. XVII. 3. Daughter of Titus.
Iulia Augusta, *see* Livia Drusilia.
Iulia Drusilla, Cal. VII., XXIV. 1, 2; Cl. XXIX. 1. Sister of Caligula.
Iulia Drusilla, Cal. XXV. 4. Daughter of Caligula.
Iulia Livilla, Cal. VII.; Cl. XXIX. 1. Daughter of Germanicus.
Iuliae, A. LXV. 1, 4, CI. 3; Cl. XXIX. 1.
Iulianus, -a, -um, *adj.* from Iulius (Caesar): *milites*, J. LXXV. 2.
Iulii, J. VI. 1.
Iulius, -a, -um, *adj.* to Iulius: *basilica*, Cal. XXXVII. 1, Pass.; *curia*, Cal. LX.; *familia*, Cl. II. 1; *lex*, J. LXXXI. 1; A. IV. 1; N. XXXIII. 2; *portus*, A. XVI. 1.
Iulius Caesar, C., the Dictator: *Caesar, J. I.* 3, IX. 2 (*bis*), X. 1 (*bis*), 2, XVII. 2, XX. 2 (*ter*), XXVIII. 3 (*bis*), XXIX. 1, XXX. 5, XXXII., XLIX. 1, 4 (*quater*), L. 2, LII. 2 (*ter*), 3, LIII., IV. 1, 3, LVI. 1, 4, LXXIX. 2, 3 (*rex*), LXXX. 2, 3, LXXXI. 1, 2, LXXXII. 2, LXXXV. (*bis*), LXXXVI. 1, LXXXVIII., LXXXIX.; A; VIII. 1. 2, X. 1, 2, XIII. 1, XVII. 5, XXXV. 1, XLV. 1, LXVIII., XCIV. 9, 11, XCV. (*bis*); T. IV. 1; N. XXXVII. 1, Gr. XX.; Rh. I.; Luc.; *Caesar dictator*, J. XLI. 2; Cl. XLI. 2; *Gaius Caesar*, J. XXX. 4; A. IV. 1, XXXI. 5, XCIV. 9; T. IV. 1; N. II. 2; Ter. V.; *Iulius Caesar*, G. III. 2, *Iulius*, J. XX. 2; *Divus Caesar*, A. XCVI. 1; *Divus Iulius*, A. II. 1, XV., XVII. 5, XXXI. 2, XCIV. 11, C. 3; Cal. XXXVIII. 1; Cl. XVII. I, XX. 1; Vit. VIII. 1; V. V. 7; Gr. VII; Rh. I.
(Iulius) mensis, J. LXXVI. 1.
Iulius Hyginus, C., Gr. XX.
Iulius Marathus, A. LXXIX. 2, XCIV. 3.
Iulius Modestus, Gr. XX.
Iulius Montanus, Verg. 29.
Iulius Saturninus, A. XXVII. 2.
Iulius Vindex, N. XI. 1, XLI. 1, 2, XLV. 2, XLVI. 3; G. IX. 2, XI., XVI. 2.
Iulius, *see* Antonius.
Iunia Calvina, V. XXIII. 4.
Iunia Claudilla, Cal. XII. 1, 2.
Iunius Novatus, A. LI. 1.
Iunius Rusticus, D. X. 3.
(Iunius) Silanus, D., J. X. 1.
(Iunius) Silanus, Appius, Cl. XXIX. 1, XXXVII. 2 (*ter*).
(Iunius) Silanus, L., Cl. XXIV. 3, XXVII. 2, XXIX. 1, 2.
(Iunius) Silanus, M., Cal. XII. 1, XXIII. 3 (*bis*).
Iuno, D. IV. 4.
Iuppiter, J. LXXXI. 3; A. LXX. 1, XCIV. 8, 9; Cal. XXXIII. (*simulacrum*), LVII. 1 (*simulacrum Olympiae*), LVII. 1, 3, LVIII. 2; G. II, IX. 2, XII. 1; D. IV. 4, XV. 3; *Optimus Maximus*, J. LXXIX. 2; A. XXIII. 2, XCIV. 6, 8; Vit. XV. 3; V. V. 7; *Capitolinus*, J. LXXXIV. 3; A. XXVI. 3, XXX. 2, XCI, 2, XCIV. 8; T. LIII. 2; Cal. XXII. 4; N. X. 2; D. IV. 4, VI. 1, VIII. 5; *Cassius*, N. XXII. 3; *Custos*, D. V.; *Latiaris*, Cal. XXII. 2; *Olympius*, A. LX.; Cal. XXII. 2; *Tonans*, A. XXIX. 1, 3, XCI. 2 (*bis*), *Tragoedus*, A. LVII. 1.
Iuvenalis, -e, *adj.* from *iuvenis: dies*, Cal. XVII. 2; a day added to the

Saturnalia by Caligula; *ludi,* N. XI. 1; games instituted by Nero to commemorate the first shaving of his beard.

KALENDAE, the first day of the month.

LABEO, SEE Antistius, Fabius.

Laberius, D., J. XXXIX. 2. A celebrated Roman writer of mimes (105–43 B.C.).

Labienus, T., Cal. XVI. 1.

Lacedaemonii, T. VI. 2. The people of Lacedaemon (Sparta).

Lacedaemonius, -a, -um, *adj.* from Lacedaemon: *medici,* Pers.

Laches, V. XXIII. 1.

Laco, *see* Cornelius.

Laelius Archelaus, Gr. II. (*bis*).

Laelius Hermas, Gr. X. (*bis*).

Laelius (Sapiens), C., Ter. I. (*ter*), II, III. (*ter*), IV., V. A friend of the younger Scipio and a distinguished patron of literature; consul in 190 B.C.

Laetorius, C., A. V.

Laetus, *see* Suetonius.

Laevius Melissa, Gr. III.

Lamia, *see* Aelius.

Lamianus, -a, -um, *adj.* from Lamia: *horti,* Cal. LIX. Gardens on the Appian Way, near Aricia.

Lampadio, *see* Octavius.

Lanuvinus, -a, -um, *adj.* from Lanuvium: Gr. II.

Lanuvium, A. LXXII. 2. An ancient city of Latium, south of Mons Albanus.

Laodiceni, T. VIII. The people of Laodicea, a city of Phrygia on the river Lycus.

Lares, N. XLVI. 2; Vit. II. 5; *cubiculi.* A. VII. 1; D. XVII. 2; *compitales,* A. XXXI. 4; *familiares,* Cal. V. Tutelary deities of a house or city, worshipped at the hearth or at the cross-roads.

Latiaris, *see* Juppiter. The tutelary deity ot the Latin League, with a temple on the summit of Mons Albanus (Monte Cavo).

Latine, A. LXXXIX. 1; T. LXXI.; Cl. XLII. 1; N. VII. 2, XXXIX. 2; Tit. III. 2; D. IV. 4; Gr. I., VII., XVI.; Rh. I., II. *Adv.* from Latinus.

Latinitas, A. XLVII (*see* note).

Latinus, -a, -um, *adj.* from Latium, meaning "of Latium," or "Latin" in various senses: *bibliotheca,* J. XLIV. 2; A. XXIX. 3; *carmen,* N. XII. 3; *coloniae,* J. VIII.; *condicio,* V. III.; *eloquentiae,* Rh. V., *facundia,* Cal. XX.; *feriae,* the Latin Festival, celebrated in April at the Alban Mount in honour of Jupiter Latiaris, J. LXXIX. 1; Cl. IV. 3; N. VII. 2; *genus,* A. XXXI. 1; *grammaticus,* Gr. X.; (*litteris*), Gr. X.; *oratio,* T. LXX. 1; *pugiles,* A. XLV. 2; *res,* Verg. 21; *rhetores,* V. XVIII.; *rhetoras,* Rh. I.; *Siren,* Gr. XI.; *sermo,* Cl. I. 2, XVI. 2; Gr. VII., XXII.; (*verbum*), Gr. XXII.; *cf.* Verg. 43; *vox,* Ter. V; *via,* D. XVII. 3, a road branching off to the eastward from the via Appia half a mile south of the porta Capena, and joining it again at Casilenum, a town near Capua. It passed through the Aurelian wall by the porta Latina.

Latium, Vit. I, 2.

Latius, -a, -um, *adj.* to Latium: *historiae,* Verg. 38.

Laureolus, Cal. LVII. 4 (*see* note). The name ot a mime, or farce.
Lavicanum (*sc. praedium*), J. LXXXIII. 1. An estate of Julius Caesar's at Lavicum (Labicum) a town of Latium east of Rome.
Lenaeus, *see* Pompeius.
Lentulus, Cn., G. IV. 1. Consul in 3 B.C.
Lentulus Augur, Cn., T. XLIX. 1.
Lentulus Gaetulicus, Cn., Cal. VIII. 1, 2; Cl. IX. 1; G. VI. 2 (*bis*).
Leontinus, -a, -um, *adj.* from Leontini, a city of eastern Sicily: *campus,* Rh. V.
Lepida, T. XLIX. 1. Wife of Quirinus.
Lepida, G. V. 1 (*bis*). Wife of Galba; *see also* Aemilia and Domitia.
Lepidus, *see* Aemilius *and* Domitius.
Leptinus, *see* Furius.
Leucadia, Ter V.
Liber, A. XCIV. 5. The Italic god identified with the Greek Dionysus, god of wine; the name is used of the Greek Dionysus.
Liberalis, *see* Flavius and Salvius.
Libertas, A. XXIX. 5, Liberty worshipped as a goddess.
Libitina, N. XXXIX. 1 (*see* note).
Libo, *see* Scribonius.
liburnica (*sc. navis*), A. XVII. 3; Cal. XXXVII. 2 (*see* note); N. XXXIV. 2.
Licinianus, *see* Calpurnius Piso Frugi.
Licinius, Ter. V.
Licinius Calvus, C., J. XLIX. 1, LXXIII.; A. LXXII. 1. A celebrated Roman orator and poet, a contemporary of Catullus and often mentioned with him by the Romans.
Licinius Crassus, L., N. II. 2; Rh. I.
(Licinius) Crassus, M., J. IX. 1 (*bis*), 2, XIX. 2, XXI., XXIV. 1; L. 1; A. XXI. 3; T. IX. 1; Verg. 2. Triumvir with Caesar and Pompey.
(Licinius) Crassus Frugi, M., Cl. XVII. 3.
Licinius Mucianus, V. VI. 4, XIII.
Licinus, A. LXVII, 1. A freedman. *See also* Clodius.
Liguria, Cl. XVII. 2. A district of Cisalpine Gaul, about the modern city of Genoa.
Livia Drusilla, A. LXII. 2; T. IV. 3; *Drusilla,* A. LXIX. 2; *Livia,* A. XXIX. 4, XL. 3, LXIII. 1, LXIX. 1, LXXXIV. 2, XCIX. 1 (*bis*), CI. 2; T. VI. 2, XIV. 2, XXII., L. 2 (*bis*); Cal. VII. Cl. I. 1, IV. 1, 4, 6 XI. 2; G. I.; *Livia Augusta* Cal. X. 1, XV. 2, XXIII. 2; G. V. 2; O. I. 1; *Iulia Augusta,* Cal. XVI. 3; *Augusta,* Cl. III. 2, XI. 2.
Livia Medullina Camilla, Cl. XXVI. 1.
Livia Ocellina, G. III. 4, IV. 1.
Livia Orestilla, Cal. XXV. 1.
Livilla, T. LXII. 1; Cl. I. 6, III. 2. Daughter of Drosus.
Livilla, Cal. VII. Daughter of Germanicus; *see* Iulia.
Livii, T. III. 1; Livii Drusi, T. III. 1; cf. Drusus.
Livius (Andronicus), L., Gr. I. A Greek slave from Tarentum, whose comedy and tragedy, put upon the stage in 240 B.C., mark the beginning of Roman literary history.
Livius, T. Cal. XXXIV. 2; Cl. XLI. 1; D. X. 3. Livy, the celebrated Roman historian (59 B.C.–17 A.D.).
Livius Drusus, T. III. 2. The first of the name.
(Livius) Drusus, T. VII. 1. Grandfather of Tiberius.

Melissa, *see* Laevius.
Melissus, C., Gr. XXI.; Verg. 16.
Memmius, C., J. XXIII. 1, XLIX. 2, LXXIII.; Gr. XIV. (*bis*), Ter. III.
Memmius, C., Cal. XXV. 2, Consul in 30 A.D.
Memphis, Tit. V. 3. A city of Egypt, on the lower course of the Nile.
Menander, Ter. II., v. (*ter*). The most distinguished writer of the Athenian New Comedy, born in 342 B.C.
Menas, A. LXXIV. A freedman.
Mendes, A. XCIV. 4. A town of Egypt in the Nile delta.
Menecrates, N. XXX. 2. A lyre-player.
meridianus, *see* gladiator.
Mero, *see* Biberius.
Messala, *see* Valerius.
Messalina, *see* Statilia *and* Valeria.
Messana, Cal. LI. 1. A city of north-eastern Sicily, modern Messina.
Mestrius Florus (Flaurus), V. XXII.
Metellus, *see* Caecilius.
Mettius Pompusianus, V. XIV.; D. X. 3.
Mettius Rufus, D. IV. 2.
Mevania. Cal. XLIII. A city of Umbria on the via Flaminia near the Clitumnus river.
Mida (Midas), Pers. A wealthy king of Phrygia, whose touch was fabled to turn everything into gold. Because he alone did not accept the decision of Tmolus, who awarded the prize to Apollo in a musical contest with Pan, Apollo changed his ears into those of an ass. Midas concealed them from all except the slave who cut his hair. The latter dug a hole in the ground and whispered into it: "King Midas has ass's ears." A reed grew up on the spot and betrayed the secret to the world.
Miletus, Cal. XXI. A city on the western coast of Asia Minor.
miliarium aureum, O. VI. (*see* note).
Milo, J. XXX. 3. The slayer of Clodius.
Minerva, Cal. XX. 4; Vit. XIII. 2. (*ποιό ιου*, *see* note); D. IV. 4 (*bis*), *XV.* 3.
Minos, T. LXX. 3; G. II. The famous king of Crete, because of his integrity made a judge in the Lower World.
Misenensis, -e, *adj.* from Misenum: *classi*, Plin.
Misenum, A. XLIX. 1; T. LXXII. 3, IXXIV; LXXV. 3; Oal. XIII.; N. XXXI. 3; Verg. 34. A promontory and town at the northern end of the Bay of Naples, an important naval station.
Misenus, Verg. 34.
Mithridates (also Mithradates), J. IV. 2, XIX. 2; N. XXIV 2; *Magni*, J. *XXXV.* 2.
Mithridaticus, -a, -um, *adj.* from Mithridates: *Bello*, T. XXXVII. 3.
Mnester, Cal. XXXVI. 1, LV. 1, LVII. 4. An actor of pantomimes.
Modestus, *see* Iulius.
Moesia, T. XII.; O. IX. 3; V. VI. 3. A country north of Thrace and Macedonia, modern Servia and Bulgaria; *Moesiae*, Vit. XV. 1, the Moesian provinces.
Moesiacus, -a, -um, *adj.* from Moesia: *acercitus*, V. VI. 2.
Molo, *see* Apollonius.
Montanus, *see* Iulius.
Morbovia, V. XIV. (*see* note).
Mucia, J. L. 1. Wife of Gnaeus Pompeius.
Mucianus, *see* Licinius.

Mummia Achaica, G. III. 4 *(bis)*. Granddaughter of Catulus.

Mummius, L., G. III. 4. The Roman consul who took and sacked Corinth in 146 B.C.

Munatius Plancus, 1., A. VII. 2, XXIX. 5; T. V.; Cl. XVI. 1; N. IV.; Rh. VI. (*bis*). Consul in 42 B.C.

(Munatius) Plancus, L., A. CI. 1. Consul in 13 A.D.

Munda, A. XCIV. 11. A town of Spain, the scene of Caesar's final victory in the Civil War.

Mundensis, -e, *adj.* from Munda; *proclium,* J. LVI. 5.

Murena, *see* Varro. murmillo, *see* gladiator.

Musa, *see* Antonius.

Musae, Gr. VI.; *see* also Hercules.

Musium (Museum), Cl. XLII. 2. An institution at Alexandria for the advancement of learning and the support of scholars, containing a lecture hall, a common dining-room, cloisters, etc.

Mutina, A. x. 2, LXXVII. A city of Cisalpine Gaul; modern Modena.

Mutinensis, -e, *adj.* from Mutina: *acies,* A. XII.; *bellum:* A. IX. 1, LXXXIV. 1; Rh. I.

Mylae, A. XVI. 1. A promontory and town in the north-eastern part of Sicily, not far from Messana.

Mytilenae, J. II.; A. IXVI. 3; T. X. 1. The chief city of Lesbos, a large island off the western coast of Asia Minor.

NAEVIA, SEE Ennia.

Naevius (Cn.), Gr. II.; Ter. V. The early Roman epic and dramatic poet (269-199 B.C.). Mais, *see* Servilia.

Nais, *see* Servilla.

Narbo, T. IV. 1. A city of southern Gaul; modern Narbonne.

Narcissus, Cl. XXVIII., XXXVII. 2; Vit. II. 5; V. IV. 1, 2; Tit. II. Freedman of Claudius.

Naso, *see* Actorius.

Naturalis Historia, Plin.

Naulochus, A. XVI. 1. A town in the north-eastern part of Sicily, near Mylae.

Nauplius, N. XXXIX. 3. Nauplius, king of Euboea and father of Palamedes. To avenge the unjust execution of his son before Troy, he caused the wreck of the returning Greek ships by false beacons.

Neapolis, A. XCVIII. 5; T. IV. 2, VI. 2; N. XX. 2, 3; XXV. 1, XL. 4; Verg. 11, 36. Modern Naples.

Neapolitani, A. XCII. 2. The inhabitants of Neapolis (Naples).

Neapolitanus, -a, -um, *adj.* from Neapolis: *certamen,* Cl. XI. 2.

Nemausenses, T. XIII. 1. The inhabitants of Nemausus, a city of southern Gaul; modern Nimes.

Nemorensis, -e, *adj.* from *nemus,* "grove," applied to the grove of Diana at Aricia, J. XLVI.; *rex,* Cal. XXXV. 3. The priest of Diana of Aricia (*see* note).

Neoptolemus, Cal. LVII. 4. A tragic actor.

Nepos, *see* Cornelius.

Neptunus, A. XVI. 2, XVIII. 2. The Italic god identified with the Greek Poseidon, god of the Sea.

Nero, a word of Sabine origin, T. 1. 2; *see* Claudius, Salvius Otho, Tiberius, Titus.

Nero, T. LIV. 1 (*bis*), 2 (*bis*); Cal. VII. (*bis*); Cl. IX. 1. Son of Germanicus.

Nero, the Emperor: *Ahenobarbus*, N. VII. 1, XLI. 1; *Augustus*, N. XLVI. 3; *Nero Caesar*, Vit. II. 2, Rh. I.; Pass.; *Nero*, Cl. XXVII. 2 (*bis*), K. 2, XLIII., XIV.; N. I. 2. V. 1. 2, VI. 2, VII. 1, XXIII. 1, XXXIX. 2, in Greek (*bis*) and in Latin, 3, XL. 2, XLI. 1, XLVIII. 2 (*bis*), 3. XLIX. 3 (in Greek) LVII. 2; G. I. (*bis*), II., VI. 1, VIII. 1, 2, IX. 1, 2, X. 1, 5, XI., XII. 2, XV. 1, 2, XXII.; O. II. 2. III. 1, IV. 1, VI. 1, X. 2; Vit. IV., XI. 2; V. IV. 4, V. 1, 5, 7, VI. 3, IX. 1, XIV., XXV.; D. I. 1, XIV. 4; Pers. (*ter*); Luc. (*ter*); Pass. (*bis*, once for Gaius); *Caesar*, Luc.

Nero falsus, N. LVII. 2.

Nerones, T. IV. 3.

Neroneus, -a, -um, *adj.* from Nero: *agona*, N. XXI. 1; *mensem*, N. LV.; *certamini*, Vit. IV.

Neronia, N. XII. 3.

Neronianus, *see* Patrobius.

Neronianus, -a, -um, *adj.* from Nero: *cantica*, Vit. XI. 2.

Neropolis, N. LV. A name which Nero proposed to give Rome.

Nerulonensis, -e, *adj.* from Nerulum, a town of Lucania on the road from Capua to Rhegium: A. IV. 2.

Nerva, D. I. 1; *Nervae forum*, D. V.; *see* note.

Nicanor, A. LXXXIX. 1; *see also* Saevius.

Nicias, *see* CUrtius.

Nicomedes, J. II., XLIX. (*sexies*). Nicomedes IV, king of Bithynia.

Nicon, A. XCVI. 2. "Victor," the name of a donkey.

Nicopolis, A. XVIII. 2.

Niger, *see* Aquillus *and* Novius.

Nigidius, P. A., XCIV. 5. P. Nigidius Figulus, a contemporary of Caesar and Cicero, called by Gellius (4. 9) the most learned of the Romans next to Varro.

Nigrinus, *see* Pontius.

Nilus, A. XVIII. 2. The Nile. Nioba, N. XXI. 2. Niobe.

Nisus, Verg. 42.

Nobllior, *see* Fulvius.

Nola, A. XCVIII. 5, C. 2; T. XL. A city of Campania, north-east of Naples.

Nomentana via, N. XLVIII. 1. A road running through the porta Colllna north-east to Nomentum in the Sabine country.

Nonae, the seventh day of March, May, July, and October, and the fifth of the other months.

Nonianus, *see* Servilius.

Nonius Asprenas Torquatus (C.), A. XLIII. 2, LVI. 3; Cal. XXXV. 1.

Nonnius, Hor.

Norbanus Flaccus, Vit. III. 2. Consul in 15 A.D.

Noricum regnum, T. XVI. 2. A country of central Europe, between Cisalpine Gaul and the upper course of the Danube. Novaria, Rh. VI. A town of Tranapadine Gaul. Novariensis, -e, *adj.* from Novaria: Rh. VI.

Novatus, *see* Iunius. November mensis, J. XL. 2; A. XXXII. 3.

Novius Niger, J. XVII. 1, 2.

Novocomensis, -e, *adj.* from Novum Comum: Plin.

Novum Comum, J. XXVIII. 3. A town of Cisalpine Gaul on lacus Larius (the Lake of Como); modern Como.

Nuceria, Vit. I. 3, II. 2. A residence of the Vitellii, probably the town of Campania, south-east of Naples.

Oppius, C., J. LII. 2 (*bis*), LIII., LVI. 1, LXXII. A friend of Caesar and a writer of biographies and other works.

Oppius Chares, Gr. III.

Oppius Sabinus, D. VI. 1.

Orbilius Pupillus, L., Gr. IV., VIII., IX. (*ter*), XIX.

Orbilius, Gr. IX. Son of Orbilius Pupillus.

Orcivi senatores, A. XXXV. 1 (*see* note).

Orcus, N. XXXIX. 3. The Lower World, abode of the dead; also its king Pluto.

Oreates, N. XXI. 3, XXXIX. 2. Son of Agamemnon, who killed his mother Clytemnestra and was pursued by the Furies.

Orestilla, *see* Livia.

Orfitus, *see* Salvidienus.

Oriens. A. XIII. 3; T. IX. 1, XII. 2; Cal. I. 2; N. V. 1, XXXIX. 1, XL. 2; V. IV. 5, V. 7, VI. 4; Tit.V. 3: D. II. 2; V. 35.

Origines, A. LXXXVI. 3. An historical work of M. Porcius Cato Censorinus, which discussed the origins of the various peoples of Italy and their history down to his own time.

Ostia, T. X. 2, XI. 1; Cal. XV. 1 LV. 1; Cl. XII. 3, XVII. 2, XX. 3 XXV. 2; N. XVI. 1, XXVII. 3 XXXI. 3; XLVII. 1; V. VIII. 3 Rh. I. The seaport of Rome at the mouth of the Tiber.

Ostiensis, -e, *adj.* from Ostia: *portum, Cl. XX.* 1; *provincia* Cl. XXIV. 2.

Ostienses, Cl. XXXVIII. 1, XL. 3 The people of Ostia.

Otho, *see* Salvius.

Ovidius (Naso, P.), Gr. XX. The famous Roman poet, 43 B.C. to 17 A.D.

PACIS TEMPLUM, V. IX 1. Begun by Vespasian in 71 A.D., and completed four years later. It lay behind the basilica Aemilia and south-east of the forum of Augustus.

Paconius, M., T. LXI. 6 (*bis*).

Pacuvius, M., J. LXXXIV. 2. An early Roman writer of tragedies (220–132 B.C.), a nephew of Ennius.

Padus, Verg. 19.

Paean, N. XXXIX. 2. An epithet of Apollo as the Healer.

paegniarius, *see* gladiator.

Paetina, *see* Aelia.

Paetus Thrasea, N. XXXVII. 1; D. X. 3; Pers. (*bis*).

Palaemon, *see* Remmius.

Palatinus, -a, -um, *adj.* from Palatium: *Apollo, see* Apollo; *atriensis,* Cal. LVII. 3; *bibliotheca, G*r. II., XX.; *domus.* A. XXIX. 3, LVII. 2; Cl. XVII. 3; V. XXV.; D. XV. 2; *ludi,* Cal. LVI. 2.

Palatium, A. V., XXIX. 1, LXXII. 1; T. V., LIV. 2; Cal. XIV. 2, XXII. 2,4, XLI. 1, XLVI., LIV. 2; Cl. XVIII. 2; N. VIII., XXV. 2, XXXI. 1, XXXIV. 1; G. XIV. 2, XVIII. 1; O. I. 3, VI. 1, 2, VII. 1, VIII. 2; Vit. XV. 2, XVI.; Tit. II.; Gr. II., XVII. (bis). The Palatine hill; applied also to the Palace of the Caesars on that hill; cf. *Palatina domus.*

Palfurius Sura, D. XIII. 1.

Philologus, Gr. X. (*bis*); *see also* Ateius.
Philopoemen, *see* Vinius.
Philus, Ter. I.
Phoebe, A. LXV. 2 (*bis*). A freed-woman
Phoebus, A. LXX. 1. An epithet of Apollo as god of light.
Phoenissae, J. XXX. 5; cf. A. XXV. 4. "The Phoenician Women," a tragedy of Euripides.
Phrygius, -a, -um, Verg. 38.
Phyllis, D. XVII. 3.
Picenum, J. XXIV. 1. A district on the eastern coast of central Italy.
Pictor, *see* Carvilius.
Pinarius, L., J. LXXXIII. 2. Grand-nephew of Julius Caesar.
Pinax, Gr. VI.; *see* note.
Piso, *see* Calpurnius.
Pisonianus, -a, -um, *adj.* from Piso: *coniuratio,* N. XXXVI. 1; Luc.
Pitholaus, J. LXXV. 5. A rhetorician and poet of the time of Julius Caesar.
Pius, T. XVII. 2, Cal. XXII. 1. A surname conferred on several of the Roman emperors.
Placentia, J. LXIX.; O. IX. 2. A town of Cisalpine Gaul on the Po; modern Piacenza.
Plancus, *see* Munatius.
Plato, Cal. XXXIV. 2. The Greek philosopher.
Plautia Urgulanilla, Cl. XXVI. 2 (*bis*), XXVII. 1. Wife of the emperor Claudius.
Plautius, A., Cl. XXIV. 2; V. IV. 1.
Plautius, A., N. XXXV. 4.
Plautius Rufus, A. XIX. 1.
Plautus (T. Maccius), Ter. V.
Plinius Secundus, (C), Cal. VIII. 1,2, 3 (*bis*); Plin. Pliny the elder, author of the Natural History. He lived from 23 to 79 A.D.
Plotia Hieria, Verg. 9.
Plotius, -a, -um, *adj. to* Plotius: *rogatio,* J. V.
Plotius Gallus, Rh. II. (*bis*).
Plotius Tucca, Verg. 37, 38, 40.
Plotus, *see* Voltacillus.
Poeni, T. II. 1. The Phoenicians and (usually) the Carthaginians, as descendants of the Phoenicians.
Polemo, N. XVIII.
Polla, *see* Vespasia.
Pollentinus, -a, -um, *adj.* from Pollentia a town of Liguria; modern Pollenza: *plebs,* T. XXXVII. 3.
Pollio, *see* Asinius, Clodius, Vespasius.
Pollux.J. X. 1; T.XX.; Cal. XXII. 2. Brother of Castor.
Polus, A. LXVII. 2. A freedman.
Polybius, A. CI. 1. A freedman of Augustus.
Polybius, Cl. XXVIII. A freedman of Claudius.
Polycrates, Cal. XXI. The celebrated tyrant of Samos, famous at first for his good fortune, but betrayed and crucified in 522 B.C.
Polyhistor, see Cornelius Alexander.
Pompeia, J. VI. 2, LXXIV. 2. Daughter of Q. Pompeius.
Pompeia, T. VI. 3. Sister of Sex. Pompeius.
Pompeianus, -a, -um, *adj.* from Pompeius: *bellum,* J. LVI. 1; *biremes, A. XVI.* 3; *curia,* J. LXXXI. 3; *domus,* T. XV. 1; *partes,* V. I. 2; *theatrum,* T. XLVII. (*see* Pompeius Magnus); Cl. XXI. 1; as subst., T. LVII. 2. Pompeii, Gr XV. The Pompey family.
Pompeii, conjecture in Cl. XXII. 1. The Campanian town.
Pompeius, T. LVII. 2. A Roman knight.

Forum, A. LXXII. 1; *gens,* Cl. XXV. 3; *habitus, A. XCVIII.* 3; *imperator,* V. IV. 5; *litterae,* Gr. X.; *nomina,* Cl. XXV. 3; *plebs,* J. XIV. 1; T. LXXVI.; POPULUS, A. XXI. 3, XXXI. 5, XLVII., LVIII. 2, LXV. 3, XCIV. 2, 3, Cl. 2; T. XXI. 2, 3, 7 (*bis*), XLIX. 2; Cal. IV., XI., XIII., XXIII. 1, XXX. 2; Cl. III. 2, VI. 2, XXV. 3, 5, XLIII.; N. XXXVII. 3; *G. X.* 1, XV. 2; *res,* Gr. X.; Verg. 19; *scriptores,* Verg. 30; *sermo,* A. XCVIII. 3; *signa,* Cal. XIV. 3; *urbs,* Verg. 21.

Romulus, A. VII. 2, XCV.; T. I. 1, LIX. 2; Cal. XXV. 1.

Rubico, J. XXXI. 2, LXXXI. 2. The river Rubicon, in north-eastern Italy, forming the boundary between Umbria and Cisalpine Gaul.

Rubria, N. XXVIII. 1. A Vestal virgin.

Rufilla, A. LXIX. 2.

Rufio, J. LXXVI. 3.

Rufrius Crispinus, N. XXXV. 5. Stepson of the emperor Nero.

Rufus, *see* Cluvius, Mettius, Octavius, Plautius, Pompeius, Rutilius, Salvidienus.

Russus (?), *see* Claudius.

Rusticus, *see* Iunius.

Rustius Caepio, D. IX. 2.

Rutilius Rufus, (P.), A. LXXXIX. 2; Gr. VI. A celebrated orator and writer, consul in 105 B.C.

SABBATA, A. LXXVI. 2; T. XXXII. 2 (*see* note). The Sabbath of the Jews; the seventh day of the week, Saturday.

Sabina, *see* Poppaea.

Sabini, T. I. 1; Vit. I. 2; V. I. 4, II. 1; Tit. X. 1. The Sabines, a people of central Italy, dwelling in the region north-east of Rome

Sabinus, -a, -um, *adj.* from Sabini: *lingua,* T. I. 2; *ruris,* Hor.

Sabinus, *see* Asellius, Cornelius, Flavius, Nymphidius, Oppius, Poppaeus.

Sabratensis, -e, *adj.* from Sabrata, a town of northern Africa, south-west of Carthage: V. III.

Sacra via, J. XLVI., LXXX. 4, Vit. XVII. 1. The oldest and most famous street of Rome, running from the Colosseum valley to the summit of the Velia (marked by the arch of Titus), and thence across the Forum to the temple of Saturn and the beginning of the clivus Capitolinus.

Saeculare carmen, Hor. An ode written by Horace for the Saeculares ludi of Augustus.

Saeculares ludi, A. XXXI. 4 (*bis*); Cl. XXI. 2; Vit. II. 5; D. IV. 3. Sacrifices to the gods of the Lower World, made in the Tarentum, a part of the campus Martius near the Tiber. In the year 249 B.C. they were made a national festival, to be celebrated every one hundred years. Augustus celebrated them in 17 B.C., Claudius in 47 A.D. and, Domitian in 88 A.D.

Saepta, A. XLIII. 1, 4; T. XVII 2 (*see* note); Cal. XVIII. 1, XXI.; Cl. XXI. 4; N. XII. 4. A large enclosure in the campus Martius, divided into smaller sections, where the comitia centuriata voted.

Saevius Nicanor, Gr. V. (*bis*); *M. Saevius Postumius,* Gr. V.

Salaria via, N. XLVIII. 1: V. XII. The road leading from Rome north-east to the Sabine territory. It derived its name from the trade in salt.

Scalae anulariae, A. LXXII. 1. A stairway in Rome, perhaps leading from the Forum to the Palatine behind the temple of Castor.

Scantinia lex, D. VIII. 3. A law of uncertain authorship and date, providing for the punishment of unnatural crimes.

Scaptiensis, -e, *adj.* from Scaptia, the name of one of the Roman tribes: *tribules, A. XL.* 2 *(see* note).

Scelerata Castra, Cl. I. 3.

Scipio (P. Cornelius Africanus Aemilianus): *Scipio,* Ter. I. III. (*bis*), IV., V.; *P. Scipio,* Ter. I; *P. Africanus,* Ter. III.; *Africanus,* Ter. I. *Scipio Africanus,* Ter. I. The younger Scipio, who destroyed Carthage in 146 B.C.

Scipio, P. (Cornelius), J. XXXV. 2, XXXVII. 1, LIX. (*bis*); T. IV. 1,

Scribonia, A. LXII. 1, LXIII. 1, LXIX.; Gr. XIX. Wife of Augustus.

Scribonianus, *see* Furius.

Scribonius, T. XIV. 2.

Scribonius Aphrodisius, Gr. XIX.

Scribonius Libo, L., T. XXV. 1, 3; Gr. XIX.

Scutarius, A. LVI. 4.

Scythae, A. XXI. 3. The people of Scythia, north of the Black and Caspian Seas.

Scytobrachion, *see* Dionysius.

Secundus, *see* Gabinius *and* Plinius. secutor, *see* Gladiator.

Seianus, *see* Aelius.

Selene, Cal. XXVI. 1, Daughter of Mark Antony and Cleopatra.

Seleucus, Cl. XXV. 3. King of Syria.

Seleucus, T. LVI. A grammarian.

Seleucus, O. IV. 1. VI. 1. An astrologer.

Semigraeci, *see* Graeci.

Semiramis, *see* Sameramis.

Seneca, L. Aunaeus, Cal. LIII. 2; N. VII. 1 (*bis*), *XXXV.* 5, LII.; Verg. 29; Pers. The well-known philosopher and tutor of Nero (c. 4 B.C.-A.D. 65.). T. LXXIII. 2 perhaps refers to his father, Seneca Rhetor.

Senones, T. III. 2; 01. LI. 3. A Gallic people dwelling in northern Umbria and the adjacent part of Cisalpine Gaul.

Sentius, Cn., Verg. 35.

September mensis, A. XXXI. 2, XXXV. 3, C. 3; T. XXVI. 2; Cal. XV. 2; D. XIII. 3.

Septimius, Hor.

Septimontale sacrum, D. IV. 5. The "Festival of the Seven Hills," celebrated in December in commemoration of the inclusion of seven hills within one wall.

Septizonium, T. I. *(see* note).

Serapis, V. VII. 1, 2. One of the principal Egyptian deities.

Sermones, Hor. *See* Saturae.

Sertorius (Q.), J. V. One of Marius's generals, who after the death of his commander carried on war in Spain against the party of Sulla for some years. He was finally assassinated in 72 B.C.

Servilia, J. L,. 2 (*bis*). Mother of M. Brutus.

Servilia Nais, N. III. 2.

Servilianus, -a, -um, *adj,* from Servilius: *horti,* N. XLVII. 1.

Servilius Caepio, J. XXI.

Servilius Isauricus, J. III.

Servilius Isauricus, P., A. LXII. 1; T. V.; Rh. IV. (*bis*).

Servilius Nonianus, Pers.

Sulla, Cal. LVII. 2. An astrologer.

Sulla, Faustus, J. XXVII. 1, LXXV. 3; Gr. XII. Son of the dictator.

Sulla, Faustus, Cl. XXVII. 2.

Sulla Felix, L. Cornelius, the Dictator, J. I .1, 2, III., V., XI., XLV. 3, LXXIV. 1, LXXV. 4, LXXVII.; T. LIX. 2; Gr. XII. (*bis*).

Sulla, P., J. IX. 1 (*bis*).

Sullanus, -a, -um, *adj.* from Sulla, referring to the Dictator: *temporis* Gr. XI.; *temporibus,* Gr. XIII.

Sulpicii (Galbae), *G. III.* 1 (III. 3).

Sulpicius, Cl. IV. 5.

Sulpicius, Ser., J. XXIX. 1, L. 1.

Sulpicius Carthaginiensis, Verg. 38.

Sulpicius Camerinus, Q., V. II. 1. Consul in A.D. 9.

Sulpicius Flavus, Cl. XLI. 1.

Sulpicius Galba, G. III. 1. The first of the name, consul in 144 B.C.

(Sulpicius) Galba, C., G. III. 4 (*bis*). Brother of the emperor Galba.

(Sulpicius) Galba, Ser., G. III. 2. Great-grandfather of the emperor Galba.

Sulpicius Galba, Ser., the Emperor: *Ser. Galba imperator, G. VI.* 1; *Servius, G. III* 4, IV. 1; *Caesar, G. XI.*; O. v. 2; *L. Livius Ocella,* G. IV. 1; *Galba,* N. XXXII. 4, XL. 3, XLII. 1, XLVII. 2, XLVIII. 2, XLIX. 3; G. II., III. 3, IV. 2, V. 1, VI. 2, XX. 2; O. IV. 1, V. 1, VI. 1, 2, 3, VII. 2, X. 1, XII. 2; Vit. VII. 1, VIII. 2, IX., X. 1; V, V. 1, 7, VI. 2, XVI. 1; Tit. V. 1; *Galba Cupido, G. XX.* 2.

Sulpicius Gallus, C., Ter. IV.

Superum mare, J. XXIV. 1, XLIV. 3, A. XLIX. 1. "The Upper Sea," a name applied to the Adriatic; cf. Inferum mare.

Sura, *see* Palfurius.

Suria, *see* Syria.

Surrentum, A. LXV. 1. A town at the southern end of the Bay of Naples, modern Sorrento.

Syracusae.T. LXXIV.; Cal. XX., XXI., XXIV. 2. The celebrated city of eastern Sicily; applied by Augustus to his study, A. LXXII. 2.

Syria (Suria), J. XXII. 2 (Suria), XXXV. 2; A. XVII. 3; T. XIV. 3, XXXIX., XLI., XLII. 1, XLIX., 2, LII. 3; Cal. II.; N. XXXIX. 1; Vit. II. 4, 5; V. IV. 5, VI. 3, XV.

Syria dea, N. LVI. (dea Syria); *see* note.

Syriacus, -a, -um, *adj,* from Syria: *legionibus,* T. XLVIII. 2; *expeditions,* Cal. X. *1; exercitum,* V. VI. 4.

Syriaticus, -a, -um, *adj.* from Syria: *exercitus,* Vit. XV. 1.

Syrus, -a, -um, *adj.* meaning "Syrian": Gr. VIII.; *pueri,* A. LXXXIII.

Syrus, Ter. III.

TALARIUS, Cal. VIII. 4

Talentum, J. IV. A Greek weight and sum of money. The latter varied according to whether it was of gold or silver, as well as in different states of Greece. The Attic talent, which is most frequently meant, contained 6000 *drachmae,* and was equal to nearly $1200.

Tanusius Geminus, J. IX. 2 (*bis*). A writer of history and the author of an epic poem (*Annales*), slightingly referred to by Seneca (*Epist. 93.* 9).

Tarentinus, -a, -um, *adj,* from Tarentum, the city of southern Italy: Gr. XVIII.

Tarichaeae. Tit. IV. 3 (*see* note).

Tarpeius, -a, -um, *adj,* from Tarpeia, who betrayed the Roman citadel to

the Sabines: *monti, J. XLIV.* 1; *culmine,* D. XXIII. 2. Applied to the Capitoline hill and to the temple of Jupiter Capitolinus.

Tarquinius Priscus, A. II. 1. The fifth king of Rome.

Tarracina, 1. XXXIX.; *G. IV.* 1. A town of Latium on the via Appia, modem Terracina.

Tarraco, A. XXVI. 3. A town of north-eastern Spain, modern Tarragona.

Tarraconenses, G. XII. 1. The people of Tarraco.

Tarraconensis, -e, *adj.* from Tarraco: *Hispania, G. VIII.* 1, one of the provinces into which Spain was divided under the empire.

Tarsensis, -e, *adj.* from Tarsus, a city of Cicilia: D. X. 1.

Tatius, T. I. 1. A Sabine king who, according to tradition, shared the throne with Romulus.

Taurus, *see* Statilius.

Tedius Ater, A. XXVII. 3.

Tegea, V. VII. 3. A city of Arcadia.

Telegenius, Cl. XL. 3 *(see* note).

Telephus, A. XIX. 1, 2.

Tellus, Gr. XV. "The Earth," worshipped as a goddess.

Teminites, *see* Apollo.

Terentia, *see* Albia.

Terentia. A. LXVI. 3. Wife of Maecenas.

Terentilla, A. LXIX. 2.

Terentius Afer, P.: Ter. I.; *Terentius,* Ter. III. (*bis*), IV., V; (*ter*) *Afer.* Ter. IV.

Terentius Lucanus, Ter. I.

(Terentius) Varro, M., *see* Varro.

Terpnus, N. XX. 1; V. XIX. 1. A lyre-player.

Terra mater, T. LXXV. 1; cf. J. VII.

Tertia, J. L. 2. Sister of M. Brutus.

Tertulla, J. L. 1. Wife of M. Craasus.

Tertulla, A. LXIX. 2.

Tertulla, V. II. 1. Grandmother of Vespasian.

Tertulla, *see* Arrecina.

Tetrinius, Cal. XXX. 2; *plur., id.*

Teucer, *see* Octavius.

Teutoni (Teutones). J. XI. A people of northern Germany, neighbours of the Cimbri, with whom they invaded Italy. They were vanquished by Marius.

Thallus, A. LXVII. 2. A slave.

Thasius, -a, -um, *adj.* from Thasos, an island in the northern part of the Aegean Sea: *lapis,* N. L. A kind of marble.

Theodorus Gadareus, T. LVII. 1.

Theogenes, A. XCIV. 12, An astrologer.

Theologumena, A. XCIV. 4 *(see* note).

Thermus, M., J. II. (*bis*).

Thessali, T. VIII.; Cl. XXI. 3; *sing.,* A. XCVL. 1. The people of Thessaly in northern Greece.

Thoranius, *see* Toranius.

Thracia, J. XLIV. 3; A. XCIV. 5; T. XVI. 2; V. II. 3.

Thraex (also Thrax), Thraeces, *see* gladiator.

Thrasea, *see* Paetus.

Thrasyllus, A. XCVIII. 4; T. XIV. 4, LXII. 3; Cal. XIX. 1.

Thurinus, A. VII. 1 (*ter*). A surname of Augustus; *see* Thurinus, *adj.*

Thurinus, -a, -um, *adj.* from Thurii, a town of southern Lucania: *pago,* A. II. 3; *agrum,* A. III. 1; *regime,* A. VII. 1.

Thyatireni, T. VIII. The people of Thyatira, a town of northern Lydia.

Tortor, *see* Apollo.
Trabeatae, Gr. XXI. (*see* note).
Trachia (Trachaea) Cilicia, V. VIII. 4. A name applied to the western part of Cilicia.
Tragoedus, *see* Iuppiter.
Tralliani, T. VIII. The people of Tralles, a city in western Asia Minor (Caria).
Transalpina, *see* Gallia.
Transalpini, J. XXIV. 2. transitoria domus, N. XXXI. 1.
Transpadani, J. IX. 3.
Transpadanus, -a, -um, *adj.* from *trans, Padum: regio,* V. I. 4.
Trebatius, C., J. LXXVIII. 1.
Trebiani T. XXXI. 1. The people of Trebia, a town of Umbria, modern Trevi.
Treveri, Cal. VIII. 1. A tribe of the Belgians.
Triton, C1. XXI. 6. A sea-god.
Troia, Troy, Verg. 38. 41. Also a game described by Verg. Aen. 5. 596 ff., and consisting of evolutions by two troops of mounted youths; J. XXXIX. 2; A. XLIII. 2; T. VI. 4; Cal. XVIII. 3; C1. XXI. 3, N. VII. 1.
Tubero, Q., J. *LXXXIII.* 1.
Tucca, *see* Plotius.
Tullius, Servius, A. II. 1. The sixth king of Rome.
Tullius Cicero, M., A. v.; *M. Cicero A. III*. 2 (*Epist. ad Q. Fr.*); Gr. VII., XIV. *(Epist. ad Dolabellam; ad Att.), XCIV.* 9; Gr. XIV. *(Ep. ad Alt.): Cicero,* J. IX. 2 *(Ep. ad Axium), XVII.* 2, XX. 4 *(Orat.* de *Domo), XXX.* 5 (De Off.), XLII. 3 (frg. inc.), XLIX. 3 *(Ep. inc.), L.* 2, LV. 1 *(Brut.), LV.* 1 (Ep. ad *Nep.), LVI.* 1 *(Brut.), LVI.* 6; T. II. 4, VII. 2; Cl. XLI. 3; Gr. IX., XVI.; Rh. I., II. (*Ep. ad Tit.*), v. *(Phil.),* Ter. v. *(Limo).*
(Tullius) Cicero, Q., J. XIV. 2; Cicero, A. III. 2. Brother of the orator.
Tusculanus, -a, -um, *adj.* from Tusculum: *Fortuna, G. XVIII.* 2; *praedium.* Gr. XI.; *villa,* Gr. XI.
Tusculum, G. *IV.* 3, XVIII. 2; Gr. XVI. An ancient town of Latium, south-east of Rome.
Tuscus, N. XXXV. 5.
Tyrius, -a, -um, *adj.* from Tyrus: *elassis,* J. *XXXIX.* 4; *coloris,* N. XXXII. 3. Tyrian purple.
Tyrrhenicon Historiae, Cl. XLII. 2 (*bis*).
Tyrus, N. XXXI. 4. Tyre, the Phoenician city.

ULIXES stolatus, Cal. XXIII. 2.
Ultor, *see* Mars.
Umbria, J. XXXIV. 1, V. I. 4. A district in the north-eastern part of Italy.
Urgulanilla, *see* Plautia.

VALERIA MESSALINA, Cl. XVII. 3, XXVI 2, XXVII. 1, XXIX 3, XXXVI., XXXVII. 2, XXXIX. 1; N. VI. 4; Vit. II. 5. Wife of the emperor Claudius.
Valerius Cato, Gr. II., IV. (*bis*), *X., XI. (quinquies).*
Valerius Catullus (C.), J. LXXIII. The celebrated Roman poet.
Valerius Catullus, Cal. XXXVI. 1.
Valerius Messala, M., Rh. I. Consul in 161 B.C.
Valerius Messala, M., G. IV. 1. Consul in 3 A.D.
Valerius Messala Barbatus, Cl. XXVI. 2.
Valerius Messala Corvinus, (M.), A. LVIII. 1, 2, LXXIV., T. LXX. 1; Cl. XIII. 2; Gr. IV.; Tibull.
Valerius Probus, M., Gr, XXIV.

Valerius Proculus, Verg. 37.
Vargunteius, Q., Gr. II.
Varianus, -a, -um, *adj. from* Varus: *clades, A. XXIII.* 1 *(bis) see* Quintilius Varus), XLIX., 1; T. XVII. 2, XVIII. 1; Cal. III. 2, XXXI.
Varius, L. Verg. 10, 37, 38, 39, 40, 41, 42. A famous Roman poet, a contemporary of Vergil.
Varro, M. (Terentius), J. XXXIV. 2, LXIV. 2; Gr. XXIII.; Ter. II. The famous scholar and encyclopaedic writer (116–28 B.C.).
Varro Murena, A. XIX., 1, LVI. 4, LXVI. 3; T. VIII.; Gr. IX. (*bis*).
Varronilla, D. VIII. 4.
Varus, *see* Alfenus and Quintilius.
Vaticanus, -a, -um, *adj.*: (*collis*), Cl. XXI. 2. The Vatican hill.
Vatinius, -a, -um, *adj.* to Vatinius: *lex,* J XXII 1; *rogatio,* J. XXVIII. 3.
Vectis, V. IV. 1. An island off the south coast of Britain, the Isle of Wight.
Veientanus, -a, -um, *adj.* from Veii: (*praedium*), *G. I.* An estate of Livia's near Veil, called *ad Gallinas.*
Veil, N. XXXIX. 2 (*bis*). A city in the southern part of Etruria.
Velabrum, J. XXXVII. 2, N. XXV. 2. The valley between the Palatine and Capitoline hills.
Veliterni, A, XCIV. 2. The people of Velitrae.
Velitrae, A. I., VI., XCIV. 2. A town of Latium, south-east of Rome.
Venerius, -a, -um, *adj.* from Venus: *loci, T. XLIII.* 2; *res.* Hor.
Veneta factio, Vit. VII. 1, XIV. 3. "The Blues," one of the factions in the Circus, *see* notes on *Calig. LV.* 2 and *Dom. VII.* 1.
Venus, J. VI. 1, XLIX. 3; Cal. III., LVI. 2; *Capitolina,* Cal. VII.; G. XVIII. 2; *Coa,* V. XVIII.; *Erycina,* Cl. XXV. 5; *Genetrix,* J. LXI., LXXVIII. 1, LXXXIV. 1; *Paphia,* Tit. V. 1; a throw at dice, A. LXXI. 2 *(see* note).
Venusinus -a, -um, *adj.* from Venusia, a small town on the borders of Lucania and Apulia: Hor.
Veranius Tiaccus, A. LXXXVI. 3
Vergilius (Maro, P.), Cal. XXXIV. 2, XLV. 2; N. LIV.; D. IX. 1; Gr. XVI., XXIII.; Verg. 1, 5, 7, 29, 38, 43, 46, 48; Tibull; Luc., of. A. XL,. 5; N. XLVII. 2.
Verginius Flavus, Pers.
Verrius Flaccus, M., Gr. XVII., XVIII., XIX.
Vespasia, V.I. 3. A place in Umbria.
Vespasia Polla, V. I. 3 (*bis*), V. 2.
Vespasianus, the Emperor: *Caesar,* V. V. 2, XIII.; *Vespasunius, Cl. XLV.*; G. XXIII.; Vit. XV. 1, 2, XVII. 1; V. I. 3, II. 1, V. 7, VI. 3 (*bis*), 4, VII. 3, XV., XXII.; D. I. 3, II. 2, XV. 2.
Vespasianus, D. XV. 1. Son of Flavius Clemens.
Vespasii, V. I. 3.
Vespasiua Pollio, V. I. 3.
Vestae aedes, T. L., 3; N. XIX. 1. The temple of Vesta in the Roman Forum.
Vestalis virgo, T. II. 4; N. XXVIII. 1 *virgo maxima, 3. LXXXIII.* 1 D. VIII. 4; *plur. Vestales virgines* J. *I.* 2; A. XXXI. 3, XLIV. 3, Cl, 1 T. LXXVI.; N. XII. 4; Vit. XVI. D. VIII. 3.
Vestinus Atticus, N. XXXV. 1.
Vesuvius mons, Tit. VIII. 3, 4 Plin. (*Vesubius*).
Vettius, L., J. XVII. 1 (*bis*), 2 cf. XX. 5.
Vettius Philocomus, Gr. II. (*bis*).

Vibius Crispus, D. III. 1.
Vicetinus, -a, -um, Gr. XXIII.
Victoria, A. C. 2; G. *X.* 4. Victory worshipped as a goddess.
Vidius, Gr. XIV.
Vienna, Vit. IX., XVIII. A town of southern Gaul on the Rhone, modern Vienne.
Vigintiviri, A. IV.; cf. J. XX.
Vindelici, A. XXI. 1; Hor. A people dwelling in the northern part of Raetia.
Vindelicus, -a, -um, *adj.* from Vindelici: *bellum, T. IX.* 1, 2.
Vindex, *see* Iulius.
Vinicianus, -a, -um, *adj.* from Vinicius: *coniuratio,* N. XXXVI 1
Vinicius, A. LXXI. 2.
Vinicius, L., A. LXIV. 2.
Vinius, T., G. XIV. 2; Vit. VII. 1.
Vinius Philopoemen, T.,A. XXVII 2.
Vipsanius, M., Verg. 44.
Viriatmus, -a, -um, *adj.* from Viriatus (Viriathus), a leader of the Lusitanians: *bellum,* G. III. 2.
Viselliensis, -e, *adj.* of uncertain origin; Pass.
Vitellia colonia, Vit. I. 3.
Vitellia, Vit. I. 2. A goddess.
Vitellia via, Vit. I. 3.
Vitellianus, -a, -um, *adj.* from Vitellius: *bellum,* D. I. 2; *milites, V. VIII.* 2.
Vitellii, Vit. I. 1, 2, 3.
Vitellius, A., Vit. II. 2. Uncle of the emperor.
Vitellius, A., the Emperor. A *Vitellius, L. filius, imperator,* Vit. III. 2; *imperator Vitellius,* Vit. I. 1, *Augustus,* Vit. VIII. 2. *Caesar,* Vit. VIII. 2; *Vitellius,* O. *VIII.* 1 (*ter*), IX. 1; Vit. VII. 3, XVII. 1, V. V. 1, VI. 2, 4, VII. 1, XIV.; *Germanicus,* Vit. VIII. 2, XIV. 4; *Concordia,* Vit. XV. 4
Vitellius, L., Vit. II. 2, 4, III. 2; Pers. Father of the emperor.
Vitellius, P., Vit. II. 2. Grandfather of the emperor.
Vitellius, P., Vit. II. 2, 3. Uncle of the emperor.
Vitellius, Q., Vit. I. 2. Uncle of the emperor.
Vitellius, *see* Petronianus.
Volaterrae, Pers. (*bis*). A town of Etruria.
Vologaesua, N. LVII. 2; V. VI. 4; D. II. 2. Vologaesus I, king of the Parthians.
Voltacilius Plotus, L., Rh. III.
Vonones, T. XLIX. 2. A king of the Parthians.
Vulcatius (Sedigitus), Ter. II. IV., V.

Xenon (commonly Zenon), T. LVI.
Xenophon, J., LXXXVII. *(Cyrop.)*
Xerxes, Cal. XIX. 3

Zenodotus, Gr. XI.
Zmyrna, Gr. XVIII. (*bis*); An epic poem of C. Helvius Cinna, a contemporary of Cicero and Caesar, on the subject of the love of Myrrha, or Zmyrna, for her father Cinyras. Although the poem was of small compass he spent nine years in elaborating it, and it abounded in obscure mythological allusions and pedantic learning; so that many grammarians acquired fame by writing commentaries on it.

Richard Clay and Sons, Ltd,, London and Bungay.

SUGGESTED READING

ADKINS, LESLEY, AND ROY A. ADKINS. *Handbook of Life in Ancient Rome.* New York: Oxford University Press, 1998.

AREIS, PHILLIPPE, GEORGE DUBY, AND PAUL VEYNE, EDS. *A History of Private Life: From Pagan Rome to Byzantium.* Cambridge, MA: Harvard University Press, 1992.

BAKER, G. P. *Tiberius Caesar: Emperor of Rome.* Latham, MD: Rowman & Littlefield, 2001.

BALSDON, J. P. *Life and Leisure in Ancient Rome.* London: Phoenix Press, 2002.

---. *Rome: The Story of an Empire.* New York: McGraw-Hill, 1970.

BARRETT, ANTHONY A. *Caligula: The Corruption of Power.* New Haven, CT: Yale University Press, 1998.

---. *Livia: First Lady of Imperial Rome.* New Haven, CT: Yale University Press, 2002.

CAESAR, JULIUS. *Civil War.* Trans. Jane F. Gardner. New York: Penguin, 1976.

---. *The Conquest of Gaul.* Trans. S. A. Hanford. New York: Penguin, 1983.

CARCOPINO, JEROME. *Daily Life in Ancient Rome.* New Haven, CT: Yale University Press, 2003.

CHAMPLIN, EDWARD. *Nero.* Cambridge, MA: Harvard University Press, 2003.

GIBBON, EDWARD. *Decline and Fall of the Roman Empire: Volumes 1, 2, 3*. New York: Knopf, 1993.

---. *Decline and Fall of the Roman Empire: Volumes 4, 5, 6*. New York: Knopf, 1994.

GRANT, MICHAEL. *Sick Caesars: Madness and Malady in Imperial Rome*. New York: Barnes & Noble Books, 2003.

---. *The Twelve Caesars*. New York: Barnes & Noble Books, 1996.

HORNBLOWER, SIMON, AND ANTONY SPAWFORTH, EDS. *Oxford Classical Dictionary*. New York: Oxford University Press, 2003.

---. *Oxford Companion to Classical Civilization*. New York: Oxford University Press, 1998.

JIMENEZ, RAMON L. *Caesar Against the Celts*. New York: Book Sales, 2001.

LEVICK, BARBARA. *Claudius*. New Haven, CT: Yale University Press, 1993.

---. *Tiberius the Politician*. New York: Routledge, 1999.

---. *Vespasian*. New York: Routledge, 1999.

MATYSZAK, PHILIP. *Chronicle of the Roman Republic*. New York: Thames and Hudson, 2003.

MURISON, CHARLES LESLIE. *Rebellion and Reconstruction – Galba to Domitian*. New York: Oxford University Press, 1999.

PLINY THE YOUNGER. *Letters of the Younger Pliny*. Trans. Betty Radice. New York: Penguin, 1990.

PLUTARCH. *Plutarch's Lives: Volume 1*. Ed. Arthur Hugh Clough. Trans. John Dryden. New York: Random House, 2001.

---. *Plutarch's Lives: Volume 2*. Ed. Arthur Hugh Clough. Trans. John Dryden. New York: Random House, 2001.

SANTOSUOSSO, ANTONIO. *Storming the Heavens: Soldiers, Emperors, and Civilians in the Roman Empire*. Boulder, CO: Westview, 2001.

SCARRE, CHRISTOPHER, AND TOBY WILKINSON. *Chronicle of the Roman Emperors*. New York: Thames and Hudson, 1995.

SCULLARD, HOWARD H. *From the Gracchi to Nero: A History of Rome from 133 B.C. to A.D. 68*. New York: Routledge, 1994.

SHELTON JO-ANN. *As the Romans Did: A Sourcebook in Roman Social History*. New York: Oxford University Press, 1997.

SOUTHERN, PAT. *Domitian: Tragic Tyrant.* Bloomington, IN: Indiana University Press, 1997.

TACITUS. *The Annals of Imperial Rome.* Trans. Michael Grant. New York: Penguin, 1976.

WALLACE-HADRILL, ANDREW. *Suetonius.* London: Bristol Classics, 1995.

WELLESLEY, KENNETH. *Year of the Four Emperors.* New York: Routledge, 2000.

WILLIAMS, JOHN EDWARD. *Augustus.* Fayetteville, AR: University of Arkansas Press, 1995.